THE JOHN NATHAN-TURNER
DOCTOR WHO PRODUCTION
DIARY 1979-1990

CONTENTS

FOREWORD

'Memory cheats,' said John Nathan-Turner.

Which, amusingly, I tend to remember as 'memory lies'. Which sort of makes his point …

John was applying this observation to fans enjoying deludedly rosy nostalgia about dodgy old *Doctor Who* classics, and using these delusions as the basis for unfavourable comparisons with his own era of the show. Of course, he was saying this in the days before mass availability of old episodes for domestic viewing at will. So he was right in one sense.

But in another sense, he'd got it quite wrong.

Because no-one is more forgiving of all the flaws in those creaky old black and white episodes than those same fans. These die-hard devotees of the show were a lot less forgiving of John's output and were often the bane of his existence.

I regarded John as a little paranoid, but it's a truism that you're not paranoid if they're out to get you. And 'they' – some sections of the fan community – were indeed out to get John, organising petitions to get him sacked and writing poisonous diatribes about him in the fan press. Witch-hunt is probably too strong a word, but …

I remember John shutting himself in his office with the latest copies of some of the most virulent fanzines and fretfully chain-smoking as he read these denunciations. He would emerge glum or angry or both, and I didn't blame him … though I did wonder why he read the damned things.

In fairness, the fans had, periodically, a lot to complain about. John had presided over some of the show's lowest moments. But it speaks to the complexity of the man that he also presided over some of the show's greatest moments, and a version of the Doctor and his companions and their adventures that would decisively provide the template for the show when it returned from its interregnum, and apparently ever after.

These flashes of greatness and genius were written by a maverick, wildly talented band of newcomers. And they were brilliantly performed by the groundbreaking partnership of Sylvester McCoy and Sophie Aldred as the Doctor and Ace.

I hired those writers. But who hired me? John did. Who hired Sylvester McCoy? John did. You get the picture. Not just Sophie and that roll-call of brilliant first-time writers, but wildly gifted musicians like Dominic Glynn and Mark Ayres …

We all got our first break because John was willing to take a gamble on new talent in a way that virtually no-one else in television drama did. Possibly before or since.

We got our chance.

And we owe it all to him.

Thank you, John.

Andrew Cartmel
London
22 September 2021

INTRODUCTION

John Nathan-Turner is perhaps the most controversial person to be involved with *Doctor Who*, certainly the most controversial person associated with the 'classic' series, which ran on the BBC between 1963 and 1989. No other single person had such a wide-ranging and long-lasting influence on the show.

Born in Birmingham in 1947, John Turner (his real name) had aspirations to either act or work in television when he left school. Despite a few early forays into acting in his youth, he quickly realised he wasn't suited to that role, and instead turned his efforts towards a career in television. He joined the BBC in London the late 1960s, working as a Floor Assistant on various studio productions. This gave him his first brush with *Doctor Who* in 1969, when he worked on the Patrick Troughton story 'The Space Pirates' in this capacity.

A promotion to Assistant Floor Manager soon followed in the early 1970s, which saw John – now self-re-named as John Nathan-Turner – return to *Doctor Who* for the Jon Pertwee stories 'The Ambassadors of Death' and 'Colony in Space'. He was promoted again to the role of Production Assistant, and then some years later Production Unit Manager.

The Production Unit Manager, back in the 1970s, was the right-hand man of the producer on any given BBC TV series, tasked with looking after budgets, booking studio facilities, and generally ensuring that everything ran smoothly. It was as Production Unit Manager that John returned to *Doctor Who* in 1977, arriving at the same time as new producer Graham Williams for the show's fifteenth season, with Tom Baker now in the title role.

John worked on every *Doctor Who* story that Williams produced during his three years on the show, while also working on *All Creatures Great and Small* between 1978 and 1980 and *Flesh and Blood* in 1980. When Graham Williams left, John applied for and successfully got the job of producing *Doctor Who* from its eighteenth season, albeit initially on a trial basis, with ex-*Doctor Who* producer Barry Letts appointed as Executive Producer to look over his shoulder.

The show's eighteenth season in 1980/81 saw a significant change of approach, with new theme music, new titles and a new style of incidental music, all instigated by John. Tom Baker left the show at the end of this year, and John had the task of casting his successor. He immediately settled on Peter Davison, an actor whose star was very much in the ascendancy at the time, and someone John knew well from his work on *All Creatures Great and Small*, in which Davison had one of the lead roles.

Davison's debut in the nineteenth season in 1982 saw *Doctor Who* moved from its traditional Saturday teatime slot for the first time in its history, to a twice-weekly midweek slot instead. This new, soap-opera-style scheduling, coupled with Davison's popularity as the Doctor, saw an upswing in ratings. The following year, the show celebrated its twentieth anniversary with a 90-minute special alongside the regular season; and, away from the screen, *Doctor Who*'s popularity seemed assured, as conventions both sides of the Atlantic began to grow in number and popularity, John being a regular attendee.

However, Davison's departure in 1984 seemed to cast a shadow over the show, as yet again John had to cast a new leading man. His choice of Colin Baker never seemed to gel with the viewing public, and suddenly *Doctor Who* began to look like it was on a downward spiral. The 1985 season was moved back to the Saturday teatime slot, but with the episodes now doubled in length, *Doctor Who* looked increasingly unsure of itself, and within a few months, the BBC announced that the show was to be cancelled, before back-peddling to a position of it merely being put on an extended hiatus.

1986 ushered in a period of turmoil from which classic-era *Doctor Who* never really recovered. The twenty-third season, when it finally arrived, was cut to nearly half its former length, with just 14 episodes, now back to 25 minutes in length. The pressures of making the series saw John's script editor, Eric Saward, resign, and a very public and messy falling-out between the two ensued. To cap it all, toward the end of the year, John was ordered not to take up the option on Colin Baker's contract for the following year, effectively sacking his leading man.

With diminishing enthusiasm for a job he couldn't seem to be able to move away from, John cast the seventh Doctor, Sylvester McCoy, and set about rebuilding *Doctor Who* from the ground-up. With only 14 episodes a year to work with, any progress was going to be slow and incremental, and while things did occasionally seem to be improving for the show, there were also missteps along the way. John produced three seasons with McCoy as the Doctor between 1987 and 1989, but always seemed to be battling to swim upstream with the show. When the axe finally came down on *Doctor Who* in 1989, it was a bitter blow to John, but one that seemed unavoidable at the time.

With no show to make, John's days at the BBC were numbered, and he was made redundant from the corporation in 1990. His post-*Doctor Who* career was mostly unedifying. He went to work for BBC Enterprises for a year or so in the early 1990s, overseeing a number of *Doctor Who* projects, including some VHS 'specials' that he scripted and directed; but a fan backlash (orchestrated in the main by the fanzine *DWB*, whose editor, Gary Leigh, had fallen out with John some years previously) saw this avenue closed off. He tried his hand at presenting, when the fledgling UK satellite TV channel BSB purchased a large number of old *Doctor Who* stories to screen and dedicated a weekend to the show. BSB's early demise closed that door for John too. He began touring *Doctor Who*-themed events, which he staged at theatres and lecture halls, and fronting 'weekends' at the permanent *Doctor Who* exhibitions at Longleat House and Llangollen. He continued to guest at *Doctor Who* conventions on both sides of the Atlantic, but was increasingly unable to divorce himself from the series he had once produced. John and his long-term partner, Gary Downie, were in the process of moving abroad to Spain to start a new life, when he became seriously ill. John Nathan-Turner died on Wednesday 1 May 2002, at the age of 54.

For anyone interested in John's life, then there is no better resource to recommend than Richard Marson's biography of the man. *JN-T: The Life and Scandalous Times of John Nathan-Turner* (published by Miwk Publishing, 2013), later retitled *Totally Tasteless,* is a fascinating and comprehensive account of John's life and career. It covers all aspects of his personality and interests, his flaws and his fascinations, and is – at times – an unsettling and troubling tome to read. This book doesn't for one minute set out to compete with Marson's superlative biography, but does at least try to complement it.

For me, John's time as producer of *Doctor Who* has always seemed uniquely and unusually worthy of close scrutiny. This is due partly to the length of time he stayed in the job, partly to the wildly differing merits of some subsections of his 'era', and partly to the contentious behind-the-scenes dramas that were never far from the show's surface during that period.

What this book sets out to do is to put a timeline together of what John was doing, and when. It seeks to explore when he made certain decisions, some of which had huge long-term consequences for the show. But it also encompasses some of the more boring minutia that his role as producer entailed. At times, it helps to explain how he reacted to certain events over which he had no control, and at others it details where things that he could influence went badly wrong.

Central to this story are John's working relationships with script editors and directors. The two biggest falling-outs that he had were, first, with his script editor Eric Saward – who left the show in 1986 in the wake of the previous year's cancellation crisis and the death of the writer Robert Holmes – and, secondly, with the writer and director Peter Grimwade, who earned John's wrath through his actions in the aftermath of the cancellation of the Saward-scripted 1983 story 'The Return'. Both of these clashes are charted with reference to contemporary paperwork and correspondence. But there are other examples too.

What this book doesn't attempt to do is to present a day-to-day history of the production of *Doctor Who* in the 1980s. John was in overall charge, but once he and his script editor had commissioned and agreed the scripts of a given story, these would be handed over to a director, who would then do a lot of the work needed to get it made. John might attend some production meetings, rehearsals, and casting sessions, but once a director had been assigned, his main involvement came during location filming and/or studio recording sessions. John would seldom miss a day of these, so their dates are noted regardless whether or not John had any notable involvement in what occurred. Usually, he just observed from the background.

But any in-depth analysis of discussions that script editors were having with writers, or conversations that directors were having with actors, is for another time and place – unless John was directly involved in one way or another.

My interest in *Doctor Who* began at an early age. By my early teens, I was a member of the *Doctor Who* Appreciation Society and had begun to pay attention to such things as the names in the show's end credits. John's appointment as the new producer was heralded with a photo-feature in the pages of an early issue of *Doctor Who Weekly*, and from then on, his work on *Doctor Who* became something of a compelling interest of mine. Graham Williams, Philip Hinchcliffe … his predecessors had been just names, but now the producer of *Doctor Who* had a *face*! John kept a very high profile for himself, both in print and on TV, and also at the first conventions I attended in the early 1980s. As his career waxed and waned, along with *Doctor Who* itself, for the remainder of the decade, the way that he worked became something I wanted to know more about.

I never really got to know John well. Our paths didn't really cross until after his tenure as *Doctor Who*'s producer was over and he had left the BBC. I'd seen him on stage at various events over the years when he was still working on the show, but during the 1990s, I was one of a small team that provided the audio-visual (A/V) services for most of the UK's premier *Doctor Who* conventions. At first slightly wary of us 'techhies', John increasingly liked to hang out with us in the bar during and after events, and the post-convention A/V crew curry with him and his partner, Gary Downie, then became something of a ritual. Through mutual friends, I would run into him from time to time at parties, and found myself increasingly revising my opinion of him.

John was a gregarious and outgoing person, who loved having fun, getting sloshed, gossiping and telling terrible shaggy-dog stories. One time, he was about to regale a group of which I was part with his favourite yarn. He had just launched into the opening spiel, which told of a speciality seafood restaurant that had all the food swimming live in a big tank, from which patrons could choose and then have their choice caught and cooked freshly for them. I whispered to John that I knew the punchline, and he whispered back that he thought I was winding him up. So I, in turn, whispered the punchline to him, and the look on his face as he realised that someone else already knew his favourite joke was pretty priceless!

John liked having fun, and he liked having a drink, and he *really* liked combining the two. And he liked to do this without constantly having to look over his shoulder or worry about letting his guard down. He'd had his fingers burnt a good many times by fans befriending him, only to discover that they had some degree of ulterior motive – be it to gain permission for set visits, or to try to get hold of the phone number of companion actress Nicola Bryant, or to cadge props or scripts. There were usually strings attached, for those wanting to become friends with John Nathan-Turner. John wanted none of that.

One person John and Gary Downie came to know and befriend in later years, when they were living in Brighton, was Stephen Cranford. Cranford lived in nearby Worthing, and was working for the police at the time they first met in 1993. Cranford was also a big *Doctor Who* fan, and was introduced to John and Gary by a colleague who knew of his interest in the show. John and Gary were fascinated by Cranford's job as a police officer, and kept in touch with him. As time went by, Cranford became a regular guest at the couple's parties, and would help them out with any odd-jobs that needed doing in their Brighton house.

When John left the BBC at the end of August 1990, one of his last tasks was to clear out the now-defunct *Doctor Who* production office in Union House. With scripts and documentation that dated back to the early 1960s, plus a whole raft of paperwork that related to John's decade as producer, the office was piled high with cabinets of pure history. And it was all scheduled to be thrown into a skip. So John and Gary hired a van, bagged everything up in rubbish sacks, and transported it all back to Brighton. The paperwork would stay bagged up in their garage, while a small selection of props that John had also retained over the years would be kept in their house. John and Gary would joke to Cranford that this all constituted their 'pension'.

When John died in 2002, Gary disposed of many of the props and items that John had kept. However, when Gary too died in 2006, it fell to Cranford to clear out their house. He discovered the production office paperwork still bagged up in the garage, along with a huge number of photographs, a sizeable collection of videotapes and a small number of films.

A few years previously, Cranford had been the conduit between the self-styled *Doctor Who* Restoration Team and another friend of his, Graham Strong, who back in the 1960s had made good-quality off-air audio recordings of many now-missing *Doctor Who* episodes. Cranford was put in touch with Restoration Team member Paul Vanezis, who at the time worked for the BBC. Vanezis arranged to meet with Cranford and Strong at BBC Television Centre in London, in order to borrow the latter's original reel-to-reel audio tapes. Vanezis was an old friend of mine, and as I was also part of the Restoration Team, he asked me to come along for the day as well.

After Gary's death, Stephen Cranford contacted Paul Vanezis again, informing him of the material that John and Gary had left, and offering it to the Restoration Team, who were, at the time, the creative force behind the

INTRODUCTION

BBC's classic *Doctor Who* DVD range. Cranford very much wanted the tapes, photos and paperwork that John had saved to be put to good use. Most of John's archive had an obvious and immediate interest value. Some items, however, initially seemed to be of little use.

One day, I was looking through an old file of John's, containing his BBC expense receipts. Now, on first examination, these weren't the most exciting pieces of *Doctor Who* production paperwork I'd ever come across. However, a closer study started throwing up interesting titbits. Working lunches and meetings with Peter Davison and Colin Baker took on greater significance when cross-referenced with production dates, as did meetings with the agents of actors such as Tom Baker and Elisabeth Sladen.

John had kept quite a few files of correspondence, and I had over the years amassed further information from the many visits I had made to the BBC Written Archives Centre to study the various *Doctor Who* production files kept there. Between them, these various sources of information enabled me to piece together a record of what John was doing, and when, during his time in charge of the show.

Suddenly, it seemed to me that it would be possible to start working out a large part of what John's professional diary must have looked like throughout the time he was *Doctor Who*'s producer. If only there was time to sit down and start compiling all the details …

And then 2020 happened. Thanks to SARS-CoV-2, the world changed for everyone in a few short months, and the UK went into its first major lockdown in March. Needing a project to help me stay sane, I decided that it was the perfect time to try to piece together John Nathan-Turner's *Doctor Who* Production Diary. I contacted Stephen James Walker and David J Howe at Telos Publishing, who liked the idea, and I asked Stephen Cranford if it would be okay to use John's paperwork as the basis for such a book. He thought it was a great idea too. Many, many months of typing and retyping then followed.

So here we go …

Richard Molesworth
2 November 2021

1979

Setting the Scene:

John Nathan-Turner officially became the producer of *Doctor Who* in late 1979. In John's own memoirs, as published in *Doctor Who Magazine*, he recalled being offered the job during the studio rehearsals for 'Shada', which would place the date as sometime in November. However, he was throwing ideas about Season 18 to his line manager as early as September, so the notion of him replacing Graham Williams as producer must have been discussed, if only informally, for some months prior to him being officially offered the role.

Although John was now officially the new producer of *Doctor Who*, his promotion to producer grade was on only a temporary 'acting' level to begin with. This was quite normal for the BBC when promoting people to more senior positions. Nevertheless, John's appointment represented something of a gamble on the part of his BBC bosses. So, alongside John, former *Doctor Who* producer Barry Letts[1] was formally appointed as that show's Executive Producer by the then-current BBC Head of Series and Serials, Graeme McDonald.[2] McDonald, as Head of Department and John's direct boss, would normally be the *de facto* (if uncredited) Executive Producer of *Doctor Who*, but at that time he was having to cope with a recent significant increase in his own responsibilities, and he felt that he didn't know as much about the show as he needed to in order to fully oversee a rookie like John. He persuaded Barry Letts, who was currently still working as a producer in the Drama

---

[1] Barry Letts directed the Patrick Troughton story 'The Enemy of the World' and was hurriedly appointed producer of *Doctor Who* in 1970, replacing Derrick Sherwin. Letts was in charge for the entirety of Jon Pertwee's run as the Doctor, and was then responsible for casting Pertwee's replacement, Tom Baker. Letts left the show after producing Baker's debut story, 'Robot' in 1974, although he did return to direct 'The Android Invasion' in 1975. He remained as a producer at the BBC, taking over their Sunday evening 'classic series' strand, on which he was working when asked to become Executive Producer of *Doctor Who* in late 1979.

[2] Graeme McDonald had joined the BBC as a producer in 1966, having worked as a director for a number of years at Granada Television. He became BBC Head of Serials in 1977, replacing Bill Slater, and as such was the line manager of the *Doctor Who* producer. He was responsible for the appointment of Graham Williams as successor to Philip Hinchcliffe. In 1979 his role was merged with that of BBC Head of Series to become BBC Head of Series and Serials. In 1981, he replaced Shaun Sutton as the BBC's Head of Drama, and then in 1983 he became Controller of BBC2, until he left the BBC in 1987.

Department, to take on this role on his behalf. However, Letts elected to keep himself very much at arm's length from Nathan-Turner from the outset, limiting himself to offering detailed notes and observations on the scripts that were commissioned for the show.

Although John's name crops up on a lot of *Doctor Who* paperwork from 1979 (and indeed before), this mainly relates to his role as Production Unit Manager on the show. Any meetings, script read-throughs, location filming days or studio sessions that he attended in the latter capacity are outside the scope of this book and so aren't recorded. Only items directly connected with his new role as producer are noted, and so our story begins in late 1979.

One of John's first moves as producer was to make the case for ditching six-part stories. These had been previously considered a logistical necessity; the show's annual allocation of 26 x 25-minute episodes had been traditionally subdivided into five four-part stories and one six-parter. Nathan-Turner asked for extra funding in order to make 28 episodes during the run of Season 18, so that he could make seven four-part adventures instead. BBC1 Controller Bill Cotton agreed to this, and so, going into the 1980s, Nathan-Turner was now responsible for producing the longest season of *Doctor Who* since the 1960s.

Another significant change John wanted to make to was to move away from the traditional-style incidental music favoured by the show's regular composer Dudley Simpson and to use instead electronic music as pioneered by the BBC Radiophonic Workshop. The increasing popularity of electronic music in the music industry in general may have played a part in his thinking. This in turn led John to consider also the arrangement of the show's theme tune, which had remained more or less the same since the 1960s. And if the theme was to be revamped, he reasoned, the title sequence ought to be revamped as well.

Even before any storylines or scripts were under consideration, in the autumn of 1979, John Nathan-Turner was planning some of the biggest changes *Doctor Who* had seen in many a year …

SEPTEMBER

Tuesday 25th:
Itinerary: John sends a memo to Graeme McDonald, Head of Series and Serials at the BBC, along with two LPs by the French musician Jean Michel Jarre. He asks McDonald to listen to the LPs, as this is the type of synthesizer music he wants to utilise on the next season of *Doctor Who*. He invites McDonald to reply with his comments.

Friday 28th:
Itinerary: Graeme McDonald replies to John, having listened to the Jean Michel Jarre LPs. He thinks the music is too ethereal and romantic, and not nearly dramatic enough for a pacey show like *Doctor Who*.

OCTOBER

John's work as Production Unit Manager keeps him busy for much of this month, as the final studio sessions for 'The Horns of Nimon' take place, along with location filming for 'Shada'.[3]

NOVEMBER

Thursday 1st:
Itinerary: John's usual place of work as Production Unit Manager is his office in Room 401 of BBC Threshold House in Shepherd's Bush, London. Today, however, he's at the BBC Television Rehearsal Rooms (a complex usually referred to as the 'Acton Hilton' by those in the BBC) in Victoria Road, Ealing. He, along with producer Graham Williams and script editor Douglas Adams, attend the 'Producer's Run' of the first studio block for 'Shada', the final story to be made for the show's Season 17.

Friday 2nd:
Itinerary: Graeme McDonald writes to John and Barry Letts, asking if there would be any mileage in trying to film a *Doctor Who* story, or even a pair of stories, for the upcoming Season 18 in Australia. Would ABC TV – the Australian channel that, at the time, purchased and screened *Doctor Who* – welcome such an involvement?, he wonders.

Monday 12th:
Itinerary: By now, John is spending more time in the *Doctor Who* Production Office in Room 204 of BBC Union House – immediately adjacent to Threshold House in Shepherd's Bush, London – preparing to take over from Graham Williams. Today, however, he takes a short walk from Union House, across

---

[3] There is no documentation that shows John making any further decisions on *Doctor Who* with regard to becoming its new producer during this month.

Shepherd's Bush Green to Shepherd's Bush tube station, and boards an eastbound tube train on the Central line. Three stops later, and he gets off at North Acton Station and walks to the BBC Television Rehearsal Rooms in Victoria Road, Ealing.[4] Here, full cast rehearsals are continuing under the auspices of director Pennant Roberts for the second studio block of 'Shada'.

Commentary: 'Shada' is to be the last *Doctor Who* story made under outgoing producer Graham Williams. Rehearsals for the second studio block of the story are well under way, but (as is something of an annual tradition at this time) the threat of union industrial action looms large at the BBC in the run-up to Christmas. This could threaten the planned studio recording dates for the second studio block, which would have a knock-on effect on the remaining third studio session.

John Nathan-Turner: 'After completing the filming [for "Shada"], studio sessions began. During the first session of rehearsal or perhaps the later aborted session, I noticed Tom [Baker] passing my office door one day and entering Graeme McDonald's office. Shortly after Tom had left, I was also summoned. "Your time has come, John," said Graeme. "I'd like you to produce *Doctor Who*. And I've told *that* man!" I was delighted, of course. Graeme went on to explain that there was to be a major reorganisation of the department, with the establishment of a group of senior executive producers overseeing younger producers' projects, Barry Letts was to be the first, producing his own strand of classic family dramas and overseeing my debut on *Doctor Who*.'[5]

Wednesday 14th:
Itinerary: John draws up a planned production schedule for 1980/81, which will see the making of seven four-part stories that will comprise Season 18. John has made the argument for abandoning the production of six-part stories, and this has been accepted. The seven stories are allocated the production codes 5N, 5P, 5Q, 5R, 5S, 5T and 5V. John's planned schedule gives the respective dates by which a director will have to be contracted for each story. The director for story 5N will need to start on 28 January 1980, and will finish on 23 May. The director for story 5P will need to start on 10 March, and will finish on 4 July. The director for story 5Q will need to start on 21 April, and will finish on 15 August. The director for story 5R will need to start on 2 June, and will finish on 26 September. The director for story 5S will need to start on 14 July, and will finish on 7 November. The director for story 5T will need to

---

[4] John would nearly always use the tube to travel around central London for any work-related duties. Taxis were a very rare expense for him.
[5] John Nathan-Turner memoirs, *Doctor Who Magazine* #233.

start on 1 September, and will finish on 26 December. The director for story 5V will need to start on 27 October, and will finish on 27 February 1981. John also writes to John Moore in the BBC's Contracts Department, asking them to negotiate a continuation of Tom Baker's contract for Season 18, encompassing all 28 episodes.

Thursday 15th:
Itinerary: John takes another short tube ride from the *Doctor Who* Production Office to the BBC Television Rehearsal Rooms at Acton, where rehearsals are continuing for the second studio block of 'Shada'. On his return to the Production Office, he sends a memo to the Organiser of Series/Serials, requesting that Lovett Bickford be engaged to direct serial 5N. At the moment, there is no script attached to story 5N, but it will be the first story to be made and shown in the eighteenth season.

John Nathan-Turner: 'Inevitably, I think, as a new producer, when I took over, I didn't want to employ anyone who might know more about the programme than I did. So for that (first) year, I veered away from directors who had done the show before, and created, if you like, my own reparatory company of directors ... Additionally, I'm very keen – and there is a responsibility on television producers – to encourage and develop new talent, be it writers or directors.'[6]

Saturday 17th:
Itinerary: John travels in to work by car for a non-duty day at Television Centre. He also makes a short car trip out to Kensington and then back to Union House. The reasons for this are unknown, but it might possibly relate to the threatened industrial action at the BBC.

Commentary: John's normal BBC contract is for him to work between Monday and Friday, 9.30am through to 5.30pm, but he is sometimes required also to work over weekends; these are referred to as 'non-duty days', and either trigger an overtime payment or – preferably – allow him to take time off in lieu the following week. Additionally, if he is required to work on a non-duty day, he is allowed to claim travel expenses to and from work, so on these days he usually travels in by car and claims mileage expenses, rather than use public transport.

Monday 19th:
Itinerary: Today should have been the first day of the second studio block of 'Shada', but studio TC6 is locked to the production due to a union strike at the

---

[6] John Nathan-Turner interview, *Doctor Who Magazine* Winter Special 1983/84.

BBC, despite all the required sets having been constructed and erected there ready for recording. Graham Williams is initially hopeful that the studio will be available for recording the following day, and is looking to extending the session by booking by an extra day beyond that, to compensate for the strike day.

Tuesday 20th:
Itinerary: The second and final studio day of the second studio block for 'Shada' is also lost due to strike action. Graham Williams looks to arrange a remount of this studio session, and asks the director and cast to return to rehearsals for the third studio block the following day. He writes to the Organiser of BBC Series/Serials asking for clarification on how he should proceed with the production, having lost the second studio block. On the same day, John hops on a tube train at Shepherd's Bush, travelling on the Hammersmith and City line. Fours stops later, he gets off at Westbourne Park station, and then walks to Warwick Avenue, where the BBC Radiophonic Workshop has its home. After his meetings there, he returns later that same day to Union House.

John Nathan-Turner: 'I had decided that with *Blake's 7* and *Doctor Who* in production, my show needed a different musical contribution – both in updating Ron Grainer's splendid theme and changing the style of the incidental music. I intended to hand over the responsibility of the latter to the Radiophonic Workshop ... '[7]

Peter Howell: 'When it came to the signature tune, I said that I was prepared to have a go, but if, in fact, it didn't work, and had I at any time received the wrong reaction when I played it to different people, it would have been buried, and no-one would have known about it! Actually, nobody even knew that I was doing it except John Nathan-Turner, who commissioned it, and Brian Hodgson (Head of the Radiophonic Workshop).'[8]

Commentary: One of the first decisions John made after being appointed producer of *Doctor Who* was to alter the musical style of the series. Not only did he want a new arrangement of the main theme tune, but he also wanted a new style of incidental music. He turned to the BBC's Radiophonic Workshop to provide him with the solution to both these issues. His early trips over to the Workshop (of which this was the first) were almost certainly so that John could have meetings in order to secure the department's involvement. Once the arrangements were fully in place for the Radiophonic Workshop to take

---

[7] John Nathan-Turner memoirs, *Doctor Who Magazine* #234.
[8] Peter Howell interview, *Doctor Who Magazine* #194.

1980

Setting the Scene:

John was taking stock of the show he had inherited. Douglas Adams had departed as script editor the previous year, and had left no stockpile of scripts or storylines in development. In his search for a new script editor to replace Adams, Nathan-Turner initially contacted the writer Johnny Byrne, whom he knew from his time working on *All Creatures Great and Small*, to which Byrne had contributed several scripts. Byrne wasn't keen on the idea of commuting or of relocating away from his native Norfolk, and so he declined the offer. However, he did offer to write a story for the show. Nathan-Turner later recalled, 'I had actually offered Johnny Byrne the position of script editor when I first started. However, he was doing so well as a writer, he felt unable to accept.'[12]

On the recommendation of former *Doctor Who* writer and current *Bergerac* producer Robert Banks Stewart, Nathan-Turner was put in touch with writer Christopher H Bidmead. Bidmead was offered the script editor's job just before Christmas 1979, and officially started in the New Year.

'Thanks to a recommendation from a fellow producer,' Nathan-Tuner later recounted, 'I met Christopher H Bidmead. I liked him enormously, as did Barry [Letts]. His ideas tallied with mine and he brought with him tremendous scientific knowledge and intelligence, and great experience of computers and word processors ... He started as soon as his contract was negotiated.'[13]

Nathan-Turner was also keen to push through the other changes he wanted to make to the show. He opted to commission new opening and closing titles – complete with a new series logo – to replace the ones that had been in use since Tom Baker's first adventure, 'Robot', in 1974. For this task, he chose BBC graphic designer Sid Sutton. He also formally commissioned the Radiophonic Workshop's Peter Howell to update the opening and closing theme music, replacing the version that had basically been in use since the 1960s. The incidental music for the series was also given a revamp, with Dudley Simpson's services disposed of in favour of electronic scores, again courtesy of the Radiophonic Workshop.

Other changes included tasking costume designer June Hudson with

---

[12] John Nathan-Turner memoirs, *Doctor Who Magazine* #234.
[13] John Nathan-Turner memoirs, *Doctor Who Magazine* #234.

creating a new costume for the fourth Doctor, keeping the same basic silhouette but using a maroon palette across nearly all the outfit, including the trademark scarf.

Nathan-Turner also thought that series regulars Romana and K-9 had both come to the end of their useful runs as companions of the Doctor. His early discussions on the subject with Romana actress Lalla Ward chimed with her own desire to move on, so the decision to have this character leave the TARDIS after twenty more episodes was essentially by mutual agreement. The fact that K-9's days were numbered was enough to tempt the character's original voice actor John Leeson to return for his remaining few stories, after David Brierley, who had replaced Leeson for Season 17, said that he was not going to be available for the new season.

John had around three months before the first story of the new season was scheduled to go into production. So far he had commissioned two prospective stories, but with Christopher H Bidmead now on board, the task of getting more scripts lined up was no longer John's sole burden.

JANUARY

Thursday 3rd:
Itinerary: John calls in to BAFTA, where he collects some tapes, and then gets a taxi back to his office at Union House.

Commentary: The British Academy of Film and Television Arts (BAFTA) have their offices in Piccadilly, Central London. It's not known what the tapes were that John collected, or why he needed to collect them.

Friday 4th:
Itinerary: Ian Oliver of BBC Children Programmes puts in a request to the *Doctor Who* Production Office. Oliver is doing a new children's quiz series, and asks John if he can use a Dalek in one of the items. Jane Judge, the production secretary on *Doctor Who*, notes that Graeme McDonald has already given his consent for this. On the same day, John writes to all directors and Production Assistants working on *Doctor Who*, laying out the protocols and procedures that need to be observed should anyone request to visit the BBC studios when *Doctor Who* is being recorded. He also writes a separate letter to all directors, stating that any script rewrites need to be agreed by the script editor either with, or on behalf of, the writer. He makes the point that such script changes must be proposed, not supposed. Paul Field of London Hospital Broadcasting also contacts the *Doctor Who* Production Office on this day. He hosts a radio

item called '*Doctor Who*'s Smarter Brother', which is proving popular with his audience, and so he asks if any of the main cast – Tom Baker, Lalla Ward or David Brierley, the voice of K-9 – could record an introduction to the item on tape for him. John replies that David Brierley is agreeable, and asks Brierley to pop into the BBC to discuss the matter. John then takes Brierley to lunch.

Commentary: It's not known if Brierley recorded the requested introduction for London Hospital Broadcasting. It's possible that John used the opportunity of meeting Brierley that day to sound out Brierley's position on potentially continuing to supply the voice of K-9 for the upcoming Season 18. John had already decided that K-9 was to be written out this year. On learning of Brierley's non-availability for future stories, John subsequently asked John Leeson – who had voiced the character for the fifteenth and sixteenth seasons – to return for the last few stories.

David Brierley: 'They stopped K-9 in the storyline, because the problem with K-9 was that he could solve any problem under the sun … I went away. Then they decided to bring him back, by which time I was working in the West End. I just wasn't able to do it.'[14]

John Leeson: 'John Nathan-Turner phoned me up, and said that David Brierley had decided that he'd had enough of K-9, and would I come back to see K-9 out over the next few stories? I said, "Yes I would."'[15]

Monday 7th:
Itinerary: Arrow Books approach the *Doctor Who* Production Office, asking for permission to publish a book entitled *The Doctor Who Technical Manual*. Despite the longstanding relationship that W H Allen and Target books have enjoyed with *Doctor Who* over the previous decade, John gives his assent.[16]

Wednesday 9th:
Itinerary: For reasons unknown, John takes a trip by tube from the *Doctor Who* Production Office to Lancaster Gate.

Monday 14th:
Itinerary: For reasons unknown, John takes a trip by tube from the *Doctor Who* Production Office to Oxford Circus. On the same day, Graeme McDonald

---

[14] David Brierley interview, *Doctor Who Magazine* #399.
[15] John Leeson interview, *Doctor Who Magazine* #228.
[16] Arrow Books were the paperback book division of Hutchinson publishing company. *The Doctor Who Technical Manual* by Mark Harris was eventually published in hardback initially, in September 1983, by Severn House, a hardback division of Hutchinson.

writes to John, turning down the modern-day *Sherlock Holmes* idea by Peter Grimwade, which John had previously pitched.

Tuesday 15th:
Itinerary: John takes a trip by tube from the *Doctor Who* Production Office to the Radiophonic Workshop in Warwick Avenue.

Commentary: It's possible that, by now, Peter Howell's work was proceeding apace on the new version of the theme tune, and John went to see (or even hear) how he was progressing.

Wednesday 16th:
Itinerary: David Fisher delivers his four scripts for 'Avalon', and Terrance Dicks delivers his storyline for 'The Vampire Mutation' to the *Doctor Who* Production Office. Also on this day, John signs off the request for Lalla Ward to be contracted to appear in twenty of the episodes of Season 18. In the evening, he goes to the Wyndham Theatre for the opening night of the play *Piaf,* performed by the Royal Shakespeare Company.

Commentary: The cast of this production of *Piaf* includes Anthony Higgins, Conrad Asquith (previously PC Quick in 'The Talons of Weng-Chiang'), Bill Buffery, Allan Hendrick, Malcolm Storry, Michael Bertenshaw, Helen Brammer, Ian Charleson, Geoffrey Freshwater, Diana Van Fossen, Valerie Testa, Ian Reddington (later to play the Chief Clown in 'The Greatest Show in the Galaxy'), Jane Lapotaire and Zoe Wanamaker.

Thursday 17th:
Itinerary: John signs off the commissioning brief for Stephen Gallagher to write a storyline for 'The Dream Time', which will eventually become the Season 18 story 'Warriors' Gate'. Pennant Roberts meanwhile delivers rewrites for the first two episodes of 'Dragons of Fear', a story he'd pitched to *Doctor Who* prior to John being appointed as producer.

Friday 18th:
Itinerary: John signs off the request for Tom Baker to be contracted to appear in all 28 episodes of Season 18.

Monday 21st:
Itinerary: John takes composer Dudley Simpson to lunch. Over the meal, he informs him that his services won't be required on the upcoming eighteenth season of *Doctor Who*.

Commentary: Dudley Simpson had regularly provided incidental music for

to receive "sealed orders" from Gallifrey indicating, as I recall, that he was to obliterate Romana.'[26]

Thursday 28th:
Itinerary: Terrance Dicks delivers his four scripts for 'The Vampire Mutation' to the *Doctor Who* Production Office.

MARCH

Tuesday 4th:
Itinerary: Andrew McCulloch and John Flanagan deliver their storyline for 'Meglos' to the *Doctor Who* Production Office.

Monday 10th:
Itinerary: John signs off the commissioning brief for Andrew McCulloch and John Flanagan to write the four scripts for 'The Golden Star' (as 'Meglos' has now been retitled). Romey Allison, the Production Associate on 'The Leisure Hive', writes to John to express concerns about the allocation of just five studio days for the story. Allison doubts that the story can be completed in this time, but thinks that six studio days would be sufficient.

Tuesday 11th:
Itinerary: John writes to the Head of Exports at BBC Enterprises, giving his feedback on artwork for *The Doctor Who Annual 1981*. He thinks the likenesses of Tom Baker and K-9 are excellent, but is disappointed that Romana generally looks nothing like Lalla Ward.

Thursday 13th:
Itinerary: John makes arrangements for photographers from the *Radio Times*, from BBC Picture Publicity and from the general press to attend the Brighton location filming for 'The Leisure Hive' on Thursday 20 March.

Friday 14th:
Itinerary: John signs off the commission for Peter Grimwade to write a story outline for 'Zanadin', and for Keith Miles to write a story outline for 'Mark of Lumos'.[27]

---

[26] John Nathan-Turner memoirs, *Doctor Who Magazine* #234.
[27] 'As previously mentioned, 'Zanadin' would become 'Time-Flight' in Season 19. 'Mark of Lumos' wouldn't proceed beyond the story outline stage.

Monday 17th:
Itinerary: John attends a planning meeting for 'The Leisure Hive' at the BBC's Lime Grove studios, along with director Lovett Bickford and the various members of the relevant BBC Departments who will work on the story. Andrew McCulloch and John Flanagan deliver their script for 'The Golden Star' Part One to the *Doctor Who* Production Office.

Tuesday 18th – Wednesday 19th:
Filming rehearsals take place at the BBC Television Rehearsal Rooms in Victoria Road, Ealing for the Brighton scenes due to be filmed later this week for 'The Leisure Hive'.

Tuesday 18th:
Itinerary: John signs off the commissions for Malcolm Edwards and Leroy Kettle to write a scene breakdown for 'Mouth of Grath', and for Andrew Stephenson to write a scene breakdown for 'Farer Nohan'.[28] In the evening, John takes a trip to Her Majesty's Theatre in London to see their production of *On the Twentieth Century*.

Commentary: The cast of this production of *On the Twentieth Century* includes Chris Melville, Carole Brook, Mark Wynter, David Bexon, Colin Thomas, Jeannie Harris, John Conroy, Teresa Wellard, Valerie Leon, Ann Beach, Richard Manuel, Bernard Martin, Julia Mckenzie, David Healy, Keith Mitchell, Peter Johnston and Fred Evans.

Thursday 20th:
Itinerary: John travels down to Brighton by train to attend the first day of filming on his first story as producer, 'The Leisure Hive'. The location is a stretch of promenade and beach known as Fishmarket Hard. After the day's filming concludes, he stays overnight in the Queens Hotel, Grand Junction Road, along with the rest of the crew. The filming at Brighton beach is attended by the various photographers who were invited by John the previous week. Unfortunately, Tom Baker fails to make an appearance at the filming due to illness, so Lalla Ward films as many of her solo scenes as she can, and also poses for the press.

Friday 21st:
Itinerary: Today's the second of the two planned filming days for 'The Leisure Hive' on Brighton beach, and once all the required shots are completed, John

---

[28] Neither of these potential stories would progress beyond the story outline stage. Leroy Kettle, known to friends as Roy, was a part-time writer whose main job was as a civil servant in the Department of Employment.

Matthew Waterhouse to be contracted to play the role of Adric, for between 20 and 24 episodes in Season 18, with an option in the BBC's favour of him appearing in between 20 and 28 more episodes in Season 19 the following year.

Commentary: Matthew Waterhouse had been seen for the role of Adric after being recommended to John by BBC casting director Jenny Jenkins. Waterhouse had recently started work as a clerk in the BBC's News Information department, but had ambitions to become an actor, and had sought out Jenkins in order to try his luck in getting any parts. She had just helped him get cast in a small role in the BBC series *To Serve Them All My Days* when it was announced in the press that John was looking to introduce a new juvenile male character into *Doctor Who*. Waterhouse asked Jenkins to put him up for the role, and he was asked to attend a couple of readings/auditions (dates unknown) before being offered the part of Adric.

Friday 4th:
Itinerary: Today is a bank holiday (Good Friday) and therefore a day off for most of the rest of the country, but it's also the third and final day of the first studio block for 'The Leisure Hive'. John arrives at Television Centre at 9.30am, and again remains until recording concludes at 10.00pm.

Monday 7th – Thursday 17th:
Rehearsals for the second studio block of 'The Leisure Hive' take place at the BBC Television Rehearsal Rooms at Acton.

Thursday 10th:
Itinerary: John signs off the commissions for Christopher Bailey to write a scene breakdown for 'The Kinda', and for John Bennett to write a scene breakdown for 'Soldar and the Plastoids'.[35] Also on the same day, John has a lunch meeting with actor Matthew Waterhouse, who has been chosen to play the role of new companion Adric. Adric will make his on-set debut in the next story in production, 'The Wasting' (formerly 'The Vampire Mutation', later 'State of Decay'). Due to production schedules, his on-screen introduction, in the preceding story 'Full Circle', will be recorded later in the season.

Commentary: In his 2010 autobiography, *Blue Box Boy*, Matthew Waterhouse recalls being taken to lunch by John to a 'modest French restaurant at the corner of Wood Lane, just off Shepherd's Bush Green'. He recalls that the

---

[35] 'The Kinda' will later be re-titled as just 'Kinda', and will enter production in the show's 19th season. 'Soldar and the Plastoids' is another potential story that gets no further than the story outline.

lunch was a rather stilted affair, and afterwards, John and he returned to the *Doctor Who* Production Office, where John played him a cassette of the new theme tune to the series, and asked what Waterhouse thought of it.

Friday 11th:
Itinerary: Graeme McDonald writes to John, expressing concerns about some elements in the scripts for 'The Wasting', specifically the potential for scenes involving blood and certain action sequences to be too gruesome and horrific for teatime viewing. He asks for assurances from John that the on-screen results will be acceptable for family viewing on BBC1, but also praises the quality of the scripts.

Monday 14th:
Itinerary: John takes a tube ride from the *Doctor Who* Production Office in Union House to the BBC Television Rehearsal Rooms at Acton. This is for another script conference regarding 'The Leisure Hive'. More issues have arisen prior to the second production block, which is due to be recorded in the studio later this week. On the same day, Jill Farnborough from *Blue Peter* contacts the *Doctor Who* Production Office, asking if they can arrange for a photoshoot of Tom Baker in costume as the Doctor, alongside a pack of cub scouts doing the washing up in a canteen, which they want to include in this year's *Blue Peter Annual* book. John contacts *Blue Peter* producer Biddy Baxter on his return from Acton, and vetoes the idea on the grounds that he doesn't want the Doctor to be seen washing dishes in a canteen. Baxter responds that, in that case, she'll use Tom Baker as Tom Baker, and not in character as the Doctor for the photo, and so John gives her Baker's agent's details. Also on the same day, Chris Crouch from BBC Enterprises contacts the *Doctor Who* Production Office on behalf of a Mrs Cameron, who is one of the organisers of the *Woman's Own* Jumbley, an event due to take place early in May at Alexandra Palace.[36] He informs John that Mrs Cameron would like K-9 to present prizes at the event, on either 3, 4 or 5 May. John Leeson has already agreed to attend the event, says Crouch, and so could provide K-9's voice. John has no objections to K-9 making an appearance, but asks Crouch to check who would be operating the K-9 prop. He also signs off the commissioning brief for Stephen Gallagher to write the four scripts for 'The Dream Time' (later 'Warriors' Gate). Andrew McCulloch and John Flanagan deliver their scripts for Parts Two, Three and Four of 'The Last Zolfa-Thuran' (the latest title for 'Golden Star', which will eventually become 'Meglos') .

---

[36] Presumably a jumble sale-type event organised by *Women's Own* magazine at Alexandra Palace in London.

Tuesday 15th:
Itinerary: Mick Jackson from the BBC1 programme *James Burke: The Real Thing* contacts the *Doctor Who* Production Office. He explains that they are using a Dalek prop for an item on the show (reciting an audition speech for *Hamlet*), but suspects they might have a problem with obtaining overseas rights to sell the programme abroad with the Dalek segment in. So Jackson wants to shoot an alternative insert, using K-9 to replace the Dalek, should the Dalek negotiations prove problematic. John refuses them permission to use K-9.

Commentary: The edition of *James Burke: The Real Thing* shown on BBC1 on 10 April 1980 did indeed feature a Dalek auditioning for Shakespeare in one segment. It's not known if the segment was replaced, or retained, for overseas sales.

Wednesday 16th:
Itinerary: Jenny O'Connor from Marvel UK sends John a proof copy of the first page of an interview that John has done for *Doctor Who Weekly*, together with the text for a story that the comic wishes to publish. She asks that John call her 'as soon as possible' to discuss them.[37]

Thursday 17th:
Itinerary: John takes a tube ride from the *Doctor Who* Production Office to the BBC Television Rehearsal Rooms at Acton to attend the Producer's Run for the second studio block of 'The Leisure Hive'. On his return to Union House, he sends copies of the scripts for 'The Last Zolfa-Thuran' out to the various BBC departments who will be contributing to the story. He also contacts Marvel UK, asking to be sent the second page of the interview article he has done for them.

Friday 18th:
Itinerary: It's the first day of the second studio block for 'The Leisure Hive', in studio TC3 at BBC Television Centre. This block would normally be scheduled to last three days but will eventually run to four. John arrives at Television Centre at 9.30am and remains until recording concludes at 10.00pm, before joining the cast in the BBC Club bar.[38]

---

[37] The article was almost certainly 'The Man Behind Dr Who', which was published in Issue 31 of *Doctor Who Weekly*, dated 14 May 1980.
[38] John regularly has an expenses claim for supplying 'hospitality for the cast' after a day in the studio, so it's reasonable to suppose that he joins the cast at the bar, and probably – given that he's the producer – is expected to buy the first round.

Saturday 19th:
Itinerary: It's the second day of the second studio block for 'The Leisure Hive', in studio TC3 at BBC Television Centre. John drives in to Television Centre, as it's a non-duty day for him.

Sunday 20th:
Itinerary: It's the third day of the second studio block for 'The Leisure Hive', in studio TC3 at BBC Television Centre. John drives in to Television Centre, again, as it's another non-duty day, and he joins the cast in the bar after recording.

Monday 21st:
Itinerary: It's the fourth and final day of the second studio block for 'The Leisure Hive', in studio TC3 at BBC Television Centre. John arrives at 9.30am, and remains until recording concludes at 10.00pm, before joining the cast in the BBC Club bar.

John Nathan-Turner: 'Production [on 'The Leisure Hive'] did, however, over-run by a whole day – for which I was carpeted by my superiors, and generally none too pleased about anyway.'[39]

Commentary: It would seem that John's first story had turned into something of a mess, production-wise. More studio days than would usually be necessary to record a four-part story have had to be allocated to the production, and such disarray would not have gone unnoticed by Barry Letts and Graeme McDonald. They obviously felt the need to take John to one side and have a chat about how things were going.

Tuesday 22nd:
Itinerary: John writes to Graeme McDonald, explaining why he justified two overruns during the recent studio sessions for 'The Leisure Hive'. He details that an overrun of 15 minutes on Saturday 19 April was in order to complete all the scenes involving a number of extras, to save having to re-book them for another day, and that an overrun of 22 minutes on Sunday 20 April was to complete scenes with artists whose contracts expired that evening, again to prevent re-booking expenses. Also on this date, John contacts Marvel UK, stating his reservations about the story he was sent for approval, as it seems too similar to 'The Leisure Hive' in some respects. He is told that the issue that would include the story had already been printed.[40]

---

[39] John Nathan-Turner memoirs, *Doctor Who Magazine* #234.
[40] It's not known which story in *Doctor Who Weekly* this refers to.

Wednesday 23rd:
Itinerary: Paul Neary from Marvel UK contacts John, informing him that the story to which he objected has been altered, but that this has incurred fines from Marvel's printers in order to accommodate the new version. John makes the point that being asked to comment 'as soon as possible' was too vague a request if an immediate response was required, especially as he was tied up on the second studio block of 'The Leisure Hive' for four days during all this.

Thursday 24th:
Itinerary: Christopher Bailey delivers his scene breakdown for 'The Kinda' to the *Doctor Who* Production Office. John also writes to Assistant Head of Merchandising at BBC Enterprises, asking them to ensure that any further material sent from Marvel for approval for publication in *Doctor Who Weekly* should have clear deadlines noted.

Friday 25th:
Itinerary: John sends memos to the Heads of the Make-Up and Visual Effects Departments, praising Dorka Nieradzik's and Andrew Lazell's recent work in their respective capacities on 'The Leisure Hive'. He also orders 80 more copies of the rehearsal scripts for 'The Last Zolfa-Thuran' from the BBC Print Room. John then attends a planning meeting for 'The Wasting' in Union House, along with director Peter Moffatt and the various members of the relevant BBC Departments who will work on the story. Andrew Smith delivers his scripts for 'The Planet that Slept' Parts Two to Four to the *Doctor Who* Production Office.

Monday 28th:
Itinerary: Julia Goodwin from the British Safety Council contacts the *Doctor Who* Production Office, asking if it would be possible to organise a special photograph of Tom Baker, in costume as the Doctor, to launch a nationwide painting competition they are running. The competition, for children, is for them to submit paintings using the theme 'Painting a Safer World'. John has no objections to this, and puts Goodwin in touch with Jean Diamond, Tom Baker's agent.

Commentary: The required photo – of Tom Baker in costume as the Doctor, next to an easel with the 'Painting a Safer World' logo prominently displayed – is eventually staged during the location filming for 'State of Decay' a few days later.

Tuesday 29th:
Today is a rehearsal day for the forthcoming location filming of 'The Wasting'. This takes place at the BBC's Television Rehearsal Rooms at Acton.

Wednesday 30th:
Itinerary: This is the first day of location filming for 'The Wasting' at Burnham Beeches, Farnham Common, Buckinghamshire. John drives to the location from his home in London, and returns home after filming concludes. On the same day, he also writes to director Pennant Roberts, enclosing revised scripts for the abandoned story 'Shada', now edited down into two fifty-minute episodes. He tells Roberts he has put in a proposal for the story to be remounted, utilising the already-filmed location footage and already-recorded studio material. With a modicum of new studio material needed to complete the shortened story, the proposal is for 'Shada' to be made and shown as a two-part *Doctor Who* Christmas special on BBC1 later that year.

Commentary: If the condensed 2 x 50 minute version of 'Shada' had been shown as proposed, it would have presumably gone out on BBC1 between 'State of Decay' and 'Warriors' Gate'. How this would have worked, given the new look of Season 18 (including the new design of the Doctor's costume) and its positioning mid-way through a trilogy of stories set in the E-Space universe, would have required some form of explanation. In his memoir *Blue Box Boy*, Matthew Waterhouse recalls John mentioning the possible remount of 'Shada' to him, telling him that it would be rewritten to include Adric in the cast. There is however no mention of Adric in the truncated scripts for 'Shada' that John prepared, and if the existing footage from Season 17 was to be utilised, it would seem that there was not much scope for including Adric in the as-yet unrecorded scenes.

MAY

Thursday 1st:
Itinerary: Today is the second day of location filming for 'The Wasting' at Burnham Beeches, Farnham Common, Buckinghamshire.

John Nathan-Turner: 'On 1 May 1980 I went to view the first day's filming rushes at Ealing, before going out to location at Burnham Beeches. By the time I'd got there, the sequence where the bat bites the Doctor on the neck had been shot, and I was told that Tom [Baker] had insisted that the make-up wound be blue, "as the Doctor has blue blood." I requested a reshoot at the end of the day. However, time ran out, so we simply didn't use the close-up shot of the hand and the blue blood – but look closely at the wide shot!'[41]

---

[41] John Nathan-Turner Memoirs, *Doctor Who Magazine* #234.

Friday 2nd:
Itinerary: Filming for 'The Wasting' resumes at Burnham Beeches, before switching to Ealing Film Studios, where the interior of its water tank doubles for the internal ladders of the *Hydrax* spaceship.

Tuesday 6th – Wednesday 14th:
Rehearsals for the first studio block of 'The Wasting' take place at the BBC Television Rehearsal Rooms at Acton.

Tuesday 6th:
Itinerary: John takes a tube ride from the *Doctor Who* Production Office to the BBC Television Rehearsal Rooms at Acton, to attend a full script read-through by the cast of 'The Wasting'.

Wednesday 7th:
Itinerary: John writes to Graeme McDonald to let him know that story 5N has had a change of name from 'Avalon' to 'The Leisure Hive', that story 5P has had several changes of name from 'The Vampire Mutation' to 'The Wasting' and now 'State of Decay', and that story 5Q has had a change of name from 'Meglos' to 'The Golden Star' and now 'The Last Zolfa-Thuran'. On the same day, Lorne Martin from BBC Enterprises contacts the *Doctor Who* Production Office, enquiring if K-9 could make an appearance at a fête on 7 June that Graham Leslie, a BBC insurance manager, is involved in organising. John agrees.

Friday 9th:
Itinerary: John takes a short tube ride from Union House to the BBC Television Rehearsal Rooms at Acton, to sit in on the continuing rehearsals for the first studio block of 'State of Decay'.

Monday 12th:
Itinerary: Again, John takes a tube ride from Union House to the BBC Television Rehearsal Rooms at Acton, to observe the continuing rehearsals for the first studio block of 'State of Decay'.

Tuesday 13th:
Itinerary: Robin Nash, Head of Variety at the BBC, writes to John, once again to dismiss his idea of a six-part series of *The Jeannie Little Show*; presumably John has been continuing to pitch this since its initial rejection.

Wednesday 14th:
Itinerary: John again takes a short tube ride from the *Doctor Who* Production Office to the BBC Television Rehearsal Rooms at Acton. Today is the

Producer's Run for the first studio block of 'State of Decay'.

John Nathan-Turner: 'At one producer's run-through of "State of Decay", Peter [Moffatt] informed me that all the bits I wanted to cut were Tom's favourite moments. He asked me to give the notes to the actors with him. All of them Tom accepted, until I mentioned a scene where the TARDIS materialised in the rebel's hide-out. As it had been rehearsed, the door opened, then the rebels threw loads of spears, and the Doctor emerged clutching them all, as if he'd caught them as they flew at him. I didn't like this at all and said so. Tom grittily asked me why. I said I thought it was more *Superman* than *Doctor Who!*[42]

Thursday 15th:
Itinerary: It's the first day of a two-day studio block for 'State of Decay' in studio TC3 at BBC Television Centre. After recording concludes, John joins the cast in the BBC Club bar.

Friday 16th:
Itinerary: It's the second day of the first studio block for 'State of Decay' in studio TC3 at BBC Television Centre. After recording, John again joins the cast in the BBC Club bar.

Sunday 18th:
Itinerary: John and Gary Downie, his partner, attend a garden party at the home of director Christopher Barry in Oxfordshire.

Monday 19th – Wednesday 28th:
Rehearsals for the second studio block of 'State of Decay' take place at the BBC Television Rehearsal Rooms at Acton.

Monday 19th:
Itinerary: John walks from Union House to the Shepherd's Bush tube station and hops on a tube on the Central line to go to Oxford Circus. From there, he walks to the offices of Equity, the actors' union, for a meeting.

Commentary: One of the earliest interactions John had with Equity, this meeting was prompted by Matthew Waterhouse joining the cast of *Doctor Who*. To be employed on a regular basis by the BBC, an actor was required to be an Equity member. Waterhouse, because of his lack of experience as an actor, had never applied for membership, and at the time, getting an Equity card was quite a difficult process. In his memoir *Blue Box Boy*, Waterhouse

---

[42] John Nathan-Turner memoirs, *Doctor Who Magazine* #234.

TARDIS set has been revamped for the eighteenth season (and is first used in 'State of Decay') as he doesn't want to pre-empt its new appearance in a programme that will go out before Season 18 airs.

Thursday 29th:
Itinerary: It's the first day of the three-day final studio block for 'State of Decay' in studio TC6 at BBC Television Centre. After recording, John joins the cast in the BBC Club bar.

Friday 30th:
Itinerary: It's the second day of the three-day final studio block for 'State of Decay' in studio TC6 at BBC Television Centre. Once again, after recording, John joins the cast in the BBC Club bar.

Saturday 31st:
Itinerary: It's the final day of the three-day final studio block for 'State of Decay' in studio TC6 at BBC Television Centre. As it's a non-duty day, John drives to Television Centre and then back home after recording concludes.

JUNE

Sunday 1st:
Itinerary: John travels in to work by car for a non-duty day at Television Centre.

Commentary: The studio recording block for 'State of Decay' had finished the previous day, so John must have had some other business relating to the making of the programme to attend to.

Saturday 7th:
Itinerary: John travels in by car for a non-duty day at Television Centre. Today is the gallery-only studio day for 'The Leisure Hive', which John presumably attends.[47]

---

performed the final song of each show while sat in a rocking chair.
[47] Gallery-only studio days had been a regular part of *Doctor Who*'s production for some years at this point. The production would utilise the equipment in the gallery of one of Television Centre's studios on a day when the studio was empty or was being prepared for another production. The videotape (VT) machines in the gallery were used to replay tapes that had been recorded in the actual studio sessions, allowing basic video effects such as laser beams to be added to the already-

Monday 9th:
Itinerary: Graeme McDonald writes to John, telling him that he enjoyed reading the scripts for 'The Planet That Slept'. He asks that the Marshmen aren't made to appear too frightening at the end of the first episode.

Tuesday 10th:
Itinerary: John writes to Graeme McDonald to explain why there was a three-minute overrun on Saturday 31 May, the final studio day for 'State of Decay'. He puts it down to the need to complete a complicated roll-back-and-mix effect.

Wednesday 11th:
Itinerary: Stephen Gallagher delivers his scripts for 'The Dream Time' to the *Doctor Who* Production Office. Dave Martin, co-creator of K-9, writes to John, enquiring if the press speculation regarding K-9 being dropped from the show has any basis. He adds that if it's all a publicity stunt, he's perfectly willing to join in for the fun of it.

Thursday 12th:
Itinerary: John takes a tube from Union House to Richmond, to have a lunch meeting with actress Elisabeth Sladen.[48]

Commentary: John must have had an inkling by now that Tom Baker would not continue with the show beyond the end of Season 18, when his current BBC contract was due to expire. John's initial idea about how to approach the impending change of lead actor was to ask Elisabeth Sladen to return as the popular companion character Sarah Jane Smith for a short run of stories that would bridge the change between the fourth and fifth Doctors. Sladen, whose original run in the show had previously helped smooth the transition between the third and fourth Doctors, gave the proposal some consideration, but eventually declined. Louise Jameson, who had played another of the fourth Doctor's earlier companions, Leela, subsequently came to the same decision when John then made the same offer to her. It's fair to assume that from this point onwards, John was starting to think long and hard about the show's future beyond Season 18, and who should be cast as the new Doctor if, as expected, Tom Baker bowed out.

---

recorded material in a cost-effective manner.
[48] In her 2011 autobiography, Elisabeth Sladen recalls going to meet John in the *Doctor Who* Production Office, where he asked her to return as Sarah Jane Smith, and she declined. If that was the case, perhaps this lunch was either a prelude to that meeting and offer, or an attempt on John's part to get Elisabeth Sladen to reconsider after her refusal.

John Nathan-Turner: 'Once I realised that recasting the Doctor was to fall to me, I had discussions with Lis Sladen and Louise Jameson with regard to rejoining the show to help us with the transition to the new Doctor. In fact, Chris Bidmead and I went to the Orange Tree Theatre in Richmond to see Lis in a play and to discuss the proposal afterwards. Both Lis and Louise felt they shouldn't retrace their steps in the show.'[49]

Louise Jameson: 'John Nathan-Turner rang me up and said would I come and meet him. I thought, "Ooh, I'm going to head my own TV series, finally." Anyway, John wanted Leela to come back for the episode in which Tom left, and to go through the next series with the new Doctor. He wanted, for the fans, something that they were familiar with, to smooth over the change of the two Doctors. I said I'd come in for one story, then probably two of the next season, but I didn't want to do a whole year. Also, he asked Lis Sladen first!'[50]

Friday 13th:
Itinerary: John signs off the commission for Terence Green to write a story breakdown for 'The Psychrons'.[51]

Saturday 14th – Tuesday 24th:
Rehearsals for the first studio block of 'Meglos' (as 'The Last Zolfa-Thuran' has now reverted to) take place at the BBC Television Rehearsal Rooms at Acton.

Saturday 14th:
Itinerary: John travels in by car (as it's a non-duty day) to the BBC Television Rehearsal Rooms at Acton, for a script read-through for the first studio block of 'Meglos'.

Monday 16th:
Itinerary: John writes to Dave Martin, confirming that K-9 is due to leave the show in January 1981, but asks that Martin keep the information to himself for the time being. He adds that should the show not work as well without K-9, then the Doctor can always go back to Gallifrey to pick up K-9 Mark I at some point.

Friday 20th:
Itinerary: John writes to the Organiser of Drama Series/Serials, asking that Paul Joyce be engaged to direct story 5S (which will eventually be 'Warriors'

---

[49] John Nathan-Turner memoirs, *Doctor Who Magazine* #234.
[50] Louise Jameson interview, *Doctor Who Magazine* #215/#136.
[51] 'The Psychrons' was another potential story that got no further than a story breakdown.

Gate') between 21 July and 14 November.

Tuesday 24th:
Itinerary: John takes a tube ride from Union House to the BBC Television Rehearsal Rooms at Acton for the Producer's Run of the first studio block of 'Meglos'. John and Christopher H Bidmead circulate their first Drama Script Classified List[52], which states that the only writers they are working with at this date for upcoming storylines and/or scripts are: Stephen Gallagher, Andrew McCulloch and John Flanagan, Christopher Priest and Andrew Smith.

Wednesday 25th:
Itinerary: It's the first day of the three-day first studio block for 'Meglos' in studio TC8 at BBC Television Centre. After recording, John joins the cast in the BBC Club bar. Also on this day, John decides that 'Destiny of the Daleks' will be selected to be repeated from 5 to 8 August on BBC1, followed by 'City of Death' on 12, 13, 19 and 20 August. John also writes to Graham Williams and Douglas Adams, informing them that his attempts to remount 'Shada' as two 50-minute episodes have now been abandoned, due to a lack of BBC studio availability in the autumn.

Thursday 26th:
Itinerary: It's the second day of the three-day first studio block for 'Meglos' in studio TC8 at BBC Television Centre. The recording overruns by 15 minutes. Afterwards, John joins the cast in the BBC Club bar.

Friday 27th:
Itinerary: It's the third and final day of the first studio block for 'Meglos' in studio TC8 at BBC Television Centre. Also on this day, Fletcher Richardson from the *It's Saturday* show on Radio Blackburn contacts the *Doctor Who* Production Office. He wants to start a 'Save K-9' petition, and seeks confirmation that K-9 is indeed leaving the show. John issues a 'No comment' response, the first of many that were to become something of a trademark of his.

Commentary: Rumours had been flying in the national tabloids that the BBC were planning on axing K-9 from *Doctor Who*, ever since the newspaper *The Sun* had run the story and started a 'Save K-9' campaign in the edition published on 7 June. John had neither confirmed nor denied the story at this point.

---

[52] The Drama Script Classified List was circulated two or three times a year around the BBC Drama Department, so that the various production offices and heads of department could see which writers were working on which programmes.

Monday 30th:
Itinerary: John writes to Graeme McDonald, to explain the 15-minute recording overrun on 26 June. He puts it down to the complexities of redressing a jungle set featured in the production. McDonald sends a handwritten reply to John, asking if these complexities had been foreseen by him in advance. John's response to this isn't recorded.

Monday 30th – Wednesday 9th July:
Rehearsals for the second studio block of 'Meglos' take place at the BBC Television Rehearsal Rooms at Acton.

JULY

Tuesday 1st:
Itinerary: Phil Chivers from the BBC programme *Ask Aspel* contacts the *Doctor Who* Production Office. The show will be having Lalla Ward on as a guest on a future edition, and is looking for some clips to use to introduce her. John recommends scenes from 'The Creature from the Pit' and 'The Horns of Nimon' for them to consider.[53] On the same date, John writes to writer Bob Baker, the other co-creator of K-9, to apprise him of the situation regarding the character being dropped from *Doctor Who*.

Commentary: John's suggestions to Phil Chivers presumably reflected the fact that he didn't want any footage from the upcoming Season 18 to be screened at this point.

Monday 7th:
Itinerary: John travels by tube from Union House to Maida Vale for a meeting at the BBC Radiophonic Workshop.

Wednesday 9th:
Itinerary: John takes a tube ride from Union House to the BBC Television Rehearsal Rooms at Acton for the Producer's Run of the second studio block of 'Meglos'. Afterwards, he takes another tube to Baker Street, where he heads to Madame Tussauds for a further meeting about the upcoming *Doctor Who* Experience exhibition.

---

[53] Lalla Ward appeared as a guest on the edition of *Ask Aspel* shown on BBC1 on 15 July 1980.

Thursday 10th:
Itinerary: It's the first day of the three-day second studio block for 'Meglos' in studio TC8 at BBC Television Centre. The session overruns by two minutes. After recording, John joins the cast in the BBC Club bar.

Friday 11th:
Itinerary: It's the second day of the three-day second studio block for 'Meglos' in studio TC8 at BBC Television Centre. After recording, John joins the cast in the BBC Club bar.

Saturday 12th:
Itinerary: It's the third and final day of the second studio block for 'Meglos' in studio TC8 at BBC Television Centre.

Monday 14th:
Itinerary: John writes to Graeme McDonald, to explain why there was a two minute recording overrun on 10 July. He puts this down to the need to complete scenes on the TARDIS set, which had then to be struck overnight. He also explains that there was a thirty-minute overrun on the final studio day, 12 July, in order to complete all the scenes needed to finish the story.

Tuesday 15th:
Itinerary: Peter Jarvis from BBC Plymouth contacts the *Doctor Who* Production Office. He's looking to use clips of the Doctor and the Loch Ness Monster from the story 'Terror of the Zygons' in an episode of the regional programme *Brain Wave*. John has no objections to the use of these clips.

Thursday 17th:
Itinerary: John attends a planning meeting for 'Full Circle' (the new title for 'The Planet That Slept') in Threshold House, along with director Peter Grimwade and the various members of the relevant BBC Departments who will work on the story.

Friday 18th:
Itinerary: John signs off the commissioning brief for Johnny Byrne to write the four scripts for 'The Keeper of Traken'.

Saturday 19th:
Itinerary: John travels in by car for a non-duty day at Television Centre.

Tuesday 22nd:
Itinerary: The actor Clifford Rose writes to John, asking if there is any chance

for him to play a 'nasty' character in *Doctor Who* in the near future.[54]

Wednesday 23rd:
Itinerary: John travels by car to Black Park Country Park in Iver, Buckinghamshire, for the first day of location filming for 'Full Circle'. He drives home after filming is concluded.

John Nathan-Turner: 'It's a little unfair of me to mention this, but on the first day of filming, Andrew [Smith, the writer of the story] travelled out on the coach to the location and threw up all over the costumes! I'm sure it was the excitement of such a young writer finally realising that his script was going to be seen on British television.'[55]

Thursday 24th:
Itinerary: John travels by car to Black Park Country Park in Iver, Buckinghamshire, for the second day of location filming for 'Full Circle'. Again, he drives home after filming is concluded.

Friday 25th:
Itinerary: John travels by car to Black Park Country Park in Iver, Buckinghamshire, for the third and final day of location filming for 'Full Circle'. Again, he drives home after filming is concluded.

Saturday 26th:
Itinerary: John travels in by car for a non-duty day at Television Centre.

Tuesday 29th – Wednesday 6th August:
Rehearsals for the first studio block of 'Full Circle' take place at the BBC Television Rehearsal Rooms at Acton.

Tuesday 29th:
Itinerary: Betty McBride from the BBC1 programme *Where Are They Now?* contacts the *Doctor Who* Production Office, looking to use clips of Ysanne Churchman as the voice of Alpha Centauri from either 'The Curse of Peladon' or 'The Monster of Peladon' in an edition of the programme. John has no objections, provided the clips they use don't feature the Doctor (Jon Pertwee) in shot as well.

---

[54] Rose's letter was passed by John to director Paul Joyce, who then wrote to Rose on 4 August, offering him the role of Rorvik in 'Warriors' Gate' as a result. Rose was best known at the time for his role as the Nazi officer Kessler in the BBC's wartime series *Secret Army* (1977-79), and would return to that role in the spin-off series *Kessler* in 1981.
[55] John Nathan-Turner memoirs, *Doctor Who Magazine* #234.

Wednesday 30th:
Itinerary: John has a lunchtime meeting at the BBC Club bar with a prospective director for the series.

Commentary: John omitted to record the name of the director in question on his expenses form, so it's unknown whether or not it was someone who eventually went on to direct for the show.

Thursday 31st:
Itinerary: John writes to the Head of the Drama Group at the BBC, lamenting the fact that it was impossible to arrange a co-production deal with ABC TV in Australia for Season 18. He requests that the idea be pursued for the upcoming Season 19, and suggests that five weeks of Australian location filming be considered, in order to make one four-part story entirely on location, and to also record film inserts for a second story.

Commentary: If there was at any time a suggestion of filming any part of Season 19 on location in Australia, it's tempting to speculate how this might have worked. Is it possible, for example, that the story 'Kinda' was originally earmarked to be made entirely on location in Australia, considering that the storyline features parallels to some elements of Aboriginal culture? Could the Aboriginal links in the story 'Four to Doomsday' have had some greater significance at some point? And which other story could possibly have had its location-only film sequences shot in Australia? Surely not 'Black Orchid' or 'The Visitation'? Which leaves only 'Earthshock' as a possibility?

AUGUST

Friday 1st:
Itinerary: John draws up a character profile for a new member of the TARDIS crew, Tegan Jovanka, who will join the show late in Season 18.

Christopher H Bidmead: 'Tegan was entirely John Nathan-Turner. It was John's idea that she should be an airline hostess, and Australian – which was not unconnected with the fact that we were getting significant sales in Australia.'[56]

John Nathan-Turner: 'The name Tegan Jovanka was, in fact, a mistake. I'd

---

[56] Christopher H Bidmead interview, *Doctor Who Magazine* #258.

written a short document about the character for Chris Bidmead to embellish. At the top I'd written "Tegan (Jovanka)", meaning: shall we call her one or the other? I knew an Australian girl called Tegan – although the origins of the name are, I believe, Welsh – and President Tito's wife was called Jovanka. Chris thought that Jovanka was an intended surname, so I decided to leave it.'[57]

Commentary: John was obviously focusing on the links that he could make with Australia at the time, especially with talk floating around of a possible co-production deal with ABC TV.

Monday 4th:
Itinerary: John writes to Keith Barnfather, organiser of the upcoming Interface I convention for the *Doctor Who* Appreciation Society (DWAS), taking place this coming weekend. He explains that he will have to cancel his planned appearance at the event, due to a family illness.

Tuesday 5th:
Itinerary: John attends a planning meeting for the studio recordings of 'Full Circle' at the BBC's Television Rehearsal Rooms in Acton, along with director Peter Grimwade and the various members of the relevant BBC Departments who will work on the story.

Wednesday 6th:
Itinerary: John takes a tube ride from Union House to the BBC Television Rehearsal Rooms at Acton for the Producer's Run of the first studio block of 'Full Circle'.

Thursday 7th:
Itinerary: It's the first day of the two-day first studio block for 'Full Circle' in studio TC3 at BBC Television Centre. After recording, John joins the cast in the BBC Club bar.

Friday 8th:
Itinerary: It's the second day of the first two-day studio block for 'Full Circle' in studio TC3 at BBC Television Centre. Recording overruns by 15 minutes, mainly due to complications with the mechanism that powers the central console on the TARDIS set. After recording, John joins the cast in the BBC Club bar.

---

[57] John Nathan-Turner Memoirs, *Doctor Who Magazine* #234.

Monday 11th – Wednesday 20th:
Rehearsals for the second studio block of 'Full Circle' take place at the BBC Television Rehearsal Rooms at Acton.

Monday 11th:
Itinerary: John writes to Graeme McDonald, to explain the 15-minute recording overrun on 8 August. He says it was due to having to complete all the scenes on a particular set, which couldn't be retained for the second studio block. McDonald writes back the same day, pointing out that John hasn't explained *why* the recording overran, as presumably he always knew the set in question couldn't be used in the next block. On the same day, John signs off the commission for Jack Gardner to write the four scripts for his story 'The Dogs of Darkness', potentially for inclusion in Season 19.[58]

Tuesday 12th: (John's thirty-third birthday)
Itinerary: Michealjohn Harris, Head of the BBC Visual Effects Department, writes to John about the recent studio session for 'Full Circle'. He outlines an issue with the gear box on the motor that drives the central rotor in the TARDIS console prop, and suggests spending money on completely rebuilding the prop to prevent losing more studio time trying to coax the existing mechanism to work. He also complains that the more complicated scenes in the story, which required intricate visual effects, were left until the final half-hour of the studio session to record, and the resultant scramble to get the scenes 'in the can' produced substandard results. He warns that if future studio sessions treat the contribution of the Visual Effects Department in a similar manner, the Department might have to reconsider its involvement in the production of *Doctor Who*.

Wednesday 13th:
Itinerary: John authorises director Paul Joyce to carry out extensive rewrites of the scripts of 'Warriors' Gate' (as 'The Dream Time' has now been re-titled) due to the 'unavailability' of writer Stephen Gallagher.

Thursday 14th:
Itinerary: Johnny Byrne delivers his script for 'The Keeper of Traken' Part One to the *Doctor Who* Production Office.

Friday 15th:
Itinerary: John writes to Graeme McDonald with more details about the 'Full Circle' studio overrun on 8 August. He gives four main reasons. The first is

---

[58] 'The Dogs of Darkness' was still being considered as a potential story as late as April 1981.

that the first studio block was deliberately overscheduled to allow more time in the second for modelwork; the second is that there was a malfunction of a two-inch videotape machine used for the recording; the third is that there was a problem with the TARDIS console mechanism, which was resolved only by having a member of the Visual Effects Department team lying on his back, out of shot, manually operating the central column. John explains that he has now decided to have the console mechanism rebuilt. The final reason he gives is the need for performance retakes by the younger members of the cast, for which he takes full responsibility. On the same day, John signs off the commission for John Flanagan and Ian McCulloch to write a story outline for an unnamed story (which will ultimately be titled 'Project Zeta-Sigma') to introduce the new fifth Doctor in Season 19.

Saturday 16th:
Itinerary: John travels in by car for a non-duty day at Television Centre.

Monday 18th:
Itinerary: John writes to Jeanne and Barry Little, a couple in Sydney, Australia, who are friends of his. Jeanne is an entertainer and comedienne with a sizable following in Australia, and is beginning to get known in the UK at the time. John has previously persuaded the *Parkinson* chat show production team to book Jeanne as a guest, with a view to pitching a series based around her, but – as previously noted – this has come to nothing. John tells the couple that he's been asked to produce another series of *Doctor Who*, but that a few details have yet to be sorted out before he agrees. He also tells them that he and Gary [Downie] hope to be over in Sydney for a holiday at the end of January 1981, and goes on to say that the idea of filming a *Doctor Who* story in Australia is starting to look like it might come to fruition. He asks if Jeanne, who is also an actress, might be free for a small role [in London] from mid-December to mid-January.[59]

Tuesday 19th:
Itinerary: Johnny Byrne delivers his script for 'The Keeper of Traken' Part Two to the *Doctor Who* Production Office. On the same day, Philip Gilbert, the Resources Planning Manager at the BBC, writes to John, asking for an explanation for the overrun on the first studio block of 'Full Circle'.

Wednesday 20th:
Itinerary: John takes a tube ride from Union House to the BBC Television Rehearsal Rooms at Acton for the Producer's Run of the second studio block

---

[59] John was clearly thinking of offering Jeanne Little the role of Tegan's Auntie Vanessa in 'Logopolis'.

of 'Full Circle'.

Thursday 21st:
Itinerary: It's the first day of the three-day second studio block for 'Full Circle' in studio TC3 at BBC Television Centre.

John Nathan-Turner: 'In one scene of this story, *Doctor Who's* new artful dodger, Adric, purloins a vital piece of equipment, which he offers to the Doctor. [The Doctor] is delighted, yet reproachful at the theft. In one take, Tom [Baker] misquoted his line and appeared to totally approve of the youngster's crime. I was unhappy about this and the possible effect on our younger viewers. A retake was called for, and when the reason was explained to Tom, he said, "What does John think I'm playing? St Francis of Assisi?" Occasionally thereafter he would refer to me as "The Vatican".'[60]

Friday 22nd:
Itinerary: In the morning, John attends a planning meeting for 'Warriors' Gate' at BBC Television Centre, along with director Paul Joyce and the various members of the relevant BBC departments who will work on the story. It's also the second day of the three-day second studio block for 'Full Circle' in studio TC3 at BBC Television Centre; John attends this after the planning meeting. After recording, John joins the cast in the BBC Club bar.

Saturday 23rd:
Itinerary: It's the third and final day of the three-day second studio block for 'Full Circle' in studio TC3 at BBC Television Centre, which overruns, mainly due to a camera breaking down. After recording, John joins the cast in the BBC Club bar.

Sunday 24th:
Itinerary: John travels in by car for a non-duty day at Television Centre.

Monday 25th:
Itinerary: Johnny Byrne delivers his script for 'The Keeper of Traken' Part Three to the *Doctor Who* Production Office.

Tuesday 26th:
Itinerary: John writes back to Philip Gilbert, the Resources Planning Manager at the BBC, to reiterate the problems encountered in the first studio block of 'Full Circle', which resulted in an overrun (as he had already outlined to Graeme McDonald). He goes on to explain that the most recent three-day

---

[60] John Nathan-Turner memoirs, *Doctor Who Magazine* #234.

studio block for 'Full Circle' was stricken by the loss of a VT machine (again), delays caused by two changes of microphones, and a camera breakdown. Despite these issues, the final studio recording overran by just six minutes.

Wednesday 27th:
Itinerary: Today is the gallery-only day for 'Full Circle'. John attends at least part of this session.

Thursday 28th:
Itinerary: John takes the tube from Union House to Baker Street, where he walks to Madame Tussauds to attend a 'launch party' to publicise the new series of *Doctor Who*, which will start in two days' time on BBC1. He is joined by Tom Baker, who poses for press photos alongside his new waxwork double. On his return to the *Doctor Who* Production Office, John writes to Graeme McDonald to outline the reasons why the studio session on 23 August overran by six minutes (as he had already explained to Philip Gilbert the previous day).

Friday 29th:
Itinerary: John writes to Lovett Bickford to thank him for his work on 'The Leisure Hive'. However, he notes that the final edit on Part Four is not, as yet, complete. On the same day, Johnny Byrne delivers his script for 'The Keeper of Traken' Part Four to the *Doctor Who* Production Office. Other scripting matters occupy John today. He requests that Christopher H Bidmead be given staff clearance to write the scripts for 'Logopolis'. Executive Producer Barry Letts writes a four-page critique of the scripts of 'Warriors' Gate', and suggests that extensive rewrites are needed. Finally, John signs off the commissioning brief for Terence Dudley to write a story outline for an untitled story (which would eventually become 'Four to Doomsday').

Saturday 30th:
'The Leisure Hive' Part One screens on BBC1.

SEPTEMBER

Tuesday 2nd:
Itinerary: John writes to Philip Gilbert, the Resources Planning Manager, to complain of losing 2 hours and 25 minutes of time during the recent gallery-only session on Wednesday 27 August for 'Full Circle'. He puts this down to the video disc equipment that had been specifically requested not being

available due to it having been removed by the Sport Department; the booking for the telecine facility that was requested getting lost in the Planning Department; and the breakdown of two two-inch videotape machines. John also writes to director Paul Joyce, enclosing the notes that Barry Letts has made about the scripts for 'Warriors' Gate'. He proposes that they deal with the issues raised by Letts after the planned script read-through with the cast on 6 September, but notes that he's also dealing with a 'major crisis' with regard to the show's 'next scripts'.

Wednesday 3rd:
Itinerary: John writes to the Head of the Design Department, to praise Janet Budden's work on 'Full Circle.'

Thursday 4th:
Itinerary: John takes a short tube ride from Union House to the BBC Television Rehearsal Rooms at Acton.

Commentary: Rehearsals for 'Warriors' Gate' have yet to begin, so it's unclear what business John would have at the Acton Rehearsal Rooms at this time. It's possible that Paul Joyce was working on his rewrites of the scripts for 'Warriors' Gate' at Acton, hence the reason for John's visit.

Saturday 6th – Saturday 20th:
Rehearsals for the first studio block of 'Warriors' Gate' take place at the BBC Television Rehearsal Rooms at Acton.

Saturday 6th:
Itinerary: John takes a tube ride from Union House to the BBC Television Rehearsal Rooms at Acton, for the first day of rehearsals for the first studio block of 'Warriors' Gate', which includes a full script read-through by the cast. 'The Leisure Hive' Part Two screens on BBC1.

Monday 8th:
Itinerary: Jane Chapman from the BBC magazine programme *Nationwide* contacts the *Doctor Who* Production Office, looking for information on Tom Baker's first story, 'Robot'. They are planning a feature on the makers of various *Doctor Who* monsters; this is currently due for transmission the following day. John gives his assent as long as Graeme McDonald is also in agreement.[61]

---

[61] This planned feature didn't go ahead.

Tuesday 9th:
Itinerary: Sheila Cronin from the Personnel Department sends John a memo, confirming that director Paul Joyce is to be paid a staff contribution fee for having performed extensive rewrites on the four scripts for Stephen Gallagher's story 'Warriors' Gate'.

Friday 12th:
Itinerary: John signs off the casting of Anthony Ainley, who is contracted to appear as the Master in eight episodes of Season 18, with an option in the BBC's favour for either a further four or eight episodes the following year.

Christopher H Bidmead: 'John did things like come in and say, "Oh, the scripts [for 'The Keeper of Traken'] are almost finished – jolly good. We ought to have the Master in it." "What a good idea, John." At the same time, you were saying [to yourself] "Oh hell," and [thinking] what a lot of work it would be, [but also] thinking about the super opportunities. "It will totally screw up that scene, this bit won't work anymore, that's a disaster – but, if we do this, it might work!" I loved those challenges.'[62]

Anthony Ainley: 'I was lucky enough to be in *The Pallisers*, which was a big BBC series. John Nathan-Turner was working on that. He remembered me and later asked me if I'd like to play the Master.'[63]

Saturday 13th:
Itinerary: John takes a tube ride from Union House to the BBC Television Rehearsal Rooms at Acton, to sit in on the rehearsals for the first studio block of 'Warriors' Gate'. 'The Leisure Hive' Part Three screens on BBC1.

Wednesday 17th:
Itinerary: Jeff Mile from the BBC show *Larry Grayson's Generation Game* contacts the *Doctor Who* Production Office. He wants to use a Dalek prop in a game for the edition of the show due to be recorded this coming Saturday, 20 September. John's response is an emphatic 'No'. John writes to the Head of Copyright, to explain that John Flanagan and Andrew McCulloch were requested to do rewrites on their scripts for 'Meglos', which amounted to scripting an extra six minutes of material, and asks that they be paid for this work. John also signs off the commission for Eric Saward to write a scene breakdown for 'Plague Rats'.[64]

---

[62] Christopher H Bidmead interview, *Doctor Who Magazine* #258.
[63] Anthony Ainley interview, *Doctor Who Magazine* Summer Special 1982.
[64] This story will eventually evolve into 'The Visitation' for Season 19.

Commentary: This should have been the first day of the first studio block for 'Warriors' Gate' in studio TC3. However, industrial action amongst the scenic crews at BBC Television Centre prevented the story's sets being erected, and the whole three-day studio session was cancelled at the last minute. The time was given over to extra rehearsals for the cast, and the studio time was rebooked for the following week. However, a different studio, TC6, was allocated, causing issues with the sets that had been designed and constructed with TC3 in mind.

Saturday 20th:
'The Leisure Hive' Part Four screens on BBC1.

Commentary: This was the final day of rehearsals for the first studio block of 'Warriors' Gate', and so would presumably have seen the Producer's Run take place. There is no record of John having travelled to Acton on this date; but with the last-minute changes to the story's production schedule, this was probably just an oversight in his usually diligent expenses claims.

Monday 22nd:
Itinerary: John signs off the commission for Peter Grimwade to write the four scripts for a story called 'Zanadin'. John then takes the tube from Union House to Oxford Circus, to meet with Jean Diamond, Tom Baker's agent.

Commentary: By now, John had a very good indication that Tom Baker would be leaving the role of the Doctor at the end of the eighteenth season. However, the fact that he attended a face-to-face meeting with the actor's agent indicated that the inevitable announcement to the press of Baker's departure, and the subsequent publicity this would generate, were now being considered and planned for by all parties.

John Nathan-Turner: 'It was sometime during [the making of] this story ["Warriors' Gate"] that Tom [Baker] announced that he did not wish to stay for an eighth season. The message came from his agent, Jean Diamond, who told me that Tom felt he'd given everything to the show and wanted to try something different. At the time, I didn't realise that recasting the Doctor would be my problem. I'd only been offered a year as producer, and I didn't really know what the powers-that-be thought of my work, though the playback sessions thus far had been reasonably successful. Tom, Jean and I had agreed that we would delay announcing Tom's departure. Madame Tussauds in London had started work on Tom's waxwork figure during "The Leisure Hive" for the *Doctor Who* Experience, for one thing, and both Tom and

the [show] could benefit from the news being held back.'[65]

Wednesday 24th:
Itinerary: Today is the first day of the delayed first studio block for 'Warriors' Gate' in studio TC6 at BBC Television Centre. After recording, John joins the cast in the BBC Club bar.

Thursday 25th:
Itinerary: John signs off the commission for Christopher Bailey to write the four scripts for 'The Kinda'. It's also the second day of the three-day first studio block for 'Warriors' Gate' in studio TC6 at BBC Television Centre. After recording, John joins the cast in the BBC Club bar.

Friday 26th:
Itinerary: John Flanagan and Ian McCulloch deliver their story outline for 'Project "4G"' to the *Doctor Who* Production Office. It's also the third and final day of the first studio block for 'Warriors' Gate' in studio TC6 at BBC Television Centre. A dispute regarding the safety of part of a scaffolding set made by an outside contractor sees recording halted for over an hour. Although some time is made up, the studio session overruns by 31 minutes as a result.

John Nathan-Turner: 'Much of the spaceship interior was based on scaffolding, and in the middle of studio rehearsal a safety officer declared the set was unsafe. We lost much time over this, and the whole thing was so frustrating. However, the artistes' safety is paramount and the set had to be checked and adjusted.'[66]

Commentary: This issue regarding the safety of the set might have been due in part to the fact that it was originally designed to be erected in a different studio, and had to be altered at the last minute to accommodate being used in TC6 instead.

Saturday 27th – Wednesday 1st October:
Shorter-than-usual rehearsal sessions for the second studio block of 'Warriors' Gate' take place at the BBC Television Rehearsal Rooms at Acton.

Saturday 27th:
Itinerary: John travels in by car for a non-duty day at Television Centre. 'Meglos' Part One screens on BBC1.

---

[65] John Nathan-Turner memoirs, *Doctor Who Magazine* #234.
[66] John Nathan-Turner memoirs, *Doctor Who Magazine* #234.

Tuesday 30th:
Itinerary: John writes to Graeme McDonald to explain that the studio session on Friday 26 overran by 31 minutes.

OCTOBER

Wednesday 1st:
Itinerary: Eric Saward delivers to the *Doctor Who* Production Office his scene breakdown for 'Plague Rats' (which will eventually become 'The Visitation'). It's also the final day of rehearsals for the second studio block of 'Warriors' Gate', and so would normally be the day of the Producer's Run.

Commentary: Again, there is no record of John having actually travelled to Acton on this date.

Thursday 2nd:
Itinerary: It's the first day of the three-day second studio block for 'Warriors' Gate' in studio TC1 at BBC Television Centre. After recording, John joins the cast in the BBC Club bar.

Friday 3rd:
Itinerary: It's the second day of the three-day second studio block for 'Warriors' Gate' in studio TC1 at BBC Television Centre. After recording, John joins the cast in the BBC Club bar.

Saturday 4th:
Itinerary: It's the third and final day of the three-day second studio block for 'Warriors' Gate' in studio TC1 at BBC Television Centre. John travels in by car, as it's a non-duty day. 'Meglos' Part Two screens on BBC1.

Sunday 5th:
Itinerary: Clifford Rose writes to John, thanking him for helping to cast him as Rorvik in 'Warriors' Gate'.

Monday 6th:
Itinerary: In the morning, John interviews actress Janet Fielding, who is under consideration for the role of new companion Tegan Jovanka. On the same day, John has a meeting at Madame Tussauds with their Public Relations Department.

Commentary: It would seem that plans for publicising the *Doctor Who* Experience exhibit at Madame Tussauds were gathering momentum at this time. Tom Baker's waxwork was already public knowledge, and the press announcement was now planned for the following week.

Tuesday 7th:
Itinerary: John signs off the commission for John Flanagan and Andrew McCulloch to write the four scripts for 'Project "4G"'. Also on the same day, Barbara Cox from *Larry Grayson's Generation Game* contacts the *Doctor Who* Production Office, seeking permission to use the Doctor's scarf and sonic screwdriver prop in a game where contestants have to guess which TV characters certain objects belong to. The show is due to be recorded in the next few days, and Cox apologises for the lateness of the request. John agrees, and puts Cox in touch with costume designer June Hudson. In the morning, John takes a tube from Union House to Oxford Circus. Then, in the afternoon, he takes a taxi from Union House to Brook Green, to meet with the actor Peter Davison. After the meeting, he gets a cab back to Union House.

Commentary: The last time John visited Oxford Circus it was to meet with Tom Baker's agent, Jean Diamond, and although not specified in his expenses, it is a reasonable assumption that this latest trip to the same location was for the same reason. With Tom Baker's departure from the show now agreed by all parties, John quickly turns his attention to the casting of his successor. He spares very little time in honing in on Peter Davison, an actor he knew very well from his time working as a Production Unit Manager on *All Creatures Great and Small*, in which Davison played vet Tristan Farnon. He offers Davison the role of the fifth Doctor, and Davison asks for time to consider this.

John Nathan-Turner: 'I knew I wanted someone totally different from the previous Doctor, both physically and in acting style. Then I hit on the idea of Peter Davison. Graeme McDonald kept repeating his name with mounting enthusiasm when I mentioned it to him. Bill Cotton also gave his blessing, and so I rang Peter at home one evening and asked him if he'd like to meet to discuss the idea. Peter was dumbstruck, and took several days to decide whether [or not] he even wanted to talk about it.'[67]

Peter Davison: 'I was rung up one day by John Nathan-Turner, and he told me that Tom Baker was leaving – which no-one else knew at the time – and said, "Will you think about doing the Doctor?" I remember being silent for some time. My first reaction was that it was a ludicrous idea. I'd often fantasised about being in *Doctor Who*, but never really thought of playing the

---

[67] John Nathan-Turner memoirs, *Doctor Who Magazine* #234.

lead! First of all, I kind of turned it down. John said, "Well, look, let me take you out to lunch and explain to you why I'd like you to do it." He said that he wanted to change the image markedly from Tom. It's no secret that he didn't really like Tom's treatment of the Doctor. He wanted someone younger.'[68]

Wednesday 8th:
Itinerary: Robin Rumberlow from the BBC series *Take Hart* contacts the *Doctor Who* Production Office. He wants to use K-9 in a sketch in which the robot dog becomes a 'Feline'. John refuses. On the same date, John sends a memo to Graeme McDonald expressing dissatisfaction with Paul Joyce's handling of the studio sessions for 'Warriors' Gate' and acknowledging that it was an error of judgment on his part to engage a director who, although imaginative, had little experience of working at the high speed demanded by *Doctor Who*.

Thursday 9th:
Itinerary: John writes to the Head of the BBC's Design Department, praising Graeme Story's work on 'Warriors' Gate'. John also appears as a guest on Radio 4's *Today* programme, to discuss with presenter Andy Price the forthcoming departure of K-9. Meanwhile, Sarah Sutton is contracted to appear as Nyssa in four episodes of Season 18, with an option in the BBC's favour for a further 12 episodes early the following year, and a second option beyond that for 16 out of 20 more episodes.

Commentary: The decision to retain the character of Nyssa, as played by Sarah Sutton, as a regular character was taken by John before any rehearsals for 'The Keeper of Traken' had taken place.

Christopher H Bidmead: 'Nyssa was a surprise to us. There was nothing particularly special about the character that dictated we bring her on board, but I certainly think Sarah Sutton was special. It was John's decision that we needed another companion. It could have been some crisis of confidence.'[69]

Friday 10th:
Itinerary: John writes to Graeme McDonald, explaining that there was a five-and-a-half minute overrun to the 'Warriors' Gate' studio recording session of Friday 3 October. He puts this down to the need to complete all the scenes on a set that was due to be struck overnight and therefore wasn't able to be used the following day.

---

[68] Peter Davison interview, *Doctor Who Magazine* #213.
[69] Christopher H Bidmead interview, *Doctor Who Magazine* #258.

Saturday 11th:
'Meglos' Part Three screens on BBC1.

Tuesday 14th:
Itinerary: John is asked by the BBC Press Office to come up with a figure for the cost of making an episode of *Doctor Who*. He estimates that an episode of the 1980/81 season came in at a cost of around £37,000.

Thursday 16th:
Itinerary: John meets Peter Davison for lunch.

Commentary: Davison had been mulling over the offer of taking on the role of the fifth Doctor for the past week. This was probably the day he informed John that he would like to accept the part.

Saturday 18th:
Itinerary: John travels in by car for a non-duty day at Television Centre. 'Meglos' Part Four screens on BBC1.

Monday 20th:
Itinerary: Crispin Evans from the BBC1 Saturday morning show *The Multi-Coloured Swap Shop* contacts the *Doctor Who* Production Office. Evans would like Tom Baker to be a guest on the show's upcoming one-hundredth edition, as he had also been a guest on the very first edition back in 1976. The suggestion is put to Evans that Matthew Waterhouse could appear alongside Baker, as publicity for the new character Adric. Evans declines this idea, electing to keep an appearance from Waterhouse back until later in the show's run, when Adric has had a chance to establish himself with the audience. Evans wants Baker's appearance to keep the focus on the show's anniversary, which will look back to its first edition.[70]

Tuesday 21st:
Itinerary: In the evening, John goes to see the play *Pal Joey* at the Albery Theatre.

Commentary: The cast of *Pal Joey* includes Jane Gurnett, Deborah Browning, Debbie Astell, Lyn Hockney, Kay Jones, Raymond Brody, Susan Kyd, Buster Skeggs, Denis Lawson, Danielle Carson, Alana Tilvern, Darlene Johnson, Christopher Munckie, Michael Fitzpatrick, Tracey Perry, Sian Phillips and Jean Hart.

---

[70] The one-hundredth edition of *The Multi-Coloured Swap Shop* ultimately did not feature an appearance by Tom Baker.

Wednesday 22nd:
Itinerary: The organisers of the Exeter Book Week event approach the *Doctor Who* Production Office, looking to arrange for K-9 to appear there. The event is being covered by BBC Plymouth, and the writers Bob Baker and Dave Martin (creators of K-9) will have some involvement in the proceedings, as will Sparrow Books, who are currently publishing a series of K-9 children's books written by Martin. John declines to get involved, or to allow the use of the K-9 prop. On the same day, Crispin Evans from *The Multi-Coloured Swap Shop* contacts the *Doctor Who* Production Office with some new proposals for *Doctor Who* items. The first is an appearance by K-9 in an edition toward the end of November, to tie in with an item about a disc jockey who has made his own K-9-type robot dog – Evans is keen for the two robot dogs to meet. John declines this idea, saying that K-9 will be nothing to do with *Doctor Who* once he's been written out of the show, but does make a handwritten note that maybe K9 Mark III could be used.[71] The second request from Evans is for Matthew Waterhouse to be a guest on the 1 November edition. This is received favourably, and quickly brought forward to this coming Saturday, 25 October.

Thursday 23rd:
Itinerary: John takes the tube from Union House to Oxford Circus, to attend the press photocall to announce the casting of Janet Fielding at the new companion, Tegan Jovanka, at Hammersmith Park. Afterwards, he takes several members of the press pack to a nearby pub for lunch. Janet Fielding is contracted to appear as Tegan in 12 episodes of Seasons 18 and 19, with an option in the BBC's favour for a further 12 out of 20 more episodes.

Friday 24th:
Itinerary: John takes the tube to Oxford Circus again, this time for a press photocall to announce the opening of Madame Tussauds' *Doctor Who* Experience attraction. Then, having heard a rumour that Baker's imminent departure from the show has been leaked to the press, he and the actor hurriedly agree to make this news fully public, and he sets up a further press conference for this purpose. Afterwards, John takes the members of the press to a nearby pub for lunch and drinks. Then he returns to the *Doctor Who* Production Office at Union House via tube. Colin Gilbert from the BBC2 comedy show *Not The Nine O'Clock News* contacts the *Doctor Who* Production Office on the same day. He wants to be able to use the Wolfweed props from the story 'The Creature from the Pit' in a song routine they're devising about

---

[71] K-9 Mark III would be the co-star of *K-9 and Company* in December 1981, so perhaps John had already begun formulating ideas for a spin-off show with K-9 at this point.

some fictional animals called Ichas. The Wolfweeds are to appear as the Ichas themselves, but will be in only a single two-second shot, without any other characters or actors involved. John gives his agreement for this. John Radcliffe, the Executive Producer of *Continuing Education*, also contacts the *Doctor Who* Production Office. He's producing a Christmas lecture at the Institute of Electrical Engineers on 17 December, aimed at Sixth Form students, and wants to have K-9 appear on stage. John passes the request to the BBC Visual Effects Department, who will have the final say on K-9's involvement. John then has to hurriedly arrange for *Doctor Who* clips to be made available for both that evening's editions of *BBC News* and *Nationwide* for their coverage of the announcement of Tom Baker's departure. The clips screened are from 'Meglos' Parts One and Four.

John Nathan-Turner: 'On 23 October 1980 Tom posed with two waxworks of himself on the pavement of the Marylebone Road, to the delight of the press. Tom was the first person to have two likenesses in the same exhibition; one with the Meglos cactus effect and one without. Terry Sampson and Lorne Martin from BBC Enterprises (who had negotiated the details of the contract with Tussauds) adjourned with Tom and myself to a nearby pub. I took a phone call there informing me there had been a leak to the *Daily Mirror*, and a news reporter, rather than a showbusiness reporter, was on his way to the pub – someone at Tussauds had told him where we were. Tom and I bolted to a cab, appropriately headed off down Baker Street, found a backstreet hostel and set about calling an emergency press conference. We agreed that if one paper had the story, why not let the rest in on the "exclusive"? Shortly afterwards, we assembled with the BBC Drama press officer, Kevin O'Shea, and the editor of Picture Publicity, Brian Clifford, at 12A Cavendish Place, and were soon joined by a barrage of reporters and photographers.'[72]

Saturday 25th – Tuesday 4th November:
Rehearsals for the first studio block of 'The Keeper of Traken' take place at the BBC Television Rehearsal Rooms at Acton.

Saturday 25th:
Itinerary: John drives to Television Centre for an early start, so he can oversee Matthew Waterhouse's appearance on that morning's edition of *The Multi-Coloured Swap Shop*. Waterhouse is to be collected by car from his home at 7.45am, and needs to be in reception at BBC Television Centre by 9.15am. He will be on air by 10.00am, and then a second car will collect him at approximately 10.20am to take him to the BBC Rehearsal Rooms for the start

---

[72] John Nathan-Turner memoirs, *Doctor Who Magazine* #234. In his memoirs, John gets the date slightly wrong – it was Friday 24 October, not Thursday 23 October.

of the rehearsals for 'The Keeper of Traken'. John has arranged for the image translator prop from 'Full Circle' to be one of the prizes that Matthew offers to viewers, and also sets the question for him to ask: 'What was the name of the Professor who made K-9 Mark I?'[73] Also on this day, Christopher H Bidmead delivers his scripts for all four episodes of 'Logopolis'. 'Full Circle' Part One screens on BBC1.

Monday 27th:
Itinerary: The Features Department from BBC Manchester contacts the *Doctor Who* Production Office. They're making a pilot for a feminist revue programme called *Revolting Women* and would like to use some archive footage of Louise Jameson as Leela to illustrate a feature on 'tough women'. John has no objections to their proposal.

Wednesday 29th:
Itinerary: Sue Mallinson from the programme *Pick of the Year*, which is due to be shown on New Year's Eve, contacts the *Doctor Who* Production Office, asking if they can have a clip of either K-9's or Romana's departure from *Doctor Who* to use in their show. As 'Warriors' Gate' isn't due to be screened until early the following year, and John doesn't want the relevant scenes screened in advance, he offers her a choice of clips from 'State of Decay' instead.

NOVEMBER

Saturday 1st:
Itinerary: John travels in by car for a non-duty day at Television Centre. 'Full Circle' Part Two screens on BBC1.

Monday 3rd:
Itinerary: Alan Russell from the BBC1 show *Record Breakers* contacts the *Doctor Who* Production Office, enquiring if K-9 can make an appearance in their Christmas episode, *All Star Record Breakers*; this is due to record during the week commencing 8 December and will be shown on BBC1 on Christmas Eve. John requests further details from Russell about K-9's proposed involvement before making a decision.

---

[73] If you knew the answer was Professor Marius, then you too could have had a chance of winning the image translator prop!

Tuesday 4th:
Itinerary: John takes a short tube ride from Union House to the BBC Television Rehearsal Rooms at Acton. Today is the Producer's Run for the first studio block of 'The Keeper of Traken'.[74]

Wednesday 5th:
Itinerary: Peter Davison is announced as the fifth Doctor on BBC news. It's also the first day of the three-day first studio block for 'The Keeper of Traken' in studio TC6 at BBC Television Centre. After recording, John joins the cast in the BBC Club bar.

Thursday 6th:
Itinerary: John writes to Jeanne and Barry Little in Sydney, Australia. He clarifies the request in his previous letter as to Jeanne's potential availability in mid-December through to mid-January – he had considered casting her as Aunt Vanessa in 'Logopolis', but couldn't get this approved by actors' union Equity. John slyly notes that he thinks Equity would have required him to consider casting every Australian actress living in London before he would be allowed to offer the role to Jeanne.[75] It's also the second day of the three-day first studio block for 'The Keeper of Traken' in studio TC6 at BBC Television Centre.

Friday 7th:
Itinerary: John writes to Graeme McDonald about a studio overrun of ten minutes on Wednesday 5 November. This was due to paint on the studio floor not drying in time, delaying the recording by over half an hour. It's also the third and final day of the first studio block for 'The Keeper of Traken' in studio TC6 at BBC Television Centre. After recording, John joins the cast in the BBC Club bar.

Saturday 8th:
Itinerary: In the evening, John and Gary Downie go to see the play *Funny Kind of Day* at the Beck Theatre in Hayes. 'Full Circle' Part Three screens on BBC1.

Monday 10th – Wednesday 19th November:
Rehearsals for the second studio block of 'The Keeper of Traken' take place at the BBC Television Rehearsal Rooms at Acton.

---

[74] John has this expense logged as 5 November, but he must have erred, as that was the start date of the first studio block for 'The Keeper of Traken'.
[75] A shortlist of ten actresses from Australia and New Zealand whose details appeared in the *Spotlight* directory was drawn up for John on 31 October.

Tuesday 11th:
Itinerary: During the day, John meets and has lunch with several members of the *Doctor Who* Appreciation Society's executive committee. Also on this day, Jenny Hughes from the Open University programme *Illusions* contacts the *Doctor Who* Production Office. *Illusions* isn't due to be shown until August 1981, but for one edition they would like to use the TARDIS prop and demonstrate the 'illusion' of how it appears and disappears. John agrees to this request. John also writes to Graeme McDonald about the studio overrun of 15 minutes on Friday 7 November for 'The Keeper of Traken'. He explains that this was in due in part to the central column mechanism of the TARDIS console breaking down once again, despite the recent repairs undertaken. Once again, the column mechanism had to be manually operated by an effects assistant lying on the floor out of shot in order to get the relevant scenes recorded. A broken studio microphone added to the delay while it was replaced. On the same day, McDonald writes to John with his thoughts on the scripts for 'Logopolis'. His main concern regards the units of measurement used by the Doctor when recording the dimensions of the police box: he notes that the inhabitants of Gallifrey and Logopolis would use something more unique than imperial or metric units.

Wednesday 12th:
Itinerary: John attends a pre-planning meeting for 'Logopolis' in Threshold House, along with director Peter Grimwade and the various members of the relevant BBC Departments who will work on the story. Jane Sampson from BBC Radio Scotland contacts the *Doctor Who* Production Office. There will be an interview with 'Full Circle' writer Andrew Smith on their programme *Sunday Club* this coming Sunday, 16 November, and she would like an audio clip from his story to use to introduce him. John arranges for a clip of Adric's first scene from the story to be made available.

Saturday 15th:
'Full Circle' Part Four screens on BBC1.

Monday 17th:
Itinerary: Dee Walter from the BBC show *Mastermind* contacts the *Doctor Who* Production Office, to check that the answer they have to the question 'Who is playing the current *Doctor Who*?' is accurate. John asks when the edition of *Mastermind* will be transmitted, as the Doctor is due to change early next year, so the correct answer will depend on when the programme will go out.

Wednesday 19th:
Itinerary: John takes a short tube ride from Union House to the BBC Television Rehearsal Rooms at Acton for the Producer's Run of the second

studio block for 'The Keeper of Traken'. Also on this day, Tom Baker and Lalla Ward announce their engagement.

Thursday 20th:
Itinerary: Helen Griffith, Senior Personnel Officer at the BBC, writes to John about the book *A Day With a TV Producer*, which is published this week.[76] She belatedly confirms that the BBC has no objection to his involvement with the book, and acknowledges that this stemmed from an approach made by the publishers through the BBC Television Publicity Office. However, she asks for much earlier warning in future if he intends to write for any other publications, or to speak in public about BBC affairs. She refers him to read clause 10 of his BBC contract, which details what he can and can't do in terms of extra-curricular commercial activities. On the same day, John also signs off the commissioning brief for Eric Saward to write the four scripts for 'Plague Rats'.

Friday 21st:
Itinerary: Sue Mallinson from *Pick of the Year* gets back in touch with the *Doctor Who* Production Office. She's not happy with the choice of clips she's been offered from 'State of Decay', and asks for something more 'spectacular'. John suggests either the 'chronic hysteresis' scene from 'Meglos' Part One, or the final scenes from 'Full Circle' Part Four. On the same day, Janet Fielding, Matthew Waterhouse and Sarah Sutton take part in a photocall to promote Sutton joining the cast. It's also the first day of the three-day second studio block for 'The Keeper of Traken' in studio TC8 at BBC Television Centre. After recording, John joins the cast in the BBC Club bar.[77] It's also the evening of the annual BBC *Children in Need* telethon. The *Children in Need* producers have requested that Tom Baker and Lalla Ward make an appearance on the programme, and so John has arranged for Ward to come into the BBC that day, and for Baker to be freed from 'The Keeper of Traken' studio session for ten minutes sometime between 7.30 and 8.00pm. However, things go awry, as John is told that Tom and Lalla are scheduled to make their *Children in Need* appearance at 8.00pm, which is unworkable with the *Doctor Who* recording. Consequently the appearance is scrapped. To make matters worse, although John has also arranged for Peter Davison and his wife, actress Sandra Dickinson, to appear on the telethon, in order to read out letters, chat, or make an appeal, neither of them end up being used on screen.

---

[76] *A Day With a TV Producer* by Graham Rickard, published 27 November 1980 by Wayland Books. The book mainly follows the production of the story 'The Leisure Hive'.
[77] John has this expense logged as 20 November, but he must have erred with the date, as this was the first day of the second studio block for 'The Keeper of Traken'.

Saturday 22nd:
Itinerary: Mary Cline from the BBC lunchtime magazine programme *Pebble Mill at One* contacts the *Doctor Who* Production Office, enquiring about having Peter Davison as a guest on the edition due to be shown on Wednesday 3 December. She tells John that she particularly wants an audience of children to appear alongside Davison, so that they can discuss their opinions on the new Doctor. It's also the second day of the three-day second studio block for 'The Keeper of Traken' in studio TC8 at BBC Television Centre. After recording, John joins the cast in the BBC Club bar. 'State of Decay' Part One screens on BBC1.

Sunday 23rd
Itinerary: Today should be the third and final studio day of the second block of 'The Keeper of Traken', but a one-day strike at BBC Television Centre means that nothing is recorded. A remount is scheduled for 17 December.

John Nathan-Turner: 'We had a remount on this story. The electricians walked out on one of our studio days because they hadn't been able to park their cars at Television Centre! I was told on the day, a Sunday I think, that we were to lose our studio time that afternoon. I went around all the dressing rooms to ask if the artistes were free for the remount, as all the guest cast were about to finish their contracts. Much to my delight, they were available. We tracked down the Head of Programme Planning to a branch of Safeways where he was shopping with his family. He came rushing in to confirm a date for the remount before the actors were offered other work.'[78]

Monday 24th:
Itinerary: John writes to Graeme McDonald about a studio overrun of two minutes on Friday 21 November, during the second studio block for 'The Keeper of Traken'. He explains that this was due to the fact that on Thursday 20 November recording had been delayed by ten minutes due to the need to track down a banging noise in the studio, which was eventually traced to an unsecured boom microphone cable. This lost time had to be made up the following day, resulting in the overrun.

Wednesday 26th:
Itinerary: Lauri Stirley from *All Star Record Breakers* contacts the *Doctor Who* Production Office, looking to use approximately 15 seconds of the *Doctor Who* title sequence, to appear on a screen behind some dancers during the programme. John refuses, on the grounds that the title sequence is too recognisable. On the same day, John writes to director Paul Joyce, asking him

---

[78] John Nathan-Turner memoirs, *Doctor Who Magazine* #234.

to undertake three re-edits on Part Four of 'Warriors' Gate'. Also on this day, a photocall for the three new companion regulars – Matthew Waterhouse, Sarah Sutton and Janet Fielding – is held in Hammersmith Park. In addition, John writes to Mark Patterson at *Children in Need*, cataloguing the problems he encountered the previous Friday in trying to co-operate with the production, stating his dissatisfaction with the attitude shown toward *Doctor Who* and his annoyance that the time and effort that he, Tom Baker, Lalla Ward, Peter Davison and Sandra Dickinson had put in for the telethon had been totally wasted. He pointedly tells Patterson and *Children in Need* not to ask for any favours from him again. Also on this day, John receives a letter from Patricia Jaques, Acting Senior Personnel Officer, informing him that his promotion to acting producer level has been extended to 31 December 1981.

Commentary: John's promotion to the role of producer was still not confirmed as permanent, and the extension of his 'acting producer' contract for a further 13 months could be taken as an indication that he was still very much 'on probation' in his position as producer of *Doctor Who*.

Thursday 27th:
Itinerary: Mary Cline contacts the *Doctor Who* Production Office, asking if a number of props could be made available for the upcoming Peter Davison edition of *Pebble Mill at One*. She specifies that costumes/props for Daleks, Cybermen, Mandrels, Nimon, Foamasi and K-9 be supplied if possible. John arranges for a selection of costumes from the two *Doctor Who* Exhibitions at Blackpool and Longleat House to be made available.[79] On the same day, John writes to the * Manager of Series and Serials, noting that he anticipates that there will be a small overspend on the current season. However, he also asks for a further £3,000 to be allocated to the budget in order to pay clearances for a selection of flashback clips of old adversaries and companions from previous stories to be used in the final episode of 'Logopolis'.

Friday 28th:
Itinerary: John writes to Graeme McDonald in response to his memo of 11 November regarding the scripts of 'Logopolis'. He says that the unit of measurement used by the Doctor when recording the dimensions of the police box will stay as 'metres', as the Doctor has got used to this system during his banishment to Earth some years ago. John also points out that he dislikes 'gobbledygook' words being invented to be used in this sort of context.

---

[79] Peter Davison appeared on the edition of *Pebble Mill at One* screened on BBC1 on Wednesday 3 December.

Saturday 29th:
'State of Decay' Part Two screens on BBC1.

DECEMBER

Undated:
Around now, Christopher H Bidmead decides to depart his *Doctor Who* script editor post at the end of the year. John tries to interest Ted Rhodes, currently script editor on *All Creatures Great and Small,* in taking over, but Rhodes declines. Instead, BBC staff member Antony Root is given a temporary attachment , until a permanent replacement for Bidmead can be found.

Christopher H Bidmead: 'I'd had several rows with John Nathan-Turner. They weren't escalating – John and I knew where we stood *vis-à-vis* each other – but there was a lot of what you might call creative tension between us. Mainly, it was the big problem that there was no job description for what I was doing. As nobody would write one for me, there was, to my mind, only one thing to do: I thought the job was actually fairly important to the show, and I wanted to test whether the BBC felt that as well, so I said I wanted another 30 percent pay to stay on another year. They said, "Thanks, but no thanks." There was no hassle over it – I think they understood what my point was – and the answer was, "No, we don't actually value script editors all that much."'[80]

Monday 1st:
Itinerary: Peter Grimwade delivers his scripts for 'Zanadin' Parts One and Two to the *Doctor Who* Production Office.

Tuesday 2nd:
Itinerary: John makes two tube journeys; one to Baker Street and back to Union House, the other to Oxford Circus and again back to Union House.

Commentary: One or both of these journeys are probably connected to the press photocall that has been arranged today for Janet Fielding.

Thursday 4th:
Itinerary: Peter Grimwade delivers his scripts for 'Zanadin' Parts Three and Four to the *Doctor Who* Production Office.

---

[80] Christopher H Bidmead interview, *Doctor Who Magazine* #258.

Friday 5th:
Itinerary: John signs off the commission for Rod Beacham to write a story breakdown for 'Hebos'.[81]

Saturday 6th:
'State of Decay' Part Three screens on BBC1.

Monday 8th:
Itinerary: John Flanagan and Andrew McCulloch deliver their four scripts for 'Project Zeta Plus' to the *Doctor Who* Production Office.

Thursday 11th:
Itinerary: John sends a bouquet of flowers to Lalla Ward, in advance of her upcoming wedding to Tom Baker.

Friday 12th:
Itinerary: Jenny Hughes from the Open University programme *Illusions* writes to John, thanking him for the loan of the TARDIS prop, and for his help with their programme. She informs him that the episode with the TARDIS in is due to be shown on Saturday 15 August 1981, at 1.05pm on BBC2.

Saturday 13th:
Itinerary: John is a guest at the wedding of Tom Baker and Lalla Ward at Chelsea Registry Office. 'State of Decay' Part Four screens on BBC1.

Monday 15th:
Itinerary: Rehearsals for the location filming for 'Logopolis' take place at BBC Television Centre. On the same day, Terence Dudley delivers his story outline for 'Day of Wrath' (which will become 'Four to Doomsday') to the *Doctor Who* Production Office, and Christopher Bailey delivers his four scripts for 'The Kinda'.

Tuesday 16th:
Itinerary: John travels by car to Ursula Street, Wandsworth, and then on to Albert Bridge in Kensington and Chelsea, for the first day of location filming for 'Logopolis'.

Wednesday 17th:
Itinerary: Today is the remount of the final day of the second studio block for

---

[81] Beacham had played Corporal Lane in the 1968 story 'The Web of Fear', and would go on to script the *Blake's 7* episode 'Assassin'. 'Hebos' was never developed beyond the story breakdown stage.

'The Keeper of Traken' in studio TC6 at BBC Television Centre. Because of this, today's planned location filming for 'Logopolis' has to be cancelled. John drives in to Television Centre by car.

Thursday 18th:
Itinerary: John travels by car to the BBC's Overseas Monitoring Station in Caversham for the second day of location filming for 'Logopolis'.

Friday 19th:
Itinerary: Today was meant to be spent filming in the A413 lay-by in Denham for 'Logopolis', but no work is done, and the filming is postponed until Monday 22 December.

Monday 22nd:
Itinerary: John travels by car to the A413 lay-by in Denham for the rescheduled final day's location filming for 'Logopolis'.

Tuesday 23rd:
Itinerary: John signs off the commissioning brief for Terence Dudley to write the four scripts for 'Day of Wrath'.

Monday 29th – Wednesday 7th January:
Rehearsals for the first studio block of 'Logopolis' take place at the BBC Television Rehearsal Rooms at Acton.

Monday 29th:
Itinerary: John takes a short tube ride from Union House to the BBC Television Rehearsal Rooms at Acton, to attend the first day of rehearsals for the first studio block of 'Logopolis'.

Tuesday 30th – Wednesday 31st:
Itinerary: John takes two days of annual leave from the BBC, while the cast continue their rehearsals for 'Logopolis'.

1981

Setting the Scene:

John is nearing the end of production on his first full season as *Doctor Who* producer. The year has certainly been something of a learning curve for him. The production of 'The Leisure Hive' could be considered as something of a failure, as the extra studio days that needed to be allocated to the story in order to get everything recorded would have sent it deeply over budget. But things seemed to have settled down, and he was by now mastering the mechanics of producing the show, with only small but regular studio overruns seemingly an inevitable blot on his copybook.

John had also overseen a complete change of regular cast, and once 'Logopolis' was completed in the early weeks of January 1981, he would be in charge of a show that he had totally cast himself. The unveiling of Peter Davison as the fifth Doctor had afforded a welcome shot of publicity, and the show now needed to capitalise on this.

One downside to all this was the departure of Christopher H Bidmead. John's relationships with his script editors were always quite fraught, but the reasons for Bidmead's exit weren't all to be laid at his door. Another downside was the low viewing figures that Season 18 was generating. ITV had gone out all-guns-blazing to compete with *Doctor Who* this year, screening the flashy US import *Buck Rogers in the 25th Century* against the show. *Doctor Who* had consequently shed a few million viewers compared to the seventeenth season. However, the latter's ratings had been artificially high, due to a mammoth strike at ITV, which had seen the rival channel go off air entirely during part of 1979. However, ratings would improve. *Doctor Who* was starting to claw back its audience.

Once work on 'Logopolis' was over, John could take a few months to draw breath and to consolidate the experience he'd gained over the past 12 months, before hurtling headlong into the production of Season 19 with renewed enthusiasm. Hopefully, at some point soon, he'd be rewarded by having his promotion to producer grade fully ratified …

JANUARY

Friday 2nd:
Itinerary: John takes a short tube ride from Union House to Westbourne Park in Notting Hill, and then back to the BBC.

Commentary: The rehearsals for 'Logopolis' were still under way at Acton on this date, so it's not known what business John was attending to at Westbourne Park.

Saturday 3rd:
'Warriors' Gate' Part One screens on BBC1.

Tuesday 6th:
Itinerary: Jonathan Dent, from the BBC programme *Friday Night, Saturday Morning*, contacts the *Doctor Who* Production Office. They are considering doing an item on *Doctor Who* companions, and want to register their interest at this stage. Dent says he will be back in touch if the idea goes any further.

Wednesday 7th:
Itinerary: John takes a short tube ride from Union House to the BBC Television Rehearsal Rooms at Acton for the Producer's Run of the first studio block for 'Logopolis'.

Thursday 8th:
Itinerary: It's the first day of the two-day first studio block for 'Logopolis' in studio TC3 at BBC Television Centre. After recording, John joins the cast in the BBC Club bar.

Friday 9th:
Itinerary: It's the second and final day of the two-day first studio block for 'Logopolis' in studio TC3 at BBC Television Centre. After recording, John joins the cast in the BBC Club bar.

Saturday 10th:
'Warriors' Gate' Part Two screens on BBC1.

Monday 12th – Wednesday 21st:
Rehearsals for the second studio block of 'Logopolis' take place at the BBC Television Rehearsal Rooms at Acton.

Monday 12th:
Itinerary: John writes to Graeme McDonald about an overrun of fifteen minutes during the studio recording of 'Logopolis' on Friday 9 January. He attributes this mainly to having to restage several TARDIS interior scenes due to the central console mechanism making excessive noise when in motion. On the same day, Terence Dudley delivers his four scripts for 'Day of Wrath' to the *Doctor Who* Production Office.

Thursday 15th:
Itinerary: John Flanagan and Andrew McCulloch deliver script rewrites on 'Project Zeta Plus' to the *Doctor Who* Production Office.

Saturday 17th:
'Warriors' Gate' Part Three screens on BBC1.

Monday 19th:
Itinerary: John writes to Michealjohn Harris, Head of the BBC's Visual Effects Department, about the ongoing, season-long problems with the TARDIS console. A new mechanism was installed for the first studio block of 'Logopolis', but in John's opinion this was far too noisy. This problem was compounded by the visual effects designer, John Horton, leaving the studio halfway through the first recording day on Thursday 8 January, and so being unavailable during the evening recording, when the excessive noise became apparent. John asks Harris for options regarding the prop, which will not now be needed again until a few months' time at the earliest, when recording for Season 19 begins. Also, on the same day, John has a meeting/working lunch with writer Christopher Priest.

Commentary: Priest was originally set to write the story 'Sealed Orders' for Season 18, but it was replaced by 'Warriors' Gate' when problems arose with it. As a consolation of sorts he was invited to pitch a story for the upcoming Season 19. That story, 'The Enemy Within', would also run into problems, being replaced by 'Earthshock' in the season's running order.

Wednesday 21st:
Itinerary: 'Sandi'[82] from *The Multi-Coloured Swap Shop* contacts the *Doctor Who* Production Office. They are planning to have visual effects designer Mat Irvine on as a guest on the edition due to be shown on Saturday 31 January, and would like to use some clips from 'Warriors' Gate' to illustrate his interview. John gives the okay for them to use clips of the Privateer spaceship

---

[82] No other name is given on the memo.

and gateway exploding, but specifically asks that they use no clips of K-9.[83] Today is also the Producer's Run for the second studio block of 'Logopolis'.

Commentary: John has no record of visiting Acton on this date in his expenses, but it's inconceivable that he didn't attend the Producer's Run.

Thursday 22nd:
Itinerary: It's the first day of the three-day second studio block for 'Logopolis' in studio TC6 at BBC Television Centre. After recording, John joins the cast in the BBC Club bar.

Friday 23rd:
Itinerary: It's the second day of the three-day second studio block for 'Logopolis' in studio TC6 at BBC Television Centre. After recording, John joins the cast in the BBC Club bar.

Saturday 24th:
Itinerary: It's the third and final day of the second studio block for 'Logopolis' in studio TC6 at BBC Television Centre. John drives to the BBC for this. After recording, he hosts a farewell party for Tom Baker, who has recorded his final scenes as the Doctor on this day. 'Warriors' Gate' Part Four screens on BBC1.

Commentary: The final studio recording of 'Logopolis' marks the conclusion of production on Season 18 of *Doctor Who*, and of John's first season as producer.

John Nathan-Turner: 'We held two parties for Tom: one at the BBC Television Centre bar where we invited companions, producers, directors and the current team, and a larger gathering at BBC Enterprises, then based in Ealing.'[84]

Monday 26th:
Itinerary: Eric Saward delivers his four scripts for 'The Visitation' (formerly 'Plague Rats') to the *Doctor Who* Production Office. On the same day, John writes to Harry Smith in the BBC Design Department, thanking him for allocating Tony Burrough to work on story 5W, which at the moment is due to be 'Project Zeta-Sigma' (formerly 'Project Zeta Plus'). On the subject of 'Project Zeta-Sigma', John also has a working pub lunch today with its writers, John Flanagan and Andrew McCulloch. Meanwhile, Paul Joyce writes to John, thanking him for the opportunity to direct 'Warriors' Gate' and for his

---

[83] In the event, it is Sarah Sutton rather than Irvine who actually guests on the 31 January edition of *The Multi-Coloured Swap Shop*.
[84] John Nathan-Turner memoirs, *Doctor Who Magazine* #234.

supportiveness when 'on and off-stage dramas' were encountered during the production. In a post-script he adds 'Hope to see you on the 29th' (though it is unknown to what this related, perhaps one explanation is that Joyce had got the date of Tom Baker's leaving party wrong).

Wednesday 28th:
Itinerary: Today is a gallery-only studio day for 'Logopolis', at least some of which John attends. John also has a working pub lunch with writer Christopher Bailey.

Commentary: The subject of discussion is almost certainly Bailey's proposed Season 19 story 'Kinda' (originally 'The Kinda').

Thursday 29th:
Itinerary: John writes to Graeme McDonald about an overrun of three minutes experienced during the previous day's gallery-only studio day for 'Logopolis', which was caused by a faulty two-inch videotape machine. Also today, John is informed that BBC1 will not screen Season 19 in the expected Saturday evening slot starting in the autumn. Instead, the show will be switched to a twice-weekly evening slot with a delayed start date of January 1982.[85] This will be a groundbreaking and controversial move; since it began in November 1963, *Doctor Who* has always been screened in a Saturday teatime slot.

John Nathan-Turner: 'Graeme explained that though the series was getting a good general reaction, the audience figures, due to the competition, had been disappointing. The Controller was thinking of moving it to a twice-weekly slot early in the evening to try and give it the audience it deserved. He went on to discuss the way the Sixth Floor thought that viewing tastes on Saturday evenings had changed. Producers don't control where their programmes are transmitted, by the way, but the thought that we might reach a larger audience certainly appealed.'[86]

Friday 30th:
Itinerary: Another party is held at Television Centre to mark Tom Baker's departure from the show. Attendees include assistant Val McCrimmon (Floor Manager on four stories from Season 18), Peter Grimwade (director of 'Full

---

[85] This change in scheduling was necessitated partly by the fact that Peter Davison was committed to record episodes of the sitcom *Sink or Swim* in the summer, requiring a break in production of *Doctor Who* and making it more difficult to get enough stories banked in advance of an autumn transmission date. However, the relatively poor ratings Season 18 had achieved in the Saturday timeslot was certainly another factor.

[86] John Nathan-Turner memoirs, *Doctor Who Magazine* #234.

Circle' and 'Logopolis'), Margot Hayhoe (Production Manager on 'Logopolis') and Pat Greenland (assistant to Peter Grimwade). Tom Baker briefly attends, but makes a quick exit.

Saturday 31st:
'The Keeper of Traken' Part One screens on BBC1.

FEBRUARY

Monday 2nd:
Itinerary: Brian Richards from BBC Cardiff contacts the *Doctor Who* Production Office. A programme that they are making for St David's Day, and that is due to be recorded on 25 February, is planned to include a comedy skit in which St David returns as a Time Lord, appearing out of thin air to the TARDIS sound effect. John agrees to this request. On the same day, Christopher Bailey delivers rewrites of his scripts of all four episodes of 'Kinda' to the *Doctor Who* Production Office.

Tuesday 3rd:
Itinerary: John sends a memo to the Assistant Head of Artist's Contracts, requesting that Peter Davison's contract to play the Doctor be reissued to cover 26 episodes rather than the 28 originally envisaged, and setting out the dates between 30 March 1981 and 5 February 1982 when the actor would be required to be available.

Friday 6th:
Itinerary: John signs off the commission for Christopher Priest to write four scripts for 'The Enemy Within', and for Tanith Lee[87] to write a story outline for an untitled story.[88]

Saturday 7th:
'The Keeper of Traken' Part Two screens on BBC1.

Monday 9th:
Itinerary: John requests that Terence Dudley be given staff clearance to write

---

[87] Tanith Lee had found great success in writing literary science fiction in the early 1970s, and had recently contributed scripts to the BBC science fiction series *Blake's 7*. The first of these, 'Sarcophagus', had been screened in March 1980, while the second, 'Sand', was yet to be recorded at this time.
[88] Lee's proposed story would get no further than this story outline commission.

the two scripts for his proposed story 'Black Orchid'.[89]

Tuesday 10th February – Tuesday 3rd March:
Itinerary: With production concluded on Season 18, and the first recording for Season 19 still some months away, John takes three weeks of annual leave from the BBC. He and Gary Downie go on holiday to the USA, and visit New Orleans for Mardi Gras. On their return to London, John discovers that their house has been burgled in their absence.

Tuesday 10th:
Itinerary: John writes to director Paul Joyce, giving him the viewing figures for 'Warriors' Gate', which he claims are the best of the season to date, and thanks him for his work on the story. John also writes to costume designer Colin Lavers. He outlines at length his thoughts on the image the fifth Doctor should have, and the way his costume should appear. He notes that it should be a period cricket outfit, and that the shirt should be the same as worn by Tom Baker in Season 18, with '?' embroidery on the lapels. He stipulates that a cricket jersey is also required for merchandise reasons. The footwear is described as white cricket shoes, and the trousers as period baggy pants with some colour, such as stripes. A top coat and hat are also suggested by John. Other ideas are put forward as possibilities, such as a morning suit and a collapsible top hat. He suggests meeting with Lavers and Davison on Friday 6 March to test the costume ideas.[90]

Friday 13th:
Itinerary: In John's absence, rehearsal scripts for all four episodes of 'Project Zeta-Sigma' are distributed by script editor Antony Root to all the BBC Departments who will be contributing to the production of this story, which is planned to be first into production for Season 19.

Saturday 14th:
'The Keeper of Traken' Part Three screens on BBC1.

Monday 16th:
Itinerary: Terence Dudley delivers his two scripts for 'Black Orchid' to the *Doctor Who* Production Office.

---

[89] Terence Dudley was directing episodes of the BBC series *Flesh and Blood* on BBC staff at the time.
[90] John was on leave at this point, so he'd probably written these memos on or prior to Monday 9 February, his last day in the *Doctor Who* Production Office.

Wednesday 18th:
Itinerary: Sarah Sutton is contracted for a further 16 episodes, and Janet Fielding for a further 18 episodes, both for Season 19.[91]

Thursday 19th:
Itinerary: In John's absence, script editor Antony Root pulls 'Project Zeta-Sigma' from the 5W production slot and announces that 'Four to Doomsday' by Terence Dudley will replace it. John Black remains as director. All work on casting, sets, props and costumes for 'Project Zeta-Sigma' is halted with immediate effect, and all Departments will now have to work against the clock to get all their elements required for 'Four to Doomsday' ready in time for the planned studio dates in April.

Commentary: 'Project Zeta-Sigma' was initially bumped further down the season's production order to allow time to try to get the scripts into a useable state, but was eventually abandoned. Its place as the fifth Doctor's first adventure was ultimately taken instead by Christopher H Bidmead's 'Castrovalva'. However, as 'Four to Doomsday' had now been assigned its original production slot, and as 'The Visitation' was already locked in as the second story to be recorded for the new season, one consequence of this change of plan was that Peter Davison would now be recording a number of other stories before the one in which he would make his on-screen debut. John Nathan-Turner managed to retrofit these events in later interviews, claiming that it was his intention all along to have Davison record his debut story out of sequence, after others were already completed.

John Nathan-Turner: 'I wasn't happy with the idea of Peter doing his debut story first. I felt he needed time to get into his character and become settled with it. And I didn't want an opening story where everyone could tune in and find out what the Doctor was like from the first episode. His character only really came through in the final episode. I wanted to keep everyone guessing so that they would watch the second, third and fourth episodes as well.'[92]

Friday 20th:
Itinerary: Peter Davison is contracted for 26 episodes of Season 19.[93]

Saturday 21st:
'The Keeper of Traken' Part Four screens on BBC1.

---

[91] Presumably this was on instructions given by John prior to his leave.
[92] John Nathan Turner interview, *Doctor Who Magazine* #68.
[93] Presumably this was on instructions given by John prior to his leave.

Tuesday 24th:
Itinerary: Terence Dudley delivers rewrites of all four episodes of 'Four to Doomsday' to the *Doctor Who* Production Office.

Wednesday 25th:
Itinerary: Matthew Waterhouse is contracted for 20 episodes of Season 19.[94]

Thursday 26th:
Itinerary: To promote the upcoming private auction on 10 March of the Whomobile car featured during his time as the third Doctor, its owner Jon Pertwee contacts the BBC to request the loan of a Dalek prop to be seen alongside the car in a photocall planned for 3 March. In John's absence, the request is refused by the *Doctor Who* Production Office.

Saturday 28th:
'Logopolis' Part One screens on BBC1.

MARCH

Wednesday 4th:
Itinerary: John returns back to work at the *Doctor Who* Production Office in Union House after his holiday in the USA. He writes to the Head of Merchandising at BBC Enterprises, stating that he'd be happy for the renewal of Marvel's licence to continue publishing *Doctor Who Monthly* to go ahead. He states how happy he is with the new style of the magazine, and with the recent fiftieth issue in particular.[95]

Saturday 7th:
'Logopolis' Part Two screens on BBC1.

Monday 9th:
Itinerary: John writes to director Peter Grimwade, thanking him for his work on 'Logopolis'. John also signs off the commissioning brief for former script editor Christopher H Bidmead to write a story outline for 'The Visitor' (which will eventually become 'Castrovalva'). In the evening, John and Gary go to see *Oklahoma* at the Palace Theatre in the West End.

---

[94] Presumably, again, this was on instructions given by John prior to his leave.
[95] Issue 50 of *Doctor Who Monthly* was published with a cover date of March 1981.

Commentary: The cast of *Oklahoma* included John Diedrich, Alfred Molina, Rosamund Shelley, Madge Ryan and Linal Haft.

Tuesday 10th:
Itinerary: Alan Bookbinder from the BBC2 review programme *Did You See …?* contacts the *Doctor Who* Production Office. They are interested in having Peter Davison as a guest reviewer on an upcoming edition of their next season (which will record from the end of April to the end of June), an d want to tie this in with a 'behind-the-scenes' feature on *Doctor Who*. John replies that he's not particularly keen on 'behind-the-scenes' items, and so his answer is no to that proposal for the moment, but he stresses that he and Bookbinder should talk again later in the year.

Friday 13th:
Itinerary: John sends Michael Checkland, the Controller of Planning and Resource Management, a memo formally requesting that BBC Enterprises contribute some 'front money' to the budget for *Doctor Who*'s 1981/82 season. To justify this, he points out the considerable income the show generates via overseas sales and merchandising.

Saturday 14th:
'Logopolis' Part Three screens on BBC1.

Wednesday 18th:
Itinerary: John takes the tube to the Television Rehearsal Rooms in Acton, and then returns to the *Doctor Who* Production Office at Union House. On the same day, Graeme McDonald sends John a memo expressing concern at the 'formidable amount' of money spent on script write-offs over the past year, albeit confined to four writers. He requests that performance in this regard be carefully monitored over the coming year.

Commentary: Rehearsals for 'Four to Doomsday' aren't due to begin for another couple of weeks, so John's visit to Acton may have been to check the general arrangements for the upcoming season's rehearsals.

Saturday 21st:
'Logopolis' Part Four screens on BBC1.

Wednesday 25th:
Itinerary: John takes the train to Blackpool to visit the *Doctor Who* Exhibition, which has been refurbished with props and costumes from Season 18, and will reopen to the public in just a few weeks. John stays overnight at a local hotel,

and is joined in the evening by the Director of the Ritz Catering Corporation.[96] John's travel and hotel expenses for this visit are paid by BBC Enterprises.

Thursday 26th:
Itinerary: John returns to London from Blackpool via train.

Friday 27th:
Itinerary: John takes the tube to the Television Rehearsal Rooms in Acton, and then returns to the *Doctor Who* Production Office at Union House.

Commentary: Rehearsals for 'Four to Doomsday' are still just over a week away, so the reason for John's visit to Acton isn't known.

Monday 30th:
Itinerary: John meets members of the executive committee of the *Doctor Who* Appreciation Society, and entertains them at the BBC bar over lunch. In the evening, he goes to see the play *Educating Rita* at the Piccadilly Theatre.

Commentary: The cast of *Educating Rita* included Mark Kingston, Julie Walters, Julia Deakin and Zoe Gonord.

APRIL

Wednesday 1st:
Itinerary: John meets up with his new incoming script editor, Eric Saward, and takes him to lunch at the BBC bar.[97] Avril Warner, a researcher on Yorkshire Television's *Extraordinary People* programme, contacts the *Doctor Who* Production Office. Duncan Goodhew[98] is planned to be a guest on an upcoming edition of the programme, and he has mentioned that his favourite TV programme as a child was *Doctor Who*. Warner asks if they could have permission to show a clip of the 'original Doctor and the Daleks'. On the same day, Christopher H Bidmead delivers his story outline for 'The Visitor' to the *Doctor Who* Production Office.

---

[96] The New Ritz Catering Company organised the physical refurbishment of the Blackpool exhibition each new 'season', sprucing up display cases, adding new exhibits, and removing old ones.
[97] Antony Root's three-month attachment to *Doctor Who* was not going to be extended.
[98] Goodhew had won a gold medal swimming the breaststroke in the 1980 Olympics in Moscow.

John Nathan-Turner: 'Eric [Saward] was an experienced radio writer who was brought in by Christopher Bidmead, nurtured by him and Antony Root, and later suggested to me by both of them for the role of script editor. I was impressed by his writing and liked him as a person. It is strange that you can work with someone for five years and never actually get to know them.'[99]

Eric Saward: 'I delivered "The Visitation" script in January 1981, Chris Bidmead had left the previous December, and Antony Root had taken over to fill in for three months ... Then one day I had a phone call from John Nathan-Turner quite out of the blue, asking me if I wouldn't mind coming in for a chat. So I went in and he asked me if I'd be interested in script editing *Doctor Who* for three months while Anthony was away.'[100]

Thursday 2nd – Friday 10th:
Rehearsals for the first studio block of 'Four to Doomsday' take place at the BBC Television Rehearsal Rooms at Acton.

Thursday 2nd:
Itinerary: John takes a short tube ride from Union House to the BBC Television Rehearsal Rooms at Acton to observe the first day of rehearsal for the first studio block of 'Four to Doomsday'.

Friday 3rd:
Itinerary: John has a pub lunch with an unnamed reporter from Marvel's *Doctor Who Monthly* magazine.[101]

Monday 6th:
Itinerary: John has a working lunch with Peter Grimwade and two unnamed researchers.

Commentary: John specifies on his expenses form for this lunch that he met Grimwade in the latter's capacity as director, not writer, and so the meeting was almost certainly with regard to Grimwade's upcoming work on 'Kinda', rather than his script for 'Time-Flight'.

Wednesday 8th:
Itinerary: Helen Griffiths, Senior Personnel Officer at the BBC, writes to John

---

[99] John Nathan-Turner memoirs, *Doctor Who Magazine* #235.
[100] Eric Saward interview, *DWB* #57. It would seem that Saward was initially told that Root would be returning to *Doctor Who* in three months' time.
[101] Issue 51 of *Doctor Who Monthly*, dated April 1981, has a lengthy interview with John, conducted by Jeremy Bentham earlier in the year. It's possible that Bentham was the person John met for lunch, and the interview was done on this day.

to inform him that there is no objection to his involvement in the upcoming book *Facts About a Television Series*.[102] On the same day, John signs off the commission for Christopher H Bidmead to write the four scripts for 'Castrovalva' (as 'The Visitor' has now been retitled).

Commentary: After coming close to getting his wrists slapped over his involvement with the Graham Rickard book *A Day With a TV Producer* the previous year, John was obviously trying to ensure that he was above reproach with this proposed book project.

Thursday 9th:
Itinerary: John takes a short tube ride from Union House to the BBC Television Rehearsal Rooms at Acton, where rehearsals for 'Four to Doomsday' are still ongoing.

Friday 10th:
Itinerary: John has a working lunch at the BBC bar with writer Lesley Thomas.

John Nathan-Tuner: 'I first went to New Orleans for a holiday in 1981 and was there during Mardi Gras. The atmosphere was wonderful – the French Quarter has an atmosphere all its own … I had initial discussions with our American distributors, Lionheart, and they were interested in a co-production deal. We initially contracted Lesley Thomas, an American writer who was working on a soap opera over here at the time, to produce a scene breakdown. However, "Way Down Yonder", as it was called, didn't have that elusive "*Who*-ish" quality about it … '[103]

Saturday 11th:
Itinerary: John drives from his home, first to the *Doctor Who* Production Office at Union House in the morning, and then to the BBC Television Rehearsal Rooms at Acton. Today is the Producer's Run for the first studio block of 'Four to Doomsday'.

Monday 13th:
Itinerary: It's the first day of the three-day first studio block for 'Four to Doomsday' in studio TC6 at BBC Television Centre. After recording, John joins the cast in the BBC Club bar. On the same day, John pitches a series to David Reid, based on the true-life story of the jockey Bob Champion.[104]

---

[102] This book, by Alan Road, would eventually be published by Andre Deutch Ltd in July 1982 under the title *Doctor Who: The Making of a Television Series*.
[103] John Nathan-Turner memoirs, *Doctor Who Magazine* #239.
[104] Bob Champion had ridden the winner in the Grand National horse race just a few days earlier, on 4 April. He'd been diagnosed with testicular cancer in 1979,

Tuesday 14th:
Itinerary: It's the second day of the three-day first studio block for 'Four to Doomsday' in studio TC6 at BBC Television Centre. After recording, John joins the cast in the BBC Club bar.

Wednesday 15th:
Itinerary: It's the third and final day of the first studio block for 'Four to Doomsday' in studio TC6 at BBC Television Centre. Also today, Marcus Mortimer from the BBC Light Entertainment Department contacts the *Doctor Who* Production Office. He is working on the BBC1 comedy series *3 of a Kind* and wants to do a sketch where a man (presumably one of the show's two male stars, Lenny Henry or David Copperfield) is in a pub, playing a Space Invaders machine. The machine stops working mid-game, and the man calls over to the bar and complains. A Mandrel from the Season 17 story 'Nightmare of Eden' comes out from behind the machine, armed with a gun, and blows the man up. Although Mortimer is very insistent that the sketch would not be 'sending up *Doctor Who*', John's response is a very firm 'No'.

Thursday 16th – Monday 27th:
Rehearsals for the second studio block of 'Four to Doomsday' take place at the BBC Television Rehearsal Rooms at Acton.

Thursday 16th:
Itinerary: In the morning, John takes a taxi from Union House to Great Russell Street to 'meet with publisher'[105]. After the meeting, he returns to Union House, again by taxi. Also on this day, John Benyon, the producer of the children's radio programme *Playday* contacts the *Doctor Who* Production Office. He would like to ask Peter Davison to guest on the programme this coming Saturday. Davison would be interviewed from approximately 9.00am at a studio in Broadcasting House, and then would take some phoned-in questions from children. John approves this, as Davison is not due to be in rehearsals that day, and refers Benyon to Davison's agent, John Mahoney, so that he can make the necessary arrangements.

Commentary: Today is also the press photocall with Peter Davison in Hammersmith Park, where the fifth Doctor's costume is unveiled in public for the first time. The park is just a short walk from BBC Television Centre, and so

---

and his win in the Grand National after overcoming his cancer battle was seen as one of the great sporting triumphs of modern times.

[105] Presumably this is Andre Deutsch Ltd, publishers of Alan Road's *Doctor Who: The Making of a TV Series*, which is being prepared at about this point in time. Road will follow the making of the next story in production, 'The Visitation', from start to finish.

(understandably) there is no travel expenses claim from John for attending. Unusually, there is no expenses claim for hospitality for the attending journalists, either.

Tuesday 21st:
Itinerary: Liz Ross from the BBC2 arts programme *Arena* contacts the *Doctor Who* Production Office. They are planning a show on the Mona Lisa, and are currently viewing the story 'City of Death'. They aren't sure if they want to use any extracts at the moment, but want to know if it's okay for them to do so, should they wish. John asks them to give him further details when they've worked out what they want – or intend – to use.

Thursday 23rd:
Itinerary: Jill Farnborough from *Blue Peter* contacts the *Doctor Who* Production Office. She wants a photo of Peter Davison in costume as the fifth Doctor for use in the upcoming *Blue Peter Annual*, due out later in the year. John agrees to send a photo, and also lets Davison's agent, John Mahoney, know about the planned feature/photo inclusion. Also on this day, John and Antony Root circulate a Drama Script Classified List, which states that the only writers they are working with at this date for upcoming storylines and/or scripts are: Christopher Bailey, Rod Beacham (storyline), Christopher H Bidmead, Terence Dudley, Jack Gardner, Terence Greer (scene breakdown), Peter Grimwade, Tanith Lee (scene breakdown), Christopher Priest, Eric Saward and Andrew Smith (scene breakdown).

Friday 24th:
Itinerary: John attends a planning meeting for 'The Visitation' in Union House, along with director Peter Moffatt and the various members of the relevant BBC Departments who will work on the story.

Monday 27th:
Itinerary: It's the final day of rehearsals for the second studio block of 'Four to Doomsday', and so is the day of the Producer's Run.

Commentary: There is no expenses record of John travelling to Acton today, although it's inconceivable that he wouldn't have attended the Producer's Run.

Tuesday 28th:
Itinerary: It's the first day of the three-day second studio block for 'Four to Doomsday' in studio TC6 at BBC Television Centre. After recording, John joins the cast in the BBC Club bar. On the same day, John writes to Graeme McDonald to inform him that he's been asked to direct a pantomime, *Puss in*

Boots, later in the year, based on a script that John himself wrote some years ago. The pantomime is scheduled to play at the Tunbridge Wells Theatre, rehearsing from 7 December, opening on 21 December, and running through to 9 January 1982. John stresses that he's had only a tentative offer at the moment, but wants approval before pursuing it further. He adds that he is confident he could cope with this outside project alongside his role as producer of *Doctor Who*, as the show is currently planned to have a production break at around the time the pantomime will be on.

Wednesday 29th:
Itinerary: It's the second day of the three-day second studio block for 'Four to Doomsday' in studio TC6 at BBC Television Centre. After recording, John joins the cast in the BBC club bar. On the same day, John writes a short treatment for *One Girl and Her Dog*, a pilot programme that will team up former companion Sarah Jane Smith, played by Elisabeth Sladen, and the recently departed robot dog, K-9.[106]

Commentary: *One Girl and Her Dog* begins with Sarah packing up her home in South Croydon and preparing to move in with her Aunt Lavinia in the remote village of Morton Harwood. The removal men leave a crate behind, in which Sarah finds K-9 Mark III, a gift from the Doctor. Aunt Lavinia arrives at Sarah's house, on her way to the airport, and hands over her ward, Brendan, to Sarah, before rushing off to catch a flight to America. Sarah, K-9 and Brendan depart in Sarah's car, heading to Morton Harwood. Upon arrival, the trio are embroiled in a black magic yarn, during which Sarah discovers that K-9 has an evil plan. The robot dog has actually been built by the Master, and sent by him to Sarah as part of an evil scheme. Brendan is able to reprogram the metal dog, and he becomes the friendly robot that the previous K-9s have also been.

Thursday 30th:
Itinerary: It's the third and final day of the second studio block for 'Four to Doomsday' in studio TC6 at BBC Television Centre. After recording, John joins the cast in the BBC Club bar.

Commentary: This date marked the official end of Antony Root's attachment as *Doctor Who*'s script editor, although in fact he would finish his work on the show the following day, when he completed a draft storyline for the 'Sarah and K-9' pilot script. He went on to join the production team of the BBC police drama *Juliet Bravo*. Eric Saward officially took over as script editor from the same date. Initially this was for three months only, as there was thought to be

---

[106] This project will eventually become *K-9 and Company*.

a possibility that Root might return to *Doctor Who*; ultimately that would not happen, and Saward would become the permanent script editor.

Eric Saward: 'I looked at the scripts [of "Kinda"] with some horror. When we weren't in the studio with "Four to Doomsday", I was in long meetings with Christopher Bailey, Peter Grimwade [the director of "Kinda"] and Antony Root, who was in the process of a week's handover. They had the first two episodes [of "Kinda"] roughly in shape, but the second two didn't really exist. They just weren't working.'[107]

MAY

Friday 1st:
Itinerary: Today is the first day of filming for 'The Visitation'. John travels by tube to Ealing Film Studios, where all the London-based scenes in Part Four are being shot on Stage 2. He returns by tube to Union House after filming concludes. On the same day, Jenny Roberts from the BBC's *Ceefax* text-page service contacts the *Doctor Who* Production Office. They want to run an interview with K-9 on their pages, but John refuses – he wants no publicity featuring K-9 at the moment. Antony Root drafts out John's treatment for the 'Sarah and K9' pilot, giving it a new title, *A Girl's Best Friend*. The storyline is a lot closer to the televised *K-9 and Company*, and the subplot about K-9 Mark III being created by the Master is dropped.

Tuesday 5th:
Itinerary: Filming for 'The Visitation' resumes, this time on location at Black Park Country Park in Iver, Buckinghamshire. John travels to and from the location by car. On the same day, Richard Eden from the technical magazine *Studio Sound* contacts the *Doctor Who* Production Office, requesting the loan of a Dalek prop to be photographed next to a mixing console for a photoshoot for the magazine. John informs him that the Dalek props are not available for lending out.

Wednesday 6th:
Itinerary: It's the second day of location filming for 'The Visitation' at Black Park Country Park. Again, John travels to and from the location by car. On the same day, John writes to Graeme McDonald about a seven-minute studio overrun on 'Four to Doomsday' on Thursday 30 April. John puts this down to

---

[107] Eric Saward interview, *Doctor Who Magazine* #346.

time lost on videotape line-up over the course of the three-day session. He also apologises for not informing McDonald about an overrun of 15 minutes on Wednesday 15 April. This, explains John, was down to (unspecified) technical breakdowns, and the need to complete all the scenes in a particular set.

Thursday 7th:
Itinerary: It's the third day of location filming for 'The Visitation' at Black Park Country Park. Again, John travels to and from the location by car. On the same day, John writes to Bob Wright, the BBC's Head of Lighting, praising both Bob Hignett and Dave Chapman for their recent work on 'Four to Doomsday'. Also on this day, Ami Halling from Walt Disney Productions replies to an enquiry John has made some time previously about the possibility of filming a portion of a *Doctor Who* story either in Disneyland in California, or Disney World in Florida. She declines the request on the basis that it's against the company's policy to allow filming for non-Disney products. Meanwhile, Michael Checkland, Controller of Planning and Resource Management, finally replies to the 13 March memo in which John requested a BBC Enterprises contribution to *Doctor Who*'s budget. Checkland refuses this request, explaining that all available Enterprises investment money for 1981/82 has already been allocated to other shows.

Friday 8th:
Itinerary: Filming for 'The Visitation' moves to a new location – Tithe Barn in Hurley, Berkshire – which will double for the main manor house seen in the story. Once again, John drives to and from the location by car. He also entertains members of the local press – from the *Slough Express* and the *South Bucks Advertiser* – over lunch.

Saturday 9th:
Itinerary: John travels in to Union House by car for a non-duty day at work, to attend a script read-through of 'The Visitation' by the cast.

Monday 11th – Tuesday 19th:
Rehearsals for the first studio block of 'The Visitation' take place at the BBC Television Rehearsal Rooms at Acton.

Wednesday 13th:
Itinerary: Steve Webber from VCL Video Services contacts the *Doctor Who* Production Office. He wants to make a programme for video release only, using a Dalek and/or K-9, to be partnered with the ITV children's robot Metal Mickey. John responds with a firm 'No'.

Thursday 14th:
Itinerary: John writes to Mickey Edwards at the BBC Visual Effects Department, asking him to send him the four prop space pack helmets used by the four main members of the cast in 'Four to Doomsday'. This is so that they can be retained in the *Doctor Who* Production Office for possible future use.

Friday 15th:
Itinerary: Helen M Griffiths, the BBC's Senior Personnel Officer, writes to John to let him know that there is no objection to him directing *Puss in Boots* at the Tunbridge Wells Theatre over this coming Christmas period. On the same day, John draws up a character profile for a new member of the TARDIS crew, Turlough, who will join the regular in the twentieth season. A 20-year old blond, skinny youth, Turlough is set to be introduced in a three-story arc. He will be revealed to be an agent in the employ of the Black Guardian, who wins the Doctor's trust but is secretly working against him. Turlough's future is left up in the air at this point, as John states that he may or may not continue with the Doctor after the initial trilogy.

Tuesday 19th:
Itinerary: John takes a short tube journey from Union House to the BBC's Television Rehearsal Rooms at Acton. Today is the Producer's Run for the first studio block of 'The Visitation'.

Wednesday 20th:
Itinerary: It's the first day of the two-day first studio block for 'The Visitation' in studio TC3 at BBC Television Centre. After recording, John joins the cast in the BBC Club bar.

Thursday 21st:
Itinerary: It's the second and final day of the first studio block for 'The Visitation' in studio TC3 at BBC Television Centre. After recording, John joins the cast in the BBC Club bar.

Friday 22nd:
Itinerary: Jane Mayes from the BBC programme *Ask Aspel* contacts the *Doctor Who* Production Office, asking if they can include a clip of the regeneration sequence from 'Logopolis' Part Four in a future edition, as they have received many requests to show this scene. John agrees to this.

Saturday 23rd – Tuesday 2nd June:
Rehearsals for the second studio block of 'The Visitation' take place at the BBC Television Rehearsal Rooms at Acton.

Saturday 23rd:
Itinerary: John travels in to Television Centre by car for a non-duty day at work.

Tuesday 26th:
Itinerary: John writes to Peter Grimwade, director of 'Kinda', to outline Peter Davison's limited availability for rehearsals for the story, due to the actor's commitment to the BBC sitcom *Sink or Swim*, which will be in rehearsals at the same time. Between Saturday 18 July and Sunday 26 July, Davison will rehearse for *Sink or Swim* in the morning, and then join the rehearsals for 'Kinda' in the afternoon, apart from on two planned studio days for the former, when he won't be available for *Doctor Who* rehearsals at all. On the same day, John writes to Peter Logan at the BBC Visual Effects Department, asking that the light atop the model TARDIS (used for effects filming) be altered to run off a 12-volt battery via a wire to be run up the pole that supports the model. This is to save time in the studio, as currently one whole side of the model needs to be detached to access the 'on/off' switch for the light.

Wednesday 27th:
Itinerary: John writes to Peter Day at the BBC Visual Effects Department, praising the work done by Peter Wragg on 'The Visitation'. He also, in a separate memo, informs Day that the upcoming story 'Black Orchid' will have minimal visual effects requirements, and so would be an ideal opportunity for an assistant designer to be assigned.

Thursday 28th:
Itinerary: John meets members of the executive committee of the *Doctor Who* Appreciation Society, and entertains them at the BBC bar.

Friday 29th:
Itinerary: 'Caroline' from the BBC1 show *Pop Quiz* contacts the *Doctor Who* Production Office, requesting a photo/slide of Peter Davison in costume as the Doctor, which is needed to illustrate the question 'Who wrote the theme music of *Doctor Who*?' in an upcoming edition of the show. On the same day, John writes to Terence Dudley, telling him that he has been given the go-ahead to produce a 50-minute special for Sarah and K-9, and that he wants Terence to write the script for this. He sends Terence the notes on the programme's format that were firmed out the previous month by Antony Root, and asks Dudley to come up with a scene breakdown for the pilot.

JUNE

Monday 1st:
Itinerary: John writes to the BBC's Head of Copyright, asking him to negotiate with the agent of writers Bob Baker and Dave Martin for the rights to use the character of K-9 in the pilot programme 'A Girl's Best Friend'.[108] John notes that a series of six or seven episodes might follow if the pilot is successful, which should be factored into negotiations. He also notes that the agent has already expressed displeasure that Baker and Martin weren't asked to write the initial treatment for the pilot programme, and that they would like to write at least three episodes of the proposed series, should it go ahead. John notes that he would be prepared to commission them for just one script if a series were to be given the green light, but that if that was judged a success, then he would be happy to offer them further episodes. On the same day, Christopher H Bidmead delivers his four scripts for 'Castrovalva' to the *Doctor Who* Production Office.

John Nathan-Turner: 'On the walls of Graeme McDonald's office were a set of Escher prints, which I didn't like. I always tried to position myself with my back to them, but this wasn't always possible. I found them disturbing, as many of them are optical illusions. I still find them so. The drawing of *Castrovalva*, which is not an optical illusion, was the inspiration for this story. It was a little joke by Chris on me.'[109]

Tuesday 2nd:
Itinerary: John writes to the BBC Artists Contract Department, asking that Elisabeth Sladen be engaged to play Sarah Jane Smith, and that John Leeson be engaged to provide the voice of K-9, in the pilot episode 'A Girl's Best Friend'. An option in the BBC's favour is included in their contracts, for an additional six or seven programmes to be made between 1 May and 31 November 1982; this option would need to be taken up by 31 January 1982.

Wednesday 3rd:
Itinerary: It's the first day of the three-day second studio block for 'The Visitation' in studio TC3 at BBC Television Centre. On the same day, Nick Fisher of Gaslight Lighting contacts the *Doctor Who* Production Office. He

---

[108] Baker and Martin created K-9 for their story 'The Invisible Enemy' in 1977, and the character remained their copyright. The BBC had to pay them a fee every time K-9 appeared in a *Doctor Who* story.
[109] John Nathan-Turner Memoirs, *Doctor Who Magazine* #235.

would like to visit the studio when they next record some TARDIS interior scenes, so that he can see how the set is lit. The reason for this is that he's organising the stage lighting for the group Wishbone Ash, for their tour at the end of the year, and they've requested that he create a similar lighting effect for them. He says that whatever he produces for the group will not directly copy whatever the BBC does. John agrees to this.

Thursday 4th:
Itinerary: It's the second day of the three-day second studio block for 'The Visitation' in studio TC3 at BBC Television Centre. After recording, John joins the cast in the BBC Club bar. On the same day, Philip Lewis from the Studio Amateur Dramatic Group (SADG) branch of the BBC Club writes to John. Lewis has written a script adaptation of the first few chapters of David Whitaker's 1964 novelisation *Doctor Who in an Exciting Adventure with the Daleks*, ending before the Daleks actually make an appearance in the story, and seeks John's permission for members of the BBC Club to record a performance of this, for the BBC Club's use only. John responds that he has no objections in principle, as long as the recording is made and played only for the SADG members. Also on this day, John writes to the Head of Copyright, informing them that the copyright negotiations for the use of K-9 have now been concluded, and that the pilot programme 'A Girl's Best Friend' will definitely be going ahead.

Friday 5th:
Itinerary: It's the third and final day of the second studio block for 'The Visitation' in studio TC3 at BBC Television Centre. Nick Fisher of Gaslight Lighting (see the entry for 3 June) visits the *Doctor Who* studio for around 30 minutes, to look at the lighting for the TARDIS set. After recording, John joins the cast in the BBC Club bar. On the same day, Virginia Brown of Lonsdale Advertising contacts the *Doctor Who* Production Office. She enquires if they could use K-9 in a TV commercial. John refuses, adding that the character has only just left the series, and that he can't discount a possible return for K-9 to *Doctor Who* at some time in the future. Also on the same day, Clive Doig, a former *Doctor Who* vision mixer who is now producer of the BBC1 children's programme *Puzzle Trail*, contacts the Production Office, asking if he could use the TARDIS prop in an upcoming edition. John agrees to this and gives Doig a list of the next *Doctor Who* studio sessions when the prop will be needed, so that Doig can plan to work around these.

Monday 8th:
Itinerary: John requests that Terence Dudley be given staff clearance to write

the script for 'A Girl's Best Friend'.[110]

Tuesday 9th:
Itinerary: John has a working lunch in the BBC bar with Elisabeth Sladen and her agent, Todd Joseph.[111]

Wednesday 10th:
Itinerary: John takes a taxi from Union House to Piccadilly for a meeting at Target Books – presumably with Christine Donougher, the range editor at the time. Target Books have been publishers of novelisations of *Doctor Who* stories since 1973. After the meeting, John returns to Union House by taxi.[112]

Friday 12th:
Itinerary: John has a working lunch at the BBC bar with writer Alan Road, who has been covering the production of 'The Visitation' for his upcoming book *Doctor Who: The Making of a TV Series.*

Monday 15th:
Itinerary: John Thornicroft from BBC Schools Programmes contacts the *Doctor Who* Production Office. Mat Irvine is to appear on an upcoming edition of one of their programmes, *Science Workshop,* to talk about his work in visual effects, and Thornicroft wants to use a clip from 'Warriors' Gate' to illustrate his chat. John agrees.[113] On the same day, Claire Mitchell from the BBC Pebble Mill religious programme *Pilgrimage* contacts the *Doctor Who* Production Office. She's looking to use a clip from 'The Brain of Morbius' to illustrate a talk on religious commitment, and John agrees as long as all the necessary clearances are obtained.

Tuesday 16th:
Itinerary: The Royal Society for the Prevention of Accidents (ROSPA) contacts the *Doctor Who* Production Office, asking if Peter Davison would be interested

---

[110] Terence Dudley was still working on episodes of the BBC series *Flesh and Blood* as a staff director at the time. Exactly when Dudley delivered his script for *K-9 and Company* is unknown, but the due date was sometime around September 1981.

[111] Presumably to discuss the upcoming pilot for *K-9 and Company,* and the tentative plans should a full series by commissioned on the back of it.

[112] Target Books were just starting to novelise stories that Nathan-Turner had produced, with *The Keeper of Traken* by Terrance Dicks having been published the previous month, and *The Leisure Hive* by David Fisher due to be published the next month. At this time, the offices of Target Books were at 44 Hill Street in Mayfair, London, close to Piccadilly Station.

[113] This edition of *Science Worksop* with Irvine aired on BBC1 on Wednesday 7 October 1981.

in heading a campaign aimed at improving road safety. On the same day, the Dental Association contact the *Doctor Who* Production Office, looking to recruit Davison for a campaign to encourage people to brush their teeth. John has no objections to either of these approaches, and refers them both to Davison's agent, John Mahoney. John also writes to the Merchandising Assistant at BBC Enterprises with a lengthy list of issues he has with the proposed artwork for a *Doctor Who* Easter Egg, with enclosed booklet, which is to be made by Suchards.

Wednesday 17th:
Itinerary: John has a working lunch with writer Johnny Byrne.

Commentary: Johnny Byrne had previously scripted 'The Keeper of Traken', and was looking to pitch another story, 'The Time of Neman'. This would later become 'The Time of Omega' and eventually 'Arc of Infinity' in the twentieth season.

Thursday 18th:
Itinerary: John writes to the Head of the BBC's Visual Effects Department, asking if he has had any joy in finding any photos of an electric car that has been under discussion for use in 'A Girl's Best Friend'.[114]

Wednesday 24th:
Itinerary: John sends a memo to the BBC Manager of Series/Serials, detailing the *Doctor Who* stories that he has chosen for repeating on BBC1 this summer. These are 'Full Circle' in week 31 and 'The Keeper of Traken' in week 32.

Commentary: For BBC planning purposes, each year was always divided into production 'weeks', week 1 being the first week of January.

Thursday 25th:
Itinerary: In the evening, John goes to see the play *Feasting with Panthers*, which stars Tom Baker as Oscar Wilde, at the Chichester Festival Theatre.

Commentary: Other members of the play's cast included Donald Houston, John Higginson, Peter Glaze, David Hitchen, Frank Shelley, Aubrey Woods, Lockwood West, Richard Evans, Keith Bartlett, Amanda Holmes, Jonathon Morris (who would play Chela in the *Doctor Who* story 'Snakedance' the following year), Sue Withers, Jeremy Anthony, Gary Fairhill, Stephen Bone,

---

[114] The electric car in question had previously been used in an episode of the long-running BBC sitcom *Last of the Summer Wine*, and was ultimately deemed unsuitable for use in *K-9 and Company*.

Michael Anthony, and Terry Sheppard.

John Nathan-Tuner: 'I had been to Chichester on an office outing a few months earlier to see Tom Baker give a spellbinding performance as Oscar Wilde in *Feasting with Panthers*. I was very impressed with a young actor in the play called Jonathon Morris. Tom introduced us when we went to celebrate afterwards … I think we gave Jonathon his TV debut in "Snakedance".'[115]

Saturday 27th:
Itinerary: John travels in to Television Centre by car for a non-duty day at work.

Monday 29th:
Itinerary: John receives a letter from Tom Baker, thanking him for coming to see him in his play the previous week. On the same day, John requests that Eric Saward be given staff clearance to write the four scripts for 'Centenal'.[116]

Tuesday 30th:
Itinerary: John has a working lunch with director Paul Seed.

Commentary: Paul Seed had played the role of Graff Vynda-K in the 1978 story 'The Ribos Operation', but at this point in time was looking to move away from acting and into directing. It's possible he was just looking for general advice from John, but it's not inconceivable that the idea of him possibly directing a *Doctor Who* story was discussed. If so, nothing ever came of such a suggestion.

JULY

Monday 6th – Friday 10th:
With the production of *Doctor Who* on a summer hiatus, John takes a week of annual leave from the BBC.

Monday 6th:
Itinerary: In John's absence from the *Doctor Who* Production Office, a letter comes in from Ian Marter, the actor who had played companion Harry Sullivan at the start of the fourth Doctor's era, returning the BBC's copies of

---

[115] John Nathan-Turner memoirs, *Doctor Who Magazine* #236.
[116] Actually a misspelling of 'Sentinel'. There is no record of when Saward delivered his scripts for the story that would become 'Earthshock'.

the scripts for the 1967/68 story 'The Enemy of the World', which had been sent to him via Target Books' parent company W H Allen. Marter has just written a novelisation of the story for them. On the same day, Avril Roberts from *The Music Arcade*, a BBC Schools programme, contacts the *Doctor Who* Production Office, floating the idea of doing a feature on how electronic music is made, and using the creation of the new *Doctor Who* theme music by Peter Howell to illustrate the process. When John returns from his leave, he agrees to this request.[117]

Wednesday 8th:
Itinerary: Susie Friend, researcher on Radio 2's John Dunn programme, contacts the *Doctor Who* Production Office, requesting details about the TARDIS – such as the history of the actual police boxes, and information about the BBC prop – for the 'Answers Please' segment of the programme. Still on leave, in the evening John goes to see *Barnum* at the London Palladium.

Commentary: *Barnum* had just opened in the West End the previous month. The cast included Michael Crawford, Deborah Grant, Jennie McGustie, Sarah Payne, William C Witter and Christopher Beck.

Saturday 11th:
Itinerary: Back from leave, John travels in to Television Centre by car for a non-duty day at work.

Tuesday 14th:
Itinerary: Barney Jones of Radio 1's *Mailbag* programme contacts the *Doctor Who* Production Office. He wants to run a special item on *Doctor Who* in the autumn, looking forward to the show's new season and delving into its history, using clips from old episodes and potentially interviewing Tom Baker and/or Peter Davison. As the new *Doctor Who* season won't actually start in the autumn, but is being held over until January 1982, John suggests instead that he ties the feature in with the upcoming 'The Five Faces of *Doctor Who*' repeat season on BBC2 in November.[118] Jones likes this idea. On the same day, John writes to Ian Marter, thanking him for returning the scripts for 'The Enemy of the World' and asking him to give him a ring so they can arrange to go for a drink sometime soon.

---

[117] The edition of *The Music Arcade* that featured the item on Peter Howell and his arrangement of the *Doctor Who* theme aired on BBC1 on 2 February 1982.
[118] 'The Five Faces of *Doctor Who*' was the umbrella title of a lengthy season of BBC2 archive repeats instigated by John, beginning on Monday 2 November 1981. The stories selected for repeat were '100,000 BC', 'The Krotons', 'Carnival of Monsters' and 'The Three Doctors'. 'Logopolis' ended the season with the only, to date, on-screen appearance of the fifth Doctor.

Friday 17th:
Itinerary: Biddy Baxter from *Blue Peter* writes to John, enclosing a copy of the latest *Blue Peter Annual*, which includes a two-page feature about *Doctor Who*. She thanks John for all the help he gave with this. On the same day, John writes to the actress Dinah Sheridan, to see if she would be interested in appearing in a *Doctor Who* story. He sends her the scripts for 'Black Orchid', and asks if she would be interested in playing the role of Lady Cranleigh.[119]

Saturday 18th – Tuesday 28th:
Rehearsals for the first studio block of 'Kinda' take place at the BBC Television Rehearsal Rooms at Acton.

Saturday 18th:
Itinerary: John travels in to Television Centre by car for a non-duty day at work. A script read-through for 'Kinda' takes place at the BBC Television Rehearsal Rooms at Acton.

Friday 24th:
Itinerary: Graeme McDonald writes to John to confirm that his promotion/appointment as producer of *Doctor Who* has at last been made permanent. McDonald offers his congratulations, but tempers this with a note that there were other contenders who were considered for the role.

Commentary: John's promotion to producer is finally made permanent and official by his bosses at the BBC. This must have been a fantastic moment for him at the time, and he could only have assumed that not only was he thought to be doing a good job, but that the post was now definitely his for as long as he wanted it. McDonald's note about other contenders might well have been accurate, but it's equally likely that he was just trying to keep John on his toes. McDonald was just in the process of leaving his own post as Head of Series and Serials, to become Head of Drama. His rubber-stamping of John's permanent appointment as producer was probably one of his last actions in the former role, before he handed over to his successor, David Reid.

Monday 27th:
Itinerary: John takes a taxi to Olympia to meet with a book publisher (unfortunately, the name of the publisher in question isn't noted on his

---

[119] Sheridan's agent was John Mahoney, who was also Peter Davison's agent at the time. John had been told by Mahoney that Sheridan might be free later in the year and agreeable to appearing in the series. This approach for 'Black Orchid' came to nothing, but Sheridan did later appear in *Doctor Who*, as Chancellor Flavia in 'The Five Doctors'.

expenses). On the same day, David Reid[120], the new BBC Head of Series and Serials, writes to John about the scripts for 'Castrovalva'. He suggests adding a voiceover recap to the start of the first episode, to remind the audience of what is happening when the action starts,[121] and also questions the effectiveness of the cliffhanger to the story's third episode.

Tuesday 28th:
Itinerary: John takes a short tube journey from Union House to the BBC's Television Rehearsal Rooms at Acton for the Producer's Run of the first studio block of 'Kinda'. Also on this day, John writes to actress Barbara Murray, asking if she would be interested in appearing in a *Doctor Who* story. He sends her the scripts of 'Black Orchid' and offers her the role of Lady Cranleigh.[122]

Wednesday 29th:
Itinerary: It's the first day of the three-day first studio block for 'Kinda' in studio TC8 at BBC Television Centre. After recording, John joins the cast in the BBC Club bar.

Commentary: Today is an extra public holiday, as it's the day of the wedding of Prince Charles and Lady Diana Spencer.

Thursday 30th:
Itinerary: It's the second day of the three-day first studio block for 'Kinda' in studio TC8 at BBC Television Centre. After recording, John joins the cast in the BBC Club bar.

Friday 31st:
Itinerary: It's the third and final day of the first studio block for 'Kinda' in studio TC8 at BBC Television Centre.

---

[120] David Reid had been directing and occasionally writing for television since the 1960s. He began producing in the late 1960s and continued for much of the 1970. Before taking over from Graeme McDonald as BBC Head of Series and Serials, he had been Executive Producer on the ITV shows *Sapphire and Steel* and *Hammer House of Horror*. He became John's new Head of Department, and therefore his new boss.

[121] A pre-credits reprise of the final moments of 'Logopolis' was ultimately used at the start of 'Castrovalva' instead.

[122] Dinah Sheridan had obviously declined the role by this point.

AUGUST

Saturday 1st – Tuesday 11th:
Rehearsals for the second studio block of 'Kinda' take place at the BBC Television Rehearsal Rooms at Acton.

Sunday 2nd:
Itinerary: John travels in to Television Centre by car for a non-duty day at work. However, he leaves Television Centre in the early afternoon to travel over to Queen Mary's College in London, for the second day of the *Doctor Who* Appreciation Society's Panopticon IV Convention. That afternoon, he makes his convention debut on stage to answer questions about his work on the show.

Monday 3rd:
Itinerary: John writes to David Reid, requesting that Season 20 be transmitted on BBC1 from autumn 1982, so that Season 21 will then be able to air on BBC1 in autumn 1983, across *Doctor Who*'s twentieth anniversary. On the same day, 'Full Circle' Part One is repeated on BBC1.

Tuesday 4th:
Itinerary: John entertains Barbara Elder, Chair of the North American *Doctor Who* Appreciation Society (NADWAS), at the BBC Club bar.[123] 'Full Circle' Part Two is repeated on BBC1.

Wednesday 5th:
'Full Circle' Part Three is repeated on BBC1.

Thursday 6th:
'Full Circle' Part Four is repeated on BBC1.

Saturday 8th:
Itinerary: Peter Moffatt writes to John with a query about the edit of 'The Visitation' Part Four, which he's just completed. He feels that the reprise at the start of the episode might need some additional music, but has elected to keep the audio mix as per the ending of Part Three so as to not upset the purists who watch the show. He takes the opportunity to thank John for asking him

---

[123] John was scheduled to make his US convention debut later this month, at the NADWAS's Panopticon West event in Tulsa, Oklahoma, and so was presumably discussing the final arrangements for the event. He would be joined at the convention by Peter Davison (and Davison's then-wife, Sandra Dickinson).

to direct the story.

Monday 10th:
Itinerary: John replies to David Reid's memo of 27 July, proposing to add a reprise of the final few moments of 'Logopolis' Part Four to the start of the first episode of 'Castrovalva'. On the same day, John signs off the commissioning brief for a story outline for 'Terminus' from Stephen Gallagher. 'The Keeper of Traken' Part One is repeated on BBC1.

Tuesday 11th:
Itinerary: John takes a short tube journey from Union House to the BBC's Television Rehearsal Rooms at Acton for the Producer's Run of the second studio block of 'Kinda'. On the same day, John Groom from the BBC2 science programme *Horizon* contacts the *Doctor Who* Production Office. Groom is looking to use the TARDIS prop in an episode about dinosaurs. John attempts to contact Groom on a number of occasions over the following weeks, but gets no reply. In mid-September he notes on Groom's memo that the programme is 'not using it' ('it' being the TARDIS prop, presumably). 'The Keeper of Traken' Part Two is repeated on BBC1.

Wednesday 12th: (John's thirty-fourth birthday)
Itinerary: It's the first day of the three-day second studio block for 'Kinda' in studio TC8 at BBC Television Centre. After recording, John joins the cast in the BBC Club bar. He also entertains Juliet Simpkins from Madame Tussauds during the day, during which they discuss the future of the *Doctor Who* Experience exhibition the waxworks is currently hosting.[124] 'The Keeper of Traken' Part Three is repeated on BBC1.

Thursday 13th:
Itinerary: It's the second day of the three-day second studio block for 'Kinda' in studio TC8 at BBC Television Centre. After recording, John joins the cast in the BBC Club bar. He also entertains Richard Farley from Andre Deutsch Publishers during the day.[125] 'The Keeper of Traken' Part Four is repeated on BBC1.

---

[124] The Madame Tussauds display was now going to become very quickly dated, given that Tom Baker's Doctor and Lalla Ward's Romana (not to mention Baker's twin portrayal of Meglos) were the main focus of the displays. Perhaps today's discussion was around whether or not it would be possible to update the exhibition with waxworks of Peter Davison's fifth Doctor and his companions?
[125] Richard Farley was the photographer who took all the photos used in the Andre Deutsch book *Doctor Who: The Making of a TV Series* by Alan Road.

Friday 14th:
Itinerary: It's the third and final day of the second studio block for 'Kinda' in studio TC8 at BBC Television Centre. After recording, John joins the cast in the BBC Club bar.

Saturday 15th:
Itinerary: John writes to the Manager of Series/Serials, asking that John Black be engaged to direct the 'K-9 Special' between 21 September and 25 December. Then John, along with Peter Davison (and his wife, Sandra Dickinson), flies out to Tulsa, Oklahoma to attend the US convention Panopticon West. An air traffic controllers' strike delays their flight's departure.

Sunday 16th:
Itinerary: Arriving later than planned in the US, John is able to take part in the final day of the three-day Panopticon West event at the Camelot Inn in Tulsa, Oklahoma.

John Nathan-Turner: 'We set off to Tulsa, Oklahoma in August 1981 as the guests of the North American *Doctor Who* Appreciation Society. We stayed at the Camelot Hotel, which was shaped like a castle and had a shield-shaped pool with Excalibur buried in a large stone in the middle of it. The building was bedecked with flags, and had a drawbridge and practical moat – and we had bodyguards with guns!'[126]

Monday 17th:
Itinerary: Still in Oklahoma, John dictates a memo by phone to his Production Secretary, Jane Judge, who is back in the *Doctor Who* Production Office in London. The memo is for David Reid, and explains why there was a studio overrun of 13 minutes on Friday 14 August, the last studio day of 'Kinda'. John attributes this to time lost when a two-inch videotape machine broke down; to having to source replacement two-inch videotapes when problems occurred with the original blanks that had been supplied; and then to problems caused by a faulty microphone during the whole three-day studio session. He also dictates a letter to director Fiona Cumming, informing her that there will be a large contingent of members of the press attending the location filming for 'Castrovalva' on Wednesday 2 September. He tells her he will endeavour to keep them out of the way of the filming itself.

Wednesday 19th:
Itinerary: David Reid writes to John to inform him that, now his appointment to producer has been made permanent, Barry Letts will no longer be Executive

---

[126] John Nathan-Turner memoirs, *Doctor Who Magazine* #235.

Producer on *Doctor Who*. Reid notes that Letts currently has two further sets of scripts to read, and will comment on them, but that in future, should John require any help or advice with any issues, he is to deal directly with Reid himself.

Friday 21st:
Itinerary: Kevin O'Shea from BBC Publicity contacts the *Doctor Who* Production Office. He discusses the upcoming Lord Mayor's Show in London, and suggests that if there was a *Doctor Who* angle to the proceedings, then he could get some good publicity out of it.[127] On the same day, Ann Throup, a Production Assistant on the Schools programme *The Music Arcade*, writes to John, forwarding a copy of the script that they will be using for filming at the Radiophonic Workshop on the 25 August.

Tuesday 25th:
Itinerary: Now back in the UK, John writes to Peter Moffatt, and asks that some additional music be added to the reprise at the start of Part Four of 'The Visitation'. John has requested composer Paddy Kingsland to provide some additional orchestration for this purpose, and wants to arrange a sypher session that Moffatt can attend in order to carry out the necessary edit. He takes the opportunity to thank Moffatt for the work he's done on 'The Visitation'. Meanwhile director John Black writes to John, thanking him for asking him to direct 'The Keeper of Traken' and 'Four to Doomsday'. He goes on to thank him for asking him to direct *Sarah and K-9* (as *K-9 and Company* was called at this point). Also on this day, David Reid writes to John, informing him that the controller of BBC1 doesn't want *Doctor Who* to return to an autumn slot. However, Reid raises the possibility of making a 90-minute special to mark *Doctor Who*'s twentieth birthday.

Thursday 27th:
Itinerary: John attends a planning meeting for 'Castrovalva' in Threshold House, along with director Fiona Cumming and the various members of the relevant BBC Departments who will work on the story.

---

[127] A *Doctor Who*-themed float, with Peter Davison, in costume as the fifth Doctor, flanked by fan-made replica costumes of various *Doctor Who* monsters, would eventually form part of the Lord Mayor's Show parade, on Saturday 14 November 1981

SEPTEMBER

Tuesday 1st:
Itinerary: Today is the first day of location filming for 'Castrovalva', starting at the Wireless and Telegraphy Station in Duddleswell, East Sussex. John drives down to the location, and then stays overnight at the Wellington Hotel in Tunbridge Wells.

Wednesday 2nd:
Itinerary: Filming for 'Castrovalva' continues, now at Buckhurst Park in Withyham, East Sussex. John again spends the night at the Wellington Hotel in Tunbridge Wells. On the same day, Stephen Gallagher delivers his story outline for 'Terminus' to the *Doctor Who* Production Office.

Thursday 3rd:
Itinerary: Filming for 'Castrovalva' continues at Buckhurst Park. John again spends the night at the Wellington Hotel in Tunbridge Wells.

John Nathan-Turner: 'One evening, after the wrap, a select few were invited for drinks in [Lord de la Warr, the owner of the estate's] library: the regular cast; Fiona Cumming, the director; Margot Hayhoe, the production manager and myself. We didn't stay long, as we were muddy and dishevelled, but the gins his lordship poured were enormous. This was not the sole reason for returning to his estate for the filming of "Black Orchid", but it may well have been the start of the evening that led to poor Matthew Waterhouse's much-discussed "illness" on location the following day. I certainly recall a group of us playing darts very badly, while imbibing way into the night.'[128]

Friday 4th:
Itinerary: Today is the final day of location filming for 'Castrovalva', at Harrison's Rocks and the surrounding woods in Groombridge, East Sussex. John entertains members of the local press at the unit hotel bar, then drives back home after filming concludes.

Saturday 5th:
Itinerary: John travels in to Television Centre by car for a non-duty day at work.

---

[128] John Nathan-Turner memoirs, *Doctor Who Magazine* #235.

Monday 7th:
Itinerary: John takes the tube from Union House to the Television Rehearsal Rooms at Acton, to attend a full read-through of the script of 'Castrovalva' by the cast.

Tuesday 8th – Monday 14th:
Rehearsals for the first studio block of 'Castrovalva' take place at the BBC Television Rehearsal Rooms at Acton.

Wednesday 9th:
Itinerary: John writes to the Head of Public Relations at British Airways, Heathrow Airport, enclosing the scripts for 'Xeraphin'[129] and asking for permission to be able to film on one of their Concorde aeroplanes. On the same day, John signs off the commission for Patrick Mills and John Wagner to write a story outline for 'Song of the Space Whale'.[130]

Saturday 12th:
Itinerary: Today is a non-duty day at work. John drives to the Television Rehearsal Rooms at Acton, to observe the ongoing rehearsals for 'Castrovalva'.

Monday 14th:
Itinerary: John takes a short tube journey from Union House to the BBC's Television Rehearsal Rooms at Acton for the Producer's Run of the first studio block of 'Castrovalva'.

Tuesday 15th:
Itinerary: Today is the first day of the two-day first studio block for 'Castrovalva' in studio TC3 at BBC Television Centre. However, in the morning, John travels by tube to the BBC Film Studios at Ealing, where he views the location film rushes for 'Castrovalva' that were shot the previous week. Once this has concluded, he returns via tube to BBC Television Centre for the remainder of the day's studio session. After recording, John joins the cast in the BBC Club bar. Also on the same day, John writes to David Platt at

---

[129] As 'Zanadin' has now been renamed. The story will eventually be titled 'Time-Flight'.

[130] Pat Mills and John Wagner had been writing comic strips for *Doctor Who Weekly/Doctor Who Monthly* for some time, and had decided to try and write for the show itself. 'The Song of the Space Whale' nearly made it into production during Season 20, before it was replaced quite late in the day by 'Mawdryn Undead'. It then was pencilled in for a time to be made as part of Season 22, before it was bumped again to make way for 'Vengeance on Varos'. At that point, 'The Song of the Space Whale' was abandoned.

BBC Programme Acquisitions, informing him that Richard Todd will be a guest star in the *Doctor Who* story that will screen over weeks 5 and 6 in 1982 ('Kinda'), and suggests that there might be some mileage in scheduling a Richard Todd film season at around the same time. Such scheduling could be beneficial to both parties, he points out. John also writes to the Manager of Series and Serials, setting out a draft production schedule for *Doctor Who*'s 1982/83 season (the twentieth). He also states that he would not be prepared to release Peter Davison for a period of 10 weeks to all him to make a series of *Sink or Swim* for the Light Entertainment Department, adding that if he were to do so, he doubts that Season 20 could be ready to air by the first week of January 1983. He goes on to say that, at this stage, he may be looking for a new Doctor.

Commentary: John's final remark in his letter to the Manager of Series and Serials is very odd. There are no clues that John was dissatisfied with Davison's portrayal of the Doctor during production of the first four stories of Season 19. The ambiguity of the phrasing ('Incidentally, at this stage we *may* be looking for a new Doctor') doesn't make clear what 'stage' is actually meant. John might have been implying that if Davison were to be taken away from *Doctor Who* to make more episodes of *Sink or Swim* without his consent, then he would look to jettison the actor and bring in another new Doctor after only a single season of the fifth incarnation. Or was he saying that by the time that Season 20 aired in January 1983, he might be looking for a new Doctor? If it was the latter, then he wasn't far wrong: Colin Baker was sounded out about succeeding Davison about six months after that date.

Wednesday 16th:
Itinerary: It's the second day of the two-day first studio block for 'Castrovalva' in studio TC3 at BBC Television Centre. After recording, John joins the cast in the BBC Club bar. On the same day, the *The Music Arcade* production team contacts the *Doctor Who* Production Office to inform them that the archived protection copy of the *Doctor Who* theme music tape that they had borrowed for their item on the creation of the new arrangement, used for the Davison-era titles, is damaged and won't play. A new protection copy of the theme music is ordered.

Thursday 17th – Monday 28th:
Rehearsals for the second studio block of 'Castrovalva' take place at the BBC Television Rehearsal Rooms at Acton.

Thursday 17th:
Itinerary: John meets with writer Bill Lyons, and the two of them have a

working lunch at the BBC bar.[131] Meanwhile David Goodman from BBC Leeds contacts the *Doctor Who* Production Office. He is working on a regional opt-out light entertainment programme called *Lifelines* and wants to use a clip from 'Destiny of the Daleks' that shows stuntgirl Sue Crossland in action. John agrees, pending approval from Roger Hancock (Terry Nation's agent).

Friday 18th:
Itinerary: John takes the tube from Union House to the Television Rehearsal Rooms at Acton for the rehearsals of the second studio block of 'Castrovalva'. On the same day, John writes to Lord de la Warr, thanking him for letting *Doctor Who* use an area of his estate for filming on 'Castrovalva'. He encloses a photo of Lord de la Warr and Peter Davison standing beside the TARDIS prop, taken by a *Radio Times* photographer who had attended the filming. He looks forward to returning to Lord de la Warr's estate for work on 'Black Orchid' next month.

John Nathan-Turner: 'The bulk of the location work [for "Castrovalva"] took place on Lord de la Warr's estate. I remember arriving on the first day and greeting what I thought was the gardener, only to discover that it was the Lord himself. He had allowed us to film on his estate, giving the fee to charity, but with one condition – he had his photograph taken with the TARDIS. A *Radio Times* photographer took the picture, which we had framed as a thank you for his co-operation.'[132]

Monday 21st:
Itinerary: David Reid writes to John with his feedback on the scripts for 'Sentinel'.[133] He finds it to be a good, exciting story, but wants to know if Adric somehow survives at the end. John writes back confirming that Adric dies, and that he wants to make the ending as moving as possible.

Tuesday 22nd:
Itinerary: John travels by tube to the BBC Film Studios at Ealing, where he again views the 16mm location film for 'Castrovalva'. He also entertains members of the press.[134] On the same day, John signs off the commission for

---

[131] Bill Lyons had written extensively for the BBC drama shows *Z Cars* and *Angels* in the late 1970s and had just broken into science fiction with his script for the story 'Games' for the fourth season of *Blake's 7*. He would later be asked to provide a scene breakdown for a proposed *Doctor Who* story, but this came to nothing.

[132] John Nathan-Turner memoirs, *Doctor Who Magazine* #235.

[133] 'Sentinel' will be renamed 'Earthshock' before transmission.

[134] With no filming or photocall today, it's unclear why John was entertaining members of the press.

Barbara Clegg to write a story outline for 'The Enlighteners'.[135]

Wednesday 23rd:
Itinerary: John attends a planning meeting for 'Black Orchid' in Union House, along with director Ron Jones and the various members of the relevant BBC Departments who will work on the story.

Thursday 24th:
Itinerary: John attends a preliminary planning meeting for 'Sentinel' in Threshold House, along with director Peter Grimwade and the various members of the relevant BBC Departments who will work on the story.

Friday 25th:
Itinerary: John takes the tube from Union House to the Television Rehearsal Rooms at Acton, to sit in on the rehearsals for the second studio block of 'Castrovalva'.

Saturday 26th:
Itinerary: John travels in to Television Centre by car for a non-duty day at work.

Monday 28th:
Itinerary: John takes the short tube journey from Union House to the BBC's Television Rehearsal Rooms at Acton, for the Producer's Run of the second studio block of 'Castrovalva'. On the same day, he also writes to the Head of BBC Copyright, stating an intention to use the Cybermen in the upcoming story 'Sentinel'.[136]

Tuesday 29th:
Itinerary: It's the first day of the three-day second studio block for 'Castrovalva' in studio TC6 at BBC Television Centre. Also on this day, John writes to Matthew Robinson, commending him on his direction of two plays that John had recently seen at the Red Lion theatre.[137] Richard Spence from the production team of BBC2's *Russell Harty* programme contacts the *Doctor Who* Production Office on this day. They are tentatively planning a show in late

---

[135] This will be renamed 'Enlightenment' before transmission.
[136] The Cybermen were the creations of Kit Pedler and Gerry Davis, and clearances needed to be made with the writers or their estates to allow their use in the story.
[137] Director Matthew Robinson had recently worked with Gary Downie on the BBC series *Angels* and had got to know John through him. John would later attempt to get the BBC interested in a drama series Robinson had devised titled *Rye Spy*, to no avail. However, this did ultimately lead to John asking Robinson to direct the story 'Resurrection of the Daleks' in 1983.

November or early December looking at visual effects, and want to be able to use K-9, a Dalek and a Cyberman. They also would like to get either Tom Baker or Peter Davison as a guest for this edition. John suggests that it might be possible to tie this in with publicity for *K-9 and Company*. However, after some further discussions, John notes that the *Russell Harty* team now seem quite indifferent to the whole idea. On the same day, John writes to Marcus Plantin, Assistant Producer on *Larry Grayson's Generation Game*, with a number of ideas/suggestions for games that would tie in with *Doctor Who*. The first is 'Who's Who?', where the contestants would have to identify, from a selection of archive clips, one of the five actors to have played the Doctor. John points out that the repeat run 'The Five Faces of *Doctor Who*' will be showing on BBC2 that November and December. The second idea is for a game called 'Who's What?', where items/props from *Doctor Who* would have to be identified by the contestants. John suggests as examples a Dalek, a Cyberman, the sonic screwdriver, the TARDIS and K-9. He points out that K-9 will be appearing in its own spin-off show over Christmas, and offers up to the *Generation Game* team the use of the show's prop store and the stock of props and costumes help at the two *Doctor Who* Exhibitions. Finally, John signs off the commission for Christopher Bailey to write a story outline for 'Snakedance'.

Wednesday 30th:
Itinerary: It's the second day of the three-day second studio block for 'Castrovalva' in studio TC6 at BBC Television Centre. After recording, John joins the cast in the BBC Club bar. Also today, John writes to the Head of Copyright, explaining that Part Four of 'Kinda' has been found to be underrunning and that Christopher Bailey has been asked to write an additional four minutes of material to fill the necessary time.

OCTOBER

Thursday 1st:
Itinerary: It's the third and final day of the second studio block for 'Castrovalva' in studio TC6 at BBC Television Centre. After recording, John joins the cast in the BBC Club bar. Also today, John writes to Sarah Bird at BBC Contracts, asking her to engage Anthony Ainley to appear (in his semi-regular role as the Master) in the story 'Time-Flight'. On the same day, Johnny Byrne is given the go-ahead to develop a story set in Amsterdam for the following season.

Friday 2nd:
Itinerary: Rehearsals for the location filming for 'Black Orchid' take place at the BBC Television Rehearsal Rooms at Acton. Also, John writes to David Reid to inform him of an overrun of 15 minutes during the final studio recording for 'Castrovalva' the previous day. He explains this was down to a scaffolding tower, which was supposed to be erected in the studio overnight, actually being moved into position in the morning, whereupon it collapsed.

Saturday 3rd:
Itinerary: John travels in to Television Centre by car for a non-duty day at work.

Monday 5th:
Itinerary: Today is the first day of location filming for 'Black Orchid'. The Railway Centre in Quainton, Buckinghamshire is the first location visited, where all the story's scenes at the railway station are shot. John drives down to the location, then stays overnight at the Wellington Hotel in Tunbridge Wells. While he is away from the *Doctor Who* Production Office, Anthony Ainley writes to John to apologise for not joining the rest of the cast in the bar after the final day of studio recording for 'Castrovalva'. He takes the opportunity to thank John for casting him as the Master, and tells him he finds playing the role the most enjoyable work he's ever done, and that he looks forward to returning to the show in January for 'Time-Flight'. David Reid writes to John, having read the script for *K-9 and Company*. He urges John to downplay the witchcraft and 'black arts' elements of the script, as these subjects always draw public complaints and criticism. He also suggests cutting any references to religion and God, and vetoes the scripted mention of Brendan being naked when about to be sacrificed on the altar at the story's conclusion. Reid summarises that he feels the story works well, but advises John to think carefully about the lines of attack that will inevitably be trotted out against the production.

Tuesday 6th:
Itinerary: Work on 'Black Orchid' switches to Buckhurst House in Withyham, Kent, which will be the main location for the rest of the filming. Again, John stays overnight at the Wellington Hotel in Tunbridge Wells.

Wednesday 7th:
Itinerary: Location filming for 'Black Orchid' resumes at Buckhurst House in Withyham, Kent. Again, John stays overnight at the Wellington Hotel in Tunbridge Wells. Back in London, Barbara Clegg delivers her story outline for 'The Enlighteners' to the *Doctor Who* Production Office.

Thursday 8th:
Itinerary: Location filming for 'Black Orchid' resumes at Buckhurst House in Withyham, Kent. John entertains members of the press at a local pub for lunch, then stays overnight once more at the Wellington Hotel in Tunbridge Wells.

Friday 9th:
Itinerary: Location filming for 'Black Orchid' concludes at Buckhurst House in Withyham, Kent. John entertains the owners of Buckhurst House for lunch, and once filming has concluded, drives back home.

Saturday 10th – Monday 19th:
Rehearsals for the single studio block of 'Black Orchid' take place at the BBC Television Rehearsal Rooms at Acton.

Saturday 10th:
Itinerary: John drives to the Television Rehearsal Rooms at Acton for the first day of rehearsals for 'Black Orchid''s single studio block. He drives in by car, as it's a non-duty day at work.

Monday 12th:
Itinerary: David Reid writes to John with his critique of the scripts for 'Xeraphin'. He asks that care be taken portraying the various disintegrating bodies seen in the story, so as to not make them too frightening. He also asks if John will really get access to Concorde for the location filming.

Tuesday 13th:
Itinerary: Liz Duckworth from the BBC Personnel Department writes to John, informing him that he is allowed to accept a fee for writing the forward for *The Doctor Who Quiz Book*.[138] Also on this day, John attends a BBC New Technology Seminar at Woodstock Grove, along with fellow producers Vere Lorimar, Mark Shivas and Guy Slater. John writes to Graham Richmond at BBC Television Film Services, asking for Peter Chapman and Bruce Galloway to be assigned to the location filming of 'Xeraphin'.[139]

---

[138] *The Doctor Who Quiz Book* by Nigel Robinson was published by Target Books in December 1981.
[139] Peter Chapman was the film cameraman on 'Black Orchid', and was indeed allocated to work on 'Time-Flight' in the same capacity. Bruce Galloway was a film sound recordist who had previously worked on 'Revenge of the Cybermen', but wasn't allocated to 'Time-Flight'.

Wednesday 14th:
Itinerary: John has a working lunch with writer Stephen Gallagher.[140]

Thursday 15th:
Itinerary: John takes the tube from Union House to Warwick Avenue, to pay a visit to the BBC Radiophonic Workshop. He returns to Union House by tube later in the day. John also signs off the commissioning brief for Stephen Gallagher to write the script for 'Terminus' Part One.

Saturday 17th:
Itinerary: John drives to the Television Rehearsal Rooms at Acton to attend the rehearsals for 'Black Orchid''s single studio session. He drives in by car, as it's a non-duty day at work.

Monday 19th:
Itinerary: John takes the short tube journey from Union House to the BBC's Television Rehearsal Rooms at Acton for the Producer's Run of the single studio block for 'Black Orchid'. He also runs up a small bill for photocopying new studio scripts for 'Black Orchid', which has been rewritten over the weekend. Graham Richmond from the BBC's Television Film Services department at Ealing Studios writes to John, complaining that the *Doctor Who* production schedules are not allowing enough time between location filming and the studio recording to edit the film sequences for most stories. He cites 'Black Orchid' as an example, where getting the location film edited in time for it to be telecined during the studio session was proving to be problematic. He gives John a rule-of-thumb guide that ten film-editing days are needed to prepare sequences shot during five days of location work. Also on this day, Christopher Bailey delivers his story outline for 'Snakedance' to the *Doctor Who* Production Office.

Tuesday 20th:
Itinerary: It's the first day of the single two-day studio block for 'Black Orchid' in studio TC3 at BBC Television Centre. After recording, John joins the cast in the BBC Club bar.

Wednesday 21st:
Itinerary: It's the second and final day of the single studio block for 'Black Orchid' in studio TC3 at BBC Television Centre. After recording, John joins the cast in the BBC Club bar.

---

[140] Gallagher had written the scripts for 'Warriors' Gate' for the eighteenth season, and was in the process of being commissioned to write the story 'Terminus' for the twentieth.

Thursday 22nd:
Itinerary: John writes to David Reid regarding a studio overrun of an hour at the end of the previous day's studio session. He puts this down to industrial action taken by the studio electricians, who walked out of the studio at 9.00am and didn't return until 4.45pm. He also replies to Graham Richmond at Ealing, undertaking to bear in mind his advice regarding the editing of filmed material. Finally for today, John signs off the commissioning brief for Barbara Clegg to write the script for Part One of 'The Enlighteners'.

Friday 23rd:
Itinerary: John attends a planning meeting for 'Sentinel' in Threshold House, along with director Peter Grimwade and the various members of the relevant BBC Departments who will work on the story.

Sunday 25th:
Itinerary: John travels in to Television Centre by car for a non-duty day at work.[141]

Monday 26th:
Itinerary: Rob Benfield from the *Blue Peter* production team contacts the *Doctor Who* Production Office. They want to do a feature on *Doctor Who* – reworking and updating one that has been used a few times previously since the show's tenth anniversary – to tie in with the 'The Five Faces of *Doctor Who*' repeat season on BBC2. John gives his assent, and asks to be informed as to when the item will be shown.[142] On the same day, Susan Vale from McCormicks advertising agency contacts the *Doctor Who* Production Office. They are working on a campaign for Philips video recorders and TV sets, and want to use Tom Baker, in character as the fourth Doctor, to present a series of adverts for these products. John vetoes the idea. Also on this day, Christopher Bailey delivers his additional four-minute scene for Part Four of 'Kinda' to the *Doctor Who* Production Office.[143]

Tuesday 27th:
Itinerary: John travels by car to Guildford to meet with representatives of the Fisher Price toy company. A photographer from the company has been following the production of 'Castrovalva', and Fisher Price will later release a series of slides from the story for their Viewmaster 3-D picture-viewer toy.

---

[141] Today is the gallery-only day for 'Black Orchid' in studio TC6, which is probably John's reason for coming into work on his day off.
[142] The item is part of the *Blue Peter* edition shown on BBC1 on 29 October.
[143] This additional scene will be done as a remount during the first studio session of 'Earthshock' on 10 November.

Today John has to sign off on the selection of 21 images to be used, out of the hundreds taken. After lunch, he drives back to BBC Television Centre, then returns home.

Wednesday 28th:
Itinerary: John writes to the Head of BBC Copyright, informing him that they have received the additional four minutes of script from Christopher Bailey for 'Kinda' Part Four.

Thursday 29th:
Itinerary: Today is the only day of location filming required for 'Earthshock' (as 'Sentinel' has now been renamed), at Springwell Lock Quarry in Rickmansworth, Buckinghamshire. Although none of the regular cast is required, John attends the filming, driving to and from Rickmansworth by car. Sue Mallinson, producer of the BBC programme *Pick of the Year*, also contacts the *Doctor Who* Production Office on this day. She wants to use a clip of the regeneration sequence from 'Logopolis' Part Four in her programme. John approves this. Finally for this day, Stephen Gallagher delivers his script for 'Terminus' Part One to the *Doctor Who* Production Office.

Friday 30th – Monday 9th November:
Rehearsals for the first studio block of 'Earthshock' take place at the BBC Television Rehearsal Rooms at Acton.

Friday 30th:
Itinerary: John takes the tube from Union House to the Television Rehearsal Rooms at Acton, to attend the first day of rehearsals for the first studio block of 'Earthshock'.

NOVEMBER

Undated:
Itinerary: Graham Stevens, who is producing the BBC's Christmas promotions, contacts the *Doctor Who* Production Office sometime in November. He requests that a five-second clip of the Doctor and his three companions wishing a 'Universally Happy Christmas' to the audience be recorded for use in the BBC's on-air Christmas promotions in December.[144]

---

[144] A clip of the four main cast members, in costume on the set of 'Earthshock', wishing the audience at home a 'Happy Christmas', is recorded during the studio

Sunday 1st:
Itinerary: John travels in to Television Centre by car for a non-duty day at work.

Monday 2nd:
'The Five Faces of *Doctor Who*' repeat season on BBC2 kicks off this evening with the first ever episode of the series, 'An Unearthly Child'. The following three episodes of this story will then be screened an episode a night, with the story concluding on Thursday 5th.

Tuesday 3rd:
Itinerary: John's movements today are something of a mystery. He lodges both lunch and dinner expenses claims for being 'outside base area' – i.e. away from Union House, and probably away from London too. It's possible he travelled to Birmingham in advance of the location filming for *K-9 and Company* the following week. On the same day, John writes to David Reid in response to his memo of 5 October regarding the script for *K-9 and Company*. He agrees to be careful with the religious and witchcraft aspects of the script, and also notes that any scenes with Brendan on the altar would be carefully shot. He also sends a second letter to Reid, asking that Ron Jones be allowed to direct the story 'Xeraphin', an engagement that will run from 16 November 1981 through to 12 March 1982. This would entail Jones being released from any Production Manager duties during that period.[145]

Wednesday 4th:
Itinerary: John entertains members of the executive committee of the *Doctor Who* Appreciation Society at the BBC bar. On the same day, he writes to Richard Bailey, who is responsible for the studio gallery observation rooms at BBC Television Centre.[146] John asks that these rooms be closed for the duration of the studio sessions for 'Earthshock', so as to prevent anyone seeing

---

sessions of that story. The clip is used as part of this year's BBC1 Christmas presentation package, alongside similar clips of the casts from other BBC programmes.

[145] Ron Jones had completed the internal BBC director's course earlier in the year, and 'Black Orchid' had been his first production as a director. He was still nominally employed by the BBC as a Production Manager, so John's request to have him back working on *Doctor Who* as a director so soon after he'd finished his first assignment was a significant endorsement.

[146] The studios at BBC Television Centre had Observation Galleries that anyone who was in the building could pop into to view what was going on in the studio. A number of well-connected fans used their contacts inside the BBC to regularly gain access to the gallery of whichever studio *Doctor Who* was recording in, so they could watch the programme being made.

the Cybermen or learning of Adric's death and leaking 'spoilers' to the fan press.[147]

Saturday 7th:
Itinerary: John travels in to Television Centre by car for a non-duty day at work.

Monday 9th:
Itinerary: John takes the short tube journey from Union House to the BBC's Television Rehearsal Rooms at Acton for the Producer's Run of the first studio block for 'Earthshock'. Also today, John writes to Greg Childs from *Larry Grayson's Generation Game*. Childs has previous been in contact with the *Doctor Who* Production Office with regard to an idea for a specific game, intended to feature robot characters from various programmes and films. From *Doctor Who*, K-9 and a Cyberman have been selected.[148] John acknowledges being informed of the planned recording date of the programme that will feature this game, Thursday 3 December. John informs Childs that the Cyberman costume will be supplied by Dinah Collin (the costume designer for 'Earthshock'), and that it will need someone inside it. Also, he nominates Mat Irvine to supply and operate the K-9 prop. Details of the copyright owners for both creations are given to Childs, so that their use in the show can be cleared. John also points out that K-9 will shortly be having his own programme, which will also star Elisabeth Sladen, and enquires if the *Larry Grayson's Generation Game* team would consider having Sladen feature in the game in some way, as publicity for *K-9 and Company*. John also writes to Dinah Collin on the same day, and asks her to ensure that the Cyberman costume used is not one of the new 'Earthshock' ones, as he doesn't want to spoil the surprise of their return by unveiling the new design prior to 'Earthshock' airing next spring; he want her to ensure that 'one of the original Cybermen – i.e. one of the horrors from the Exhibition' is used instead for the *Generation Game* recording. John then writes to Mat Irvine at the BBC Visual Effects Department to inform him that the fully-operational K-9 prop will be required for that recording. John also writes to Peter Grimwade, to ask that *Earthshock* guest star Beryl Reid be allowed to leave rehearsals early on Friday 20 November, so that she can appear on BBC1's *Children In Need* programme later that evening. He also points out that Peter Davison will not be in rehearsals on Saturday 14 November, due to his participation in the Lord Mayor's Show

---

[147] Perhaps there was a comment made by the DWAS Executive members during his meeting with them, which prompted John to take this action regarding the studio gallery Observation Rooms.
[148] This is the first documented piece of correspondence between the two programmes, but obviously earlier conversations had taken place.

that day. Also on the same day, John signs off the commission for Christopher Bailey to write the four scripts for 'Snakedance'. 'The Five Faces of *Doctor Who*' repeat season on BBC2 continues with the four-part story 'The Krotons', which screens one episode per evening from Monday through to Thursday.

Tuesday 10th:
Itinerary: It's the first day of the three-day first studio block for 'Earthshock' in studio TC8 at BBC Television Centre. This includes the aforementioned remount of a single set from 'Kinda', needed to record the additional scene to ensure that the final episode doesn't underrun. Today is also the first day of rehearsal at the BBC Rehearsal Rooms in Acton for the location filming of *K-9 and Company*.

Wednesday 11th:
Itinerary: It's the second day of the three-day first studio block for 'Earthshock' in studio TC8 at BBC Television Centre. After recording, John joins the cast in the BBC Club bar.

Thursday 12th:
Itinerary: John has a lunchtime meeting in the Bridge Lounge at BBC Television Centre with a contingent from the Public Relations Office of British Airways to discuss their co-operation with the filming of 'Xeraphin' at Heathrow airport early next year. Today is also the third and final day of the first studio block for 'Earthshock' in studio TC8 at BBC Television Centre. After the recording, John briefly joins the cast in the BBC Club bar. He then jumps into a hire car and drives to Gloucestershire, to join up with the cast and crew of *K-9 and Company* at the unit hotel. Today they've been filming in the roads around Gloucestershire, mainly getting shots to be used in the programme's title sequence.

John Nathan-Turner: 'My associate and I entertained British Airways and British Airways Authority executives in Television Centre's Bridge Lounge. I remember the famous Biddy Baxter sitting at the next table with her *Blue Peter* cast, having a row about the quality of the grapefruit! The lunch and the meeting went reasonably well and both sets of executives requested approval of the script. I explained that the BBC was not prepared to part with editorial control, but that we would listen to any objections they might have. One of them was a bit off about this, so I simply whispered to my associate, just loud enough to be overheard, "What time are we meeting the Air France people?" Within a couple of days, we had been granted full use of a British Airways Concorde on the ground, unlimited stock footage, as many Concorde models as we wanted and all for no charge.'[149]

Friday 13th – Monday 23rd:
Rehearsals for the second studio block of 'Earthshock' take place at the BBC Television Rehearsal Rooms at Acton.

Friday 13th:
Itinerary: John attends the second day of location filming for *K-9 and Company*, with action switching to Miserdern Nursery and Lodge in Gloucestershire. Sometime during the day, he dictates a letter to his secretary, Jane Judge, back in London, to be sent to David Reid. John explains to Reid that on Thursday 12 November there was an overrun of 15 minutes during the final studio day for 'Earthshock', and attributes this to a late start on the previous day due to artists arriving late on set, and to complexities with costumes and visual effects. John spends the night at the unit hotel in Gloucester. On the same date, John is sent a letter by Peter Bryant, who back in the 1960s was one of his predecessors as *Doctor Who* producer but is now working at the Jim Thompson literary agency. Bryant explains that the agency are currently in dispute with Eric Saward, a former client of theirs, and says that he hopes this will not impact negatively on consideration of two outlines that he submitted to the *Doctor Who* Production Office back in August on behalf of another of their clients, Eric Pringle, for proposed stories called 'War Game' and 'The Darkness'.

Saturday 14th:
Itinerary: John attends the third day of location filming for *K-9 and Company*, with action switching to Wishanger Farm in Gloucestershire. Again, John spends the night at the unit hotel. Back in London, Peter Davison appears in costume as the fifth Doctor on a float at the Lord Mayor's Show, alongside a selection of *Doctor Who* monsters, mainly supplied by fan-turned-reproduction-costume-maker Toby Chamberlain.

Sunday 15th:
Itinerary: John attends the fourth day of location filming for *K-9 and Company*, with action now switching to a church in North Woodchester, Gloucestershire. John spends the night at the unit hotel.

Monday 16th:
Itinerary: John attends the fifth day of location filming for *K-9 and Company*, with action switching to various locations around Miserdern, Gloucestershire. Again, John spends the night at the unit hotel. Back in London, Barbara Clegg

---

[149] John Nathan-Turner memoirs, *Doctor Who Magazine* #235.

delivers her script for 'The Enlighteners' Part One to the *Doctor Who* Production Office. 'The Five Faces of *Doctor Who*' repeat season on BBC2 continues with the four-part story 'Carnival of Monsters', which screens one episode per evening from Monday through to Thursday.

John Nathan-Turner: 'I had to return to London during the filming of *K-9 and Company*, and when I got back to location, the shoot was way behind. I returned for the sacrifice sequences … We got so far behind on our last night shoot that instead of travelling to several different graveyards as planned, we shot all the sequences in the same one, with John Black choosing clever angles so as not to make it obvious. As a result, we got back on schedule.'[150]

Tuesday 17th:
Itinerary: John attends the final day of location filming for *K-9 and Company*, with action now focusing on the police station and post office in Bisley, Gloucestershire. Once filming concludes, John drives back to London in his hire car. Very late in the day, the BBC1 early evening magazine programme *Nationwide* contacts the *Doctor Who* Production Office and invites John Leeson and Elisabeth Sladen to appear on the following night's programme to talk about *K-9 and Company*. Both agree to appear.

Wednesday 18th:
Itinerary: *Nationwide* have a change of mind, and almost at the last minute cancel the planned appearance by Elisabeth Sladen and John Leeson. As Leeson was booked via his agent, he is still due a fee for the appearance, despite the cancellation.[151]

Thursday 19th – Friday 27th:
Rehearsals for the sole studio session of *K-9 and Company* take place at the BBC Television Rehearsal Rooms at Acton.

Thursday 19th:
John and Eric Saward circulate a Drama Script Classified List, which states that the only writers they are working with at this date for upcoming storylines and/or scripts are: Christopher Bailey, Christopher H Bidmead, Barbara Clegg, Terence Dudley, Stephen Gallagher, Peter Grimwade, Bill Lyons (scene breakdown), Pat Mills and John Wagner (one episode), Eric Saward, Andrew Smith (scene breakdown), and Lesley Elizabeth Thomas (scene breakdown).

---

[150] John Nathan-Turner memoirs, *Doctor Who Magazine* #235.
[151] Issues surrounding this cancellation, and the outstanding fee owed to Leeson because of it, will crop up a number of times in the future.

Friday 20th:
Itinerary: John takes the tube from Union House to the Television Rehearsal Rooms at Acton to sit in on the rehearsals for the studio session of *K-9 and Company.*

Saturday 21st:
Itinerary: John travels in to Threshold House by car for a non-duty day at work.

Sunday 22nd:
Itinerary: John travels in to Television Centre by car for a non-duty day at work.

Monday 23rd:
Itinerary: Today is the final day of rehearsals for the second studio block of 'Earthshock', and so would normally be the day of the Producer's Run. There is no record of John travelling to Acton today; however, it's highly unlikely that he wouldn't have attended. 'The Five Faces of *Doctor Who*' repeat season on BBC2 continues with the four-part story 'The Three Doctors', which screens one episode per evening from Monday through to Thursday.

Tuesday 24th:
Itinerary: It's the first day of the three-day second studio block for 'Earthshock' in studio TC8 at BBC Television Centre. Peter Davison's agent, John Mahoney, attends, and brings with him a box of *Doctor Who* Easter Eggs, which he hands out to the cast. After recording, John joins the cast in the BBC Club bar.

Wednesday 25th:
Itinerary: It's the second day of the three-day second studio block for 'Earthshock' in studio TC8 at BBC Television Centre. After recording, John joins the cast in the BBC Club bar.

Thursday 26th:
Itinerary: Today is the third and final day of the second studio block for 'Earthshock' in studio TC8 at BBC Television Centre. There is a small farewell party for Matthew Waterhouse held after the studio session is concluded. John writes to BBC Enterprises, complaining that Peter Davison's agent was sent examples of *Doctor Who* merchandise before he had been sent samples himself.

Friday 27th:
Itinerary: John takes the short tube journey from Union House to the BBC's Television Rehearsal Rooms at Acton for the Producer's Run of the single

studio block for *K-9 and Company*. On the same day, he writes to David Reid about a studio overrun of 26 minutes on the final day of recording on 'Earthshock' the previous evening. He attributes this to three things: time lost because the studio floor was not ready on the first studio day, which had a knock-on effect; to additional time needed to attach 'periscopes' to the studio cameras and lights on the final two studio days; and finally to a sound problem on the last day.

Saturday 28th:
Itinerary: John travels in to Television Centre by car for a non-duty day at work. He also picks up a cash expenses advance to cover his travel to, and accommodation in, Birmingham in the coming week for the studio sessions for *K-9 and Company* at BBC Pebble Mill.

Sunday 29th:
Itinerary: John drives from London to BBC Pebble Mill in Birmingham. Today is the first day of the single two-day studio block for *K-9 and Company* in Studio A at BBC Pebble Mill. John stays overnight in Birmingham.[152]

Monday 30th:
Itinerary: Today is the second and final day of the two-day studio block for *K-9 and Company* in Studio A at BBC Pebble Mill. Again, John stays overnight in Birmingham when recording concludes. David Reid writes to John after watching a VHS of Part One of 'Castrovalva'. He thinks the episode is a very good start for the fifth Doctor, although he is unsure of one shot, which he surmises is Adric's point-of-view seen through the Master's eyes. 'The Five Faces of *Doctor Who*' repeat season on BBC2 concludes with the four-part story 'Logopolis', which screens one episode per evening from Monday through to Thursday.

DECEMBER

Tuesday 1st:
Itinerary: John drives back to London from Birmingham.

---

152 John's parents lived in Birmingham at the time, only a few miles away from BBC Pebble Mill. It's possible that he stayed with them during the *K-9 and Company* recordings. However, given that studio work could run until very late in the evening, it's also possible that he arranged a hotel near Pebble Mill, in order to spare his parents his unsociable hours.

Wednesday 2nd:
Itinerary: John writes to director Ron Jones to inform him that Peter Davison will be making an appearance on the BBC1 show *The Multi-Coloured Swap Shop* on the morning of Saturday 9 January 1982, and so will need to be released from rehearsals for 'Time-Flight' for that. John also signs off the commission for Patrick Mills and John Wagner to write the four scripts for 'Song of the Space Whale'.

Thursday 3rd:
Itinerary: The PR firm Burson-Marsteller contacts the *Doctor Who* Production Office. They are working with the Department of Industry on a series of events throughout 1982 to promote the country's various technology industries. They explain that they would like to use K-9 for the launch of an event due to be held in the Bristol region in January next year, as one of the robot dog's creators, Bob Baker, lives locally. John gives his assent for this. Also on this day, John writes to the BBC's Senior Designer, praising Nigel Jones's work on *K=9 and Company*, but also querying the number of design man-hours clocked up in the studio, which will be charged to the production. John also writes to Peter Grimwade, instructing him that for the flashback sequence planned for Part Two of 'Earthshock', none of the clips selected can include extras or walk-ons, and that permission needs to be sought and obtained from all the artists included in the final sequence. John also signs off the commissioning brief for Stephen Gallagher to write the scripts for 'Terminus' Parts Two to Four.

Monday 7th:
Itinerary: Greg Childs from the *Larry Grayson's Generation Game* production team writes to John, to thank him for his help with the 'Robots' game, which was recorded the previous Thursday.

Tuesday 8th:
Itinerary: John spends the morning working at BBC Television Centre, then takes a train to Birmingham to oversee the edit of *K-9 and Company*, which is being done at BBC Pebble Mill. John spends the rest of the week in Birmingham.[153]

Friday 11th:
Itinerary: John books two days of annual leave, covering today and Monday 14 December.[154]

---

[153] It's safe to assume that, on this occasion, John stayed with his parents.
[154] John probably stayed in Birmingham, enjoying a long weekend with his parents.

Saturday 12th:
Itinerary: Barbara Clegg delivers her revised script for 'The Enlighteners' Part One to the *Doctor Who* Production Office.

Monday 14th:
Itinerary: Today is John's second day of booked annual leave. He returns to London in the evening to be in the office the following day.

Wednesday 16th:
Itinerary: John writes to the BBC's Personnel Department, informing them that one minute of footage from the climax of 'Logopolis' Part Four is being used as a reprise at the start of 'Castrovalva' Part One. John surmises that no extra payments are required for the cast, but that director Peter Grimwade might be entitled to an additional fee as a result. John also writes to the Manager of Drama Series and Serials, requesting that Tony Virgo be allocated to direct the two-part story 6J at the end of next year. In addition, he sends BBC Enterprises a memo expressing doubts about the wisdom of agreeing to a request that has been received from the Australian company Streets to be allowed to make an animated 30-second television commercial for a *Doctor Who*-branded 'ice treat'. He explains that he wasn't happy with the previous Australian commercials produced by Prime Computers, which were initially agreed by his predecessor Graham Williams.

Friday 18th:
Itinerary: John returns to Birmingham by train to oversee sypher dubbing of *K-9 and Company* at BBC Pebble Mill. He spends the night in Birmingham.[155]

Saturday 19th:
Itinerary: John remains in Birmingham for sypher dubbing of *K-9 and Company*. Again, he spends the night in Birmingham.

Tuesday 22nd:
Itinerary: After a few days back in London, John again travels by train to Birmingham to oversee sypher dubbing of *K-9 and Company* at BBC Pebble Mill. He spends the night in Birmingham.[156]

---

[155] John was almost certainly staying with his parents again. His recollection that the final dubbing on *K-9 and Company* was done the day before transmission appears to have been amiss.

[156] Although John claims expenses for an overnight stay in Birmingham on this date, he also claims for two tickets at the Mermaid Theatre in London on the same date. Either he didn't stay in Birmingham after all, or his plans changed at the last minute, after he had already booked the tickets for whatever was on at the Mermaid Theatre.

John Nathan-Turner: 'I also recall that we had to dub a final section of [*K-9 and Company*] the day before it went out. As I was spending Christmas in Birmingham, I finished it off myself to save John Black from having to travel to Birmingham over Christmas for a couple of hours' work.'[157]

Wednesday 23rd:
Itinerary: John returns to London from Birmingham by train. Once back, he takes the tube to Oxford Circus, then gets a cab in Oxford Street to take him back to the *Doctor Who* Production Office in Shepherd's Bush.

Monday 28th:
K-9 and Company: 'A Girl's Best Friend' screens on BBC1.

---

[157] John Nathan-Turner memoirs, *Doctor Who Magazine* #235.

1982

Setting the Scene:

If 1981 had been a year of consolidation for John, 1982 would be a year of settled routine. Now that his promotion to producer had been confirmed, and John had got to grips with the logistics and daily headaches of producing *Doctor Who*, he could think about flexing his muscles a little.

He had already begun work on assembling scripts for Season 20, most of which would be made this year, and was now thinking ahead to the show's twentieth anniversary in 1983, David Reid having dangled the carrot of a potential special anniversary story in addition to the normal run.

The previous year had given John his first taste of *Doctor Who* conventions on both sides of the Atlantic, and they really appealed to his ego. His job on the show was very much back-of-the-house, but on stage at a convention, he was given nearly as much adulation as the likes of Tom Baker and Peter Davison. As a frustrated actor, he loved the attention.

1981 had ended in frantic fashion, due to the twin demands of *K-9 and Company* and *Doctor Who*. With just one more story to complete before production concluded on Season 19, the between-seasons break couldn't come quickly enough. Once production got under way again on Season 20, it wouldn't be entirely problem-free. Peter Davison's commitments to other projects would begin boxing in *Doctor Who*'s schedules, and toward the end of the year this would be coupled with an increase in internal BBC strife, with industrial action and strikes becoming the norm again. However, John had a settled cast, his working relationship with his new script editor seemed to be going well, and all could be considered rosy in the world of *Doctor Who*, as the show enjoyed perhaps it peak period of popularity with the television debut of Peter Davison's fifth Doctor in the first week of January 1982.

JANUARY

Monday 4th:
'Castrovalva' Part One screens on BBC1.

Tuesday 5th:
Itinerary: Graeme McDonald, now Head of BBC Drama, writes to David Reid, having watched 'Castrovalva' Part One go out on BBC1 the previous evening. McDonald thinks the difference in production standards between this episode and *K-9 and Company* is measurable, and not in *Doctor Who*'s favour – he thinks that standards on *Doctor Who* have slipped noticeably since the previous season. He wants Reid to ensure that John is made aware of the episode's shortcomings, and also asks Reid to see that John's choices of scripts and directors are monitored more carefully in the future. On the same day, John signs off the commissioning brief for Barbara Clegg to write the scripts for 'The Enlighteners' Parts Two to Four. 'Castrovalva' Part Two screens on BBC1.

Wednesday 6th:
Itinerary: John drives to Heathrow Airport, to oversee the first day of location filming for 'Time-Flight'. He drives home in the evening after filming.

Thursday 7th:
Itinerary: John returns to Heathrow Airport by car, for the second day of location filming for 'Time-Flight', then drives home in the evening. John also writes to the BBC Contracts Department, notifying them that Matthew Waterhouse has agreed to make a cameo appearance in Part Two of 'Time-Flight'. He asks that a script of the story be sent to Waterhouse, subject to negotiations.

Friday 8th:
Itinerary: Today was planned to be the third day of location filming for 'Time-Flight' at Heathrow Airport, but heavy snow overnight causes it to be postponed. Instead, John travels in to the *Doctor Who* Production Office in Union House, then takes a tube over to the Television Rehearsal Rooms in Acton.[158] On the same day, Stephen Gallagher delivers his script for 'Terminus' Part Two to the *Doctor Who* Production Office.

Saturday 9th – Monday 18th:
Rehearsals for the first studio block of 'Time-Flight' take place at the BBC Television Rehearsal Rooms at Acton.

Saturday 9th:
Itinerary: John travels in to Threshold House by car for a non-duty day at work. During the morning, he's on hand at BBC Television Centre, attending

---

[158] It's possible that the cast and director of 'Time-Flight' had reconvened at Acton and had decided to use the cancelled filming day as an extra rehearsal day instead.

the live broadcast of the BBC1 children's programme *The Multi-Coloured Swap Shop*, on which Peter Davison appears as a studio guest.

Sunday 10th:
Itinerary: John drives to Heathrow Airport for the rescheduled final day of location filming for 'Time-Flight'. He then drives home in the evening. At some point between Wednesday 6 January and today, John also drives to Great Russell Street to meet with 'publishers'.[159]

Monday 11th:
Itinerary: John has a working lunch with writer James Duke at the BBC.[160] 'Castrovalva' Part Three screens on BBC1.

Tuesday 12th:
Itinerary: John has a working lunch with writer Eric Pringle at the BBC.[161] 'Castrovalva' Part Four screens on BBC1.

Wednesday 13th:
Itinerary: John takes the tube from Union House to Oxford Circus and walks to the BBC's Portland Place studios to take part in the *AM* radio programme. However, it would appear that things don't go quite as planned for John … Also on this day, John signs off the commission for Johnny Byrne to write the four scripts for 'The Time of Omega'.[162]

Thursday 14th:
Itinerary: Angela Jenner, a researcher for the BBC's *AM* radio programme, writes to John, apologising for a mix-up the previous day. She explains that she had left a message with the secretary at the *Doctor Who* Production Office, saying that she had booked a studio at Portland Place to do an interview about the new series of *Doctor Who*, and requesting that someone notify her if there was anyone available to do it. No-one phoned her back, so she assumed that no such interview would go ahead. It would seem that wires had been crossed, and that John had gone over to the Portland Place studios to record

---

[159] The name of the publishers in question isn't recorded in John's expenses. It could well have been W H Allen, the parent company of Target Books, responsible for the *Doctor Who* novelisations.

[160] James Duke appears not to have worked extensively in television; there is no known record of any scripts or books attributed to a writer of that name working at this time.

[161] Eric Pringle would eventually write the two part story 'The Awakening' for Season 21.

[162] 'The Time of Omega' would be renamed 'Arc of Infinity' by the time it was broadcast.

the interview, only to find that no-one was expecting him.

Monday 18th:
Itinerary: John takes the short tube journey from Union House to the BBC's Television Rehearsal Rooms at Acton for the Producer's Run of the first studio block for 'Time-Flight'. 'Four to Doomsday' Part One screens on BBC1.

Tuesday 19th:
Itinerary: Today is the first day of the two-day first studio block for 'Time-Flight' in studio TC8 at BBC Television Centre. During the day, John entertains writer Christopher Bailey, and takes him to lunch at the BBC Club bar.[163] After the studio recording concludes, John joins the cast, again in the BBC Club bar. 'Four to Doomsday' Part Two screens on BBC1.

Wednesday 20th:
Itinerary: It's the second and last day of the first studio block for 'Time-Flight' in studio TC8 at BBC Television Centre. Problems with various effects in the studio see a good number of scenes unrecorded, and so a remount on Sunday 24 January is hastily arranged. After recording, John joins the cast in the BBC Club bar.

Thursday 21st – Saturday 30th:
Rehearsals for the second studio block of 'Time-Flight' take place at the BBC Television Rehearsal Rooms at Acton.

Friday 22nd:
Itinerary: John takes the tube from Shepherd's Bush to Oxford Circus for a 'business lunch'.[164]

Sunday 24th:
Itinerary: A remount of unrecorded studio scenes from the first recording block of 'Time-Flight' is hastily arranged on this day.

Monday 25th:
Itinerary: Catherine Robbins, who is working on the BBC educational show *The Computer Programme* at Villiers House, contacts the *Doctor Who* Production Office. She would like to use K-9 in her programme, and John gives his assent.[165] Part Three of 'Time-Flight' is found to be underrunning, so John

---

[163] Christopher Bailey had written the story 'Kinda' for this season, and was in the process of writing 'Snakedance' for the following one.
[164] No further details of this lunch are given in John's expenses.
[165] The edition of *The Computer Programme* that screened on BBC2 on 1 March 1982 includes a segment where K-9 and the show's presenter, Ian McNaught-Davis, get

writes to the BBC's Head of Copyright, asking that Peter Grimwade be engaged to write an additional seven minutes of material for the story. 'Four to Doomsday' Part Three screens on BBC1.

Tuesday 26th:
'Four to Doomsday' Part Four screens on BBC1.

Thursday 28th:
Itinerary: Vivien Devlin from BBC Edinburgh contacts the *Doctor Who* Production Office. She's working on an edition of the radio science magazine series *What's New*, and in a feature looking at the use of computers, wants to use approximately 30 seconds of K-9 speaking, which can be obtained from an old episode of *Doctor Who*. John agrees to send an episode featuring K-9 to the *What's New* team, so that they can lift the robot dog's dialogue from the tape. On the same day, John receives a letter from Geoffrey C D Wilson, producer of the BBC game show *It's A Knockout*. Wilson thanks John for his prior help and advice concerning the possible use of *Doctor Who* in his 1982 series.[166] He goes on to assure John that if this were to happen, he would ensure that it was done in a way that did not undermine the credibility of the characters.

Friday 29th:
Itinerary: Christopher Bailey delivers his scripts for 'Snakedance' Parts One and Two to the *Doctor Who* Production Office.

Saturday 30th:
Itinerary: John travels in to Television Centre by car for a non-duty day at work. It's the final day of rehearsals for the second studio block of 'Time-Flight', and so would normally be the day of the Producer's Run. There is no record of John travelling to Acton today – however, it's really inconceivable that he wouldn't be present, so this must be an oversight in his expenses.

FEBRUARY

Monday 1st:
Itinerary: It's the first day of the three-day second studio block for 'Time-Flight' in studio TC8 at BBC Television Centre. After recording, John joins the cast in the BBC Club bar. Also today, John writes to David Reid, asking that

---

lost in a maze.
[166] The nature of this help and advice is unknown.

Ron Jones be engaged to direct 'Arc of Infinity'. This engagement is to run between 15 March and 30 July. Barbara Clegg delivers her scripts for 'The Enlighteners' Parts Two and Three to the *Doctor Who* Production Office. 'Kinda' Part One screens on BBC1.

Tuesday 2nd:
Itinerary: It's the second day of the three-day second studio block for 'Time-Flight' in studio TC8 at BBC Television Centre. After recording, John joins the cast in the BBC Club bar. 'Kinda' Part Two screens on BBC1.

Wednesday 3rd:
Itinerary: It's the third and final day of the second studio block for 'Time-Flight' in studio TC8 at BBC Television Centre. The recording brings to an end production on the show's nineteenth season, although post-production on the final episodes still remains to be done. John Leeson's agent contacts the *Doctor Who* Production Office to inform them that the fee for Leeson's cancelled appearance on *Nationwide* on 18 November 1981 is still outstanding. John chases the matter with the *Nationwide* production team.

Thursday 4th:
Itinerary: John writes to David Reid regarding a studio overrun of 37 minutes during the previous day's final studio session for 'Time-Flight'. He attributes this to an inaccurate setting-up of the TARDIS interior set on the first studio day, which had a knock-on effect for the rest of the block.

Monday 8th:
Itinerary: Christopher Bailey delivers his scripts for 'Snakedance' Parts Three and Four to the *Doctor Who* Production Office. On the same day, Stephen Gallagher delivers his scripts for 'Terminus' Parts Three and Four, alongside a revised version of Part One. In addition, David Reid sends John a memo requesting his assessment of director Ron Jones's work, to help him write Jones's annual report. 'Kinda' Part Three screens on BBC1.

Tuesday 9th:
'Kinda' Part Four screens on BBC1.

Wednesday 10th:
Itinerary: On John's instruction, Sarah Sutton is contracted for 20 episodes out of 26 for Season 20, and Janet Fielding for 18 episodes out of 26.[167]

---

[167] In the end, Sutton appears in only 16 episodes, and Fielding in only 22 episodes, due to the final four-part story, 'The Return', being abandoned.

Thursday 11th:
Itinerary: Peter Davison is contracted to appear in all 26 episodes of Season 20.[168]

Monday 15th:
Itinerary: John writes to David Reid with a critique of Ron Jones's direction of the stories 'Black Orchid' and 'Time-Flight'. On 'Black Orchid', Jones's first job as a director, John found him to be competent and calm during a troubled studio session (due to industrial action by the studio electricians), but also thought he lacked a certain 'drive' at times. Nevertheless John was happy enough to offer him the chance to direct 'Time–Flight', and found his work much improved on this. John finishes by saying that he looks forward to working with Jones again later this year.[169] 'The Visitation' Part One screens on BBC1.

Tuesday 16th:
'The Visitation' Part Two screens on BBC1.

Friday 19th:
Itinerary: John writes to the Assistant to the Head of Design at the BBC, asking that Tom Yardley-Jones be assigned to design 'Arc of Infinity'. He goes on to ask that, should Yardley-Jones not be available, Tony Burrough be assigned instead.[170] On the same day, John submits a format pitch to David Reid for a bi-weekly drama series entitled *Lives*, focused on the lives of eight school-leavers sharing a house divided into apartments in London.

Saturday 20th:
Itinerary: In the evening, John goes to the Players' Theatre in Charing Cross to see their production of *Robin Hood or The Forester's Fate*.

Commentary: The cast of *Robin Hood* included Deryk Parkin, Eleanor McReady, Debbie Goody, Zoe Bright, Anthony Bateman, David Bluestone, Debbie Goodman, John Rutland, Graham Richards, Angela Easterling, Christopher Connah, Daphne Anderson, Peter Sutherland, Mairi Armstrong, Victoria Duncan, Susan Flannery, Shirley Greenwood, Shirley Rayner, John Denton, Harold Lorenzelli and Patrick McCarthy.

---

[168] Again, due to the season's curtailment to the loss of 'The Return', Davison eventually appears in only 22 episodes.
[169] Jones had already been asked to direct 'Arc of Infinity' at this point.
[170] In the event, neither was assigned to 'Arc of Infinity' – Marjorie Pratt ended up being the story's designer.

Monday 22nd:
Itinerary: David Reid writes to John after reading the scripts for 'Snakedance'. He says that he thinks John is making a mistake with this story, as he finds it too abstract and obscure, and that he hasn't a clue what actually happens in the final episode. He thinks the various appearances of Dojjen in the first three episodes are confusing, and that the end of Part Three is very week. He suggests spelling out far more clearly what the Mara is, and how it takes people over via their dreams in order to become physically real. On the same day, John signs off the commissioning brief for Terence Dudley to write the scripts of 'The Android', a two-part story.[171] 'The Visitation' Part Three screens on BBC1.

Tuesday 23rd:
Itinerary: John has a working lunch with John Mahoney, Peter Davison's agent. 'The Visitation' Part Four screens on BBC1.

Wednesday 24th:
Itinerary: John entertains David Saunders and Gary Russell of the *Doctor Who* Appreciation Society at the BBC Club bar.[172] John co-writes a letter with Eric Saward to David Reid, presenting a robust defence of the scripts for 'Snakedance'.[173]

Thursday 25th:
Itinerary: In the morning, John drives to the *Doctor Who* Production Office at Union House and picks up script editor Eric Saward. They both then drive up to Oxford, to the workshop of Richard Gregory's company Imagineering, where they are met by writer Terence Dudley. The reason for this visit is so that Gregory can give them a demonstration of an animatronic android that has been created by two associates of his, Chris Padmore and Mike Powers of CP Cybernetics, which he thinks might be suitable for use in *Doctor Who*.[174] After the demonstration, John, Saward, Dudley and Gregory all go for lunch

---

[171] This story will be renamed 'The King's Demons' by the time that it's screened.
[172] At the time, David Saunders was the Society's Coordinator, and Gary Russell edited its monthly newsletter, *Celestial Toyroom*. Russell would go on to edit *Doctor Who Magazine*, write several original *Doctor Who* novels, and in 2009 script edit *Doctor Who* itself, along with episodes of *Torchwood* and *The Sarah Jane Adventures*.
[173] Saward was the main writer of the letter; John merely added a few notes to his lengthy defence of the scripts.
[174] Chris Padmore was responsible for the prop android's hardware, whilst Mike Powers had designed the software. Powers later died in a boating accident, which meant that no-one had a working knowledge of how to programme the prop to move correctly, which had a knock-on effect of ensuring Kamelion was written out of the series almost as quickly as it was written in.

to continue their discussions, then John drives back to London with Saward. On the same day, John replies to an (undated) card from Elisabeth Sladen, which thanks him for all his work on getting *K-9 and Company* off the ground and gives her stoic response to the news that it isn't being commissioned for a full series. John says that he shares her disappointment, but voices optimism that the project isn't quite fully dead and buried.

Commentary: Imagineering had recently supplied the Terileptil costumes for 'The Visitation', the Castrovalvan hunting helmets for 'Castrovalva', the redesigned Cyberman costumes for 'Earthshock' and the Plasmatons for 'Time-Flight'. The android that Gregory demonstrated this day would eventually be christened Kamelion, and would debut in Terence Dudley's story 'The King's Demons' in the upcoming twentieth season.

John Nathan-Turner: 'Kamelion, as it was to later become known, first came to the *Doctor Who* studio a long time before "The Kings Demons". It was demonstrated to [Eric] Saward and myself in the management room just off our studio, wearing an old-fashioned '50s swimming costume. I believe it had been created for a film that had been cancelled. Richard Gregory, who had done a lot of costume/effects work for us, and Mike Powers and Chris Padmore put the machine through its paces. It really was quite impressive, and later we took writer Terence Dudley down to the Imagineering workshop to see it again.'[175]

Friday 26th:
Itinerary: John writes to David Read's office, requesting that the temporary additional secretarial help the *Doctor Who* Production Office has had over the last 18 months be made permanent, in light of the additional fan mail that Peter Davison's casting has generated.

Saturday 27th:
Itinerary: In the evening, John goes to see the play *Local Affairs* at the Theatre Royal, Drury Lane.

MARCH

Monday 1st:
Itinerary: John writes to David Reid, explaining that he was given permission

---

[175] John Nathan-Turner memoirs, *Doctor Who Magazine* #236.

last year to write and direct a pantomime at Tunbridge Wells, although the project was eventually cancelled and came to nothing. He tells Reid that the project has been resurrected for Christmas 1982, and that he has once more been asked to write and direct. He asks if he can he assume that there would be no objection to him doing so. The memo is returned to him with a handwritten note by Reid, saying that he sees no problem with this.[176] On the same day, Johnny Byrne delivers his scripts for 'The Time of Omega' Parts One to Three to the *Doctor Who* Production Office. 'Black Orchid' Part One screens on BBC1.

Tuesday 2nd:
Itinerary: John writes to the various relevant department heads at the BBC, asking that Peter Wragg (Visual Effects), Norma Hill (Make-Up), Amy Roberts (Costumes) and Dick Coles or, as a standby, Malcolm Thornton (Design) be allocated to work on story 6F.[177] 'Black Orchid' Part Two screens on BBC1.

Wednesday 3rd:
Itinerary: Barbara Clegg delivers her script for 'The Enlighteners' Part Four to the *Doctor Who* Production Office. John signs off the commission for Eric Pringle to write a scene breakdown for the proposed story 'War Game', about which Peter Bryant wrote to him on 13 November 1981.[178] Also on the same day, John writes to Sarah Sutton, telling her that he will not be extending her contract on the series, and that her character, Nyssa, will be written out during the new season. Elizabeth Western from David Reid's office writes to John, refusing his request for a permanent 'fan mail' secretary to be appointed to the *Doctor Who* Production Office. She does, however, suggest assigning a trainee to the team to look after this side of things.

Thursday 4th:
Itinerary: Sarah Ramsden from the production team of the BBC2 review programme *Did You See..?* contacts the *Doctor Who* Production Office. They are

---

[176] John would indeed be involved in a panto later in the year, although not quite in the capacity he outlined here. *Cinderella* would star Peter Davison, Sandra Dickinson and Anthony Ainley, and would run at the Tunbridge Wells Assembly Hall from 23 December 1982 to 15 January 1983. John would be producer of the show, while Lovett Bickford (director of 'The Leisure Hive') would direct and Gary Downie would provide choreography.

[177] At this point, story 6F was scheduled to be 'Song of the Space Whale' by Pat Mills (original co-writer John Wagner having dropped out of the project). This will be dropped from the schedule and replaced by 'Mawdryn Undead' in just a few months time.

[178] This story will be renamed as 'The Awakening' by the time it's screened on BBC1.

keen to do a feature on the history of *Doctor Who* monsters, and want to tie it in with the upcoming reappearance of the Cybermen in 'Earthshock'. Gavin Scott is confirmed as the presenter of the item, and consideration is also given to having a Cyberman in-costume in the *Did You See..?* studio. For clearance purposes, Ramsden is given details of the copyright owners of a list of monsters, including Daleks, Cybermen, Ice Warriors, Sea Devils, Krynoids, Yeti, Mandrels, Sontarans, Terileptils and Marshmen. She is also given details of the agent of Cyberman actor David Banks, in case they should decide to go ahead with the costumed Cyberman idea.[179] In the evening, John and Gary Downie join former script editor Christopher H Bidmead and his wife Ros for the opening gala night at the new Barbican Centre in London.

Commentary: The gala performance at the Barbican was attended by the Prince and Princess of Wales, and the headline act was the veteran American comedian George Burns.

Monday 8th:
Itinerary: John has lunch with actor Mark Lester. 'Earthshock' Part One screens on BBC1.

Commentary: Mark Lester had risen to fame, aged just eight, for his portrayal of Oliver Twist in the 1967 film *Oliver!*. He had subsequently found it difficult to escape from the shadow of this; when he had turned 18, and finally had access to his earnings from the role, he had started living a lifestyle of fast cars and late-night partying, which in turn had brought him unwanted scrutiny from the tabloid press. At the time of this meeting with John, he was in his early twenties, and had largely turned his back on acting. Although the reasons for the meeting can only be speculated upon, it's hard not to suspect that John might have been thinking of casting Lester as the new male companion, Turlough, who was due to join the TARDIS crew in the upcoming season.

Tuesday 9th:
Itinerary: John has a working lunch with writer Eric Pringle. On the same day, he writes to Christopher H Bidmead, belatedly thanking him for the evening at the Barbican Centre the previous week. He adds that he thought the show was terrific, especially George Burns. 'Earthshock' Part Two screens on BBC1.

---

[179] The edition of *Did You See ... ?* Broadcast on BBC2 on 14th March 1982 did include a 10-minute feature by Gavin Scott, giving a potted history of *Doctor Who* monsters, but didn't include a Cyberman in the studio.

Wednesday 10th:
Itinerary: The *It's a Knockout* production team contact the *Doctor Who* Production Office. Serious consideration is now being given to potentially having Peter Davison, Janet Fielding and Sarah Sutton appear in character in a game in a future edition of the show. Use of the *Doctor Who* theme music is requested, to be used to introduce the three characters. John gives his clearance for this.[180]

Thursday 11th:
Itinerary: John gets a letter from Yvonne Lugg, Senior Personnel Officer at the BBC. She confirms that there is no objection to him producing a pantomime at Tunbridge Wells next Christmas, and asks that nearer the time he provides her with the exact dates of his absence from the BBC while working on the project. On the same day, Johnny Byrne delivers the third draft of his script for 'Arc of Infinity' Part One to the *Doctor Who* Production Office.

Friday 12th:
Itinerary: Jane Marriot from *Pebble Mill at One* contacts the *Doctor Who* Production Office. They plan to have Peter Davison as a guest on the show next Tuesday, 16 March, and want to use a clip from *Doctor Who*. John agrees to the use of a clip from Part Two of 'Earthshock' (of the Doctor and Adric diffusing a Cyberbomb), but vetoes them having the TARDIS prop in the studio on the day.[181] Johnny Byrne delivers the second draft of his script for 'Arc of Infinity' Part Three to the *Doctor Who* Production Office.

Saturday 13th:
Itinerary: In the evening, John goes to see a play (title unknown) at the Theatre Royal, Drury Lane.

Monday 15th:
Itinerary: John has a working lunch with writer Ben Steed.[182] 'Earthshock' Part

---

[180] No further conversations take place between the *Doctor Who* and *It's a Knockout* production offices, and the idea is eventually dropped.
[181] This planned appearance by Davison doesn't go ahead; Nathan-Turner instead takes Davison out for lunch on Tuesday 16 March. His refusal of permission for the TARDIS prop to be sent to the *Pebble Mill at One* studio in Birmingham on that date might be linked to its planned use in London just two days later.
[182] Ben Steed had written a few drama scripts for television, including an episode of *Crown Court* in 1977 and two of *Buccaneer* in 1980. In the science-fiction field, he had scripted three *Blake's 7* episodes ('The Harvest of Kairos', 'Moloch', and 'Power'). He would later pitch a story, 'Circus of Destiny', to *Doctor Who*, delivering a storyline in January 1983 for consideration for inclusion in Season 21. However, this idea would not be taken forward.

Three screens on BBC1.

Tuesday 16th:
Itinerary: John takes Peter Davison out for lunch. 'Earthshock' Part Four screens on BBC1.

Commentary: Although this lunch engagement could have been nothing more than a convivial chat between colleagues, it's possible that John discussed with Davison some early ideas regarding the show's upcoming twentieth anniversary. It's also possible that he was trying to ascertain the actor's long-term commitment to the show, now that he'd done a full season. However, it's also possible that John was laying the groundwork for that Thursday's activities …

Thursday 18th:
Itinerary: On the pretext of filming a promotional trailer for *Doctor Who,* aimed at boosting overseas sales of the show to Australia, John has arranged for the TARDIS prop to be taken to Trafalgar Square in London. With cameras dotted about the square, Peter Davison, Sarah Sutton, Janet Fielding and Matthew Waterhouse arrive, attired in their *Doctor Who* costumes. Davison is all ready to perform his dialogue for the trailer, when the TARDIS doors open to reveal Eamonn Andrews, host of the ITV show *This Is Your Life.* Davison is the surprise 'star guest' of the programme this week, and John and the rest of the cast are whisked off to Thames Television's studios to record the rest of the show.[183]

John Nathan-Turner: 'I had to live with the secret of the red book for several months. Sandra Dickinson was, of course, in on the secret, but my staff – also kept in the dark for several weeks – couldn't understand why Thames TV kept calling. On the day of the surprise, I had to get Peter to Trafalgar Square in costume on some pretext, where the TARDIS would be erected. I told Peter we were doing a presentation trailer for Australia. I even wrote a script for it! It was arranged that I would take Peter to lunch and then we'd travel by limo to central London. Early that day Sandra rang the office in a panic; she was needed at the *This Is Your Life* rehearsal as soon as possible. Could I get Peter out of the house? I obliged. I asked him to come early to the office to deal with urgent fan mail. We made him sign letters, books, records – anything we could find. Then we went to lunch … Anyway, it all went well in the end, and gave *Doctor Who* some excellent publicity. It's sad that they cut off the Trafalgar Square pick-up sequence so quickly, as Peter looked around for me and

---

[183] Peter Davison's edition of *This is Your Life* was screened on ITV on Thursday 25 March.

shouted, "Where is he? I'll kill him!"'[184]

Friday 19th:
Itinerary: John writes to David Reid and argues the case for a short series of six or seven episodes of *K-9 and Company* to be made by the BBC in 1983/84, based on the pilot episode.

Monday 22nd:
'Time-Flight' Part One screens on BBC1.

Tuesday 23rd:
'Time-Flight' Part Two screens on BBC1.

Wednesday 24th:
Itinerary: John attends a planning meeting for 'Snakedance' in Threshold House, along with director Fiona Cumming and the various members of the relevant BBC Departments who will work on the story.

Friday 26th:
Itinerary: John has a working lunch with writer Ben Steed at the BBC Club bar. In the evening, he goes to see a play (title unknown) at the Theatre Royal, Drury Lane.[185]

Saturday 27th:
Itinerary: John travels in to Television Centre by car for a non-duty day at work.

Monday 29th:
Itinerary: John requests that Eric Saward be given staff clearance to write the four scripts for 'The Return'.[186] 'Time-Flight' Part Three screens on BBC1.

---

[184] John Nathan-Turner memoirs, *Doctor Who Magazine* #235.

[185] This was the second time in a matter of weeks that John had gone to see a play at the Theatre Royal. It's possible he attended previews of *The Pirates of Penzance*, which officially opened there at the end of May 1982. If so, then it's perhaps a significant show of interest, as the cast included future *Doctor Who* regulars Sylvester McCoy and Bonnie Langford, along with Tim Curry, Michael Praed, Annie Ross, Carolyn Allen, Jackie Downey, Gaynor Miles, Janet Shaw, Karen Lancaster, Louise Gold, Pamela Stephenson, George Cole and Chris Langham.

[186] It's not known when Eric Saward delivered his scripts for 'The Return', which was a Dalek story planned to close the show's twentieth season. After industrial action forced its abandonment, Saward rewrote the four scripts as 'Resurrection of the Daleks' for the twenty-first season. Again, the rewrite and delivery dates for these scripts aren't known.

Tuesday 30th:
Itinerary: John takes the short tube journey from Union House to the BBC's Television Rehearsal Rooms at Acton. Today are rehearsals for tomorrow's single day of filming for 'Snakedance' at Ealing Film Studios. On the same day, Johnny Byrne delivers his script for 'Arc of Infinity' Part Four to the *Doctor Who* Production Office. 'Time-Flight' Part Four screens on BBC1.

Wednesday 31st:
Itinerary: John takes the tube from Union House to the BBC's Ealing Film Studios for the first and only day of filming for 'Snakedance'. All the scenes featuring the character Dojjen, mainly from Part Four, are filmed on a soundstage there. On the same day, John receives a memo from Alan Hart, Controller of BBC1. Hart thanks John for producing a very successful series (the recently-concluded Season 19), which on his instructions was the first to be shown mid-week. Hart goes on to say that the fact that the mid-week timeslots have worked so well does not preclude further debate about the following year's schedule (indicating that it isn't yet firmly decided what day/timeslot the Season 20 episodes would occupy in the BBC1 schedules in 1983). Hart concludes by stating how well he thought Peter Davison did in his first season as the Doctor, and praising the general quality of the stories. Also on this day, John writes to Graham Richmond at the BBC's Ealing Film Studios, asking that John Baker be allocated as cameraman for story 6J ('The Android'). He also writes to the Head of Design, asking that Michael Burdle be allocated as designer for this story, and to the Head of the Make-Up Department, asking that Liz Rowell be allocated as make-up artist.[187] Also on the same day, John is sent the cover of *Doctor Who Monthly* issue 65 by Marvel UK for his approval. This features a photograph of the Terileptil leader from 'The Visitation', in which the join between the top half and bottom half of the costume is quite noticeable. Also, the way the costume is lit makes the groin area look … not as intended! Because of this, John rejects the cover.

APRIL

Thursday 1st – Saturday 10th:
Rehearsals for the first studio block of 'Snakedance' take place at the BBC Television Rehearsal Rooms at Acton.

---

[187] John got his wish with Elizabeth Rowell, but Ken Ledsham was allocated as this story's designer.

Thursday 1st:
Itinerary: In the morning, John travels by tube from Union House to the BBC's Television Rehearsal Rooms at Acton, to sit in on the rehearsals for the first studio block of 'Snakedance' for a few hours. He then takes a taxi to Heathrow Airport, where he flies to Amsterdam to take part in the location recce for 'Arc of Infinity'. He takes with him his luggage, briefcase, scripts, and traveller's cheques to the value of £90 for his expenses. He meets up with Ron Jones (director) and Ralph Wilton (Production Manager), who have both travelled over to Amsterdam the previous day, and stays overnight at a hotel in the city centre. In John's absence, his secretary rings Marvel UK and informs editor Alan McKenzie that the proposed cover for issue 65 of *Doctor Who Monthly* is to be rejected.

Friday 2nd:
Itinerary: John spends the day visiting the planned filming locations for 'Arc of Infinity' in Amsterdam, then flies back to Heathrow in the evening. He gets a taxi from the airport to BBC Television Centre, arriving at around 8.00pm, before heading for home.

Tuesday 6th:
Itinerary: In the morning, John takes the tube from Union House to the BBC Television Rehearsal Rooms at Acton, where rehearsals for the first studio block of 'Snakedance' are ongoing. John returns to BBC Television Centre in the afternoon, where he has a meeting with writer Tudor George over drinks at the BBC Club bar.[188]

Wednesday 7th:
Itinerary: John writes to Yvonne Lugg of the BBC Personnel Department regarding his planned pantomime work later in the year at Tunbridge Wells, responding to her memo of 11 March. He says that there appears to be some confusion, as he's not asking to be released from his *Doctor Who* duties during the period he'll be producing the pantomime, as there will be filming and studio sessions during that time. He states that he intends to do the pantomime project in his own free time, during the evenings and at weekends. On the same day, John also chases up with Eamon Matthews from the *Nationwide* production team, on the issue of the non-payment of John Leeson's fee for his cancelled appearance on *Nationwide* back in November 1981.

---

[188] John stipulated on his expenses form that Tudor George was a writer, but I can find no record of a writer of that name. However, there was a costume designer named Tudor George, who worked on *Gangsters*, *Who Pays the Ferryman* and, most recently at this point in time, *The Long Good Friday*. Perhaps George was looking to branch out into scriptwriting? If so, he didn't pursue that career change, but remained a prolific costume designer.

Thursday 8th:
Itinerary: John attends a pre-planning meeting for 'Arc of Infinity' in Threshold House, along with director Ron Jones and the various members of the relevant BBC Departments who will work on the story. He also travels to the Television Rehearsal Rooms at Acton to attend a planning meeting for the studio sessions of 'Snakedance', along with director Fiona Cumming and the various members of the relevant BBC Departments who will work on that story. Brian Babani, the Managing Director of Marvel UK, writes to John regarding the cover of *Doctor Who Monthly* issue 65. To enable the magazine to meet printing deadlines over the upcoming Easter period, the issue has already gone to print with the Terileptil cover that John rejected, and the cost of reprinting or overprinting it now would be prohibitively expensive – so much so that, should John insist on the cover not seeing the light of day, the costs would force Marvel UK to shelve several of their titles and make several members of staff redundant as a result. He assures John that he's put in place stringent instructions to ensure that nothing like this happens again, but asks him allow the issue to be published with the cover as it stands. He offers to meet with John, and with Martin Hussey from BBC Enterprises, to discuss this matter as soon as possible.

Friday 9th (bank holiday – Good Friday):
Itinerary: John takes the short tube journey from Union House to the BBC's Television Rehearsal Rooms at Acton for the Producer's Run of the first studio block for 'Snakedance'.

Monday 12th:
Itinerary: It's the first day of the three-day first studio block for 'Snakedance' in studio TC6 at BBC Television Centre. After recording, John joins the cast in the BBC Club bar. On the same day John writes to director John Black ('The Keeper of Traken', 'Four to Doomsday' and *K-9 and Company*) and Amy Roberts (costume designer on a number of *Doctor Who* stories and the then girlfriend of Black) thanking them for a 'super evening'.[189]

John Nathan-Turner: 'I particularly liked Nyssa's beautiful yet bizarre costume [for "Snakedance"]. Just before its first appearance at a studio recording (the desert landscape sequences had been filmed at Ealing), Sandra Dickinson (Peter Davison's wife, who was visiting to watch the recording) told Sarah Sutton – just as she left the sandwich bar heading for make-up check – that she thought the outfit was hideous. I was furious, and told Sandra so, adding that it was none of her business. Sandra didn't visit the studio again, a fact about which many people were pleased, especially the vision mixer, as Ms

---

[189] John and Gary had presumably been entertained recently by the couple.

Dickinson was prone to sit at the back of the gallery knitting loudly.'[190]

Tuesday 13th:
Itinerary: It's the second day of the three-day first studio block for 'Snakedance' in studio TC6 at BBC Television Centre. After recording, John joins the cast in the BBC Club bar. On the same day, John writes to Biddy Baxter, the producer of the BBC children's magazine programme *Blue Peter*. He asks her to consider running an item showing behind the scenes at a pantomime, and tells her of the upcoming run of *Cinderella* he'll be producing, later in the year, and of its *Doctor Who* connections.[191] Also on the same day, John signs off the commission for Philip Martin to write a scene breakdown for a story entitled 'Domain'.[192]

Wednesday 14th:
Itinerary: It's the third and final day of the first studio block for 'Snakedance' in studio TC6 at BBC Television Centre. On the same day, John submits a format pitch to David Reid for a bi-weekly drama series entitled *Catwalk*, devised by him and Gary Downie, which focuses on the behind-the-scenes intrigues at a London fashion house.

Thursday 15th – Saturday 24th:
Rehearsals for the second studio block of 'Snakedance' take place at the BBC Television Rehearsal Rooms at Acton.

Thursday 15th:
Itinerary: John replies to Brian Babani at Marvel UK, reluctantly allowing issue 65 of *Doctor Who Monthly* to go ahead with the offending Terileptil cover. He points out other problems that have recently occurred with the magazine, such as Peter Davison's surname being misspelled 'Davidson' on the cover of issue 61, and his own credit as an 'Adviser' on the title being regularly misspelled 'Advisor'. He looks forward to meeting Babani, along with Martin Hussey of BBC Enterprises, at the earliest convenience.

Tuesday 20th:
Itinerary: A lady identified simply as 'Adaire' from TV Features at BBC Manchester calls the *Doctor Who* Production Office. She's a researcher for a programme called *In Search of Troy*,[193] and wants to know if any *Doctor Who*

---

[190] John Nathan-Turner memoirs, *Doctor Who Magazine* #236.
[191] Biddy Baxter did not take up this offer.
[192] This story will eventually get made under the title 'Vengeance on Varos' during Season 22.
[193] A six-part documentary series titled *In Search of the Trojan War* was eventually made by BBC Manchester, airing on BBC2 from February 1985.

stories have been set in the time of ancient Greece, especially during the Trojan War. John tells her that William Hartnell's Doctor visited ancient Troy in the story 'The Myth Makers', and refers her to Sue Malden at the BBC Film and Videotape Library.[194] Brian Babani from Marvel UK responds to John's letter of the previous Thursday, thanking him for allowing issue 65 of *Doctor Who Monthly* to go ahead with the Terileptil cover. He adds that circulation for the magazine has been in decline, and the hoped-for boost in sales with Peter Davison's arrival as the fifth Doctor has not materialised.

Thursday 22nd:
Itinerary: John takes the tube from Shepherd's Bush to Ealing, to visit the BBC's Film Studios, where he views the 16mm film sequences that have been shot and edited for 'Snakedance'. On the same day, Terence Dudley delivers his two scripts for 'The Android' to the *Doctor Who* Production Office.

Friday 23rd:
Itinerary: John travels by tube from Shepherd's Bush to Hammersmith for a working lunch with the musician Paddy Kingsland at his studio, then returns to the *Doctor Who* Production Office. He then takes the short tube journey from Union House to the BBC's Television Rehearsal Rooms at Acton for the Producer's Run of the second studio block for 'Snakedance'.

Commentary: As a member of the BBC's Radiophonic Workshop, Paddy Kingsland had previously provided the incidental music for a number of *Doctor Who* stories in Seasons 18 and 19. By this point in time, he had left the BBC to go freelance, but was still keen to continue contributing music to the show. In just a few days' time, John would ask Kingsland to provide the music for story 6F later in Season 20; this was probably the subject of today's meeting.

Monday 26th:
Itinerary: It's the first day of the three-day second studio block for 'Snakedance' in studio TC6 at BBC Television Centre. After recording, John joins the cast in the BBC Club bar.

Tuesday 27th:
Itinerary: It's the second day of the three-day second studio block for 'Snakedance' in studio TC6 at BBC Television Centre. After recording, John joins the cast in the BBC Club bar.

---

[194] John obviously didn't have the details of the BBC's archive holdings of past *Doctor Who* episodes at his fingertips, or he'd have known that this story was completely missing.

Wednesday 28th:
Itinerary: It's the third and final day of the second studio block for 'Snakedance' in studio TC6 at BBC Television Centre. After recording, John writes to the Head of the BBC's Design Department to discuss problems with the sets. He states that the designer, Jan Spotczynski, requested several weeks ago that these be built by an outside contractor, only to have the request refused. It was then decided at the eleventh hour to allocate half of the sets to the outside contractor after all. John says that, given that this was a rush job, it was amazing that the end results were so good. On the same day, Jane Treays, a researcher for *Jim'll Fix It*, contacts the *Doctor Who* Production Office. They've received a letter from a girl who wants her mother to be helped by an android for a day – specifically an android from *Doctor Who*. Treays wants to know if *Doctor Who* has ever featured an android, and if so, could *Jim'll Fix It* use it? John sends her a VHS tape of 'The Visitation' Part Four, and offers to have a further discussion specifically about the Terileptil Android once the tape has been viewed. John also lets Terry Sampson at BBC Enterprises know that the Terileptil Android costume might need to be borrowed back from the Blackpool *Doctor Who* Exhibition (where it currently is on display) should the *Jim'll Fix It* team want to use it. Eventually, it is decided that this 'fix' is to be postponed – at least – until the next series of *Jim'll Fix It*. Also on this day, Marjorie Abel, John Leeson's agent, contacts the *Doctor Who* Production Office to let them know that Leeson's cancellation payment from *Nationwide* dating back to November 1981 still hasn't been forthcoming.

Thursday 29th:
Itinerary: In the morning, John attends a planning meeting for 'Arc of Infinity' in Threshold House, along with director Ron Jones and the various members of the relevant BBC Departments who will work on the story. John then entertains members of the executive committee of the *Doctor Who* Appreciation Society in the BBC Club bar over lunch. Later that day, John writes to Paddy Kingsland and asks him to provide the incidental music for story 6F.[195]

---

[195] At this point, story 6F is still planned to be 'The Song of the Space Whale', but this story will eventually be dropped from the schedule and replaced with 'Mawdryn Undead'.

MAY

Sunday 2nd:
Itinerary: John travels in to Television Centre by car for a non-duty day at work.

Monday 3rd (bank holiday):
Itinerary: It's an early start for John, as he gets a minicab from home to take him to Heathrow Airport. His flight departs at 8.15am and takes him, along with the cast and film crew of 'Arc of Infinity', to Schipol Airport in Amsterdam for the first day's location filming. John stays in the Sheraton Schipol Inn in Hoofdorp overnight.

Tuesday 4th:
Itinerary: Today is the second day of location filming for 'Arc of Infinity' in Amsterdam. John again stays in the Sheraton Schipol Inn overnight.

Wednesday 5th:
Itinerary: Today is the third day of location filming for 'Arc of Infinity' in Amsterdam. John arranges for the loan of two bicycles for use by Peter Davison, Janet Fielding and Sarah Sutton for a press photocall to promote the overseas filming for this story, and the new season of *Doctor Who* in general. Sarah Sutton is given her 'Snakedance' costume to wear for this photoshoot. John spends a third night in the Sheraton Schipol Inn.

John Nathan-Turner: 'A large press party accompanied us on this shoot, chiefly to capture Nyssa's and Tegan's new costumes, but Her Majesty's Press do love a foreign jaunt in any case. One of the party, a photographer called Alistair Loos, is exceedingly charming but a little gullible. The BBC Press and Publicity Department, with my help, devised a plan whereby I would tell Alistair that Janet Fielding was to wear a very revealing peignoir in the main story and, as he was an old friend, that I had wanted his paper, the *Daily Star*, to have a picture exclusive, as we had the costume with us in Amsterdam. I added apologetically that the Press Office, however, thought it was too sensational and had banned the idea. Janet confirmed the story, and throughout the day everyone could see that Alistair had fallen for the story hook, line and sinker. By the end of shooting that day, Alistair had called what is known as a "lens meeting", telling the other reporters and photographers – who were all in on the gag – of the scandalous interference by the publicity officer. It wasn't till he finally lost control so much that he was about to ring his editor that he was told the truth.'[196]

Thursday 6th:
Itinerary: Today is the fourth day of location filming for 'Arc of Infinity' in Amsterdam. John spends part of the day entertaining members of the British press[197], who have travelled over to Amsterdam to cover the filming. John arranges an evening out for the cast and crew after filming; this begins with a meal and ends with a tour of the city's notorious 'red light' district. John again stays in the Sheraton Schipol Inn overnight.

Sarah Sutton: 'I quite enjoyed filming in Amsterdam. We did go sightseeing. There was Peter, Janet, myself, and some crew, and we went out for a meal, and then we traipsed around the red light area, which was quite funny. I wanted to sit in a window, but nobody would let me. Imagine the headlines!'[198]

Friday 7th:
Itinerary: Today is the fifth and final day of location filming for 'Arc of Infinity' in Amsterdam. One of the scenes filmed today involves the Doctor and Nyssa using a public telephone kiosk, and John can be seen walking into shot at the back of the scene (as transmitted) to try and prevent a pedestrian from doing exactly the same thing. Once filming is concluded, the cast and crew head back to Schipol Airport to catch their flight back to Heathrow airport in London, which lands at approximately 10.15pm.

John Nathan-Turner: 'It was in this story that I made my only on-screen appearance in *Doctor Who*. A long tracking shot in the middle of a busy thoroughfare of Amsterdam kept being ruined by passers-by pointing at the camera. We decided to have one final attempt after which, if it failed, the shooting method would be simplified. In mid-take I saw a large lady laden with bags suddenly turn as if to head straight toward the actors ... so, in a sheepskin coat, I marched forward and turned her round the other way. The camera moved on and didn't see what happened next. She thought I was a thief and attacked me with her shopping!'[199]

Saturday 8th – Sunday 16th:
Rehearsals for the first studio block of 'Arc of Infinity' take place at the BBC

---

[196] John Nathan-Turner memoirs, *Doctor Who Magazine* #236.
[197] Representatives from the *Daily Telegraph*, the *Sun*, the *Daily Mirror*, the *Daily Express*, the *Daily Mail*, the *Daily Record* and the Press Association flew over from the UK to cover the Amsterdam filming.
[198] Sarah Sutton interview, *Doctor Who Magazine* #218.
[199] John Nathan-Turner memoirs, *Doctor Who Magazine* #236.

Television Rehearsal Rooms at Acton.

Saturday 8th:
Itinerary: John travels in to the Television Rehearsal Rooms at Acton by car for a non-duty day at work, to observe the first day of rehearsals for the first studio block of 'Arc of Infinity'.

Tuesday 11th:
Itinerary: In the evening, John attends the opening night of the play *The Little Foxes* at the Victoria Palace Theatre in London's West End.

Commentary: The cast of *The Little Foxes* included Elizabeth Taylor, Novella Nelson, Hugh L Hurd, Sada Thompson, Nicholas Coster, William Youmans, Humbert Allen Astredo, Robert Lansing, Ann Talman and J D Cannon.

Thursday 13th:
Itinerary: John has a working lunch with Alan McKenzie, the editor of Marvel's *Doctor Who Monthly*, at the BBC Club bar.

Friday 14th:
Itinerary: John takes the short tube journey from Union House to the BBC's Television Rehearsal Rooms at Acton for the Producer's Run of the first studio block for 'Arc of Infinity'. On the same day, Dennis Slater, the props buyer for the Johnny Ball-fronted BBC1 programme *Think of a Number*, contacts the *Doctor Who* Production Office. He would like to borrow the TARDIS prop for use in an episode of the programme, due to be recorded at BBC Manchester on Monday 24 May. John agrees. He arranges for the TARDIS prop to be collected from BBC Television Centre on Friday 21 May, and stipulates that it needs to be returned to London on or before Thursday 27 May. Brian Clifford from BBC Picture Publicity also writes to John on this day, thanking him for the arrangements he made to accommodate the members of the press contingent on the recent location filming for 'Arc of Infinity'. The subsequent press coverage was quite substantial, which delights Clifford.

Monday 17th:
Itinerary: It's the first day of the two-day first studio block for 'Arc of Infinity' in studio TC1 at BBC Television Centre. After recording, John joins the cast in the BBC Club bar. A BBC producer named John Smith contacts the *Doctor Who* Production Office, looking to borrow the TARDIS prop and to use the *Doctor Who* theme music for an item in his programme, the title of which is currently unknown. John agrees to the use of the theme music, but has to decline the use

of the TARDIS prop as it's about to go on a week's loan to BBC Manchester.[200] Barbara Clegg delivers her revised script for 'The Enlighteners' Part Two to the *Doctor Who* Production Office.

Tuesday 18th:
Itinerary: It's the second and last day of the first studio block for 'Arc of Infinity' in studio TC1 at BBC Television Centre. After recording, John joins the cast in the BBC Club bar.

Thursday 20th – Sunday 30th:
Rehearsals for the second studio block of 'Arc of Infinity' take place at the BBC Television Rehearsal Rooms at Acton.

Thursday 20th:
Itinerary: John sends a memo to Graeme McDonald, asking him to consider a drama proposal entitled *The Prince* by Ben Steed, which John suggests can be made entirely on film.[201] On the same day, Peter Seddon, Head of the BBC's Television Design Department, writes to John to counter the concerns he raised on 28 April about the construction of the studio sets for 'Snakedance'. Seddon informs John that the initial request to have the sets made by an outside contractor couldn't be met, as the contractor in question was committed to work on other programmes.

Saturday 22nd:
Itinerary: John purchases a sturdy anorak for use on location, and charges it to *Doctor Who*'s budget.

Monday 24th:
Itinerary: John has a working lunch with writer Peter Ling to discuss a 'new project'.

Commentary: Peter Ling had written the *Doctor Who* story 'The Mind Robber'

---

[200] There was in fact more than one TARDIS prop at the time at the BBC. John had overseen the construction of a new, lightweight one that was easier to transport and erect when filming on location, which had debuted in 'The Leisure Hive'. The old prop that had debuted in Season 14 and been used up until 'Shada' was also still at the BBC. Both had been seen side-by-side on screen in 'Logopolis', and the old prop had for some reason ended up being used for the filming of 'Black Orchid'. Perhaps John didn't want to be in a situation where both TARDIS props were out on loan at the same time, just in case …

[201] It's known that Ben Steed was pitching ideas for *Doctor Who* stories at around this time, and had already had a couple of meetings with John, but it would appear that this proposal for *The Prince* was unconnected to *Doctor Who*.

in 1968. He was also the co-creator of the soap-operas *Crossroads* and *Compact*, which both began in the 1960s. John was a big soap-opera fan, and wanted to revive *Compact*. This meeting with Ling was probably to discuss the early ideas for this revival, but it would also see Ling begin pitching ideas for new *Doctor Who* stories, although none would ever be taken up by John.

John Nathan-Turner: 'I knew that around this time the BBC was searching for a new twice-weekly serial to run throughout the year. In fact, [Eric] Saward and I worked with writers Hazel Adair and Peter Ling on a revamp of the '60s soap-opera *Compact*, which was to be called *Impact*, but sadly it never got off the ground. I always suspected that the annual change of transmission days for *Doctor Who* during its three years of twice-weekly broadcasts was used by the BBC to establish the best days to transmit the favoured soap-opera, which eventually emerged as *EastEnders*.'[202]

Tuesday 25th:
Itinerary: Barry Green from HTV Wales contacts the *Doctor Who* Production Office. He's working on a children's quiz programme, and asks for the production team to set one question (and provide the answer) about *Doctor Who*. On the same day, John writes to the Assistant Head of TV Design, asking that Tony Burrough be allocated to work on 'The Enlighteners'.[203]

Wednesday 26th:
Itinerary: John takes the short tube journey from Union House to the BBC's Television Rehearsal Rooms at Acton, where the rehearsals for the second studio block of 'Arc of Infinity' are ongoing. On the same day, John writes to actress Colette O'Neil, thanking her for her performance in 'Snakedance'.

Thursday 27th:
Itinerary: John signs off the commissioning brief for Peter Grimwade to write a story outline for 'Mawdryn Undead'.

Friday 28th:
Itinerary: John takes the short tube journey from Union House to the BBC's Television Rehearsal Rooms at Acton. Today is the Producer's Run for the second studio block of 'Arc of Infinity'. On the same day, John writes to Paddy Kingsland, asking him to provide the incidental music for 'The Enlighteners'.

---

[202] John Nathan-Turner memoirs, *Doctor Who Magazine* #235.
[203] Colin Green was ultimately allocated as designer on 'Enlightenment'. However, as the plan at this point seems to have been to make 'The Enlighteners' in the production slot eventually given to 'Mawdryn Undead', then perhaps Burrough would have been requested to tackle that story instead? 'Mawdryn Undead' had Stephen Scott allocated as designer.

He tells Kingsland that the director of the story is to be Peter Moffatt.

Commentary: It would appear that 'The Enlighteners' was now being considered as the story that would be made in the slot for 6F. 'The Song of the Space Whale' had probably been dropped by this point – or at least pushed back in production order – and 'Mawdryn Undead' had only just been commissioned as a story outline.

Monday 31st:
Itinerary: It's the first day of the three-day second studio block for 'Arc of Infinity' in studio TC1 at BBC Television Centre. After recording, John joins the cast in the BBC Club bar.

JUNE

Tuesday 1st:
Itinerary: It's the second day of the three-day second studio block for 'Arc of Infinity' in studio TC1 at BBC Television Centre. After recording, John joins the cast in the BBC Club bar. On the same day, John writes to the Manager of BBC Drama Series and Serials, asking that Margot Hayhoe be allocated to 'The Enlighteners' as Production Manager.[204]

Wednesday 2nd:
Itinerary: It's the third and final day of the second studio block for 'Arc of Infinity' in studio TC1 at BBC Television Centre. Peter Grimwade delivers his story outline for 'Mawdryn Undead' to the *Doctor Who* Production Office.

Commentary: After this, there is a three-month break in recording of *Doctor Who*, as Peter Davison is committed to making the six episodes of the final season of his BBC comedy series *Sink or Swim*. This break allows time for the Production Office to sort out the scripts and story order for the remainder of Season 20.

Thursday 3rd:
Itinerary: John travels by tube from Shepherd's Bush to Hammersmith, then returns to the *Doctor Who* Production Office.

---

[204] Again, the production slot planned for 'The Enlighteners' was soon to be reassigned to 'Mawdryn Undead'. Ann Aronsohn was allocated as Production Manager for 'Mawdryn Undead'.

Friday 4th:
Itinerary: John again travels by tube from Shepherd's Bush to Hammersmith, then returns to the *Doctor Who* Production Office. On the same day, John writes to David Reid about a studio overrun of 17 minutes during the final recording of 'Arc of Infinity' on Wednesday 2 June. He attributes this to a 50-minute late start on the first studio day, due to the studio sets being incomplete, which had a knock-on effect for the rest of the studio block. John also signs off the commission for Peter Grimwade to write the four scripts for 'Mawdryn Undead'. On the same day, he writes to the BBC Contracts Department, asking that Nicholas Courtney be engaged to appear in 'Mawdryn Undead'. Also on this day, Philip Martin delivers his scene breakdown for 'Domain' to the *Doctor Who* Production Office. In addition, John and Eric Saward circulate a Drama Script Classified List, which states that the only writers they are working with at this date for upcoming storylines and/or scripts are: Christopher Bailey, Rod Beacham (one episode), Johnny Byrne, Barbara Clegg, Terence Dudley, Stephen Gallagher, Bill Lyons, Philip Martin (scene breakdown), Pat Mills and John Wagner, Eric Pringle, Eric Saward and Peter Grimwade.

Commentary: Although the reasons for John's trips to Hammersmith at the end of this week aren't recorded, it's most likely that he was having further meetings with Paddy Kingsland, whose studios were there.

Sunday 6th:
Itinerary: John takes the tube to Euston Station, and then travels by train – 1st Class – to Blackpool. He visits the *Doctor Who* Exhibition, which has recently been refurbished with new props and costumes from the show's nineteenth season. He stays overnight in Blackpool.

Monday 7th:
Itinerary: John returns to London from Blackpool by train, and goes home.

Thursday 10th:
Itinerary: Peter Grimwade delivers his script for 'Mawdryn Undead' Part One to the *Doctor Who* Production Office.

Monday 14th:
Itinerary: Mark Strickson is contracted to appear as Turlough in 18 episodes of Season 20.[205]

---

[205] Because of the cancellation of 'The Return', the final planned story, Strickson appeared in only 14 episodes of the season.

John Nathan-Turner: 'I had quite a depressing time casting the new companion, Turlough, until Mark Strickson turned up; and even then it looked as though it might not work out … Mark was coming to see me mid-afternoon on a Friday. One of my fellow producers, Julia Smith, was having problems on her medical soap, *Angels*. One of her cast had contracted a contagious disease and Julia was writing him out. At the time, Mark had just completed a couple of episodes as an ambulance driver. Mark was sitting down in reception at Union House waiting to see me when Julia burst into my office, saying there was no point in my seeing Mark because she was about to offer him a regular part in *Angels*, to take over the storylines of the sick actor. I insisted on seeing him, however, and was very impressed. I told him I was interested and would be in touch with his agent. It transpired that Julia, meanwhile, had jumped the gun somewhat, and had invited all her production team to join her in her office at 5.30pm to meet the new regular in *Angels*. I saw the last candidate for Turlough and rang Mark's agent to offer him the role. The agent explained that Mark was in a phone box in Shepherd's Bush somewhere, dithering over whether or not to accept the offer from *Angels*. Ten minutes later Mark rang me to say he needed time to think. I suggested he contact me with an answer by lunchtime the following Monday. By now Julia Smith was in a state, with an office full of people drinking BBC wine last thing on a Friday and wondering why they'd been invited. Eventually, Julia, Mark, Julia's script editor and myself were discussing the situation in an empty office nearby. I explained that I'd given Mark time to think things over, and she agreed to do the same. I recall Julia being very dismissive of *Doctor Who* and repeatedly saying it wasn't drama. In the end, Mark was heading home with two offers of long-term work, whereas two hours earlier he'd been on the dole. As he left the office, Julia said, "Mark, if you're interested in money, do *Doctor Who*, but if you're interested in acting, do *Angels*!" I couldn't resist the bait, I'm afraid. I felt compelled to say, "If you want to be one of 12 regulars, do *Angels*, but if you want to be one of four leading parts, do *Doctor Who*!" The following Monday, Mark was going out and got knocked off his bicycle, probably because he was so preoccupied. But before the appointed deadline, he telephoned me to say he'd love to play Turlough. Julia didn't telephone me at all!'[206]

Commentary: At an earlier point in her career, Julia Smith had directed two 1960s *Doctor Who* stories, 'The Smugglers' and 'The Underwater Menace'.

Monday 14th – Friday 25th:
John takes two weeks of annual leave from the BBC, while production of *Doctor Who* takes a summer break.

---

[206] John Nathan-Turner memoirs, *Doctor Who Magazine* #236.

Thursday 17th:
Itinerary: Peter Grimwade delivers his script for 'Mawdryn Undead' Part Two to the *Doctor Who* Production Office.

Monday 21st:
Itinerary: Barbara Clegg delivers her revised script for 'The Enlighteners' Part Four to the *Doctor Who* Production Office.

Thursday 24th:
Itinerary: Peter Grimwade delivers his script for 'Mawdryn Undead' Part Three to the *Doctor Who* Production Office.

Wednesday 30th:
Itinerary: Now back from leave, John entertains four members of the executive committee of the *Doctor Who* Appreciation Society in the BBC Club bar during the day. Afterwards, for reasons unknown, he travels by taxi from BBC Threshold House to Earl's Court. On the same day, he writes to Jon Pertwee to inform him of the upcoming screening of 'The Curse of Peladon' on BBC1 as part of the *Doctor Who and the Monsters* season of repeats.

JULY

Friday 2nd:
Itinerary: John replies to a letter from John Ostrander in Chicago, USA. Ostrander is looking to produce a *Doctor Who* stage play in the city and wants to contact Terrance Dicks. John passes Ostrander's details to Martin Hussey of BBC Merchandising and asks if they could meet up for a drink when John is in Chicago later this month.

Commentary: Terrance Dicks had scripted the stage play *Doctor Who and the Daleks in Seven Keys to Doomsday*, which had run in London in 1974. Ostrander might have been considering resurrecting this in Chicago. On the other hand, he might have been looking to sound Dicks out about writing a new play.

Wednesday 7th:
Itinerary: Peter Grimwade delivers his script for 'Mawdryn Undead' Part Four to the *Doctor Who* Production Office.

Thursday 8th:
Itinerary: David Reid writes to John after reading the scripts for 'Mawdryn

Undead'. He asks if there are more episodes to come, as he doesn't think the plot is fully resolved by the end of Part Four.

Friday 9th:
Itinerary: John writes to David Reid, confirming that 'Mawdryn Undead' is a four-part story but stating that rewrites are being done on the scripts of the final two episodes.

Commentary: It's probably around this point that 'Mawdryn Undead' was fast-tracked into the production slot for story 6F.

Monday 12th:
The *Doctor Who and the Monsters* repeat season on BBC1 begins with a 50-minute compilation of Episodes One and Two of 'The Curse of Peladon'.

Wednesday 14th
Itinerary: Phil Chivers, producer of *Take Two*, notifies the Production Office that his show will be using a *Doctor Who* clip in an edition due to be screened on 20 July. Jon Pertwee writes to John, thinking him for alerting him to the repeat of 'The Curse of Peladon' and suggesting that he could perhaps appear again in a multi-Doctor story. Patrick Troughton writes to John on the same day, also regarding appearing in a multi-Doctor story. John has previously floated the idea with Troughton, and suggested that any such story would be made between April and July 1983. Troughton informs him that he's under an option for Granada TV's *Foxy Lady* comedy series during those months, but adds that he really doesn't want to miss being in the multi-Doctor story if possible. However, John is not in the *Doctor Who* Production Office to note this information. In the morning, he takes a taxi from his home to Heathrow Airport, to board a flight bound for Chicago USA, to attend the Panopticon West II convention.

Thursday 15th:
Itinerary: David Reid writes to John, informing him that he has the go-ahead to make a 90-minute multi-Doctor special for the *Doctror Who*'s twentieth anniversary the following year.

Commentary: John had probably had an inkling for some time that the multi-Doctor special would be green-lit, following Reid's suggestion the previous August. He had obviously done a degree of groundwork with Patrick Troughton and Jon Pertwee to see how receptive they would be to the idea.

Friday 16th:
Itinerary: Eric Pringle delivers his scene breakdown for 'War Game' to the

Doctor Who Production Office.

Friday 16th – Sunday 18th:
Itinerary: John is ensconced in the Americana Congress Hotel in Chicago, Illinois, which is hosting the Panopticon West II convention this weekend. While at the event, John entertains on expenses the following people: Bob Greenstein (from Lionheart, the US distributor of *Doctor Who* episodes to PBS TV stations), Greenstein's wife, Harvey Chertok (Vice President of Television Promotion and Publicity at Time-Life Films), Chertok's wife, Barbara Elder (head of NADWAS, the North American *Doctor Who* Appreciation Society), Anne Shelby (also part of the NADWAS convention team), Larry Chevet (ComiCon Organiser), Terry Nation (writer, creator of the Daleks and guest of the event), Sarah Sutton and Anthony Ainley (also guesting at the event, by virtue of their roles as Nyssa and the Master respectively), Ken Bussametts (from *TV Guide* magazine), David Ryan[207] and staff (who are making the Denver PBS station KRMA's TV documentary *Once Upon a Time Lord*), John Ostrander (producer of the planned US *Doctor Who* stage play *The Inheritors of Time*), Terry Sampson and Lorne Martin (of BBC Enterprises) and Alan Bilyard (of BBC Records and Tapes). While at the event, John talks to Terry Nation and gets his agreement in principle for the Daleks to be used in Eric Saward's scripts for 'The Return'. He is also interviewed for the *Once Upon a Time Lord* documentary.

Monday 19th:
The *Doctor Who and the Monsters* repeat season on BBC1 continues with a 50-minute compilation of Episodes Three and Four of 'The Curse of Peladon'.

Tuesday 20th:
Itinerary: John returns to London, arriving back at Heathrow Airport, then gets a taxi to his office at the BBC. On the same day, Roderick Graham, Head of Drama at BBC Scotland, writes to John to turn down a pitch he has made to produce a series based on John Christopher's *The Sword of the Spirits* book trilogy.[208]

Friday 23rd:
Itinerary: John writes to Patrick Troughton, informing him that he's changed the provisional production dates of the anniversary special to March next year,

---

[207] Incorrectly named as David Pullman in John's expenses claim.
[208] John had previously pitched this to his own boss David Reid, but Reid had turned it down as he'd just optioned another book trilogy by John Christopher, *The Tripods*, to be made as a BBC series. Reid had suggested to John that he try pitching his idea to BBC Scotland instead.

in order to accommodate Troughton's availability. He also writes to Jon Pertwee, informing him of the anniversary special and stating how pleased he is to know he is already interested in such a project.

Monday 26th:
The *Doctor Who and the Monsters* repeat season on BBC1 continues with a 50-minute compilation of Episodes One, Two and Three of 'Genesis of the Daleks'.

Wednesday 28th:
Itinerary: John writes to Anne Vie, the BBC's Assistant for Planning and Rights, saying that he has no objection to a proposal from publishers Methuen for a *Doctor Who Quiz Book of Dinosaurs*, noting that when he was previously contacted about this on 14 May the title was simply *The Doctor Who Quiz Book*. He says, though, that he is unhappy with the shot of Peter Davison used on the draft cover, and that Davison's agent is bound to feel the same way. He also requests a small amendment to the back cover blurb and points out that the character and name Nyssa are the copyright of writer Johnny Byrne, not the BBC.[209]

Thursday 29th:
Itinerary: John is joined for lunch at the BBC bar by actor Mark Strickson, cast the previous month as the new male companion Turlough. On the same day, John writes to the BBC Contracts Department, asking that Jon Pertwee, Peter Davison, Mark Strickson, Janet Fielding and Anthony Ainley all be engaged to appear in the special, which now has the working title 'The Six Doctors'.[210]

Friday 30th:
Itinerary: John meets with writer Robert Holmes and script editor Eric Saward in the *Doctor Who* Production Office, to discuss Holmes writing the script of 'The Six Doctors'.

John Nathan-Turner: 'Eric Saward and I had originally approached Robert Holmes to write the special, and provided him with an ever-changing list of Doctors, companions and villains planned to appear. Bob found the list of essential ingredients in this rather rich story too much and withdrew from the project amicably. Our standby writer was Terrance Dicks, who, with typical enthusiasm, seized the chance and came up with a terrific script.'[211]

---

[209] Anne Vie passed these comments on to Methuen in a letter dated 2 August.
[210] The title altered to 'The Five Doctors' when Terrance Dicks ended up writing the final version.
[211] John Nathan-Turner memoirs, *Doctor Who Magazine* #237.

Eric Saward: 'I remember when Bob walked into the office. He came in – a big man, tall, ex-policeman many years ago, and he still had the presence. I think he looked at John and me and thought, "Crikey, a couple of real jerks here"! He was wrong [in that] he shouldn't have made it so obvious; but he was right in that we were being silly about what we wanted. John wanted the Cybermen, the Master and all the other bits and pieces that came into it, and Bob said, "Forget it, the Cybermen are stupid, they don't work very well and I like creating original characters." John hated this because he hated being challenged. Still we asked Bob to continue, and we said we'd commission him to do it, but he wasn't certain he could make the story work. John was then furious Bob had the audacity to say he wasn't happy in this honest and outspoken way.'[212]

Saturday 31st – Sunday 1st August:
Itinerary: John attends the *Doctor Who* Appreciation Society's Panopticon V convention at the Grand Hotel in Birmingham. On the Saturday afternoon, the society's Coordinator David Saunders and Convention Organiser Paul Zeus present him with a painting of himself surrounded by many of the villains from the eighteenth and nineteenth seasons, in recognition of his recent work on the show.

AUGUST

Monday 2nd:
Itinerary: John attends a pre-planning meeting for 'Mawdryn Undead' in Threshold House, along with director Peter Moffatt and the various members of the relevant BBC Departments who will work on the story. John also writes to the BBC Contracts Department, asking that Patrick Troughton be engaged to appear in 'The Six Doctors'. On the same day, he signs off the commissioning brief for Robert Holmes to write a scene breakdown for 'The Six Doctors'. The *Doctor Who and the Monsters* repeat season on BBC1 continues with a 50-minute compilation of Episodes Four, Five and Six of 'Genesis of the Daleks'.

Tuesday 3rd:
Itinerary: John entertains Barbara Elder, head of NADWAS, at the BBC Club bar.

---

[212] Eric Saward interview, *DWB* #57.

Wednesday 4th:
Itinerary: John entertains actor Nicholas Courtney over lunch at the BBC Club bar.[213]

Thursday 5th:
Itinerary: John entertains actor Anthony Ainley over lunch at the BBC Club bar.[214]

Monday 9th:
Itinerary: John writes to Tom Baker, whose agent Jean Diamond has recently relayed in a phone call the actor's decision not to appear in the twentieth anniversary special.[215] This decision has come as a surprise to John, as Baker seemed keen on the idea when he had informal talks with him a few months earlier. John urges Baker to reconsider, and asks him to keep free in his diary the five weeks between the last week of February and the end of March 1983. On the same day, the *Doctor Who and the Monsters* repeat season on BBC1 continues with a 50-minute compilation of Parts One and Two of 'Earthshock'.

Thursday 12th (John's thirty-fifth birthday):
Itinerary: *Once Upon a Time Lord* documentary-maker David Ryan writes to John, thanking him for his cooperation during the recent Panopticon West II convention in Chicago and telling him that the footage they recorded at the event looks very good.[216] He goes on to say that he hopes they can meet up again on Friday 17 September, when John is due to be back in the US to attend a convention in Denver, as he wants to discuss the use of *Doctor Who* clips in the documentary and to record an on-camera promo with John for the show, the documentary and a PBS pledge pitch due to run in November.

Friday 13th:
Itinerary: John writes to the Head of the BBC Design Department, asking that Ken Ledsham be allocated as designer on 'The King's Demons'. If he isn't

---

[213] Courtney had already signed up to appear in 'Mawdryn Undead', which was due to begin filming later this month, so John was probably talking to him about a possible further return in 'The Six Doctors'.

[214] Ainley was probably also given the pitch for 'The Six Doctors' during this lunch.

[215] The prior discussions that John had had with Baker and his agent about the special had presumably all taken place via telephone. There is no documented correspondence to help pin down exact dates of what was discussed and when.

[216] Ryan produced the KRMA-TV documentary *Once Upon a Time Lord*, which featured interviews with Nathan-Turner and the other guests recorded at the Panopticon West II convention and was shown extensively on PBS stations in the US in the months afterwards.

available, John suggests Ken Starkey as his second choice.[217] John also writes to John Ostrander in Chicago about his proposed *Doctor Who* stage play *The Inheritors of Time*. Ostrander has previously written to John to enquire about using the BBC's own Dalek props in the production. John refers Ostrander to Julie Jones of BBC Exhibitions.

Sunday 15th:
Itinerary: Tom Baker writes to John and gives him a small ray of hope over his possible appearance in the twentieth anniversary special. He says that nothing is absolute and praises John's ambition for the production. But he also intimates that he is in negotiations with the Royal Shakespeare Company for a lengthy engagement in 1983, cutting across the proposed filming dates. He asks that he, his agent Jean Diamond and Nathan-Turner continue discussing the matter in the coming weeks.

Monday 16th:
The *Doctor Who and the Monsters* repeat season on BBC1 concludes with a 50-minute compilation of Parts Three and Four of 'Earthshock'.

Tuesday 17th:
Itinerary: John sends a telex to Basil Sands at the BBC's office in Sydney, Australia, asking him to try to get contact details for the actress Katy Manning, who played Jo Grant during the Jon Pertwee era and who now lives 'down under'. John wants to approach her to discuss her potentially appearing in 'The Six Doctors'.

Wednesday 18th:
Itinerary: John writes to Anthony Ainley, thanking him for a 'super card and present'.[218] On the same day, he writes to the BBC Contracts Department, asking that Carole Ann Ford be engaged to appear in 'The Six Doctors'. Ford had played one of the Doctor's first companions, his granddaughter Susan, in 1963/64.

Friday 20th:
Itinerary: John attends a planning meeting for 'Mawdryn Undead' in Threshold House, along with director Peter Moffatt and the various members of the relevant BBC Departments who will work on the story. On the same day, he writes to the BBC's Head of Copyright, asking them to negotiate with

---

[217] Ken Ledsham was evidently available, as he was allocated to 'The King's Demons'.
[218] John's birthday was on 12 August, so presumably Ainley's recent card and gift were to mark that occasion.

writers Mervyn Haisman and Henry Lincoln for the use of their character Lethbridge-Stewart in the story.

Sunday 22nd:
Commentary: John, along with Gary Downie, attends the wedding reception of Lynn Richards, who was AFM on 'Arc of Infinity' amongst other stories. Also in attendance are Peter Davison, Sarah Sutton, Eric Saward, Jane Judge (*Doctor Who*'s production secretary), director Ron Jones and Colin Baker (who'd played Maxil in 'Arc of Infinity'). Also on this day, while attending a *Doctor Who* convention in New Orleans, USA, Terrance Dicks is contacted by phone by script editor Eric Saward, asking him if he would like to write the script for the twentieth anniversary special. Dicks arranges to meet with Saward on his return to the BBC the following day.

Colin Baker: 'The lady who'd been assistant floor manager on "Arc of Infinity", Lynn Richards, invited us to her wedding, and it was one of those days – we all have them now and again, though not often – when I was really up for it. I enjoyed myself. I wasn't pushy, but I was amusing. People liked me. I was awake – as if I'd taken cocaine, even though I hadn't, but it was that kind of high. It was on the way home from that party, apparently, that John said to Gary [Downie], "I think I've found my new Doctor Who." I didn't know I was auditioning at the time.'[219]

Monday 23rd:
Itinerary: John attends a cast script read-through of the location material for 'Mawdryn Undead' at Threshold House.

Commentary: Eric Saward meets with Terrance Dicks to discuss the anniversary special.

Terrance Dicks: 'I got back to the office and spoke to Eric about what he wanted. He looked a bit shifty. "We've got Bob Holmes working on a storyline for us, but we're having problems," he said. "What we thought we might do is get you to write a storyline while Bob goes on with his, and then we can compare and see which one we like best." I was outraged! I said, "Certainly not. This is no way to treat a writer like Bob Holmes. Come to think of it, it's no way to treat a writer like me. Make your mind up!" Off I stormed.'[220]

Tuesday 24th:
Itinerary: John drives to Middlesex Polytechnic in Trent Park, in the London

---

[219] Colin Baker interview, *Doctor Who Magazine* #322.
[220] Terrance Dicks interview, *Doctor Who Magazine* #272.

Borough of Barnet, for the first day of location filming for 'Mawdryn Undead.' On the same day, he writes to the Head of the Television Design Department, lamenting that neither of his two preferred designers (Ken Ledsham or Ken Starkey) has been allocated to 'The King's Demons', with Graham Lough instead being given the assignment. He notes that he has only once been successful in obtaining his preferred designer (Malcolm Thornton on 'The Return') out of seven requests this year, which he thinks is a poor record. He asks how far in advance he needs to make his requests in order to have a chance of obtaining his preferred designer.[221] John also signs off the commission for Christopher H Bidmead to write a scene breakdown for 'The Wanderers'.[222]

Wednesday 25th:
Itinerary: John returns by car to Middlesex Polytechnic in Trent Park for the second day of location filming for 'Mawdryn Undead.'

Thursday 26th:
Itinerary: John returns by car to Middlesex Polytechnic in Trent Park for the third day of location filming for 'Mawdryn Undead.'

Friday 27th:
Itinerary: John returns by car to Middlesex Polytechnic in Trent Park for the fourth and final day of location filming for 'Mawdryn Undead.'

Saturday 28th – Tuesday 7th September:
Rehearsals for the first studio block of 'Mawdryn Undead' take place at the BBC Television Rehearsal Rooms in Acton.

Saturday 28th:
Itinerary: John drives down to Longleat House in Wiltshire to accompany Peter Davison, who is making several in-costume appearances at the *Doctor Who* Exhibition there over the weekend. John stays overnight, courtesy of BBC Enterprises, who have organised Davison's visit to the venue.

Commentary: It's possible that John's visit to Longleat this weekend might have had an ulterior motive. Plans were by now under way for BBC Enterprises to host a celebratory event to mark the *Doctor Who*'s twentieth anniversary the following year, and the Longleat House estate was considered

---

[221] Ken Ledsham is eventually allocated to 'The King's Demons', so John's complaint obviously worked.
[222] It's not known when Bidmead delivered his scene breakdown for what would become 'Frontios'.

a prime potential venue. The decision to host the event at Longleat might have been already agreed by this point.

Sunday 29th:
Itinerary: John accompanies Peter Davison as he makes further Longleat *Doctor Who* Exhibition appearances during the day. He then drives back home to London in the evening.

Tuesday 31st:
Itinerary: John writes to Malcolm Clarke and Dick Mills of the BBC Radiophonic Workshop, trying to track down the Production Office's VHS copies of several old Cyberman episodes/stories. Director Peter Grimwade has informed John that he loaned the tapes to either of the two men for reference during the production of 'Earthshock'.

SEPTEMBER

Wednesday 1st:
Itinerary: John entertains David Saunders, Coordinator of the *Doctor Who Appreciation Society*, at the BBC Club bar. Later this day, he and Eric Saward have a meeting with Robert Holmes to discuss the storyline for 'The Six Doctors'.

Thursday 2nd:
Itinerary: John signs off the commission for Eric Pringle to write the script for 'War Game' Part One.

Friday 3rd:
Itinerary: John writes to Tom Baker, thanking him for agreeing to meet to discuss 'The Six Doctors'. He tells Baker that once he has a script, he will arrange to meet up for a meal during the tour of his play *Educating Rita,* so they can discuss things further. John also writes to Heather Hartnell, wife of the late William Hartnell. He outlines his plans for the show's twentieth anniversary special, which at this point include using archive clips of Hartnell as the Doctor, and re-casting the part of the first Doctor with another actor. He assures her that this will be done in the best possible taste, and that the 'new' first Doctor will be unveiled as an imposter as part of the plot of the story. On the same day, John also signs off the commission for Eric Pringle to write the script for 'War Game' Part Two.

Monday 6th:
Itinerary: John writes to the Planning Manager of BBC1, suggesting that *K-9 and Company* be selected for repeat over the Christmas period, due to the original broadcast being affected by a transmission failure in the North East of England.[223] It's also the final day of rehearsals for the first studio block of 'Mawdryn Undead', and the Producer's Run. Also on this date, Heather Hartnell, the widow of actor William Hartnell, writes to John, thanking him for a letter he has sent her and telling him that she has no objections to the role of the first Doctor being recast.

Tuesday 7th:
Itinerary: John writes to Patrick Troughton, thanking him for agreeing to appear in the twentieth anniversary special.

Wednesday 8th:
Itinerary: It's the first day of the two-day first studio block for 'Mawdryn Undead' in studio TC6 at BBC Television Centre. After recording, John joins the cast in the BBC Club bar.

Thursday 9th:
Itinerary: It's the second and final day of the first studio block for 'Mawdryn Undead' in studio TC6 at BBC Television Centre. After recording, John joins the cast in the BBC Club bar.

Friday 10th:
Itinerary: John signs off the commission for Johnny Byrne to write the four scripts for 'Warriors of the Deep'.

Saturday 11th – Tuesday 21st:
Rehearsals for the second studio block of 'Mawdryn Undead' take place at the BBC Television Rehearsal Rooms at Acton.

Tuesday 14th:
Itinerary: For reasons unknown, John goes by tube from Union House to High Street Kensington and back. Andrew Sewell, a producer at the BBC Studio Amateur Dramatic Group at the Langham[224], writes to John, asking for sound recording excerpts of old episodes of *Doctor Who* for use in a quiz he is producing.

---

[223] *K-9 and Company* is indeed selected for repeat on 24 December 1982, albeit on BBC2, perhaps as a result of John's suggestion.

[224] The BBC purchased the Langham Hotel, opposite Broadcasting House, in 1965, after renting parts of the building for several decades previously. It was used mainly for radio administration purposes in the 1970s and 1980s, before being sold by the BBC in 1986 and returned to being a hotel.

Wednesday 15th:
Itinerary: John travels by tube to the BBC Rehearsal Rooms in Acton to supervise a press photocall with Sarah Sutton and Mark Strickson, to publicise the departure of Nyssa and the arrival of Turlough.

Thursday 16th:
Itinerary: John travels by taxi to Heathrow Airport, to catch a flight to Denver, Colorado, USA.

Saturday 18th – Sunday 19th:
Itinerary: John is a guest at the Star Con-Denver VI convention in Denver, Colorado, USA. Amongst other things, he meets up with David Ryan, the PBS documentary maker, and continues discussing possible projects to exploit *Doctor Who*'s popularity on the US PBS networks. He also meets up with Ron Katz, who is in the process of setting up the *Doctor Who* Fan Club of America (DWFCA), to be based in Denver. Katz plans for his club to be a profit-making business, and he seeks John's approval and agreement to do this.

Tuesday 21st:
Itinerary: John flies back from Denver to Heathrow Airport. He gets a taxi home, then catches a tube to the BBC Television Rehearsal Rooms at Acton. Today is the Producer's Run for the second studio block of 'Mawdryn Undead'.

Wednesday 22nd:
Itinerary: It's the first day of the three-day second studio block for 'Mawdryn Undead' in studio TC8 at BBC Television Centre. After recording, John joins the cast in the BBC Club bar.

Thursday 23rd:
Itinerary: It's the second day of the three-day second studio block for 'Mawdryn Undead' in studio TC8 at BBC Television Centre. After recording, John joins the cast in the BBC Club bar.

Friday 24th:
Itinerary: It's the third and final day of the second studio block for 'Mawdryn Undead' in studio TC8 at BBC Television Centre. After recording, John joins the cast in the BBC Club bar.

Monday 27th:
Itinerary: John takes a tube from Union House to the BBC's Television Rehearsal Rooms at Acton, to attend a full cast script read-through of 'Terminus'.

Tuesday 28th:
Itinerary: John writes to Stephen Scott (Designer), Amy Roberts (Costume Designer), Sheelagh Wells (Make-Up), Stuart Brisdon (Visual Effects), Don Babbage (Studio Lighting), Carol Johnson (Vision Mixer), Martin Ridout (Studio Sound) and Alan Arbuthnott (Technical Manager), thanking them for their work on 'Mawdryn Undead'.

Wednesday 29th:
Itinerary: John travels by tube from Union House to the BBC Film Studios at Ealing for the first day of filming for 'Terminus' on Stage 3B there.[225] On the same day, the *Doctor Who* Production Office receives a letter from a Chicago-based fan in the USA, Nick Telizya, who informs the BBC that 'BBC Canada' have colour 525-line two-inch videotape copies of the Jon Pertwee stories 'Colony in Space' and 'The Sea Devils'. John forwards Telizya's letter on to Sue Malden, the BBC's Archive Selector at the BBC Film and Videotape Library.

Commentary: At the time, the BBC held only 16mm black and white film prints of 'Colony in Space' and the first three episodes of 'The Sea Devils' (although episodes four to six of the latter still survived on their original colour 625-line two-inch tapes). As a result of this letter, Sue Malden contacted BBC Toronto, who confirmed that they did indeed still hold the colour 525-line tapes. She arranged to have them shipped back to the UK, and they arrived at the BBC Film and Videotape Library in February 1983.

Thursday 30th:
Itinerary: John again travels by tube from Union House to the BBC Film Studios at Ealing, for the second and final day of filming for 'Terminus' on Stage 3B.

OCTOBER

Friday 1st – Saturday 9th:
Rehearsals for the first studio block of 'Terminus' take place at the BBC Television Rehearsal Rooms at Acton.

---

[225] John noted this date as Tuesday 28 September in his expenses, but this must have been an error.

Sunday 3rd:
Itinerary: Anthony Ainley writes to John, wishing him well on his upcoming trips to America, and asking if there any lines he could be learning in the meantime. John sends him the scripts of 'The King's Demons'.

Monday 4th:
Itinerary: John writes to the Coordinator of the BBC Costume Department to complain that Colin Lavers has been allocated to begin work on the costumes for 'The King's Demons' a full week before the director joins the production, and that therefore is a week of wasted cost, which John argues about having to pay. He also complains of not being officially informed who had been allocated to the story as costume designer, only discovering that Lavers had been allocated after his secretary had contacted the Costume Department with a separate query. On the same day, John writes to the BBC Contracts Department, asking that Nicholas Courtney be engaged to appear in 'The Six Doctors'. He also writes to the BBC Head of Copyright, requesting that negotiations take place with Mervyn Haisman and Henry Lincoln for the use of their character the Brigadier in the twentieth anniversary special.

Wednesday 6th:
Itinerary: John writes to the BBC's Head of Copyright, clarifying the terms of usage of the various clips from old episodes of *Doctor Who* seen in a 'flashback' sequence in 'Mawdryn Undead' Part Two.

Thursday 7th:
Itinerary: John scripts the questions to be put to Peter Davison in an interview to be filmed in England sometime in the next few weeks for the KRMA-TV documentary *Once Upon A Time Lord*. On the same day, John writes to Gerald Flood, thanking him for a recent meeting in Brighton, along with Colin Baker.[226] As a result of this, John asks Flood if he would like to play the King in 'The King's Demons'. Also on this day, John writes to Roger Hancock, the agent of Terry Nation. He encloses Eric Saward's storyline for 'The Return', which he needs Nation to approve.

Friday 8th:
Itinerary: It's the final day of rehearsals for the first studio block of 'Terminus', and so would normally be the day of the Producer's Run. There is no record of

---

[226] John wanted to know if Flood would be interested in voicing the new robot companion Kamelion, and had arranged to meet up with him to discuss this via Colin Baker, a mutual friend, whom he had got to know during recording of 'Arc of Infinity'. At the time, Flood and Baker were touring the UK in the play *Relatively Speaking*. Baker, Flood and Nathan-Turner had obviously met up just prior to this date.

John travelling to Acton today; however, it's not really conceivable that he wouldn't attend the Producer's Run.

Saturday 9th:
Itinerary: In the evening, John goes to see the play *The Anniversary* at the Alfred Beck Theatre in Hayes.

Monday 11th:
Itinerary: Today is the first day of the two-day first studio block for 'Terminus' in studio TC6 at BBC Television Centre.

John Nathan-Tuner: 'I had first worked with [director] Mary Ridge when I was an AFM, and somewhere I still have a note from her thanking me for my work. Mary is a wonderful character, extremely organised in her work and methodical in her approach, which really is essential in working on *Doctor Who*. I remember on the first studio day her telling the scenic supervisor that the entire set was three inches off its marks, and proving it.'[227]

Mary Ridge: 'There were to be six studio days, with no location filming. A fortnight before I started, John phoned me up and asked if I could do it in the studio in just five days. I hadn't seen the script by then, so I couldn't answer that. But John said that there was no choice, so it was a very solid six days crammed into five ... '[228]

Tuesday 12th:
Itinerary: It's the second and final day of the first studio block for 'Terminus' in studio TC6 at BBC Television Centre. Also on this day, John is sent a cover proof for issue 71 of *Doctor Who Monthly*, which features a shot of Peter Davison as Omega from 'Arc of Infinity' – Omega's costume is clearly visible. John objects to its use, as it spoils the surprise that Omega takes on the Doctor's form in the story. He asks Martin Hussey to contact Marvel UK and request that they alter the cover.

Wednesday 13th:
Itinerary: Robert Holmes delivers his story outline for 'The Six Doctors' to the *Doctor Who* Production Office. Martin Hussey of BBC Enterprises has several phone conversations with Tim Hampson of Marvel UK, in which Hampson initially resists dropping the planned cover for issue 71 of *Doctor Who Monthly*. Hussey insists, reminding Hampson of the assurance that Brian Babani gave earlier in the year, so Hampson eventually agrees to withdraw the cover and

[227] John Nathan-Turner memoirs, *Doctor Who Magazine* #236.
[228] Mary Ridge interview, *Doctor Who Magazine Yearbook* 1996.

reprint the magazine. Hussey informs John of the events of the day in a memo for his files.

Thursday 14th – Friday 22nd:
Rehearsals for the second studio block of 'Terminus' take place at the BBC Television Rehearsal Rooms at Acton.

Thursday 14th:
Itinerary: John writes to Jon Pertwee, thanking him for agreeing to appear in 'The Six Doctors'. John also signs off the commission for Philip Martin to write the script for 'Domain' Part One.

Friday 15th:
Itinerary: John writes to David Ryan at KRMA-TV to agree the list of archive clips from *Doctor Who* that can be used in his documentary *Once Upon a Time Lord.* He also informs Ryan that he intends to shoot the interview with Peter Davison, for use in the documentary, on 16mm film sometime in early November.

Monday 18th:
Itinerary: John requests that Terrance Dicks be given staff clearance to write a scene breakdown for the twentieth anniversary special, which is still at this stage titled 'The Six Doctors'.[229]

Tuesday 19th:
Itinerary: Frank Murphy from the RTE programme *Anything Goes* contacts the *Doctor Who* Production Office to request clips of the first five Doctors to use in conjunction with an interview with Peter Davison that they have already recorded the previous week. John offers the opinion that clips of the first three Doctors shouldn't be used, but has no objection to providing clips of the fourth and fifth. He suggests that clips from 'Logopolis' Part Four and 'Black Orchid' Part One be used, depending on the appropriate clearance through BBC Television Sales. On the same day, John writes to Tom Baker, apologising for not yet having a script to show him for the twentieth anniversary special. He promises that as soon as there is something to show him, he will arrange an evening to discuss it over a meal.

---

[229] At the time, Dicks was working as script editor on the BBC classic Sunday serial productions. His office was in the same Union House building as the *Doctor Who* Production Office. Sometime between 13 October and this date, Robert Holmes must have decided he didn't want to continue trying to write the special, so Dicks had now become the only candidate to do so.

Thursday 21st:
Itinerary: John writes to David Ryan at KRMA-TV to inform him that the Peter Davison interview has now been filmed and is being converted to NTSC videotape before being sent to him for use in the *Once Upon A Time Lord* documentary. On the same day, David Reid writes to John, having read the scripts for 'The King's Demons'. Reid notes that most *Doctor Who* scripts have one page where all is revealed and the plot is explained. He pointedly comments that with 'The King's Demons', this must be page 63, and asks why the copy of the script he was sent has no page 63 included, as it finishes on page 62 ...

Friday 22nd:
Itinerary: It's the final day of rehearsals for the second studio block of 'Terminus', and so would normally be the day of the Producer's Run. There is no record of John travelling to Acton on this date; however, it's not really conceivable that he wouldn't attend the Producer's Run.

Monday 25th:
Itinerary: It's the first day of the three-day second studio block for 'Terminus' in studio TC8 at BBC Television Centre. On the same day, Johnny Byrne delivers his scripts for 'Warriors of the Deep' Parts One and Two to the *Doctor Who* Production Office. Tom Baker writes to John from Belfast (where his tour of *Educating Rita* is currently playing), telling him that he hopes the script problems on the proposed special are soon resolved.

Tuesday 26th:
Itinerary: It's the second day of the three-day second studio block for 'Terminus' in studio TC8 at BBC Television Centre.

Wednesday 27th:
Itinerary: It's the third and final day of the second studio block for 'Terminus' in studio TC8 at BBC Television Centre. This block hasn't gone according to plan, and several scenes from the story are still left unrecorded, necessitating a costly remount. After the evening's recording concludes, John hosts a farewell party for Sarah Sutton, although the remount means the actress will have to return to complete her scenes as Nyssa in mid-December. On the same day, John contacts Deborah Watling's agent to check if she would potentially be available to appear in the twentieth anniversary special.

John Nathan-Turner: 'We didn't actually finish this story on our last studio day. There was not a huge amount of material left behind, but it was an irritation. Sections of set had to be stored and re-erected, which costs money. Design staff also had to be re-engaged, etc, etc. This was all unexpected expenditure. However, we caught up with an early start to the next story's recording.'[230]

Mary Ridge: 'There were something like 348 shots to do on the first day, and I think we dropped about 80, which wasn't bad considering we'd lost two hours in the morning because the mains had blown ... Over the next three days, we had something like 400 shots to do. John had said that he could get me an extra hour's recording at the end of the third night, to make up for the two hours that I'd lost on the morning of the first studio day ... Everyone agreed to it, and we were bowling along absolutely splendidly. I was within 25 shots of the end of the show, when John said, "You haven't got the extra hour." That meant I had five minutes left to complete 25 shots, which was absolutely impossible. As the clock came up to 10pm, which is the time I would normally finish, John sort of slammed down the script on the counter, and they all went off to a party – to which I refused to go. I've never been so upset in my entire life, because I've never not finished on time.'[231]

Eric Saward: 'I was only aware of [Peter Davison and John Nathan-Turner] having one argument. That was when Sarah Sutton left and John was in one of his sulky moods because of an incident in the gallery, and Peter was very angry that John wasn't coming down to Sarah's farewell. I mean, it was a glass of red wine and a piece of French bread, it was no big deal, but it was the attitude that was shown – Sarah had been in the series for two years and just to let her go without saying goodbye seemed to be rather rude. That was the only argument I was aware of them having, which John recovered from quite quickly.'[232]

NOVEMBER

Monday 1st:
Itinerary: Terrance Dicks delivers his scene breakdown for 'The Six Doctors' to the *Doctor Who* Production Office.

Wednesday 3rd:
Itinerary: It's the first day of filming for 'Enlightenment' (as 'The Enlighteners' has now been renamed) on Stage 3B at the BBC Film Studios in Ealing

---

[230] John Nathan-Turner memoirs, *Doctor Who Magazine* #236.
[231] Mary Ridge interview, *Doctor Who Magazine Yearbook* 1996.
[232] Eric Saward interview, *DWB* #57.

Thursday 4th:
Itinerary: It's the second day of filming for 'Enlightenment' on Stage 3B at the BBC Film Studios in Ealing.

Friday 5th:
Itinerary: It's the third and final day of filming for 'Enlightenment' on Stage 3B at the BBC Film Studios in Ealing.

Saturday 6th:
Itinerary: Rehearsals for the first studio block of 'Enlightenment' begin at the BBC Television Rehearsal Rooms at Acton. They are due to continue through to Monday 15 November, but industrial action by the union EEPTU forces the cancellation of the planned studio dates, so on Sunday 7 November the rehearsals are abandoned.

Commentary: Peter Sallis was originally cast in the role of Striker in this story, but attended just one day of rehearsals before the planned studio dates were lost due to the strike. Sallis wasn't available for the remounted dates, so his part was recast, with Keith Barron taking his place.

Monday 8th:
Itinerary: Peter Davison is contracted to appear in 26 episodes of Season 21, but has no option for a fourth season included in his contract. Mark Strickson is contracted to appear in 20 out of 26 episodes of Season 21.

Peter Davison: 'I was very unhappy with the second season, script-wise and concept-wise. I just felt it didn't go anywhere, and I wasn't very happy with me in it. It was then – in the second year – that I had to decide if I wanted to do a fourth year, but I wasn't sure … John and I have always got on well, but we did a creative difference over the direction in which he wanted *Doctor Who* to go, and the direction I thought it should take. We talked it through, and I decided that it would be better … if I left.'[233]

Tuesday 9th:
Itinerary: John writes to Alan McKenzie at Marvel UK following a recent meeting that he's had with Richard Landen, who is to take over as contributing editor of *Doctor Who Monthly*. At this meeting, Landen has asked John to write a regular 'Producer's Column' for the publication, which John is happy to do. However, he tells McKenzie he feels he should be paid a fee for it.[234]

---

[233] Peter Davison interview, *Doctor Who Magazine* #134.
[234] No 'Producer's Column' was ever written by John for *Doctor Who Monthly*.

Wednesday 10th:
Itinerary: Elena Mathius, a researcher at BBC Wales, contacts the *Doctor Who* Production Office, asking if they can use K-9 on a programme they are making about dogs, due to be recorded on 21 November. John declines the request. On the same day, Eric Pringle delivers his script for 'War Game' Part One to the *Doctor Who* Production Office.

Thursday 11th:
Itinerary: Bill Wilson, producer of the *The Kenny Everett Television Show*, contacts the *Doctor Who* Production Office to ask permission to do a *Doctor Who* sketch. In this, the TARDIS would materialise to the sound of a toilet flushing, and then Peter Davison in character as the fifth Doctor would open the door and make a quick exit. John replies with a blunt 'No!'. On the same day, John writes to David Reid regarding overruns during the first studio block for 'Terminus'. He explains that there was a power failure in TC6 at Television Centre on 11 October, which delayed the start of recording by two hours. As a result of this, John contacted Programme Planning, who granted an extra half-hour's extension on both 11 and 12 October.[235]

Friday 12th:
Itinerary: John writes to Dalek creator Terry Nation, thanking him for his permission to proceed with Eric Saward's forthcoming story featuring the Daleks and Davros; acknowledging comments made by Nation on aspects of the story breakdown; enclosing draft scripts of the first three episodes; thanking him also for his agreement to the inclusion of a brief Dalek appearance in 'The Six Doctors'; and wishing him luck with a series he is working on with actress Farrah Fawcett. On the same date, Eric Sheddon, an Assistant in the Design Department, replies to a request John has made for *Doctor Who* to be reimbursed for the cost of damage caused to a computer prop hired in from the external Trading Post company. The damage occurred during the second studio recording block for 'Terminus' when the prop was cut down, with designer Dick Coles' approval, to accommodate some visual effects. Sheddon says that if John wishes to pursue the matter, he should do so with Michealjohn Harris of the Visual Effects Department.[236]

Saturday 13th:
Itinerary: John is a guest at the DWAS's Interface II convention, held at the

---

[235] Although, according to Mary Ridge, the extension was meant to be an hour on the final day of recording, and this was withdrawn at the last moment.
[236] A line was drawn under this matter on 17 September, when after further investigation Seddon concluded that the damage was Dick Coles' responsibility and would have to be charged to the production in the usual way.

Central London Polytechnic.

Monday 15th:
Itinerary: Philip Martin delivers his script for 'Domain' Part One to the *Doctor Who* Production Office.

Tuesday 16th:
Itinerary: Richard Simpson from *Saturday Superstore*[237] contacts the *Doctor Who* Production Office, requesting two clips of Peter Davison as the Doctor for use in the programme. John authorises the use of two clips from 'Arc of Infinity' Part One, which has yet to be broadcast on BBC1.[238]

Commentary: This was meant to be the first day of the two-day first studio recording block for 'Enlightenment'. However, as previously noted, industrial action at the BBC caused its cancellation. The three-day second studio block planned for 30 November to 2 December was also cancelled, as were the preceding rehearsals due to run from 18 to 29 November. John decided to remount all these rehearsals and studio sessions in early January, using the time previously allocated to 'The Return', the Eric Saward-scripted four-part Dalek story meant to be the final story of the twentieth season. 'Enlightenment' was accorded precedence over 'The Return' as a) it had already had all of its Ealing filming completed, and b) it tied up the Black Guardian trilogy and Turlough's introductory story arc. As a result, 'The Return' was axed[239], and the twentieth season would now comprise only 22 episodes instead of the usual 26.

John Nathan-Turner: 'Peter Grimwade had been engaged to direct the script written by Eric Saward. It was such a frustrating time; first dates were shunted, then re-shunted. Again and again it went on; post-production schedules were amended, and then even condensed in order to allow us to hang onto the project. However, in the end, the Planning Department simply said, "The final four-part story is cancelled." After liaison with my production associate, we went down to Grimwade's office, where Saward was taking coffee, and broke the news. Everyone was very depressed. I can't describe the frustration that everyone concerned feels when a project finally bites the dust. A feeling of emptiness, a feeling of "Could we have done *anything* else to keep the show on the road?" Later, I went to ask Saward and Grimwade for a

---

[237] *Saturday Superstore* was the BBC's new Saturday morning children's programme, which had replaced the long-running *The Multi-Coloured Swap Shop*.
[238] The two clips were used in the edition of *Saturday Superstore* that aired on BBC1 on Saturday 20 November and featured Peter Davison as a studio guest.
[239] The story would be quickly revived for the twenty-first season, under the new title 'Resurrection of the Daleks'.

lunchtime drink to drown our sorrows and commiserate, only to discover that they had already left with the rest of the production team on a similar mission to Television Centre, excluding only myself and the [production] associate [June Collins]. I had not been invited to the wake. I was deeply upset and annoyed ... I blame Saward. If one insists on playing two roles on a production, i.e. being the script editor and the writer, then one makes sure [one doesn't] have two faces as well ... It's not at all attractive. I tackled him about this later, and he simply didn't appreciate that the producer, or indeed the associate, could be affected by the situation as much as he, the writer. It took a long while for us to recover from my outburst about loyalty, and in some ways, I don't think we ever properly did.'[240]

Eric Saward: 'Peter [Grimwade] took his assistant, production manager, and myself out to lunch, and when we came back to the office we heard that John had been ranting and screaming all over the building and generally making a thorough ass of himself: "*I* hire and fire on this show, how dare *my* director go off and have lunch with *my* script editor and *my* production team!" None of us could make head nor tail of it, because John hadn't actually been available that lunchtime. Peter was basically saying sorry to his team for the show going down; but to John that was unacceptable, and that was why Peter wasn't invited back to direct it when it was remounted the following season, even though he wanted to. John never invited him back to the show again, but I succeeded in commissioning him for one more script. It was pure spite [on John's part]. He evidently couldn't cope with the fact that here were two people getting along together without involving him.'[241]

Monday 22nd:
Itinerary: John writes to Brian Mahoney, producer of the STV programme *Take The High Road*, thanking him for allowing Fiona Cumming to be released from planned directing duties on that show in January and February 1983, so that she can continue directing the remount of 'Enlightenment'. He also writes to the Head of Design, requesting that Malcolm Thornton be allocated as designer on 'The Six Doctors'. The twentieth season is officially confirmed as now comprising only 22 episodes, with 'The Return' being cancelled.

Thursday 25th
Itinerary: John writes to the Manager of Series and Serials, informing him that due to the postponement of 'The Return', the production code 6K, which had been allocated to that story, will now be abandoned. On the same day, John writes to the BBC Contracts Department, asking that Richard Hurndall be

---

240 John Nathan-Turner memoirs, *Doctor Who Magazine* #236.
241 Eric Saward and Ian Levine interview, *DWB* #106.

engaged to appear in 'The Six Doctors'.

Commentary: Contrary to John's suggestion here, production code 6K will later be given to 'The Six Doctors'.

Friday 26th:
Itinerary: John signs off the commission for Christopher H Bidmead to write the four scripts for 'Frontios'.

Tuesday 30th:
Itinerary: John writes to Patrick Troughton, asking him to reconsider his decision not to attend the *Doctor Who* Celebration event at Longleat House next Easter. He promises that if Troughton reconsiders, he will endeavor to make his appearance as 'painless' as possible.

Commentary: This is the first mention in John's paperwork of the planned BBC Enterprises-organised *Doctor Who* convention to be held at Longleat House over the Easter bank holiday weekend of 1983. John was very much involved in the planning of the event, and in helping to secure the appearances of past and present cast members.

DECEMBER

Wednesday 1st:
Itinerary: John writes to the BBC Copyright Department, asking them to negotiate for the use of the Daleks, the Cybermen, the Autons, K-9 and Brigadier Lethbridge-Stewart in 'The Six Doctors'.[242] John also requests that Terrance Dicks be given staff clearance to write the full script for the twentieth anniversary special, still at this stage titled 'The Six Doctors'.[243]

Commentary: It presumably slipped John's mind that he had already made a request of this kind in relation to Lethbridge-Stewart, back on 4 October.

Thursday 2nd:
Itinerary: A request from the BBC1 children's quiz show *Finders Keepers* is made to the *Doctor Who* Production Office, for permission to show a clip of the

---

[242] Although the Autons appeared in a single scene in Terrance Dicks' first draft of 'The Five Doctors', they were cut from the final version due to cost.
[243] There is no record of the date when Dicks delivered his script for what would become 'The Five Doctors' to the *Doctor Who* Production Office.

regeneration sequence from 'Logopolis' Part Four. John agrees. David Ryan from KRMA-TV in Denver writes to John on the same day, clarifying some points regarding the *Once Upon A Time Lord* documentary. He adds that KRMA-TV are interested in him producing another documentary once work on this one has concluded, either about the making of *Doctor Who* in general or about the upcoming Longleat *Doctor Who* convention due to be held over Easter 1983. Also on this day, John writes to Pat O'Leary (Production Associate), and Jennie Osborn (Production Manager), thanking them for reorganising their planned leave so that they can resume work on 'Enlightenment' when the production is remounted next year. John writes to David Reid, asking that Peter Moffatt be contracted to direct 'The Six Doctors', the engagement to run from 17 January to 13 May 1983.

Friday 3rd:
Itinerary: Andrew Sewell from the BBC Studio Amateur Dramatic Society at The Langham sends John a memo. He pitches the idea of producing a newly-recorded radio version of the story 'Genesis of the Daleks', and asks to be put in touch with Terry Nation (the writer of the story, and creator of the Daleks) in order to discuss the idea. Also on this day, John writes to director Fiona Cumming, thanking her for agreeing to continue as director for the remounted studio sessions of 'Enlightenment' in the new year. Rehearsals for the location filming for 'The King's Demons' take place at St Mary Abbot's church hall in Kensington & Chelsea, London. Finally for today, John signs off the commission for Eric Pringle to write the scripts for 'War Game' Parts Two to Four.[244]

Saturday 4th:
Itinerary: John travels by car to Bodiam Castle in East Sussex, which will be the location for the next few days of filming for 'The King's Demons'. He spends the night at the unit hotel.

Sunday 5th:
Itinerary: It's the first day of location filming for 'The King's Demons' at Bodiam Castle. After filming concludes, John travels to meet up with Tom Baker in Brighton, where his touring production of *Educating Rita* is now playing, and the two of them enjoy a meal together. John attempts to convince Baker to take part in the upcoming twentieth anniversary special, which is due into production at the end of next February. After his meal with Baker, John returns to the unit hotel for the evening.

---

[244] Although originally envisaged as a four-parter, the story was soon shortened to just two episodes.

John Nathan Turner: 'While filming "The King's Demons", I'd arranged to go see [Tom Baker] in *Educating Rita* at a Brighton theatre. Tom was splendid in the play. Afterwards, we went back to his hotel, where he read the available script to date (which was about a third of it). He liked it, agreed to do it, and we heartily drank pints of lager with large chasers of Benedictine into the night. Back in London a few days later, I took a call from Jean Diamond (Baker's agent) in the sypher dubbing suite. She apologised for not calling sooner – she'd been snowed under – but said that Tom didn't want to do "The Five Doctors". I said, "Have you spoken to him since I saw him a few days ago in Brighton?" "No," she replied. "Ah, well, in that case you need to speak to him, as he's agreed to do it!" I said. I felt confident, but there was a niggling doubt in my mind …'[245]

Monday 6th:
Itinerary: Today is the second day of location filming for 'The King's Demons' at Bodiam Castle. John again spends the night at the unit hotel.

Tuesday 7th:
Itinerary: Today is the third and final day of location filming for 'The King's Demons' at Bodiam Castle. Sarah Sutton attends the location today, so that she can appear, along with the rest of the cast, in a BBC1 Christmas promotion item filmed at the castle. After filming concludes, John drives back to London.

Wednesday 8th – Friday 17th:
Rehearsals for the single studio block of 'The King's Demons' take place at the BBC Television Rehearsal Rooms at Acton.

Thursday 9th:
Itinerary: John writes to Tom Baker, thanking him for meeting up with him the previous week. He encloses a section of early script pages from 'The Six Doctors', showing how all the Doctors and other characters are introduced to the story. He tells Baker that the fourth Doctor takes a more dominant role in the story as it develops, and hopes that he can agree to appear. He asks that Baker let him know soon, as time is running out before Peter Moffatt joins the production in early January, by which point casting needs to be settled.

Monday 13th:
Itinerary: John writes to the BBC Contracts Department, asking that Elisabeth Sladen be engaged to appear in 'The Six Doctors'. He also writes to the Manager of Series and Serials, asking that Margot Hayhoe be allocated to the special as Production Manager. John signs off a re-commission for Eric Pringle

---

[245] John Nathan-Turner memoirs, *Doctor Who Magazine* #237.

to rewrite his script for 'War Game' Part One, now as the first installment of a two-part part story rather than a four-part one. Finally for today, Johnny Byrne delivers his script for 'Warriors of the Deep' Part Three to the *Doctor Who* Production Office.

Eric Saward: 'Eric Pringle's submission started out as a four-part story for the previous season. The central idea of the history in the stones was all his. However, through lack of experience, Eric had problems realising it … When the script arrived, it was in pretty bad shape. I talked to John, and we decided that it would be too much work to pull it together as a four-parter, so it went down to two parts.'[246]

Tuesday 14th:
Itinerary: A member of staff from BBC Southampton contacts the *Doctor Who* Production Office, requesting a clip of Tom Baker from 'The Keeper of Traken' Part One to use in a regional magazine programme that will have Baker as a guest. John gives his okay for the clip to be used.

Wednesday 15th – Thursday 16th:
Rehearsals for the remounted studio day of 'Terminus' take place at the BBC Television Rehearsal Rooms at Acton.

Wednesday 15th:
Itinerary: John writes to the Assistant to the BBC's Head of Drama, asking if David Ryan (from KRMA-TV) cam be given some sort of official attachment to the BBC, so that Ryan can trail him at work. On the same day, he writes to David Reid, informing him that David Ryan is interested in producing another documentary based around either the making of *Doctor Who*, or the forthcoming Longleat convention. He asks Reid if he has any objections, and Reid replies that he does not. John then writes to David Ryan, informing him that he's looking into setting him up an internship for him at the BBC and investigating if there is any objection to him making a further *Doctor Who*-related documentary.

Thursday 16th:
Itinerary: The *Doctor Who* Production Office is sent a request for K-9 to appear with some children on a BBC Outside Broadcast programme, planned to go out live on Christmas Day morning. John has no objection.

Saturday 18th:
Itinerary: Today is the extra remount studio day for 'Terminus' in studio TC1

---

[246] Eric Saward interview, *Doctor Who Magazine* #347.

at BBC Television Centre. Completing all the scenes that were unfinished from the second studio block, it sees the return of Sarah Sutton for what is now her final day working on the series. Today should have been the first day of a three-day studio block for 'The King's Demons', but the studio session for that story has been squeezed down into just two days.

Sunday 19th:
Itinerary: It's the first day of the two-day studio block for 'The King's Demons' in studio TC1 at BBC Television Centre.

Monday 20th:
Itinerary: It's the second and final day of the sole studio block for 'The King's Demons' in studio TC1 at BBC Television Centre. Unsurprisingly, not all the required scenes are completed, and a remount will be required early the following month to complete the story. Also on this day, the *Doctor Who* Production Office is approached by Philip Bachelor, an associate advert consultant working on a poster campaign for the Ready Brek breakfast cereal. He wants to produce a poster of Peter Davison's Doctor plus a Dalek, alongside some text suggesting that the Doctor's boundless energy for saving the universe time and time again is linked to his choice of breakfast cereal each morning. John contacts Christopher Crouch at BBC Enterprises, who in turn contacts Roger Hancock, Terry Nation's agent, about the proposed use of Daleks, and John Mahoney, Peter Davison's agent, about the use of the actor's likeness. The following day, John will decide that, although the campaign would have some promotional value for *Doctor Who*, the complications involved leave him no choice but to refuse the idea. Also on this day, John writes to director Waris Hussein, expressing his regret that Hussein is unable to direct the twentieth anniversary special.

John Nathan-Turner: 'I had actually wanted Waris Hussein to direct "The Five Doctors". I knew him, and I felt it would be a charming case of full circle – to coin a phrase – if, having directed the very first episode twenty years before, he were to direct the anniversary story. It looked for a while as if he was going to do it, but he was, and is, much sought-after for all manner of glossy, stylish mini-series Stateside.'[247]

Eric Saward: '[John] actually met the director of the first story, Waris Hussein, and asked him if he was interested in directing the twentieth anniversary story. Waris didn't reply, yet we waited weeks and weeks until John eventually had to accept that he wasn't interested.'[248]

---

[247] John Nathan-Turner memoirs, *Doctor Who Magazine* #237.
[248] Eric Saward and Ian Levine interview, *DWB* #107.

Tuesday 21st:
Itinerary: John writes to David Reid, explaining that studio time during the recording block for 'The King's Demons' was lost due to members of VT staff walking out of the studio for 11 minutes on Sunday 19 December, along with other timekeeping issues with (unnamed) members of the cast, resulting in them being late arriving on set on both days. John explains that he asked the scene crew for an overrun to complete the material not yet recorded on the final evening, but that the request was refused, necessitating a remount to be organised.

Wednesday 22nd:
Itinerary: Brian Turner in the Copyright Department sends John a memo confirming that the rights have been obtained for the Autons to be featured in a short scene in the forthcoming *Doctor Who* special.

Thursday 23rd:
Itinerary: The pantomime *Cinderella* opens at the Assembly Theatre in Tunbridge Wells. Written and produced by John, it stars Peter Davison as Buttons, his wife Sandra Dickinson as the Fairy Godmother and Anthony Ainley as Baron Hardup.

Friday 24th:
K-9 and Company: 'A Girl's Best Friend' is repeated on BBC2.

1983

Setting the Scene:

The previous 12 months had not been as easy for John as he would have liked. The union-related problems that had seen the curtailment of Season 20 had been outside his control, as had the disruption to the early part of the season's production due to Peter Davison's obligations on other projects. But the reduced production time left to him had given him very little room for manoeuvre, and the knock-on effects were studio overruns and remounts that must have had a corrosive effect on the goodwill that he needed to get *Doctor Who* made on time and to budget.

The coming year looked to be an even tougher ask for him. On top of the usual 26 episodes, he had a 90-minute special to produce too. Coupled with this were the events marking the show's twentieth anniversary, the biggest of which in the UK was the Longleat convention planned for Easter 1983.

John had by now embraced the convention circuit in both the UK and the US, and had made one crucial discovery: whereas in the UK the fan scene was very much a cottage industry, with conventions relying on the goodwill of the invited guests as they usually received no payment other than (if they were lucky) their expenses, in the US it was very much a professional and money-led business, with guests receiving fees, travel expenses and hotel accommodation. Although John endeavored to keep himself as onside as possible with UK fandom, his allegiance was obviously where the money was. His involvement with past cast members, gathered for 'The Five Doctors' and the Longleat event, enabled him suddenly to become a conduit between them and the US convention organisers, a position he undoubtedly used to his financial advantage.

In the eyes of many British fans, John's 'pandering' to their US counterparts became highly noticeable at the Longleat event. Certainly before the year was out, UK fandom found that it was playing second fiddle to US fandom. The DWAS had planned its own celebratory convention for the twentieth anniversary, but soon discovered that all the guests it wished to invite had already been signed up to appear at an American event instead, many being paid big fees to do so. John's popularity with the UK fans, which had seemed pretty solid up to this point, was suddenly looking very fragile.[249]

---

[249] John didn't attend the DWAS's 20th Anniversary Party convention at the Grand Hotel, Birmingham in September 1983. This author was at that event, however, and

John's involvement with US conventions, and dealings with members of US fandom, certainly became a big part of his life in 1983, and would take on an even greater importance in the years to come. Fan commentators started to question if the time he now spent on these 'side projects' was actually impacting on his focus on producing *Doctor Who* itself. John would always strenuously deny that was the case.

If John's relationship with UK fandom was becoming strained, then so too was his relationship with his script editor, Eric Saward, in the wake of the cancellation of 'The Return' as the final story of Season 20. Although the two men obviously patched things up to the extent that they could continue working together for some years to come, things had permanently altered between them, and tensions were simmering away under the surface.

If John was aware of these shifts in his standing with fandom and his colleagues, he didn't seem to react to them. His relationship with his new Head of Department, David Reid, is also worthy of comment. Outwardly, his interactions with Reid might appear little different from those with his predecessor Graeme McDonald, frequently consisting of memos explaining studio overruns. But Reid was a lot more critical than McDonald of the scripts he was sent to read. John seems to have adopted the 'I'm right and you're wrong' attitude in most cases, and to have largely disregarded the messages that Reid was trying to put across. It's tempting to think that the seeds of the events of early 1985 had already been sown ...

John also must have known that Peter Davison was going to leave the show this year, as there was no contract option on the BBC's side for him to do a fourth season as the Doctor. So John must have begun some degree of contingency planning for casting a new leading man. Perhaps his meeting with Gerald Flood and Colin Baker in early October 1982, just a few months after the wedding reception at which Baker had so impressed John, wasn't only an opportunity to offer Flood the role of Kamelion? Could it have been also John's way of getting confirmation of his hunch about Baker's suitability for the role of the sixth Doctor..?

---

whenever John's name was mentioned on stage, it was always met with very audible boos from some sections of the audience.

JANUARY

Monday 3rd:
'Arc of Infinity' Part One screens on BBC1.

Tuesday 4th:
Itinerary: Today should have been the first day of location filming for 'The Return', but this has been cancelled due to the story being dropped from production. John writes to directors Fiona Cumming and Tony Virgo about the upcoming rehearsals for the remounts of 'The King's Demons' and 'Enlightenment', due to start on Sunday 9 January. He informs them that Peter Davison and Anthony Ainley will still be performing in pantomime in Tunbridge Wells between 10 and 15 January, with matinee performances on Wednesday 12 and Saturday 15 January, thus limiting their involvement. John also writes to the BBC Contracts Department, asking that Tom Baker be engaged to appear in 'The Six Doctors'.

Wednesday 5th:
Itinerary: Today should have been the second and final day of location filming for 'The Return'. 'Arc of Infinity' Part Two screens on BBC1.

Thursday 6th:
Itinerary: John has a meeting with 'J Black' over lunch at the BBC Club bar.[250] Johnny Byrne delivers his script for 'Warriors of the Deep' Part Four to the *Doctor Who* Production Office.

Friday 7th:
Itinerary: Eric Pringle delivers his scripts for 'The Awakening' Parts One and Two to the *Doctor Who* Production Office.

Sunday 9th – Friday 14th:
Rehearsals at Acton for the first studio block of 'The Return' should have taken place over this period. Instead, the booking has been given over to rehearsals for the first studio block of 'Enlightenment', although some of the time is also used for rehearsals for the unrecorded segments of 'The King's Demons'.

---

[250] Presumably John Black, who had previously directed 'The Keeper of Traken', 'Four to Doomsday' and *K-9 and Company*. It's possible that Nathan-Turner was looking to engage Black to direct a story for the upcoming twenty-first season, but if so, nothing came of it. On the other hand, they could have been just a couple of pals having a catch-up.

Monday 10th:

Itinerary: John has a lengthy telephone conversation with Tom Baker in the morning, with Baker now deciding for certain that he doesn't want to appear in 'The Six Doctors'. John then writes to Baker later the same day, thanking him for allowing the programme to use two minutes of previously unseen material from the abandoned story 'Shada' in lieu of the fourth Doctor's appearance – something that was presumably discussed and agreed during the earlier phone call. John also writes to Lalla Ward to ask her permission to use material from 'Shada' in 'The Six Doctors'. John then has a working lunch with the artist Andrew Skilleter.[251] Also on this day, Andrew Sewell from the Langham writes to John again, regarding his proposal to make a new radio adaption of 'Genesis of the Daleks'. The following day, John will send him copies of the scripts of the 1975 story.

Terrance Dicks: 'I'd just about got the first draft [of "The Five Doctors"] done when Eric [Saward] rang and said, "How's it going, Terrance?" I said, "Fine. Just about finished," and there was this long silence before Eric said, "Oh my God, Tom's not going to do it."[252]

Tuesday 11th:

'Arc of Infinity' Part Three screens on BBC1.

Wednesday 12th:

'Arc of Infinity' Part Four screens on BBC1.

Thursday 13th:

Itinerary: John has a working lunch with Richard Landen, who has just taken over as the main feature writer for Marvel's *Doctor Who Monthly*, at the BBC Club bar. On the same day, John writes to the BBC Contracts Department, asking that Paul Jerricho be engaged to appear in 'The Six Doctors'.

Friday 14th:

Itinerary: Today is the Producer's Run at Acton for the first studio block of 'Enlightenment', plus the remounted scenes of 'The King's Demons'. [253]

---

[251] Skilleter was, at this point in time, the main cover artist used by Target Books for their range of *Doctor Who* novelisations. He was also in the process of setting up his own company, Who Dares, which over the coming few years would release various products including licensed art prints of *Doctor Who* characters; this was probably the subject of today's meeting. Skilleter would also be the artist chosen to provide the *Radio Times* with its cover artwork for 'The Five Doctors' later in the year.

[252] Terrance Dicks interview, *Doctor Who Magazine* #272.

[253] From this point on, John's expenses paperwork is incomplete, so it's not known for certain which meetings, working lunches, rehearsals and studio sessions he

John Nathan-Tuner: 'The day before my run-through, Fiona [Cumming] called me to say that Peter Davison was unhappy and asked if I would come out to rehearsal. I explained my diary was full but that Peter could call me. He did so. His concern was that there was little or no rapport between the characters, and I stress the *characters*, of Tegan, Turlough and the Doctor. I said I would keep a close eye on this at my run-through. After the Producer's Run, I gave notes to Fiona, and then sent the AFM to call Peter, Janet and Mark. Peter was absolutely right. I addressed the regulars, stressing that if Tegan was going to be so very bolshy, it raised the question as to why the Doctor didn't dump her immediately. Similarly, we discussed how good an actor Turlough was; we, the audience knew he was up to no good, but he must make an attempt to endear himself to the Doctor. Also, as we all know he is about to do a *volte-face* at the end of Part Four and become totally loyal to the Doctor, we should get more than a glimmer of his endearing qualities. This was one of the few times I formally addressed the regulars *en masse*; the results speak for themselves. I do emphasise here that the three actors got on extremely well; it was a case of three positive characters being too strong and pulling in three separate directions.'[254]

Saturday 15th:
Itinerary: Today is the final performance of John's pantomime *Cinderella* in Tunbridge Wells.

Sunday 16th:
Itinerary: John travels in to work by car for the first day of a three-day studio block in Studio TC1 at BBC Television Centre. This should have been the start of recording for 'The Return', but the day is now given over to completing all the remaining scenes needed for 'The King's Demons'.

Monday 17th:
Itinerary: It's the second day of the three-day studio block in studio TC1 at BBC Television Centre, and the first for 'Enlightenment'. Also on this day, John writes to the BBC Contracts Department, letting them know that director Pennant Roberts and writer Douglas Adams, along with Tom Baker and Lalla Ward, have given their permission for two minutes of material from 'Shada' to be used in 'The Six Doctors', and so he authorises the necessary payments as per their original contracts.

---

attended. The assumption will be made that he attended all Producer's Runs and studio sessions unless he is known to have been elsewhere (e.g at US conventions) at the time.
254 John Nathan-Turner memoirs, *Doctor Who Magazine* #236.

Tuesday 18th:
Itinerary: It's the final day of the first studio block for 'Enlightenment' in studio TC1 at BBC Television Centre. 'Snakedance' Part One screens on BBC1.

Wednesday 19th:
Itinerary: John writes to David Reid regarding a studio overrun of 30 minutes at the end of the previous two days' recording for 'Enlightenment'. He explains that a late start on the first day due to waiting for paint on the studio floor to dry, and a VT fault on the second day, led to a knock-on delay at the end of the recording. Today should have been the first day of rehearsals at Acton for the second studio block of 'The Return'. 'Snakedance' Part Two screens on BBC1.

Thursday 20th – Saturday 29th:
Rehearsals for the second studio block of 'Enlightenment' take place at the BBC Television Rehearsal Rooms at Acton.

Thursday 20th:
Itinerary: Barbara Howard from BBC Appointments contacts the *Doctor Who* Production Office, asking for the use of a Dalek prop to accompany a BBC stand at a careers exhibition due to take place in Edinburgh in early March. John declines, as at least one Dalek prop will be needed in March during production of 'The Five Doctors'.[255] Rehearsals begin at Acton for the second studio block of 'Enlightenment'.

Friday 21st:
Itinerary: John writes to Lalla Ward, thanking her for giving permission to use material from 'Shada' in the twentieth anniversary special. He also asks if she would consider attending the upcoming event at Longleat House in early April. He notes that Tom Baker will be appearing on Sunday 3 April, and tactfully suggests that Ward consider appearing on Monday 4 April.[256]

Monday 24th:
Itinerary: Aubrey Singer, Managing Director of Television, sends John a letter, telling him he has accepted a recommendation to award him a bonus payment of £300 on top of his annual salary, in recognition of his outstanding work on *Doctor Who*.

---

[255] It's around this time that the twentieth anniversary special begins to be referred to as 'The Five Doctors' instead of 'The Six Doctors'.

[256] Ward and Baker had, by now, separated and would soon divorce. Lalla Ward ultimately did not attend the Longleat event.

Tuesday 25th:
Itinerary: John writes to Andrew Sewell with details of how to contact Terry Nation's agent, Roger Hancock, in regard to producing an audio version of 'Genesis of the Daleks'. 'Snakedance' Part Three screens on BBC1.

Wednesday 26th:
Itinerary: John entertains two members of the executive committee of the *Doctor Who* Appreciation Society in the BBC Club bar. 'Snakedance' Part Four screens on BBC1.

Thursday 27th:
Itinerary: John entertains the actor Nicholas Courtney over lunch in the BBC Club bar. He also (for reasons unknown) travels by tube to Chancery Lane and then back to Union House. John then writes to Bob Baker and Dave Martin, apologising for the fact that the character Omega (created by them in 1972 for 'The Three Doctors') was used in 'Arc of Infinity' without their prior permission being obtained. He states that he had thought Omega was BBC copyright, but assures them he has instructed the Copyright Department to make belated arrangements and payments for the character's use. John signs off the commission for Philip Martin to write the scripts for 'Domain' Parts Two to Four.

Friday 28th:
Itinerary: John takes the short tube journey from Union House to the BBC' Television Rehearsal Rooms at Acton. Today is the Producer's Run for the second studio block of 'Enlightenment'.

Sunday 30th:
Itinerary: John travels to Television Centre by car for the first day of the three-day second studio block for 'Enlightenment' (originally allocated to 'The Return') in studio TC1 at BBC Television Centre.

Monday 31st:
Itinerary: Today is the second day of the three-day second studio block for 'Enlightenment' in studio TC1 at BBC Television Centre. Also on this day, Fiona Trier from Jennie & Co, a film production company, contacts the *Doctor Who* Production Office, requesting either viewing tapes of, or copies of the scripts for, the 1966 story 'The Celestial Toymaker'. She asks who the copyright holder of the Toymaker character is, and explains that her enquiries are for a 'film idea'. John informs her that there are no tapes available – the story is missing from the BBC Film and Videotape Library – and that Brian Hayles wrote the story, and is therefore the copyright holder. On the same day, John writes to the Head of BBC Publicity, reporting that the American

PBS station KRMA-TV's general manager, who was a longstanding advocate of *Doctor Who*, has been replaced, and consequently the station has withdrawn its interest in allowing David Ryan to make any further documentaries relating to the show. John states that Ryan is still keen to make a programme about the upcoming Longleat convention, and is now seeking instead a production deal from Lionheart (the BBC's US distributor of *Doctor Who*). If that fails, however, John has asked Ryan to contact the BBC Publicity Department directly, as he thinks that the Longleat event needs to be filmed and the footage made available to the US to promote the show. John also writes to the Manager of Series and Serials, asking that Peter Moffatt's contract for directing 'The Five Doctors' be extended by three weeks, due to the large amount of post-production work needed on the story. Finally, John writes to the General Manager of Design and Scenic Services to complain about his inability to select designers from the Visual Effects Department for particular stories. He explains that he feels it important to marry specific designers to specific directors on projects, and says that he recently had a meeting with Michealjohn Harris and Peter Day from the Visual Effects Department at which he thought the matter had been resolved; since then, however, none of his requests has been met, an attitude he greatly resents.

FEBRUARY

Tuesday 1st:
Itinerary: Today is the third and final day of the three-day second studio block for 'Enlightenment' in studio TC1 at BBC Television Centre. This concludes production on *Doctor Who*'s curtailed Season 20, although some post-production and editing work is still required. 'Mawdryn Undead' Part One screens on BBC1.

Wednesday 2nd:
Itinerary: Ian Squires, Deputy Editor of *Nationwide,* writes to John. The non-payment to John Leeson for his cancelled appearance on that programme back in November 1981 has still not been resolved. Squires promises to ensure that the payment is made in all due haste. 'Mawdryn Undead' Part Two screens on BBC1.

Friday 4th:
Itinerary: John writes to Barry Brown, Executive Producer, BBC Network Features, informing him that he's about to fly to the US for a *Doctor Who* convention, but asking to meet after his return on 14 February to discuss

Brown's planned *Doctor Who* documentary.[257] John then returns home, grabs his luggage, and gets a taxi to take him to Heathrow Airport. He catches a flight to Fort Lauderdale in Florida.

Saturday 5th – Sunday 6th:
Itinerary: John attends the Omnicon IV convention at the Oceanside Holiday Inn, Fort Lauderdale, Florida. Peter Davison (along with his wife, Sandra Dickinson) also guests. Once this convention is over, John stays in America for the rest of the week, as he has another event to attend the following weekend.

Tuesday 8th:
'Mawdryn Undead' Part Three screens on BBC1.

Wednesday 9th:
'Mawdryn Undead' Part Four screens on BBC1.

Friday 11th:
Itinerary: While John is in America, the show's production secretary Jane Judge on his instruction sends a Study Visit Application Form to David Ryan at KRMA-TV. On the same day, Barbara Levy from Severn House Publishers writes to John, thanking him for writing the introduction to their upcoming book *The Doctor Who Technical Manual*.[258]

Saturday 12th:
Itinerary: Patrick Troughton writes to John, asking if he could be sent a quantity of postcard-sized photos of himself as the Doctor, which he can then use to reply to requests from fans. He also suggests that if none are available, he could pose for some during the upcoming filming for 'The Five Doctors', which might also be useful to have printed up for the Longleat event in April. He says he's looking forward to both the filming and the Longleat convention.[259]

Sunday 13th:
Itinerary: John does a personal appearance/signing session at the New Fantasy Shop in Chicago, Illinois.

---

[257] Barry Brown had presumably mentioned to John, in earlier, undocumented discussions, the idea of the BBC making a documentary about *Doctor Who* to mark the show's twentieth anniversary.

[258] *The Doctor Who Technical Manual* by Mark Harris was published by Severn House in September 1983.

[259] Troughton, along with Jon Pertwee, Richard Hurndall, Carole Ann Ford and Elisabeth Sladen, all had BBC postcards produced from photos taken during the filming of 'The Five Doctors'.

Monday 14th:
Itinerary: John takes a flight back home to Heathrow Airport. From there, he gets a taxi back home.

Tuesday 15th:
Itinerary: John entertains the writer Alan Road in the BBC Club bar.[260] 'Terminus' Part One screens on BBC1.

Wednesday 16th:
Itinerary: John entertains director Ron Jones in the BBC Club bar.[261] He also writes to BBC Enterprises, complaining about the print quality of the cover of issue 74 of *Doctor Who Monthly*. Christopher H Bidmead delivers his four scripts for 'Frontios' to the *Doctor Who* Production Office. 'Terminus' Part Two screens on BBC1.

Monday 21st:
Itinerary: John writes to the BBC Contracts Department, asking that Deborah Watling, Wendy Padbury and Caroline John be engaged to appear in cameo roles in 'The Five Doctors'.

Tuesday 22nd:
Itinerary: John (for reasons unknown) travels by tube to Baker Street, then back to the *Doctor Who* Production Office at Union House. Barry Brown of BBC Network Features writes to John. He had recently viewed the *Once Upon A Time Lord* KRMA-TV documentary, and has discovered that 35 PBS stations in America have already purchased this programme, which causes him problems. Brown had proposed making a documentary about *Doctor Who* for its twentieth anniversary year, and had secured an offer of funding from BBC Enterprises in order to do so. In return for the funding, BBC Enterprises want to sell this new documentary to the rest of the world, and to the USA in particular, and Brown now feels that the existence of a 'rival' documentary might cause them to withdraw their offer. Brown informs John that Peter Armstrong has been appointed senior producer on the proposed documentary, but asks that they delay their meeting to discuss the project for a month, in order for BBC Enterprises to make a final decision on their financial commitment. 'Terminus' Part Three screens on BBC1.

---

[260] Alan Road had previously written the book *Doctor Who: The Making of a Television Series*, published in 1982. At this time, he was writing for the *Observer* newspaper/magazine, and was presumably preparing an article about *Doctor Who*.
[261] Ron Jones had already directed the stories 'Black Orchid', 'Time-Flight' and 'Arc of Infinity', and would go on to direct 'Frontios' in the upcoming Season 21.

Wednesday 23rd:
Itinerary: John writes to the company Tannoy Ltd to apologise for including the credit 'Tannoy Voice' in the closing credits of 'Terminus'. The word 'Tannoy' is trademarked to the company, and so shouldn't have been used without their consent. He also writes to the Incorporated Liverpool School of Tropical Medicine, noting a recent letter of complaint they sent in regarding the depiction of lepers and leprosy in 'Terminus', but defending the story. In addition, he writes to the BBC Contracts Department, asking that Richard Franklin be engaged to appear in a cameo role in 'The Five Doctors'. 'Terminus' Part Four screens on BBC1.

Thursday 24th:
Itinerary: Roger Hughes from *Radio Times* writes to John to inform him of a number of letters received by the magazine, taking issue with the references to leprosy in 'Terminus'. He includes one that he intends to publish in the next issue and invites John to pen a reply that he can run alongside it. John explains that he felt it was made clear that the story's Lazar's Disease was not the same as leprosy, and that by the end of the story a cure for the condition had been discovered. John also writes to Peter Moffatt to inform him that Peter Davison and Patrick Troughton will be appearing on the BBC's *Breakfast* show on Tuesday 1 March, but that this won't affect the rehearsals for 'The Five Doctors' in any way. John then writes to Bill Sellers, the producer of *All Creatures Great and Small*, informing him that Peter Davison won't be working on *Doctor Who* between 25 April and 3 June this year, and so will be free to film for Sellers during that period. John does request that Davison's hair isn't cut during this time, to maintain continuity on *Doctor Who*.[262]

Friday 25th – Thursday 3rd March:
Rehearsals for the location filming for 'The Five Doctors' take place at the BBC Television Rehearsal Rooms at Acton.

---

[262] Davison had played Tristan Farnon in all three series of *All Creatures Great and Small* between 1977 and 1980 – which is when the series' original run finished, having exhausted all the stories in the source novels by James Herriot. However, a 90-minute Christmas special was planned to be shown on BBC1 on Christmas Day 1983, and Davison was asked to return as Tristan, alongside the other main cast members. Filming for this was done after Davison had finished his work on 'The Five Doctors'. A further Christmas special was made in 1985, and the series returned to full production in 1988, with Davison back in the role of Tristan, with new scripts now specially written and not based on Herriot's novels. Four more series of *All Creatures Great and Small* were made, running through to 1990. Bill Sellars produced every episode from 1977 through to 1990.

Friday 25th:
Itinerary: John travels by tube from the *Doctor Who* Production Office in Union House to the BBC's Television Rehearsal Rooms in Acton for the first day of location rehearsals for 'The Five Doctors'.

Monday 28th:
Itinerary: Bill Sellars, producer of *All Creatures Great and Small,* writes to John, thanking him for confirming the dates of Peter Davison's availability for the filming of his show's Christmas special. Sellars also says that an acceptable compromise on Davison's hair length should be possible.

MARCH

Tuesday 1st:
Itinerary: John sends the BBC1 Planning Manager his suggestions for a further 'The Five Faces of *Doctor Who*' repeat season that summer, something they have previously discussed. The stories he proposes be included are 'The Daleks', 'The Seeds of Death', 'The Claws of Axos', 'The Ark in Space' and 'The Visitation'. On the same day, Peter Davison and Patrick Troughton appear on the BBC's early morning TV programme *Breakfast Time*, and talk about the upcoming 20th anniversary special. 'Enlightenment' Part One screens on BBC1.

Wednesday 2nd:
'Enlightenment' Part Two screens on BBC1.

Friday 4th:
Itinerary: Deborah Watling's agent contacts John, explaining that due to a clash of commitments, Watling won't be free for the proposed recording dates for 'The Five Doctors'. John contacts the producer of *Emmerdale Farm* at Yorkshire Television, Anne Gibbons, and asks if it would be possible for Frazer Hines to be released from his contract to the series for a few days, in order to make a cameo appearance as Jamie in 'The Five Doctors'.

Saturday 5th:
Itinerary: David Ryan returns his application for a Study Visit to John. In his covering letter, he informs John that *Once Upon A Time Lord* has now sold to 47 PBS stations. However, due to management changes at KRMA-TV, their interest in producing a new 'making of *Doctor Who*' documentary has been put on hold. Ryan enquires if there is any possibility that *Once Upon A Time Lord*

could be aired by the BBC. Meanwhile, in Wales, today is the first day of location filming for 'The Five Doctors' at Plas Brondanw, Llanfrothen, Gwynedd. The opening Eye of Orion scenes are shot, plus some material with the first Doctor and Tegan. John is still in London at this point – he will not join the location filming until Tuesday 8 March.

Sunday 6th:
The cast and crew of 'The Five Doctors' have a day off from location filming. However, they all stay on in Wales for the day.

Monday 7th:
Itinerary: John writes to Bill Sellars, echoing his hope that an acceptable compromise can be reached over Peter Davison's hair length, as the first story of the next season ('Warriors of the Deep') will feature Davison swimming underwater. Sellars writes back the same day, suggesting that Davison's hair underwater could perhaps be covered by a bathing cap. He jokingly wonders if he can actually *guarantee* that Davison will have any hair left at all by the time he returns to filming *Doctor Who*, but endeavors to ensure that the actor doesn't get his hair caught in – say – a threshing machine while filming on *All Creatures Great and Small* ... Also today, John writes to *Emmerdale Farm*'s producer Anne Gibbons and executive producer Michael Glynn at Yorkshire Television, thanking them for agreeing to release Frazer Hines from their programme for a few days so that he can make a cameo appearance in 'The Five Doctors'. On the same day, Alan Bilyard from BBC Records writes to John, in response to criticism that both John and Peter Davison have apparently given with regards to the artwork depiction of Davison on the jacket of the new *Doctor Who: The Music* LP. Bilyard defends the artwork, and mentions that he likes it so much, he's thinking of issuing it as a poster. Location filming for 'The Five Doctors' continues at Carreg Y Foel-Gron, Gwynedd. Scenes shot include the first Doctor and Susan finding the TARDIS, and the ambush of the fifth Doctor, Tegan and Susan by the Master and the Cybermen.

Tuesday 8th:
Itinerary: Location filming for 'The Five Doctors' resumes at Carreg Y Foel-Gron, Gwynedd. Mainly scenes with the Master meeting the Cybermen, and the Cybermen surrounding the TARDIS with cyberbombs, are filmed today. John finally travels to Wales to join up with the cast and crew, and stays there for the rest of location filming. Peter Davison, Janet Fielding, Mark Strickson, Richard Hurndall and Carole Ann Ford all return to London, while Patrick Troughton and Nicholas Courtney arrive at the unit hotel. John spends the night at the Oakley Arms Hotel in Maentwrog. 'Enlightenment' Part Three screens on BBC1.

John Nathan-Turner: 'Patrick Troughton was very excited about returning to the programme. On the evening of his first shooting day, we sat having a "noglette" – as Pat referred to a drink – in one of the unit hotels, and he told me that when he'd got up that morning, he'd felt that he couldn't play the Doctor; he couldn't remember how he'd done it and he felt insecure. When he'd arrived on location, however, and seen the visual effects team unloading explosives and artifacts, seen the Yeti and Cyberman outfits hanging on costume rails, he'd felt instantly at home and knew then and there that he could play the Doctor again.'[263]

Wednesday 9th:
Itinerary: Location filming for 'The Five Doctors' resumes once more at Carreg Y Foel-Gron, Gwynedd, today with Patrick Troughton and Nicholas Courtney. John spends the night at the Oakley Arms Hotel in Maentwrog. Anthony Ainley returns to London. John writes to the Editor of Programme Adaptions at the BBC, suggesting either a one-off special or a series of *Doctor Who* releases on video tape/video disc. He proposes a programme (or programmes) comprising a selection of clips from the show's history, including notable moments such as the first appearances of the Daleks and other monsters, along with the earliest appearances of all the Doctors. The clips are to be linked by a presenter, and he nominates himself for the role, in light of the 'celebrity' status he has with *Doctor Who* fans due to his convention appearances in the UK and the USA. He also suggests he should get to pick the clips used. Richard Franklin writes to John, thanking him for asking him to appear in 'The Five Doctors' and for sending him a copy of the script. 'Enlightenment' Part Four screens on BBC1.

Thursday 10th:
Itinerary: Filming for 'The Five Doctors' continues, now at the Monod Quarries, Gwynedd, with Patrick Troughton, Nicholas Courtney and the Yeti. However, John spends much of the day directing a second unit, filming cutaways of the fight between the Raston Robot and the Cybermen. John then spends the night at the Oakley Arms Hotel in Maentwrog.

Friday 11th:
Itinerary: Location filming for 'The Five Doctors' continues at the Monod Quarries, Gwynedd, with more Cyber-massacre sequences. Some of the opening Eye of Orion sequences are also refilmed today – Peter Davison, Janet Fielding and Mark Strickson having been rushed back to Wales the previous evening for this purpose – as the original 16mm rushes have been found to be scratched. John spends the night in the Oakley Arms Hotel in Maentwrog.

---

[263] John Nathan-Turner memoirs, *Doctor Who Magazine* #237.

Saturday 12th:
Itinerary: It's a day off from filming 'The Five Doctors', but the crew remain in Wales. Cast members Peter Davison, Janet Fielding, Mark Strickson, Patrick Troughton and Nicholas Courtney all leave Wales and return to London, while Jon Pertwee and Elisabeth Sladen arrive on location in order begin filming their material tomorrow. John spends the night in the Oakley Arms Hotel in Maentwrog.

Sunday 13th:
Itinerary: Location filming for 'The Five Doctors' resumes at the Monod Quarries, Gwynedd. The scenes of the third Doctor and Sarah with the Raston Robot are filmed, along with the remaining Cyber-massacre material. Anthony Ainley returns to Wales. John spends the night in the Oakley Arms Hotel in Maentwrog.

Monday 14th:
Itinerary: Location filming for 'The Five Doctors' continues at the Monod Quarries, Gwynedd. Material of the third Doctor and Sarah making their 'death slide' to the Dark Tower, with the Master then spotting them, is shot today. John again spends the night in the Oakley Arms Hotel in Maentwrog.

Tuesday 15th:
Itinerary: Location filming for 'The Five Doctors' continues, now at Cwm Bychan Llanbedr, Gwynedd, with the third Doctor and Sarah meeting the Master. Once more, John spends the night in the Oakley Arms Hotel in Maentwrog. Trevor Barnes from *Nationwide* contacts the *Doctor Who* Production Office with details of a feature the programme intends to run this Thursday, 17 March. They will be interviewing Verity Lambert live in the studio and want to have the four surviving Doctors together there to be interviewed too.[264] They also request a Dalek prop for the studio, and the use of a clip from *Doctor Who*'s opening episode, 'An Unearthly Child'. Barnes is supplied with the details of the agents of Troughton, Pertwee, Baker and Davison. 'The King's Demons' Part One screens on BBC1.

Wednesday 16th:
Itinerary: Today is the final day of the Wales location filming for 'The Five Doctors'. The cast and crew – including John – return to London in the evening.

Thursday 17th:
Itinerary: Location filming for 'The Five Doctors' resumes, first in Tilehouse

---

[264] In the end, only Troughton, Pertwee and Davison took part in the programme.

Lane, Denham Green in Buckinghamshire, then at West Common Road, Uxbridge in Middlesex. Scenes filmed are the time-scoop abductions of the third Doctor in Bessie, the second Doctor and the Brigadier from the grounds of UNIT HQ, and Sarah from her local bus stop. Today is also the press photocall for 'The Five Doctors', with Tom Baker's waxwork from Madame Tussauds pressed into service alongside Messrs Hurndall, Troughton, Pertwee and Davison. Elisabeth Sladen, K-9 and Carole Ann Ford also take part in some of the group photos, as does John himself. In the evening, Peter Davison, Jon Pertwee and Patrick Troughton appear as guests on the live BBC1 magazine programme *Nationwide*.

John Nathan-Turner: 'Naturally, I invited Tom to join us for a "The Five Doctors" photocall, and again his agent confirmed he would attend. At the time, we had a temporary *Doctor Who* exhibition at Madame Tussauds, which included a full-sized waxwork of Tom. I asked if I could borrow Tom's waxwork as a standby should Tom withdraw (the other Doctors were all under contract for the photocall). On the day of the photocall, Lorne Martin of BBC Enterprises arrived with the dummy in the back of his van, covered by a rug. I was fairly sure that Tom wouldn't show up; a few days earlier, via his agent, I'd offered him a chauffeur-driven car, and she'd said that he would be happy making his own way to the call. Anyway, we waited a full ten minutes for Tom before the dummy was manhandled into position.'[265]

Friday 18th:
Itinerary: Today is the last day of filming for 'The Five Doctors'; this takes place at the BBC Ealing Film Studios in Acton. The UNIT HQ interiors are shot, along with the arrival of the third Doctor and Sarah on the roof of the Dark Tower.

Saturday 19th – Monday 28th:
Rehearsals for the single studio block of 'The Five Doctors' take place at the BBC Television Rehearsal Rooms at Acton.

Wednesday 23rd:
Itinerary: John entertains two members of the executive committee of the *Doctor Who* Appreciation Society at the BBC Club bar. 'The King's Demons' Part Two screens on BBC1.

Thursday 24th:
Itinerary: John takes the tube from the *Doctor Who* Production Office at Union House to the BBC Television Rehearsal Rooms at Acton, to sit in on the

---

[265] John Nathan-Turner memoirs, *Doctor Who Magazine* #237.

rehearsals for the studio session of 'The Five Doctors'.

Saturday 26th:
Itinerary: Peter Davison, Mark Strickson and Janet Fielding are excused from the rehearsals of 'The Five Doctors' in the morning, to appear as guests on the live BBC1 programme *Saturday Superstore*.

Monday 28th:
Itinerary: John takes the tube from the *Doctor Who* Production Office at Union House to the BBC Television Rehearsal Rooms at Acton. Today is the Producer's Run for the studio session of 'The Five Doctors'. John also takes the tube to Maida Vale, where the BBC Radiophonic Workshop is located, before returning to Union House.[266]

Tuesday 29th:
Itinerary: Today is the first day of the three-day studio block for 'The Five Doctors' in studio TC6 at BBC Television Centre. After recording, John joins the cast in the BBC Club bar. Also on this day, John forwards David Ryan's Study Visit application to Stephen Kanocz, the BBC's Senior Liaison Officer. John signs off the commission for Peter Grimwade to write a scene breakdown for 'Planet of Fire'.

Wednesday 30th:
Itinerary: Today is the second day of the three-day studio block for 'The Five Doctors' in studio TC6 at BBC Television Centre. After recording, John joins the Cast in the BBC club bar. John writes to Mike Kelt to thank him for the work he's done in creating the new TARDIS console prop.[267] He hopes that Kelt can return to work on *Doctor Who* soon.

Thursday 31st:
Itinerary: Today is the final day of the three-day studio block for 'The Five Doctors' in studio TC6 at BBC Television Centre. After recording, John joins the cast in the BBC Club bar. Stephen Kanocz writes to John to let him know that he can offer David Ryan an attachment to the *Doctor Who* Production Office for as long as John wants. However, there are strict regulations on allowing people on attachment from overseas to do any work, so he asks John to ensure that Ryan does not breach any Department of Employment regulations or union agreements.

---

[266] The BBC Radiophonic Workshop was where Peter Howell worked. He would provide the incidental music and the one-off version of the closing music for 'The Five Doctors', so presumably John's visit was to meet with him to discuss this.
[267] The new TARDIS console prop had made its debut in 'The Five Doctors'.

APRIL

Friday 1st (Good Friday – bank holiday):
Itinerary: John drives down to Longleat House in Wiltshire, in readiness for the upcoming *Doctor Who* Celebration event that BBC Enterprises are staging over the coming weekend. John's hotel is being provided by BBC Enterprises for the next few days. On the evening, John dines out with Terry Sampson (Head of Public Relations), Lorne Martin (Assistant Head of Public Relations) and Julie Jones (Organiser, BBC Exhibitions).

Saturday 2nd:
Itinerary: John spends the day helping to organise with the BBC Enterprises staff the finer details of the upcoming Celebration event. During the day, he's interviewed by Patrick Stoddard for the Radio 4 programme *Breakaway*, and encourages listeners to attend the event. He spends the night in a hotel close to Longleat House.

John Nathan-Tuner: 'Terry [Sampson], Lorne [Martin] and I all asked the Presentation Department, who are responsible for all those trails between BBC programmes, to promote our event. (I don't think that we television professionals realised just how effective these plugs were; never mind.) On the eve of the two-day event we had pre-sold some 13,000 tickets. We all agreed that this meant an eventual attendance of probably double that. How wrong we were! There were, in the end, in excess of 56,000 people. Wiltshire itself ground to a halt. We had a monster on our hands, but this one we couldn't control.'[268]

Sunday 3rd:
Itinerary: It's the first day of the *Doctor Who* Celebration event, and John has to travel to Longleat House by taxi because of the huge crowds. John spends most of his time in the forum tent, where members of the cast are interviewed and then answer questions posed by the attendees. He acts mainly as an MC, introducing each guest as they come onto the stage, but he joins Patrick Troughton on stage for the latter's solo panel. He spends the night in a hotel close to Longleat House.

John Nathan-Turner: 'After the first day's bedlam, a select few had adjourned to the nearby Bath Arms Hotel for a debriefing and a drink, and I remember being verbally attacked by some of the fan glitterati. I recall thinking how I'd

---

[268] John Nathan-Turner memoirs, *Doctor Who Magazine* #237.

wished that I'd said "no" to Terry [Sampson] and Lorne [Martin] at the outset.'[269]

Monday 4th (bank holiday):
Itinerary: It's the second and final day of the *Doctor Who* Celebration event at Longleat House. Again, John spends most of the day in the forum tent, but he's also interviewed by Ed Stewart for his Radio Two programme, which is broadcast live from the event. John stays overnight again, but this time his hotel is not paid for by BBC Enterprises, so he claims the stay on expenses.

John Nathan-Turner: 'On the second day of the event, things went a little smoother, though Longleat was still under siege. Ed Stewart from Radio Two arrived to present his radio show live from the event. Peter [Davison], Bryon Parkin (General Manager of BBC Enterprises) and I went on the show to ask people without tickets not to turn up, but still the vehicles poured in ... The worst part of the whole thing for me was witnessing an argument flaring up between a companion and a Doctor. I was forced to intervene, and tell the two of them to behave or leave! Somewhere there is a beautiful sweater covered with indelible ink marks ... which, fortunately, is as far as the fisticuffs went, and one of them left!'[270]

Tuesday 5th:
Itinerary: John drives back to London from Longleat House.

Wednesday 6th:
Itinerary: John entertains George Breo and his wife at the BBC Club bar.[271] On the same day, John writes to Stephen Kanocz, asking him to pen the formal invite to David Ryan, offering him an attachment to the *Doctor Who* Production Office. John writes to David Reid, informing him of a studio overrun of 17 minutes on the final day of recording 'The Five Doctors' on

---

[269] John Nathan-Turner memoirs, *Doctor Who Magazine* #237. John was lambasted by some British fans upset at the preferential treatment some American fans were seemingly getting at the event. He also said something to Jan Vincent-Rudzki (co-founder of the DWAS) that Vincent-Rudzki took as an insult, and the two of them had a big row as a result.

[270] John Nathan-Turner memoirs, *Doctor Who Magazine* #237. It's believed that the 'flare-up' was between Tom Baker and Mark Strickson. Strickson has said in subsequent interviews that he was upset at the time, because of what he perceived as poor treatment of the event's attendees due to extreme overcrowding, and that the incident almost resulted in him being dismissed from his role as Turlough.

[271] George Breo was the proprietor of the New Fantasy Shop in Chicago, who had hosted signing sessions by John and Peter Davison during their February trip to the US. The Breos had travelled to the UK to attend the Longleat convention.

Wednesday 31 March. He attributes this to a complex studio session featuring Daleks and Cybermen, and says it was necessary to get the special completed.

Thursday 7th:
Itinerary: Philip Martin delivers his scripts for 'Domain' Parts Two to Four to the *Doctor Who* Production Office.

Friday 8th:
Itinerary: Stephen Kanocz writes to David Ryan, informing him that his Study Visit application has been successful, and he is welcome to spend a number of weeks on attachment to *Doctor Who*, starting from 23 May. He tells Ryan that he needs to pay for his own travel and subsistence, and that he needs to clarify the exact details and duration of his attachment with John.

Monday 11th:
Itinerary: Bryon Parkin, Managing Director of BBC Enterprises writes to John to thank him for his guidance, help and total involvement in the *Doctor Who* Celebration at Longleat over the Easter weekend. He goes on to say that without John's full cooperation and enthusiasm, he is sure that the event would not have got off the ground. On the same day, Peter Grimwade delivers his scene breakdown for 'Planet of Fire' to the *Doctor Who* Production Office.

Tuesday 12th:
Itinerary: John writes to David Reid, informing him that it has now been agreed that David Ryan from KRMA-TV will be attached to the *Doctor Who* Production Office to follow through the production of a *Doctor Who* story. He adds that KRMA-TV have now decided to back Ryan to make a new documentary, *The Making of Doctor Who*, which Ryan intends to film during his internship, over two weeks in July, covering location filming, rehearsals, studio recording and post production of 'The Awakening'. Ryan plans to bring a crew consisting of one cameraman, one sound recordist and one assistant, and he would direct the documentary himself.

Wednesday 13th:
Itinerary: John writes to Richard Gregory, proposing the inclusion of the Kamelion android in two forthcoming stories.

Monday 18th – Monday 25th:
Itinerary: Judging by the stamps in his passport, John takes a week's annual leave from the BBC and goes on holiday to Spain (presumably with Gary Downie).

Monday 18th:
Itinerary: John writes to Martin Ridout (Studio Sound), Dave Chapman (Video Effects), Derek Thompson (Technical Manager), Don Babbage (Studio Lighting), Jill Haggar (Make-Up), Malcolm Thornton (Designer), Colin Lavers (Costumes) and John Brace (Visual Effects Designer), thanking them for their work on the studio sessions of 'The Five Doctors'.[272]

Wednesday 20th:
Itinerary: John signs off the commission for Peter Grimwade to write the four scripts for 'Planet of Fire'.[273]

Tuesday 26th:
Itinerary: Andrew Sewell writes to John, thanking him for the loan of a videotape copy of 'Genesis of the Daleks'. Sewell updates John on his progress with the radio version of the story: he hopes to have the scripts finished by June, and ready to go into production in August. The production will be for the BBC Studio Amateur Dramatic Group, but he hopes to interest BBC Radio Drama with the project nearer the time. He also suggests that he would like to organise a playback of the production around *Doctor Who*'s twentieth anniversary in November.

Wednesday 27th:
Itinerary: Richard Gregory's colleague Chris Padmore replies to John's letter of 13 April, confirming that Kamelion can be included in the two forthcoming stories proposed.[274]

---

[272] If John was indeed on annual leave at this time, he would presumably have written the memos of thanks before his departure, and post-dated them.

[273] The exact delivery date of Grimwade's scripts for 'Planet of Fire' isn't recorded, but the commissioning paperwork states they were due for delivery on Wednesday 25 May 1983. Again, John may have authorised this either before he went on leave, or after his return.

[274] One of these two stories would certainly have been 'Planet of Fire', which had just been commissioned. The second story isn't known, but most probably refers to 'The Awakening', in which Kamelion appeared in one scene which was filmed but cut from the final edit of the story. Ultimately, Kamelion was written out of the show in 'Planet of Fire'.

MAY

Wednesday 4th:
Itinerary: John entertains three members of the executive committee of the *Doctor Who* Appreciation Society in the BBC Club bar. On the same day, David Meldrum from the Schools Programme unit at Villiers House contacts the *Doctor Who* Production Office. He wants to use a sequence from *Doctor Who* showing two or three aliens, for a series of four programmes his department are making on the theme of 'space'. John refers him to the edition of *Did You See … ?* from 14 March 1982, which included a *Doctor Who* aliens clips montage that might be of use to him.

Thursday 5th:
Itinerary: John takes the tube from Union House to Maida Vale, where the BBC Radiophonic Workshop is based.[275] On the same day, John writes to Andrew Sewell, offering enthusiastic support for the idea of a playback of the radio version of 'Genesis of the Daleks' somewhere near the show's twentieth anniversary, and pledges to attend. John writes to David Ryan, informing him that although his upcoming internship is now all sorted, there are other issues he needs to discuss. Ryan won't be covered by any BBC insurance while he is attached to the *Doctor Who* Production Office, so needs to arrange his own cover. When it comes to filming for the planned documentary, UK union rules require a UK lighting assistant to be employed by Ryan's unit, whether he requires one or not, for each day's filming. If a member of BBC staff is filmed doing their job, then they need to be paid a fee. If actors are filmed doing their job, then they need to be paid a fee as well. These fees all need to be negotiated by Ryan separately. John states that, if this is acceptable to KRMA-TV, the BBC would pay all of Ryan's production costs as work goes along, then present KRMA-TV with a single, final bill at the end of the shoot.

John Nathan-Turner: 'I'd met David Ryan, a producer in Denver who was extremely keen to be attached to the BBC in general, and *Doctor Who* in particular. David joined us for several months, attaching himself to Michael Owen Morris's production ["The Awakening"], then getting involved with both "Frontios" and the Dalek yarn ["Resurrection of the Daleks"]. He was a delight to have on the team and was very popular with the production teams.'[276]

---

[275] Presumably to meet with Peter Howell, who was working on the incidental music for 'The Five Doctors' at the time.
[276] John Nathan-Turner memoirs, *Doctor Who Magazine* #238.

Friday 6th:
Itinerary: John travels by tube from Union House to Baker Street, for a meeting at the offices of the *Radio Times*, whose extensive promotion of *Doctor Who* over the coming year will include a one-off *20th Anniversary Special* magazine. On the same day, he signs off the commission for Robert Holmes to write a scene breakdown for 'Chain Reaction'.[277] Ian Oliver from the BBC2 programme *The Adventure Game* contacts the *Doctor Who* Production Office, asking if Janet Fielding would like to appear in an upcoming edition of the programme, due to be recorded at BBC Bristol; a selection of recording dates in June, July and August are suggested, and John chooses 1 July as the most suitable, given *Doctor Who*'s upcoming filming and recording commitments.[278]

Monday 9th:
Itinerary: Following up on the previous Friday's meeting, *Radio Times* editor Brian Gearing sends John and features writer Gay Search a lengthy memo recording what was discussed about proposed items for inclusion in the forthcoming *Doctor Who 20th Anniversary Special* publication.

Wednesday 11th:
Itinerary: John entertains Richard Landen, the main feature writer for Marvel's *Doctor Who Monthly*, in the BBC Club bar. On the same day, he signs-off the commission for Glen McCoy to write a scene breakdown for 'Timelash'.[279]

Friday 13th:
Itinerary: John entertains Terry Sampson and Lorne Martin of BBC Enterprises in the BBC Club bar.

Wednesday 18th:
Itinerary: John travels by tube from Union House to Baker Street, to meet once more with the publishers of the *Radio Times*.

Thursday 19th:
Itinerary: John writes to Roger Brunskill at BBC Enterprises, enclosing a cassette of clips from early *Doctor Who* stories featuring the first Doctor. He suggests using this as the basis for a video release called *Doctor Who – The*

---

[277] The precise delivery date of Holmes' scene breakdown for 'Chain Reaction' isn't recorded.

[278] Janet Fielding's edition of *The Adventure Game* was screened on 1 March 1984 on BBC2.

[279] The precise delivery date of McCoy's scene breakdown for 'Timelash' isn't recorded, although the commission stipulated delivery by Tuesday 31 May. At this point, the story was planned to consist of four 25-minute episodes.

Hartnell Years, with the addition of specially-shot linking material. He also proposes a sequel, *The Troughton Years*, should this prove a success.[280] Also on this day, John entertains Norman Rubinstein in the BBC Club bar.

Commentary: Rubinstein's organisation, Spirit of Light, was planning to organise a massive US convention in Chicago in November, to celebrate *Doctor Who*'s twentieth anniversary.

JUNE

Thursday 2nd:
Itinerary: In the evening, John and Gary Downie go out to the One Tun pub in Farringdon, London.

Commentary: The One Tun pub was, at the time, the regular haunt of members of the London science fiction fan community, of which a sizeable contingent were DWAS members/*Doctor Who* fans. There was a regular meeting night, which was historically the first Thursday of every month. John and Gary attended tonight to try and smooth over the rows and issues that had erupted on the Saturday night at the Longleat convention over Easter.

Friday 10th:
Itinerary: John entertains the actor Colin Baker at the BBC Club bar.

Commentary: Peter Davison had recently informed John that he intended to leave the show at the end of his third year as the Doctor. There was no option in his contract for a fourth year, but John had hoped he could nevertheless persuade the actor to stay on. Now, though, the search was on for an actor to play the sixth Doctor. John's first inclination was Colin Baker, who had played Maxil in the story 'Arc of Infinity'. He had since encountered Baker at the wedding of Lynn Richards, the production assistant on 'Arc of Infinity', and been impressed by his ability to amuse those in attendance without trying to dominate the situation. He'd also subsequently met Baker at a party that Sarah Sutton had thrown at her flat, and had formed the opinion that he was potential 'Doctor' material. He'd seen him again when he'd met up with

---

[280] John did eventually preside over video releases with these titles, based on this loose concept, but not until after he finished his stint as *Doctor Who*'s producer. Released in 1991, *The Hartnell Years* was presented by Sylvester McCoy, and *The Troughton Years* by Jon Pertwee.

Gerald Flood to discuss his potential role on 'The King's Demons'. Over lunch with Baker today, John asks him if he'd be interested in becoming the new Doctor.

John Nathan-Turner: 'I'd decided by this time that if Peter Davison was leaving, I certainly didn't want to wait nine months before the new Doctor had a full adventure. However, Peter wasn't too happy about not completing three full seasons. I must be honest and say that Peter had always said he'd only do three seasons in the show, and when I'd taken up the option on his contract for the twenty-first season, his agent, the late John Mahoney, informed me that Peter wasn't prepared to grant me another option. At the time he wasn't saying he wouldn't do a fourth season, just that he wouldn't grant me an option on one. A few months after that discussion, I had to know for our planning purposes whether, in fact, Peter would be interested in staying on for Season 22. His answer was in the negative, so the search was on for Doctor number six.'[281]

Commentary: John's decision to have the sixth Doctor do a full debut story at the end of Season 21 was probably informed by the strikes that had befallen the tail-end of Season 20 the previous year. If similar problems had forced the final story of Season 21 to be cancelled, and if that story had also been the fifth Doctor's swansong, then that would have presented all sorts of logistical problems, not least of which would have been trying to write out the fifth Doctor in the first story of Season 22, for which Peter Davison wouldn't have been under contract. The way John arranged things, if the last story in production had been lost (in the same way that 'The Return' had been), then the sixth Doctor's debut adventure would have been the first in Season 22, and the curtailed Season 21 would have ended with 'The Caves of Androzani'.

Monday 13th:
Itinerary: John has an (expensive) lunch at the Balzac restaurant in London with Hazel Adair, Peter Ling and Eric Saward.

Commentary: The purpose of this lunch was probably to try to further along the proposed relaunch of the soap opera *Compact*, which John was looking to helm.

Tuesday 14th – Wednesday 22nd:
Rehearsals for the first studio block of 'Warriors of the Deep' take place at the BBC Television Rehearsal Rooms at Acton.

---

[281] John Nathan-Turner memoirs, *Doctor Who Magazine* #238.

Tuesday 14th:
Itinerary: John travels by tube from Union House to the BBC's Television Rehearsal Rooms at Acton, to sit in on the first day of rehearsals for the first studio block of 'Warriors of the Deep'.[282]

Wednesday 15th:
Itinerary: For reasons unknown, John travels by tube from Union House to Oxford Circus.

Commentary: This day was meant to be the first of three days of filming for 'Warriors of the Deep' in the water tank at the BBC's Ealing Film Studios. The filming was cancelled due to last-minute studio rescheduling caused by the BBC's General Election coverage the previous week.[283]

Monday 20th:
Itinerary: John entertains Mae Broadley from World International Books, the publishers of the *Doctor Who Annual*, at the BBC Club bar.

Tuesday 21st:
Itinerary: John travels by tube from Union House to the BBC's Television Rehearsal Rooms at Acton for the Producer's Run of the first studio block for 'Warriors of the Deep'. Also on this day, Pat Dyer, the BBC's Senior Personnel Officer, writes to John to inform him that the BBC has no objection to his attendance at the upcoming Whovian Festival convention on 9 and 10 July in Florida.[284] Nor is there any reason why he should not be paid a fee for his attendance on this occasion, although Dyer notes that since these events are clearly BBC PR occasions that benefit the BBC accordingly, it follows that any payment that John receives should be consistent with that premise.

Wednesday 22nd:
Itinerary: Colin Baker returns to the BBC's Union and Threshold House in the afternoon, for a meeting with John and David Reid. John has informed Reid of his wish to cast Baker as Davison's replacement, and Reid has asked to meet

---

[282] Rehearsals for 'Warriors of the Deep' were originally scheduled to begin on Monday 20 June, but a snap General Election was called in the UK, forcing the BBC to alter many of its schedules at the last minute, including the planned studio recording dates for this story.
[283] Mrs Thatcher's Conservative Government had announced on 9 May a snap General Election, which was then held on 9 June. The BBC found that it had to cancel and rearrange the studio facilities for many of its programmes in order to provide election coverage, and this had a knock-on effect on shows such as *Doctor Who* for many months following.
[284] Organised by the Doctor Who Fan Club of America.

the actor before signing off on this.

Thursday 23rd:
Itinerary: It's the first day of the two-day first studio block for 'Warriors of the Deep' in studio TC6 at BBC Television Centre.

John Nathan-Tuner: 'It was during the studio session that I received a phone-call from Visual Effects to say that the Myrka would not be ready for the studio the following day. I had known that there were problems with the effects on this story, due to the sheer volume of work, but this was a bombshell. There was no way we could abandon all the Myrka scenes and not have a whole day's studio remount. The Planning Department, quite rightly, said they couldn't bear the cost. Visual Effects, who virtually attempted to forbid the use of the Myrka (something not within their remit), wouldn't pay for the inconvenience caused, and our programme budget simply didn't have enough "knicker elastic" money to finance a remount. The telephone discussions went on for several hours. In the end I had to insist that the Myrka was recorded as scheduled. It was thoroughly unsatisfactory, but I had no alternative ... Of course, after the event there was a post-mortem; memos, apologies and all the rest of it, but the fact remains we were let down badly by a department that failed to pay for its own mistakes.'[285]

Friday 24th:
Itinerary: It's the second and final day of the first studio block for 'Warriors of the Deep' in studio TC6 at BBC Television Centre. John signs off the commission for Glen McCoy to write a single 25-minute script for 'Timelash' Part One.[286]

Eric Saward: 'I don't know whose idea it was to have Ingrid Pitt do the karate kick. All I can say is that it was not scripted. In a way, it marred everything. John Nathan-Turner was there in the studio, but the kick came and went, and we were all waiting for him to say something, we all knew how ludicrous it looked ... but nothing. Maybe he wasn't focused that day?'[287]

Monday 27th:
Itinerary: Today is the first day of OB shooting for 'Warriors of the Deep' at the Royal Engineers Diving Establishment, McMullen Barracks, Marchwood

---

[285] John Nathan-Turner memoirs, *Doctor Who Magazine* #238.
[286] The exact delivery date of McCoy's script for 'Timelash' Part One isn't recorded, although the commission stipulates delivery by Monday 25 July. The decision was taken, sometime around this date, for Season 22 of *Doctor Who* to switch to thirteen 50-minute episodes, rather than twenty-six 25 minute episodes.
[287] Eric Saward interview, *Doctor Who Magazine* #347.

in Hampshire.

Tuesday 28th:
Itinerary: Today is the second day of OB shooting for 'Warriors of the Deep', now based at Stage A (Water Tank) at Shepperton Studios. Also on this day, Colin Baker joins John for lunch, where he is formally offered the role of the sixth Doctor. The lunching duo are spotted by Peter Davison, who guesses that Baker is being lined up as his replacement.

Wednesday 29th:
Itinerary: Today is the third day of OB shooting for 'Warriors of the Deep', at Stage A (Water Tank) at Shepperton Studios.

Thursday 30th:
Itinerary: Today is the fourth day of OB shooting for 'Warriors of the Deep', at Stage A (Water Tank) at Shepperton Studios. Also on this day, John writes to Terry Nation to thank him for confirming to Eric Saward that he is now happy with the scripts for the forthcoming Dalek story. He says that he will meet Nation for a gin on some future occasion.

JULY

Friday 1st:
Itinerary: Today is the fifth and final day of OB shooting for 'Warriors of the Deep', at Stage A (Water Tank) at Shepperton Studios.

Saturday 2nd – Tuesday 12th:
Rehearsals for the second studio block of 'Warriors of the Deep' take place at the BBC Television Rehearsal Rooms at Acton.

Tuesday 5th:
Itinerary: Today there is a press photocall, presided over by John, to unveil Nicola Bryant as the Doctor's new companion, Peri.

Wednesday 6th:
Itinerary: Nicola Bryant appears on BBC1's *Breakfast Time* to discuss her casting as Peri.

Friday 8th:
Itinerary: David Reid writes to John to inform him that he's agreeing to sign

off his Balzac lunch expenses from 13 June, but cautions him never again to spend so much on lunch for three people, especially at the Balzac restaurant. John takes a flight to the USA to be a guest at the Whovian Festival Tour event in Tampa.

Saturday 9th – Sunday 10th:
Itinerary: John is a guest of the Whovian Festival Tour at the McKay Auditorium, Tampa, Florida, alongside Jon Pertwee and Elisabeth Sladen. He flies back to the UK after the event.

Tuesday 12th:
Itinerary: John travels by tube from Union House to the BBC's Television Rehearsal Rooms at Acton for the Producer's Run of the second studio block for 'Warriors of the Deep'.

John Nathan-Turner: 'I'd been on a trip to America during the rehearsal of this story, with Jon Pertwee. A favourite pastime of mine was to bring back US candy bars with very peculiar names … Jon was riveted with the fun of this shopping spree and joined in. I'd been telling him who was in the guest cast of "Warriors of the Deep", and as the voluptuous Ingrid Pitt was an old chum and he'd worked with her on *Doctor Who*, he gave me a bar called "Mounds", which he said I was to give to Ingrid with his love. The cast and crew were hysterical, as was Ingrid, when her Mounds were presented just before the producer's run-through.'[288]

Wednesday 13th:
Itinerary: Today is the first day of the three-day second studio block for 'Warriors of the Deep' in studio TC6 at BBC Television Centre.

Thursday 14th:
Itinerary: Today is the second day of the three-day second studio block for 'Warriors of the Deep' in studio TC6 at BBC Television Centre.

Friday 15th:
Itinerary: John writes a memo to David Reid to apologise for the excessive Balzac lunch bill, but points out it was for four people, not three. Today is also the third and final day of the second studio block for 'Warriors of the Deep' in studio TC6 at BBC Television Centre.

Saturday 16th:
Itinerary: John and Gary host a party at their Brighton home, attended by

---

[288] John Nathan-Turner memoirs, *Doctor Who Magazine* #238.

Peter Davison, Mark Strickson and director Fiona Cumming amongst others. Ian Levine drives down from London to attend, and brings with him a fan he'd met in the nightclub Heaven the previous evening, Gary Levy.[289]

Commentary: Gary Levy used titbits of news and gossip he overheard at this party to fill the pages of the first issue of his fanzine *Doctor Who Bulletin* (*DWB*), launched early the next month. *DWB* – and its editor – would become a significant thorn in John's side in later years.

Tuesday 19th:
Itinerary: Today is the first day of location filming in Blandford Forum and Wimborne Minster, Dorset for 'The Awakening'.

Wednesday 20th:
Itinerary: John dictates a memo to Sarah Lee for the Manager of BBC Drama Series and Serials, informing him that Peter Moffatt will be working for an additional 10 days on 'The Five Doctors' in order to edit the special into a four-part story for overseas sale. It has been agreed with BBC Enterprises that they will pay for this additional work to be carried out. Today is also the second day of location filming in Wimborne Minster, Dorset for 'The Awakening'.

John Nathan-Turner: 'Most of you will know of the famous outtake from ["The Awakening"], featuring the horse demolishing the prop lych-gate. I stood and watched it happen with abject horror, though, of course, in retrospect it was terribly funny. No-one, including the horse, was hurt.'[290]

Thursday 21st:
Itinerary: Today is the third day of location filming for 'The Awakening', now

---

[289] Ian Levine had been introduced by Graham Williams as a fan of the show when John had first become producer, and John had since used him extensively as an unofficial sounding board when it came to checking elements of new stories in case they upset established continuity. Levine was also a successful record producer, and the resident DJ at one of London's biggest nightclubs at the time, Heaven. Levine was also introduced by John to script editor Eric Saward, and the two of them often exchanged ideas on possible storylines. Later, Levine was used as a 'front man' by John to pass information to the UK press when the show was cancelled in 1985. However, the two of them later fell out over the casting of Bonnie Langford as companion Mel. Gary Levy (later known as Gary Leigh) would continue editing and publishing *DWB* for the rest of John's tenure as producer of *Doctor Who*. At first the fanzine was cordial toward John and the direction in which he was taking the show, but after the events of the 1985 hiatus, it became vociferously critical.
[290] John Nathan-Turner memoirs, *Doctor Who Magazine* #238.

in Martin, near Fordingbridge in Hampshire.

Friday 22nd:
Itinerary: Today is the fourth and final day of location filming for 'The Awakening', at Damers Cottage in Martin, near Fordingbridge in Hampshire. After filming concludes, John returns to London, then flies from London to Columbus, Ohio, USA.

Friday 22nd – Sunday 24th:
Itinerary: John is a guest at the Panopticon West III convention, held at the Quality Inn, Columbus, Ohio. Other guests include Anthony Ainley, Fiona Cumming and Ian Fraser. John returns to the UK on Monday 25 July.

Commentary: Rumours began circulating at this convention that Colin Baker had been cast as the sixth Doctor. At this point, Davison's decision to leave the show hadn't been made public.

Saturday 23rd – Tuesday 2nd August:
Rehearsals for the single studio block of 'The Awakening' take place at the BBC Television Rehearsal Rooms at Acton.

Tuesday 26th:
Itinerary: John and Peter Moffatt attend a gallery-only session for 'The Five Doctors' in studio TC6, while the studio is being prepared to record that week's edition of *Top of the Pops*.

Thursday 28th:
Itinerary: John signs off the commission for Robert Holmes to write the four scripts of 'The Caves of Androzani'.[291] Peter Davison's departure from the shows is announced.

Friday 29th:
Itinerary: Peter Davison, along with John, appears on the on the BBC1 regional opt-out news programme *South East at Six*, where they are interviewed by Fran Morrison about Davison's decision to leave *Doctor Who*. John gives his thoughts on what attributes the sixth Doctor might need to have.

---

[291] The precise delivery dates of Holmes' scripts for 'The Caves of Androzani' aren't recorded, but the original commission states they were to be delivered by Tuesday 30 August 1983.

AUGUST

Tuesday 2nd:
Itinerary: Today is the Producer's Run at the BBC Television Rehearsal Rooms at Acton for the single studio session of 'The Awakening'. On the same day, John signs off the commission for Anthony Steven to write the script for 'A Switch in Time' Part One.[292]

Commentary: Also on this day, actor Peter Arne was found dead in his flat, having been killed by an intruder. Arne had just signed up to appear as Mr Range in the story 'Frontios'. Some newspaper headlines, notably in that day's edition of London's *Evening Standard*, proclaimed the 'Death of *Doctor Who* Actor', which caused problems, as many people initially wrongly assumed this referred to Peter Davison.

Thursday 4th:
Itinerary: Today is the first day of a three-day studio session for 'The Awakening' in studio TC6 at BBC Television Centre. Julia Smith, now the producer of the BBC series *District Nurse*, writes to John, enclosing a copy of a letter she has received from writer Jeremy Bentham, asking if he can borrow any photos and slides she might have from her time working on *Doctor Who*, for use in *Doctor Who Monthly*. She is unsure about this, and asks John for guidance.

Friday 5th:
Itinerary: Today is the second day of the three-day studio session for 'The Awakening' in studio TC6 at BBC Television Centre.

Saturday 6th:
Itinerary: Today is the third and final day of the studio session for 'The Awakening' in studio TC6 at BBC Television Centre.

Tuesday 9th:
Itinerary: Nicola Bryant is contracted to appear in 12 episodes of Season 21.

Thursday 11th:
Itinerary: Philip Martin delivers his revised pair of 50-minute scripts for 'Planet of Fear' to the *Doctor Who* Production Office.

---

[292] This story would have its title switched to 'The Twin Dilemma' by the time it was screened on BBC1.

Friday 12th – Sunday 14th:
Itinerary: John flies out to the US at some point before Friday 12 August (his thirty-sixth birthday). He is a guest at the The Authorized Doctor Who 20th Anniversary Celebration convention at the Ramada O'Hare Hotel, Chicago, Illinois. Other guests include Peter Davison, Ian Marter, Janet Fielding and Nicholas Courtney. He returns to the UK sometime after Monday 15 August.

Peter Davison: 'John kept the show in the public eye. "We've been invited to a convention [in America] … ," he'd say, "so we're going to cancel rehearsals on Friday, fly out instead, come back on Sunday night and go back into rehearsals on Monday!"'[293]

Saturday 13th – Tuesday 23rd:
Rehearsals for the first studio block of 'Frontios' take place at the BBC Television Rehearsal Rooms at Acton.

Monday 15th:
Itinerary: Anthony Steven delivers his script for 'A Switch in Time' Part One to the *Doctor Who* Production Office. 'The Visitation' Part One is repeated on BBC1.

Tuesday 16th:
'The Visitation' Part Two is repeated on BBC1.

Wednesday 17th:
'The Visitation' Part Three is repeated on BBC1.

Thursday 18th:
'The Visitation' Part Four is repeated on BBC1.

Friday 19th:
Itinerary: John attends a press photocall with Colin Baker and Nicola Bryant, where Baker is unveiled as the actor to portray the sixth Doctor.

Colin Baker: 'John rang me up on a Friday afternoon, and said, "The news has been leaked! We need you to come down to Television Centre immediately. We have Nicola Bryant coming in, and we'll do some photographs." I didn't even have time to change, so those photographs of me are awful. Every time I see them, I think, "Oh God, I'm wearing *that* suit." I look so bloody casual. I stood there in a horrible suit, with Nicola Bryant and hundreds of

---

[293] Peter Davison interview, *Doctor Who Magazine* #313.

photographers. I was chucked in at the deep end.'[294]

Monday 22nd:
'Kinda' Part One is repeated on BBC1.

Tuesday 23rd:
Itinerary: Today is the Producer's Run at the BBC Television Rehearsal Rooms at Acton for the first studio block of 'Frontios'. 'Kinda' Part Two is repeated on BBC1.

Wednesday 24th:
Itinerary: Today is the first day of the three-day first studio block for 'Frontios' in studio TC6 at BBC Television Centre. On the same day, John signs off the commission for Anthony Steven to write the scripts for 'The Twin Dilemma' Parts Two to Four. 'Kinda' Part Three is repeated on BBC1.

Thursday 25th:
Itinerary: Today is the second day of the three-day first studio block for 'Frontios' in studio TC6 at BBC Television Centre. 'Kinda' Part Four is repeated on BBC1.

Friday 26th:
Itinerary: Today is the third and final day of the first studio block for 'Frontios' in studio TC6 at BBC Television Centre. Anthony Steven delivers his scripts for 'The Twin Dilemma' Parts Two to Four to the *Doctor Who* Production Office.

Saturday 27th – Tuesday 6th September:
Rehearsals for the second studio block of 'Frontios' take place at the BBC Television Rehearsal Rooms at Acton.

Wednesday 31st:
Itinerary: John writes to Julia Smith, producer of *District Nurse*, to vouch for Jeremy Bentham's credentials as a writer for *Doctor Who Monthly*. 'Black Orchid' Part One is repeated on BBC1.

---

[294] Colin Baker interview, *Doctor Who Magazine* #321.

SEPTEMBER

Thursday 1st:
'Black Orchid' Part Two is repeated on BBC1.

Tuesday 6th:
Itinerary: Today is the Producer's Run at the BBC Television Rehearsal Rooms at Acton for the second studio block of 'Frontios'.

Wednesday 7th:
Itinerary: Today is the first day of the three-day second studio block for 'Frontios' in studio TC6 at BBC Television Centre.

Thursday 8th:
Itinerary: Today is the second day of the three-day second studio block for 'Frontios' in studio TC6 at BBC Television Centre.

Friday 9th:
Itinerary: Today is the third and final day of the second studio block for 'Frontios' in studio TC6 at BBC Television Centre.

Sunday 11th:
Itinerary: Today is the first day of location filming for 'Resurrection of the Daleks' in and around Shad Thames, Southwark in London, with Matthew Robinson directing.

Matthew Robinson: 'The biggest row I had was on the first or second day of shooting. It was a shot with the two policemen coming out of an archway at the warehouses on the South Bank, and Eric Saward was watching [alongside] John. I think I was doing something shot-wise that wasn't absolutely in accordance with the script. Eric was pulling a slightly wry face, so I went over to him and explained why I was doing it. Eric said, "Oh fine, absolutely fine," but John overheard and beckoned me to one side – and absolutely tore me to pieces! He said I had no reason whatsoever to be discussing shots with the writer. If I wanted to discuss shots, I should do it with him! Well, I thought it was an absolutely ludicrous point. You might have these sorts of divisions in Hollywood, but certainly not in BBC television drama … He was very, very angry – shaking with anger. I thought I was going to be sacked. I wouldn't have minded, really. Frankly, I almost walked off the show. You can't go around treating people like that. It's quite ridiculous. John didn't actually apologise either.'[295]

Monday 12th:
Itinerary: Today is the second and final day of location filming for 'Resurrection of the Daleks' in and around Shad Thames, Southwark in London.

Tuesday 13th – Tuesday 20th:
Rehearsals for the first studio block of 'Resurrection of the Daleks' take place at the BBC Television Rehearsal Rooms at Acton.

Tuesday 20th:
Itinerary: Today is the Producer's Run at the BBC Television Rehearsal Rooms at Acton for the first studio block of 'Resurrection of the Daleks'.

Wednesday 21st:
Itinerary: Today is the first day of the three-day first studio block for 'Resurrection of the Daleks' in studio TC8 at BBC Television Centre.

Thursday 22nd:
Itinerary: Today is the second day of the three-day first studio block for 'Resurrection of the Daleks' in studio TC8 at BBC Television Centre.

Friday 23rd:
Itinerary: Today is the third and final day of the first studio block for 'Resurrection of the Daleks' in studio TC8 at BBC Television Centre.

Sunday 25th – Tuesday 4th October:
Rehearsals for the second studio block of 'Resurrection of the Daleks' take place at the BBC Television Rehearsal Rooms at Acton.

Friday 30th:
Itinerary: John writes to the BBC Artists' Payments department, to inform them that Peter Davison, Janet Fielding and Mark Strickson attended a special photocall for *Radio Times* magazine on Tuesday 9 August. He asks that they be paid the appropriate fees for this. On the same day, John signs off the commission for Pip and Jane Baker to write a scene breakdown for 'Too Clever By Far'.[296] Colin Baker is contracted to appear as the Doctor in five 25-minute episodes of Season 21. Philip Martin writes to John, telling him that he is writing a book entitled *How to Write for TV* for the publishers A & C Black,

---

[295] Matthew Robinson interview, *Doctor Who Magazine* #232
[296] This story will be retitled 'The Mark of the Rani' by the time it is screened.

and wants to detail his experiences writing 'Planet of Fear' as part of the text. He asks if he could meet with John during October to discuss the matter.[297]

OCTOBER

Tuesday 4th:
Itinerary: Today is the Producer's Run at the BBC Television Rehearsal Rooms at Acton for the second studio block of 'Resurrection of the Daleks'. Colin Baker is contracted to play the Doctor in thirteen 50-minute episodes of Season 22, with an option in the BBC's favour for three more years, at a similar amount of episodes per season.

Wednesday 5th:
Itinerary: Today is the first day of the three-day second studio block for 'Resurrection of the Daleks' in studio TC8 at BBC Television Centre.

Thursday 6th:
Itinerary: Today is the second day of the three-day second studio block for 'Resurrection of the Daleks' in studio TC8 at BBC Television Centre.

Friday 7th:
Itinerary: Today is the third and final day of the second studio block for 'Resurrection of the Daleks' in studio TC8 at BBC Television Centre. John hosts a farewell party for Janet Fielding after recording concludes.

Wednesday 12th:
Itinerary: John, along with the cast and crew of 'Planet of Fire', flies out from London's Gatwick Airport at 8.00am, arriving at Arrecife Airport, Lanzarote in the Canary islands at 10.45am local time.

John Nathan-Turner: 'Originally, there was to be a major press group accompanying us, but the marvellous deal that June (Collins, the production associate) had negotiated meant that the party would have to stay for the full five-day shoot (a seven-day trip), which most Fleet Street editors weren't prepared to condone. I say most, but *The Daily Star* was determined to have first crack at the publicity and launch of Nicola Bryant as Peri. I was delighted when the photographer was announced to be Alistair Loos (of Tegan's nightie fame ("Arc of Infinity")) and the scribbler was to be someone I knew well too.

---

[297] *How to Write for TV* by Philip Martin appears never to have been published.

At the last minute the reporter was changed to someone I didn't know and whom I didn't take to at all. During the flight, the *Star* team invited me to join them for champagne. Half an hour from touchdown, the reporter revealed he'd been … researching old cuttings … and had dug up all manner of dirt on certain cast individuals … I knew I had to deal with this, and before stories were filed back to the *Daily Star*'s London office.'[298]

Thursday 13th:
Itinerary: Terry Sampson from BBC Enterprises writes to John, offering to get BBC Enterprises involved if there is to be a party at the BBC to celebrate *Doctor Who*'s twentieth anniversary. In Lanzarote, today is a day of preparation in readiness for the first day of filming on 'Planet of Fire' tomorrow.

Friday 14th:
Itinerary: John dictates a letter to Sarah Lee in London for Philip Martin, apologising for not being able to meet up to discuss Martin's planned book. Today is the first day of location filming for 'Planet of Fire', at Papagayo Beach and Bay on the island of Lanzarote.

John Nathan-Turner: 'Nicola Bryant went through an ordeal in her debut story. She was cut and grazed, bashed and pulled because of the requirements of the action; even during the drowning sequence, all wasn't smooth; a male nudist, thinking she was genuinely in trouble, attempted to rescue her. When he finally discovered we were filming, he was incensed. While we were doing the TARDIS departure shot, he brazenly walked through the shot stark naked … The Visual Effects boys threw a terrific party on the second evening, which went on very late. The *Star* writer was quite inebriated and came to my room to discuss an idea for a photoshoot of Peter as James Bond and Nicola as Honey Rider recreating the most famous scene from *Dr No* (geddit?) … and then promptly passed out on one of the beds.'[299]

Saturday 15th:
Itinerary: Today is the second day of location filming for 'Planet of Fire', now at Mirador del Rio and Orzola Quay on the island of Lanzarote.

John Nathan-Turner: 'In the converted restraint we were using for the royal apartment, our Fleet Street reporter fell asleep on top of the stunt mattresses that were lying next to the bar. I waited until just before lunch break, loudly ordered two Bloody Marys, and accidentally kicked him as I made the order. He groaned, then, realising how hung-over he was, said he felt nauseous. I

---

[298] John Nathan-Turner memoirs, *Doctor Who Magazine* #238.
[299] John Nathan-Turner memoirs, *Doctor Who Magazine* #238.

leant down, pulled him up by the collar and whispered to him that if he printed just one bad word about my cast in his newspaper, I would tell everyone I knew in Fleet Street that we had slept together the previous evening – starting with his photographer, who was on the balcony taking snaps of Peter Wyngarde. He called my bluff. I yelled for Alistair, a *very* chatty individual. Alistair left Mr Wyngarde and yelled from a distance, "Be with you in a second, guv'nor." The hung-over journalist said, "Okay, John, you win – and I'd better have that Bloody Mary!"'[300]

Sunday 16th:
Itinerary: Today is a day off for the cast and crew. Some of them visit the nearby island of Graciosa on a day-long excursion.

Nicola Bryant: 'The press came with us to Lanzarote, and they were right on our tail all the time. Of course, I had all the stuff in bikinis, and I think they were desperate for the old Page Three shot. In Lanzarote, you can do topless sunbathing, and I remember John saying to me, "If you take your top off for one second, I'll kill you – because they'll be there!" The newspapers paid for all those "James Bond" shots. That was entirely their idea. They hired Peter a tuxedo and bought me a white bikini.'[301]

Peter Davison: 'John could get the press to turn up to anything. He knew what he wanted. I didn't always agree with him. He'd made promises to the press. He was a dealmaker. He made a promise about what we would do if they came out to Lanzarote.'[302]

Monday 17th:
Itinerary: Today is the third day of location filming for 'Planet of Fire', at the Montanas de Fuego on the island of Lanzarote.

Tuesday 18th:
Itinerary: Today is the fourth day of location filming for 'Planet of Fire', again at the Montanas de Fuego.

Wednesday 19th:
Itinerary: Today is the fifth and final day of location filming for 'Planet of Fire', once more at the Montanas de Fuego. Once filming is concluded, John hosts a wrap party back at the unit hotel.

---

[300] John Nathan-Turner Memoirs, *Doctor Who Magazine* #238.
[301] Nicola Bryant Interview, *Doctor Who Magazine* #236
[302] Peter Davison Interview, *Doctor Who Magazine* #313

Thursday 20th:
The cast and crew of 'Planet of Fire' return to Gatwick Airport from Lanzarote, arriving back in the UK at 5.00pm local time.

Friday 21st – Tuesday 25th:
Rehearsals for the first studio block of 'Planet of Fire' take place at the BBC Television Rehearsal Rooms at Acton.

Monday 24th:
Itinerary: John replies to Terry Sampson, thanking him for his offer of helping with a party for *Doctor Who*'s twentieth anniversary. John reminds him that the party has already taken place in March, and that Terry and some of his staff attended it.

Tuesday 25th:
Itinerary: Today is the Producer's Run at the BBC Television Rehearsal Rooms at Acton for the first studio block of 'Planet of Fire'. John writes to Gay Search and Brian Thomas at *Radio Times*, expressing his appreciation for the magazine's *Doctor Who 20th Anniversary Special* publication. John also writes to the Head of Series and Serials, asking that Michael Morris be booked to direct story '6V', from 14 May to 7 September 1984.[303]

Wednesday 26th:
Itinerary: Today is the first day of the two-day first studio block for 'Planet of Fire' in studio TC1 at BBC Television Centre. John and Eric Saward circulate a Drama Script Classified List, which states that the only writers they are working with at this date for upcoming storylines and/or scripts are: Christopher Bailey, Pip and Jane Baker (scene breakdown), Christopher H Bidmead, Terrance Dicks (*Doctor Who* special), Brian Finch, Peter Grimwade, Robert Holmes, Glen McCoy (one episode), Philip Martin, Pat Mills, Eric Pringle, Eric Saward, Robin Squire, and Anthony Steven. On the same day, John writes to the Manager of Series and Serials, asking that Pennant Roberts be engaged to direct story 6T, between 9 April and 3 August 1984.[304]

Thursday 27th:
Itinerary: Today is the second and final day of the first studio block for 'Planet of Fire' in studio TC1 at BBC Television Centre.

---

[303] Michael Morris had recently directed 'The Awakening'. Story '6V' would eventually become 'Vengeance on Varos', and be directed by Ron Jones.
[304] Pennant Roberts had recently directed 'Warriors of the Deep'. For whatever reason, Roberts wasn't assigned this story but eventually directed 'Timelash' later in the season. The 6T code would eventually be allocated 'Attack of the Cybermen', which would be directed by Matthew Robinson.

Saturday 29th – Tuesday 8th November:
Rehearsals for the second studio block of 'Planet of Fire' take place at the BBC Television Rehearsal Rooms at Acton.

Sunday 30th:
Itinerary: John is a guest speaker at the *Doctor Who* – The Developing Art event at the National Film Theatre in London. Also guesting are Heather Hartnell, Patrick Troughton and Anthony Ainley.

NOVEMBER

Tuesday 1st:
Itinerary: Pip and Jane Baker deliver their scene breakdown for 'Too Clever By Far' to the *Doctor Who* Production Office. On the same day, John writes to the Head of Series and Serials, asking that Peter Moffatt be booked to direct story 6W, consisting of three 45-minute episodes, between 28 May and 16 November 1984.

Friday 4th:
Itinerary: John writes to the BBC Contract Department, asking them to engage Patrick Troughton to appear as the Doctor in story 6W – three 45-minute episodes.

Monday 7th:
Itinerary: John signs off the commission for Pip and Jane Baker to write two 50-minute scripts for 'Enter the Rani'.[305]

Tuesday 8th:
Itinerary: Today is the Producer's Run at the BBC Television Rehearsal Rooms at Acton for the second studio block of 'Planet of Fire'.

Wednesday 9th:
Itinerary: Today is the first day of the three-day second studio block for 'Planet of Fire' in studio TC6 at BBC Television Centre.

---

[305] This was the new title for 'Too Clever By Far', the story that would eventually become 'The Mark of the Rani'. The exact delivery date for these two scripts isn't recorded, but the original commission specified delivery by Monday 30 January 1984.

Thursday 10th:
Itinerary: Today is the second day of the three-day second studio block for 'Planet of Fire' in studio TC6 at BBC Television Centre.

Friday 11th:
Itinerary: Today is the third and final day of the second studio block for 'Planet of Fire' in studio TC6 at BBC Television Centre. After recording concludes, John hosts a farewell party for Mark Strickson.

Sunday 13th:
Colin Baker's son Jack, who'd been born in September, dies of cot death, aged just seven weeks.

Monday 14th:
Itinerary: Peter Davison records an insert with Terry Wogan at BBC Broadcasting House to be shown as part of the *Children in Need* fundraising night on BBC1 on the evening of 25 November. He donates his coat (part of the costume as worn by him as the Doctor up until 'Warriors of the Deep' – a new coat was made for 'The Awakening' onwards) to be auctioned off to raise money for the charity.

Tuesday 15th:
Itinerary: Today is the first day of location filming for 'The Caves of Androzani', at Masters Pit, Stokeford Heath, Wareham in Dorset.

Nicola Bryant: 'It was so cold. I had no way of wrapping up, because my costume was in direct continuity from the last story, wearing the clothes that I wore in Lanzarote. I remember the cameraman saying, "Slap your face, love, you're going blue!" I got frostbite, and then I got pneumonia, and then Peter [Davison] fell ill. It was a pretty rough shoot.'[306]

Wednesday 16th:
Itinerary: Today is the second day of location filming for 'The Caves of Androzani' at Masters Pit, Stokeford Heath, Wareham in Dorset. A special press screening of 'The Five Doctors' is organised in London. Richard Hurndall and Nicholas Courtney attend, but Jon Pertwee is away in America and so sends his apologies.

Thursday 17th:
Itinerary: Today is the third and final day of location filming for 'The Caves of Androzani' at Masters Pit, Stokeford Heath, Wareham in Dorset. Sometime on

---

[306] Nicola Bryant interview, *Doctor Who Magazine* #96.

or before this date, John flies from the UK to Canada.

Friday 18th – Sunday 20th:
Itinerary: John is a guest at the Who Party 6 convention held at the Ramada Inn in Toronto, Ontario in Canada. The other guest at the event is Janet Fielding.

Wednesday 23rd:
Itinerary: John signs off the commission for Glen McCoy to write a single 45-minute script for 'Timelash' Part Two[307]. Sometime before this date, he flies from Canada to Chicago, Illinois, USA. 'The Five Doctors' screens on PBS Stations throughout the US, two days before it airs on BBC1 in the UK. John watches it with many of the guests of the upcoming The Ultimate Celebration Convention in the Hyatt Regency O'Hare Hotel in Chicago, other guests at which include most of the cast of 'The Five Doctors' plus director Peter Moffatt.

Thursday 24th:
Itinerary: Still ensconced in the Hyatt Regency Hotel in Chicago, John celebrates US Thanksgiving day with his fellow convention guests. After dinner that evening, he guests along with Jon Pertwee, Anthony Ainley and Sarah Sutton on a late-night live radio show in Chicago to promote the event that weekend.

Friday 25th:
'The Five Doctors' screens on BBC1.

Saturday 26th – Sunday 27th:
Itinerary: John is a guest at The Ultimate Celebration convention, organised by Spirit of Light at the Hyatt Regency O'Hare hotel in Chicago. The other guests include Patrick Troughton, Jon Pertwee, Tom Baker, Peter Davison, Carole Ann Ford, Nicholas Courtney, Elisabeth Sladen, Ian Marter, Louise Jameson, John Leeson, Mary Tamm, Matthew Waterhouse, Janet Fielding, Mark Strickson (and wife Julie Brennan), Nicola Bryant, Anthony Ainley, Terry Nation, Peter Moffatt, Fiona Cumming, Ian Fraser and John's partner, Gary Downie. John returns to the UK soon after the event finishes.

John Nathan-Turner: 'I asked Patrick [Troughton] if he'd do "The Two Doctors" at the first big convention in Chicago in 1983. He said yes, so we

---

[307] The exact delivery date of McCoy's script for 'Timelash' Part Two isn't recorded. 23 November was the date on the commissioning form, but John must have signed this before or after his trip to Canada and the US.

went ahead and commissioned it without getting Frazer under contract, because we knew that he'd be keen.'[308]

Wednesday 30th:
Colin Baker attends his first costume fitting for the sixth Doctor.

DECEMBER

Thursday 1st:
Commentary: Today was meant to be the first day of the two-day first studio block for 'The Caves of Androzani' at BBC Television Centre, but this has had to be postponed.

Sunday 4th – Tuesday 13th:
Rehearsals for the first studio block of 'The Caves of Androzani' take place at the BBC Television Rehearsal Rooms at Acton, having been postponed from November owing to the loss of the original studio dates.

Wednesday 7th:
Itinerary: Ilinca Bossy from BBC Head of Rights and Exports writes to John regarding the *Radio Times*'s *Doctor Who 20th Anniversary Special*. The magazine has done very well overseas, with 25,000 copies sold to Pitman in Australia, 5,000 to Pitman in New Zealand, 5,000 to Methuen in Canada and 200 to Merican in Singapore. In addition, a contract has been signed with *Starlog* magazine in the USA, allowing them to print copies from their own negatives of the pages, and an initial run of 25,000 has been produced.

Tuesday 13th:
Itinerary: Today is the Producer's Run at the BBC Television Rehearsal Rooms at Acton for the first studio block of 'The Caves of Androzani'. John writes to David Reid, asking that Ron Jones be booked to direct story 6V. He also writes to Alan Hart, the Controller of BBC1, thanking him for a recent dinner he hosted to celebrate twenty years of *Doctor Who*.[309]

Wednesday 14th:
Itinerary: John writes to the Manager of Series and Serials at the BBC,

---

[308] John Nathan Turner interview, *Doctor Who Magazine* #243.
[309] The exact date and location of this dinner, and who else was in attendance, aren't known.

requesting that Matthew Robinson be engaged to direct story 6T from 9 April to 3 August 1984.[310] On the same day, Brian Turner, from the BBC Copyright Department writes to John, noting that his Department has still yet to be informed of details relating to the use of the Autons, or of extracts from 'Shada', in 'The Five Doctors' and so can't pay the usage fees. He asks John to confirm that both were used, and also for the duration of the 'Shada' material.

Commentary: The decision to remove the one scene involving the Autons from 'The Five Doctors' prior to production obviously hadn't been communicated back to the Copyright Department.

Thursday 15th:
Itinerary: Today is the first day of the three-day first studio block for 'The Caves of Androzani' in studio TC6 at BBC Television Centre.

Friday 16th:
Itinerary: Today is the second day of the three-day first studio block for 'The Caves of Androzani' in studio TC6 at BBC Television Centre.

Saturday 17th:
Itinerary: Today is the third and final day of the first studio block for 'The Caves of Androzani' in studio TC6 at BBC Television Centre.

Tuesday 20th:
Itinerary: Roger Hughes from the *Radio Times* writes to John, thanking him for penning a reply to viewers' letters about 'The Five Doctors' in the latest issue of the magazine.

Friday 30th – Monday 9th January:
Rehearsals for the second studio block of 'The Caves of Androzani' take place at the BBC Television Rehearsal Rooms at Acton.

---

[310] Production 6T will eventually be allocated to the story 'Attack of the Cybermen'

1984

Setting the Scene:

In the previous 12 months, John's fan-orientated activities had really taken off. He'd made no fewer than five trips to the US to attend conventions during the year, and had been the pivotal figure in ensuring the BBC's own event at Longleat House at Easter got off the ground. It could be argued that he was now in danger of spreading himself too thinly, given the needs of his 'day job', which had become ever more demanding.

John was overseeing arguably the biggest overhaul of the show in its history, with Tegan, Turlough, Kamelion and the fifth Doctor all bowing out, and Peri and the sixth Doctor being introduced, all within the space of four stories. His casting of Colin Baker to succeed Peter Davison as the Doctor had met with a lukewarm response within fandom, and there was evidence that the general public were not completely enthused by the decision. On top of all this, John was soon to be forced to reformat Baker's first full run in the TARDIS as a season of thirteen 45-minute episodes.

Not only had John managed to get the anniversary special made this past year, he had also had the final season of 26 traditional-duration 25-minute episodes to navigate, and by the end of December, Davison's last story was almost mid-way through production. Colin Baker had yet to step foot inside the studio, but John had already made the decision to have his new costume designed to be as tasteless as possible; a move that could be argued to have completely undermined the sixth Doctor's characterisation from the outset.

Stripped of its usual recognisable format, and of its popular leading man, and with the hearty backslapping of the twentieth anniversary quickly fading away, *Doctor Who* was suddenly looking a very vulnerable show. Now, more than ever, it needed a producer who could stay focused on the job in hand. Cheap gimmicks and an increase in fan involvement, coupled with a business-as-usual approach, could be a very dangerous gambit indeed …

JANUARY

Thursday 5th:
'Warriors of the Deep' Part One screens on BBC1.

Friday 6th:
Itinerary: Brian Turner from BBC Copyright writes to John, again asking for the duration of the 'Shada' material used in 'The Five Doctors', so that the appropriate fees can be paid. 'Warriors of the Deep' Part Two screens on BBC1.

Monday 9th:
Itinerary: Today is the Producer's Run at the BBC Television Rehearsal Rooms at Acton for the second studio block of 'The Caves of Androzani'.

Tuesday 10th:
Itinerary: This was meant to be the first day of the three-day first studio block for 'The Twin Dilemma' at BBC Television Centre. Instead, these dates have been reallocated to 'The Caves of Androzani', so recording of 'The Twin Dilemma' has been put back. Colin Baker is unveiled to press in the sixth Doctor's costume for the first time, at a photocall in Hammersmith Park. During the photocall, John starts spreading a rumour amongst the attending members of the press that he's considering changing the TARDIS's appearance, and ditching the police box exterior for good. The idea has no basis in fact – John is merely using it as a way of grabbing press headlines. On the same day, John signs off the commissions for Paula Woolsey to write one 50 minute script for 'The Cold War' Part One[311], and for Andrew Smith to write a scene breakdown for 'The First Sontarans'.[312]

Eric Saward: 'Ian Levine … produced a couple of pages that contained an idea [for "The Cold War"] – a very brief outline. I effectively wrote the whole script. Yes, Ian came up with some ideas, I will give him that credit, but he gives the impression that the whole concept was his. Ian is so keen to be seen as a major contributor to the story of *Doctor Who*. Hah, I wish him luck! Despite what Ian has said [to the contrary], Paula [Woolsey] *did* make a minor contribution, although she gets all the money, which isn't particularly fair. We

---

[311] 'The Cold War' would eventually become 'Attack of the Cybermen'. The writer was credited as 'Paula Moore' on screen.
[312] 'The First Sontarans' would be abandoned once Robert Holmes was asked to incorporate the Sontarans into 'The Two Doctors'.

don't talk anymore. Ian's contribution to *Doctor Who* was small and relatively superficial. He likes to call himself "script executive", but that would mean that John and I consulted him on scripts and stories, which we never did. We asked him about historical facts, because he had it all in his head. That was his function. He was invaluable to me, as a script editor who just didn't have time to sit down and look at a lot of old episodes.'[313]

John Nathan-Turner: 'I met the credited writer, Paula Moore, several times at meetings in my office, and she was often in script editor Eric Saward's office discussing the script. I knew that Paula was a friend of Saward's, he was honest about that, but if this script was totally written by Saward and Ian Levine, and not Ms Moore, as has been claimed, then I know nothing about it … What the hell was going on I do not know, but Ms Moore did come along to the studio recordings. If some backstage deal had been struck, I was blissfully unaware and still am.'[314]

Commentary: The exact machinations that went on between Eric Saward, Ian Levine and Paula Moore/Woolsey regarding the writing of the scripts for 'Attack of the Cybermen' are clouded by claim and counter-claim. What *is* clear is that, for whatever reason, Saward felt that he couldn't be entirely honest and open with John about the scripting of the story. This was surely a sign that things were not entirely rosy behind the scenes on *Doctor Who*.

Wednesday 11th:
Itinerary: Today is the first day of the two-day second studio block for 'The Caves of Androzani' in studio TC6 at BBC Television Centre.

Thursday 12th:
Itinerary: Today is the second and final day of the second studio block for 'The Caves of Androzani' in studio TC6 at BBC Television Centre. Colin Baker records his first scene as the sixth Doctor. 'Warriors of the Deep' Part Three screens on BBC1.

Commentary: A party is held in one of the BBC's hospitality suites for Peter Davison as he departs from the role of the Doctor for the last time today. In attendance are Matthew Waterhouse, Sarah Sutton, Janet Fielding, Mark Strickson, Gerald Flood and Anthony Ainley, all of whom also recorded earlier in the day their cameo appearances as disembodied character heads for the regeneration sequence. Colin Baker also attends the party.

---

[313] Eric Saward interview, *Doctor Who Magazine* #348.
[314] John Nathan-Turner memoirs, *Doctor Who Magazine* #239.

Friday 13th:
'Warriors of the Deep' Part Four screens on BBC1.

Saturday 14th – Monday 23rd:
Rehearsals for the first studio block of 'The Twin Dilemma' take place at the BBC Television Rehearsal Rooms at Acton.

Thursday 19th:
Itinerary: John signs off the commission for Tony Rudlin and Ingrid Pitt to write a 50-minute script for 'The Macro Men' Part One.[315] 'The Awakening' Part One screens on BBC1.

Friday 20th:
Itinerary: John writes to David Reid, asking that Sarah Hellings be engaged to direct story 6X, on dates between 28 August and 28 December 1984. 'The Awakening' Part Two screens on BBC1.

Monday 23rd:
Itinerary: Today is the Producer's Run at the BBC Television Rehearsal Rooms at Acton for the first studio block of 'The Twin Dilemma'.

Tuesday 24th:
Itinerary: John writes to the BBC Contract Department, asking them to engage Frazer Hines to appear as Jamie in story 6W – three 45-minute episodes. Today is the first day of the three-day first studio block for 'The Twin Dilemma' in studio TC8 at BBC Television Centre.

Wednesday 25th:
Itinerary: Today is the second day of the three-day first studio block for 'The Twin Dilemma' in studio TC8 at BBC Television Centre.

Thursday 26th:
Itinerary: John fully costs the projected filming of part of story 6W in America. Today is the third and final day of the first studio block for 'The Twin Dilemma' in studio TC8 at BBC Television Centre. 'Frontios' Part One screens on BBC1.

Friday 27th:
Itinerary: John Leeson's agent, Marjorie Abel, contacts the *Doctor Who* Production Office to inform John that the cancellation fee due from *Nationwide*

---

[315] 'The Macro Men' was developed no further as a potential story after this script – which was retitled 'The Macros' on delivery.

to John Leeson going back to November 1981 has *still* not been paid. John writes a furious letter to the editor of *Nationwide*, pointing out that both Leeson and Elisabeth Sladen cooperated to their fullest and set aside part of their day off to appear on the programme. He demands to know why Leeson still has yet to receive his fee. On the same day, he signs off the commission for Eric Saward to write a scene breakdown for 'The End of the Road'.[316] 'Frontios' Part Two screens on BBC1.

Saturday 28th – Monday 13th February:
Rehearsals for the second studio block of 'The Twin Dilemma' take place at the BBC Television Rehearsal Rooms at Acton.

FEBRUARY

Thursday 2nd:
Itinerary: John writes to Brain Turner at the BBC Copyright Department, confirming the duration of the 'Shada' material used in 'The Five Doctors'. On the dame day, he signs off the commission for Ian Marter to write a scene breakdown for 'Strange Encounter'.[317] 'Frontios' Part Three screens on BBC1. Sometime on or before this date, John flies from the UK to Florida, USA.

Friday 3rd:
'Frontios' Part Four screens on BBC1.

Friday 3rd – Sunday 5th:
Itinerary: John is a guest at the Omnicon V convention, held at the Oceanside Holiday Inn, Fort Lauderdale in Florida. Other guests include Colin Baker, Nicola Bryant, Nicholas Courtney and Anthony Ainley. Baker and Bryant have been released from rehearsals for 'The Twin Dilemma' in order to attend the event.

Monday 6th:
Itinerary: John (along with Colin Baker and Nicola Bryant) flies back from Florida to London, to be back in time for the location filming for 'The Twin Dilemma'.

---

[316] The exact delivery date of the scene breakdown of what would eventually become 'Revelation of the Daleks' isn't known.
[317] This potential story idea is soon abandoned.

Tuesday 7th:
Itinerary: Today is the first day of location filming for the 'The Twin Dilemma', at C J Wren & Sons, Springwell Quarry in Rickmansworth, Hertfordshire. On the same day, John signs off the commission for Chris Boucher to write a scene breakdown for an untitled story.[318]

Commentary: Unusually, the location filming for this story takes place between the first and second studio blocks, rather than in advance. This is a knock-on effect of the late-in-the-day rescheduling of the studio dates.

Wednesday 8th:
Itinerary: Today is the second and final day of location filming for 'The Twin Dilemma', now at Gerrards Cross Sand Pit and Gravel Pit, Wapsey's Wood in Buckinghamshire. 'Resurrection of the Daleks' Part One screens on BBC1.[319]

Thursday 9th:
Itinerary: John writes to BBC Contracts, asking that Graeme Harper be booked to direct story 6Z, between 12 December 1984 and 8 March 1985.

Monday 13th:
Itinerary: Today is the Producer's Run at the BBC Television Rehearsal Rooms at Acton for the second studio block of 'The Twin Dilemma'. Andrew Smith delivers his story outline for 'The Last Sontaran' to the *Doctor Who* Production Office. John signs off the commission for Robert Holmes to write a 45-minute script for 'The Kraalon Inheritance' Part One.[320]

Tuesday 14th:
Itinerary: Today is the first day of the three-day second studio block for 'The Twin Dilemma' in studio TC3 at BBC Television Centre. On the same day, John writes to Brian Turner at the BBC legal Department, asking that he negotiate for the rights to use the Cybermen in story 6T ('Attack of the Cybermen').

---

[318] This unnamed story never gets developed further.
[319] 'Resurrection of the Daleks' was written and made as a traditional four-part story, which should have been shown on BBC1 on Thursday 9th, Friday 10th, Thursday 16th and Friday 17th February 1984. However, the BBC made a late change in their TV schedules to allow coverage of the Winter Olympics in Sarajevo, which claimed these transmission slots. Rather than have a two-week pause in Season 21, John instead took up the option of re-editing the story into two 50-minute episodes which were given a Wednesday evening slot on BBC1.
[320] The exact delivery date of Holmes' script for Part One of what would become 'The Two Doctors' isn't recorded, although the commission stipulated delivery by Monday 5 March.

Wednesday 15th:
Itinerary: Today is the second day of the three-day second studio block for 'The Twin Dilemma' in studio TC3 at BBC Television Centre. On the same day, John writes to Marcia Wheeler at BBC Enterprises, outlining his proposal to film the location material for 'The Kraalon Inheritance' in New Orleans, USA, and includes his budget calculations. He asks that BBC Enterprises consider providing some co-funding, to meet the projected additional costs involved. 'Resurrection of the Daleks' Part Two screens on BBC1.

Thursday 16th:
Itinerary: Today is the third and final day of the second studio block for 'The Twin Dilemma' in studio TC8 at BBC Television Centre. This concludes production on *Doctor Who*'s twenty-first season, although there is some post-production and editing work still to be done.

Friday 17th:
Itinerary: John is a guest on Radio 4's *Feedback* programme, presented by Simon Bates. The main topic of conversation is the rumoured change of appearance of the TARDIS, John having hinted at Colin Baker's introductory press photocall that he was considering ditching the police box for good.

Saturday 18th:
Itinerary: John is a guest at the DWAS's Inter-Face III convention, held at the Bloomsbury Crest Hotel in London. He assures the attendees that the TARDIS will not be changing shape.

Tuesday 21st:
Itinerary: Paula Woolsey delivers her script for 'The Cold War' Part One to the *Doctor Who* Production Office. John signs off the commission for her to write the 50-minute script for Part Two.

Thursday 23rd:
'Planet of Fire' Part One screens on BBC1.

Friday 24th:
'Planet of Fire' Part Two screens on BBC1.

Saturday 25th:
Itinerary: John appears as a sole guest from *Doctor Who* on the BBC1 Saturday morning programme *Saturday Superstore*. He discusses the idea of changing the TARDIS's shape away from that of a police box. He says that his favourite story of those he's produced to date is 'The Keeper of Traken', although he promises that 'The Twin Dilemma' will be very good too. Later, he joins the

Pop Panel, and offers his thoughts on three new single releases: 'Breaking Point' by Bourgie Bourgie, 'Don't Answer Me' by the Alan Parsons Project and 'Burning Flame' by Vitamin Z.

MARCH

Thursday 1st:
'Planet of Fire' Part Three screens on BBC1.

Friday 2nd:
'Planet of Fire' Part Four screens on BBC1.

Thursday 8th:
Itinerary: Robert Holmes delivers his script for 'The Kraalon Inheritance' Part One to the *Doctor Who* Production Office. 'The Caves of Androzani' Part One screens on BBC1.

Friday 9th:
Itinerary: John signs off the commission for Robert Holmes to write the 45-minute scripts for 'The Kraalon Inheritance' Parts Two and Three.[321] 'The Caves of Androzani' Part Two screens on BBC1.

Tuesday 13th:
Itinerary: Philip Martin delivers his third-draft 50-minute scripts for 'Planet of Fear' Parts One and Two to the *Doctor Who* Production Office.

Wednesday 14th:
Itinerary: Paula Woolsey delivers her script for 'The Cold War' Part Two to the *Doctor Who* Production Office.

Thursday 15th:
Itinerary: Colin Baker and Nicola Bryant attend a press photocall in their 'The Twin Dilemma' costumes. Colin Baker – still in costume – later appears live on the edition of *Blue Peter* shown that evening on BBC1, interviewed by Janet Ellis. 'The Caves of Androzani' Part Three screens on BBC1.

---

[321] The exact delivery date of Holmes' script for Parts Two and Three of what would become 'The Two Doctors' isn't recorded.

Friday 16th:
'The Caves of Androzani' Part Four screens on BBC1.

Saturday 17th:
Itinerary: Colin Baker and Nicola Bryant are guests on the live BBC1 morning programme *Saturday Superstore*. They are both in their 'The Twin Dilemma' costumes, and Anthony Ainley phones in, in character as the Master.

Monday 19th:
Itinerary: Writer Anthony Steven writes to John to thank him for allowing him to bring his children in for a studio visit on the afternoon of 16 February, the final recording day for his story 'The Twin Dilemma'. He also refutes rumours that Eric Saward has told him are circulating within the BBC to the effect that he is angry and bitter about script editing changes made to the story's last episode; he assures John that this is not the case, and that he considers Saward an excellent and innovative editor. Also on this date, Brenda Gardner of Piccadilly Press writes to John, inviting him to author a non-fiction *Doctor Who* book for them, possibly to include illustrations by Andrew Skilleter.[322]

Tuesday 20th:
Itinerary: Peter Davison and Colin Baker appear as guests on the live early-evening BBC1 chat show *Harty*.

Thursday 22nd:
Itinerary: Colin Baker and Nicola Bryant are guests on the BBC's *Breakfast Time* programme. 'The Twin Dilemma' Part One screens on BBC1.

Friday 23rd:
'The Twin Dilemma' Part Two screens on BBC1.

Monday 26th:
Itinerary: John's secretary Sarah Lee signs on his behalf a reply he has written to the 19 March letter from Piccadilly Press's Brenda Gardner, in which he tells her that he is interested in her proposal for him to write a *Doctor Who* book and will see about getting an appropriate license agreed. He says that he would like to meet Gardner and Skilleter in early May to talk over ideas, after he has returned from a period out of the country. On the same date, John sends Sarah Bird of BBC Contracts a memo, asking her to book David Banks to play the Cyberleader in 'Attack of the Cybermen'.

---

[322] John would agree to this request, eventually resulting in the publication of his book *The TARDIS Inside Out* the following year.

Tuesday 27th:
Itinerary: John writes to Jonathan Powell, thanking him for allowing him to commission Eric Saward to write a story, in two 45-minute episodes, for Season 22.[323] He suggests that the commission be made when Saward's current contract as script editor expires on 27 July, and that he then be given a break of six weeks to write the scripts before being re-contracted.

Eric Saward: 'My scripts certainly got darker and more violent as the years went by. "Revelation of the Daleks" is almost cannibalistic! I'd been disappointed with "Resurrection [of the Daleks]" and felt I was sitting on the back of "Earthshock", so I told John that I wanted to write another story. Jonathan Powell [the Head of Series and Serials] insisted that I come off contract to write it. I didn't mind, although I greatly appreciated John fighting my corner. He got very angry on my behalf.'[324]

Thursday 29th:
'The Twin Dilemma' Part Three screens on BBC1.

Friday 30th:
Itinerary: John writes to the Head of Series and Serials, requesting that Peter Moffatt's engagement for directing story 6W be bought forward by two extra weeks, and also asks that Gary Downie be allocated as Production Manager to the story, at Peter's request. 'The Twin Dilemma' Part Four screens on BBC1.

APRIL

Undated:
John goes on annual leave from the BBC in late March, and spends much of April travelling with his partner, Gary Downie. They visit San Francisco and Hawaii in America, Sydney in Australia, and Hong Kong. While in Australia, John makes a trip to ABC TV, who have just in February returned a previously-missing 1960s episode of *Doctor Who*[325], to see if there is any possibility of other missing BBC material still residing in their archives. Unfortunately, his enquiries draw a blank.

---

323 The story would eventually become 'Revelation of the Daleks'.
324 Eric Saward interview, *Doctor Who Magazine* #348.
325 The recovered episode was a 16mm film print of the fourth instalment of the William Hartnell story 'The Celestial Toymaker', entitled 'The Final Test'.

Tuesday 3rd:
Itinerary: John writes to Sarah Bird of BBC Contracts, asking that Maurice Colbourne be engaged to play Lytton in 'Attack of the Cybermen'.

Commentary: The memo is written in the third person, so was probably dictated to, and sent by, John's secretary, Sarah Lee, in John's absence.

Wednesday 4th:
Itinerary: Director Sarah Hellings writes to John, thanking him for inviting her to direct 'The Mark of the Rani' later in the year, which she is looking forward to doing.

Wednesday 11th:
Itinerary: David Lloyd from BBC Contracts writes to John to inform him that he's as yet received no response from Graeme Harper regarding the offer to direct story 6Z.

Monday 16th:
Itinerary: Ronnie Marsh, acting as assistant to the new BBC Head of Serials, Jonathan Powell, informs the *Doctor Who* Production Office that extra funding would not be forthcoming from BBC Enterprises for the filming of 'The Kraalon Inheritance' in New Orleans.

John Nathan-Turner: 'I went away on my annual leave and, as usual, regularly rang base camp to see how things were progressing. My new production associate, Sue Anstruther, told me we'd lost the co-production money, which meant we couldn't afford all those US flights and accommodation. She asked me where I wanted to re-set the story. Venice was my first choice, but we were unable to find attractive (i.e. cheap) transportation. Sue suggested Seville in Spain as an economical alternative, which would mean the scripts wouldn't have to be totally rewritten. For "plantation house" read "hacienda", Missouri banks became olive groves and French Quarter became old Spanish Quarter. This is an over-simplification, of course, but the Spanish choice did mean the work on the scripts could be achieved more rapidly.'[326]

Eric Saward: 'John was away somewhere, probably at a US convention, and Sue Anstruther and I had this conversation about St Louis. She'd done the costings and it was horrendously expensive. So it had to be somewhere in Europe, and the first choice was Venice until it was pointed out that it would be impossible to do this in August, but John was adamant that the story was

---

[326] John Nathan-Turner memoirs, *Doctor Who Magazine* #239.

set abroad. Now Bob [Holmes] had written the original story set in St Louis, and there were quite serious changes to be made because, in spite of what John thought, you can't transfer a story from an English-speaking country to a Spanish-speaking country, particularly when you have verbal jokes and play on words and so on. It was quite a major rethink. Anyway, Bob went away after discussion and reworked the material to be set in Spain.'[327]

Tuesday 17th:
Itinerary: Eric Saward writes to John, informing him that he will be writing additional material for 'Attack of the Cybermen' as Matthew Robinson has found both episodes to be under-running.

Tuesday 24th:
Itinerary: Jonathan Powell [328], the new BBC Head of Series and Serials – and John's new boss – writes to John, having read the scripts for 'Attack of the Cybermen'. He praises the scripts, thinking the story is 'well told' with 'decent characterisation'.

Wednesday 25th:
Itinerary: Now in Australia, John attends a *Doctor Who* fan event in Sydney. On the same day, he dictates a letter to his secretary, Sarah Lee, to send to actor Tim Raynham, who has written in to the *Doctor Who* Production Office enclosing his details. John asks that Raynham contact Lee and arrange for a meeting in May.[329]

MAY

Tuesday 8th:
Itinerary: John returns to the *Doctor Who* Production Office after over a month of annual leave.

---

[327] Eric Saward interview, *DWB* #58.
[328] Jonathan Powell had been the producer of 'serious' BBC dramas, such as *Tinker, Tailor, Soldier, Spy* and *Smiley's People*, in the 1970s and early 1980s. He had succeeded David Reid as BBC Head of Series and Serials in late 1983, becoming John Nathan-Turner's immediate boss. He would later be promoted to BBC Head of Drama in 1985, replacing Graeme McDonald. For whatever reason, Powell was no fan of *Doctor Who*, and his dislike of the show would soon become apparent …
[329] Raynham would be offered the role of a Sontaran named Varl in 'The Two Doctors' later in the year.

Wednesday 9th:
Itinerary: John writes to Sarah Bird in the BBC Contracts Department, asking that John Lewis be engaged to compose the music for story 6X.[330]

Friday 11th:
Itinerary: Nicola Bryant is contracted to appear in a minimum of ten 45-minute episodes of Season 22, with an option on the BBC's side for the entirety of the season.[331]

Monday 14th:
Itinerary: John receives a (typed) letter from Paula Woolsey, thanking him for letting her write 'Attack of the Cybermen'. She says that she might not be able to attend the script read-through but hopes to meet him during the studio recordings.

Tuesday 15th:
Itinerary: John writes to Patrick Troughton, sending him the draft scripts of 'The Kraalon Inheritance', explaining that it will be retitled 'The Two Doctors', and that filming will now be in Spain and not America. On the same day, John requests that Alec Wheal and Camera Crew 11 be allocated to *Doctor Who* for the entirety of the studio recordings for Season 22. From 2.30pm he attends a preliminary planning meeting for 'Attack of the Cybermen' in the Conference Room at Threshold House.

Wednesday 16th:
Itinerary: John informs the BBC Copyright Department that, due to the location moving from New Orleans to Spain, Robert Holmes has had to be re-briefed to rewrite his scripts for 'The Kraalon Inheritance', now renamed 'The Androgum Inheritance'.

Thursday 17th:
Itinerary: At the request of Graeme Harper, John writes to Roger Reece at the BBC Costume Department, requesting that Andrew Rose be allocated as costume designer to story 6Z.[332]

---

[330] Lewis completed almost 21 minutes' worth of incidental music for the story before falling ill and being forced to withdraw from the project. Jonathan Gibbs was bought in as a late replacement to provide the score.
[331] This option was taken up, and Nicola Bryant featured in all 13 episodes of the season.
[332] Rose had previously designed the costumes for 'The Caves of Androzani', which Harper directed. Pat Godfrey would eventually be allocated as costume designer for 'Revelation of the Daleks'.

Monday 28th:
Itinerary: Rehearsals for the location filming of 'Attack of the Cybermen' take place at the BBC Television Rehearsal Rooms at Acton.

Tuesday 29th:
Itinerary: Today is the first day of location filming for 'Attack of the Cybermen', on Glenthorne Road, Hammersmith in London.

Wednesday 30th:
Itinerary: Patrick Troughton writes to John, thanking him for sending him the scripts of 'The Two Doctors'. He thinks they're very good, and very funny, but requests a double for any running sequences shot in Spain in the summer heat. He also suggests some ideas for comedic moments during location filming. Today is the second day of location filming for 'Attack of the Cybermen', now at Gerrards Cross Sand and Gravel Pit in Wapsey's Wood, Buckinghamshire.

Thursday 31st:
Itinerary: Today is the third and final day of location filming for 'Attack of the Cybermen', at Gerrards Cross Sand and Gravel Pit in Wapsey's Wood, Buckinghamshire. On the same day, John writes to Jenny Hanley, offering her the role of Rost in the studio sequences of 'Attack of the Cybermen'. John mentions they'd previously met at a party hosted by John Mahoney (Peter Davison's agent). [333]

JUNE

Wednesday 6th:
Itinerary: John confirms to the BBC Head of Copyright that Robert Holmes' story – previously titled 'The Kraalon Inheritance' and 'The Androgum Inheritance' – is now called 'The Two Doctors'. On the same day, he writes to Sarah Bird in the BBC Contracts department, asking that Anthony Ainley be engaged to play the Master in story 6X.

Friday 8th – Wednesday 20th:
Rehearsals for the first studio block of 'Attack of the Cybermen' take place at

---

[333] Jenny Hanley was best known at this point for her work presenting the ITV children's magazine programme *Magpie* in the 1970s. Koo Stark was eventually cast as Rost, but then dropped out due to contractual issues, leaving little time for the role to be recast. Sarah Berger eventually took the role.

the BBC Television Rehearsal Rooms at Acton.

Tuesday 12th:
Itinerary: Jonathan Powell writes to John, authorising him to record some material for 'Attack of the Cybermen' in the afternoon when in the studio. Powell adds that such deviations from the norm usually occur only when children are required in the studio, and warns that such a move should not become a norm on *Doctor Who*. Today is also a photocall for 'Attack of the Cybermen', where Colin Baker is joined by Faith Brown and Koo Stark, who in the story will be playing the Cryons Flast and Rost respectively. Solicitors acting for Koo Stark write to John today, confirming last-minute demands made to him over the phone the previous evening, that only BBC photographers be present at the photocall; that no press be allowed to attend; that, prior to publication, Stark be given final approval on all photos and any quotes she might have given; and that Stark's own photographer be allowed to take shots of her, but no-one else.

Commentary: Koo Stark had dated Prince Andrew between 1981 and 1983, and consequently her life and career were of great interest to the tabloid newspapers. John's decision to cast her in 'Attack of the Cybermen' would have been taken in full knowledge of this, and presumably he sought to profit from the resulting publicity. However, it seems he failed to anticipate the demands the actress would make regarding how the publicity was handled.

Wednesday 13th:
Itinerary: John contacts Koo Stark's solicitors, stating that he is not prepared to offer her any privileges above and beyond those he would give any other actress engaged on a standard Equity contract. If Stark is not prepared to accept this, then he insists that she withdraw from the role. He asks for an answer by 3.00pm.

Thursday 14th:
Itinerary: John writes to Cheryl Dural of Type-Forty Graphics in New Orleans[334], thanking her for her catalogue of products. From this, John orders forty Sontaran badges to give to the cast and crew of 'The Two Doctors'. Solicitors acting on behalf of Koo Stark write to John, saying that her agent has been notified that the offer of the role of Rost has been withdrawn, but that she should still be paid her fee for it. The solicitors request that the publicity photos she has posed for not be used by the BBC. Sometime on or before this date, John flies from the UK to Ohio, USA.

---

[334] Presumably one of the many US-based fans who at this time had their own cottage industries making *Doctor Who* merchandise.

Friday 15th:
Itinerary: Jonathan Powell writes to John, having read the scripts for 'Vengeance on Varos' Part One and 'The Two Doctors' Part One. He states he has enjoyed the latter, and found the former to be 'excellent.'

Friday 15th – Sunday 17th:
Itinerary: John is a guest at the Time Festival – Panopticon West IV (aka DWExpo '84) convention, held at the Quality Inn Hotel, Columbus in Ohio. Other guests include Colin Baker (and his wife, Marion Wyatt) and Gary Downie (John's partner). Baker is released from rehearsals for 'Attack of the Cybermen' so he can attend the event.

Commentary: John subsequently wrote a lengthy review of this event for #94 of Marvel's *Doctor Who Magazine*.

Monday 18th:
Itinerary: John and Gary (along with Colin Baker and his wife) fly back from Ohio to London.

Tuesday 19th:
Itinerary: John signs off the commission for Christopher H Bidmead to write a scene breakdown for an untitled story.[335]

Wednesday 20th:
Itinerary: Jonathan Powell writes to John after reading the scripts for 'Vengeance on Varos' Part Two and 'The Two Doctors' Part Three, saying he found them enjoyable. From 10.30am, John attends the Producer's Run at the BBC Television Rehearsal Rooms at Acton for the first studio block of 'Attack of the Cybermen'.

Thursday 21st:
Itinerary: Today is the first day of the two-day first studio block for 'Attack of the Cybermen' in studio TC6 at BBC Television Centre. John drafts a response to Koo Stark's solicitors and sends it to Stephen Hanlon at the BBC Legal Department for his thoughts.

Friday 22nd:
Itinerary: Today is the second and final day of the first studio block for 'Attack of the Cybermen' in studio TC6 at BBC Television Centre.

---

[335] This would eventually become 'In the Hollows of Time', featuring the returns both of the Master and of the Tractators from 'Frontios'.

Monday 25th – Wednesday 4th July:
Rehearsals for the second studio block of 'Attack of the Cybermen' take place at the BBC Television Rehearsal Rooms at Acton.

JULY

Monday 2nd:
Itinerary: In the morning, John attends a planning meeting at BBC Television Centre for the first studio block of 'Vengeance on Varos'. Later in the day, he writes to Jonathan Powell, informing him that the first studio block of 'Attack of the Cybermen' went without a hitch, and without any overrun. Stephen Hanlon from the BBC Legal Department writes to John with a revised draft reply for Koo Stark's solicitors.

Wednesday 4th:
Itinerary: Today is the Producer's Run at the BBC Television Rehearsal Rooms at Acton for the second studio block of 'Attack of the Cybermen'.

Friday 6th:
Itinerary: Today is the first day of the three-day second studio block for 'Attack of the Cybermen' in studio TC6 at BBC Television Centre. 'The King's Demons' Part One is repeated on BBC1.

Saturday 7th:
Itinerary: Today is the second day of the three-day second studio block for 'Attack of the Cybermen' in studio TC6 at BBC Television Centre.

Sunday 8th:
Itinerary: Today is the third and final day of the second studio block for 'Attack of the Cybermen' in studio TC6 at BBC Television Centre.

Monday 9th:
Itinerary: In the morning, John attends a full cast read-through of the script of 'Vengeance on Varos' at the BBC Rehearsal Rooms at Acton. The same day, John writes to Koo Stark's solicitors, assuring them that the photos of Stark, taken with Colin Baker and Faith Brown, will not be published.

Monday 9th – Tuesday 17th:
Rehearsals for the first studio block of 'Vengeance on Varos' take place at the BBC Television Rehearsal Rooms at Acton.

Wednesday 11th:
Itinerary: John writes Brian Clifford at BBC Picture Publicity, instructing that the photos taken of Faith Brown as Flast during the studio recording on Friday 6 July must not be used for publicity, as Brown's costume and make-up were altered after the photos were taken.

Thursday 12th:
Itinerary: John writes a lengthy 'Producer's Diary' article for the DWFCA newsletter. He writes as if he's already in Seville, mid-way through the filming of 'The Two Doctors', although this is still nearly a month away. He also mentions his upcoming appearance at the Stoneleigh Agricultural Show at the National Agricultural Centre over the coming August bank holiday.

Friday 13th:
Itinerary: John signs off the commission for Eric Saward to write the two 45-minute scripts for 'The End of the Road.'[336] He also writes to BBC Contracts, asking for them to negotiate with Terry Nation's agent, Roger Hancock, for the rights to use Davros and the Daleks in Saward's story. On the same day, he writes to the actress Sarah Badel, with whom he worked on *The Pallisers*, offering her the role of the Rani in 'The Mark of the Rani'. He also writes to Pennie Bloomfield, thanking her for her work as AFM on 'Attack of the Cybermen'. 'The King's Demons' Part Two is repeated on BBC1.

Monday 16th:
Itinerary: In the morning, John attends a planning meeting at the BBC Rehearsal Rooms in Acton for the second studio block of 'Vengeance on Varos'.

Tuesday 17th:
Itinerary: Today is the Producer's Run at the BBC Television Rehearsal Rooms at Acton for the first studio block of 'Vengeance on Varos'. Charles Jeanes from the BBC Visual Effects Department writes to John regarding the buggy to be used in the studio for 'Vengeance on Varos'. The chassis has already been purchased by BBC Enterprises, but the cost of converting it into the required form needs agreeing separately from the rest of the design budget for this story.

Wednesday 18th:
Itinerary: Today is the first day of the three-day first studio block for

---

[336] The exact delivery date of Saward's scripts for what will eventually be titled 'Revelation of the Daleks' isn't known. The scripts were formally accepted on Saturday 10 November 1984.

'Vengeance on Varos' in studio TC6 at BBC Television Centre.

Thursday 19th:
Itinerary: Details are finalised for the filming in Spain for 'The Two Doctors', with the cast and crew agreeing to reduced expenses rates for the shoot. Today is the second day of the three-day first studio block for 'Vengeance on Varos' in studio TC6 at BBC Television Centre.

Friday 20th:
Itinerary: Today is the third and final day of the first studio block for 'Vengeance on Varos' in studio TC6 at BBC Television Centre. A 50-minute compilation repeat of 'The Awakening' Parts One and Two is transmitted on BBC1.

Saturday 21st – Monday 30th:
Rehearsals for the second studio block of 'Vengeance on Varos' take place at the BBC Television Rehearsal Rooms at Acton.

Tuesday 24th:
Itinerary: John writes to Peter Pegrum at the BBC Visual Effects Department with a proposal to cover the budget shortfall incurred on the conversion of the guards' buggy for 'Vengeance on Varos', contingent on Charles Jeanes being allocated to work on the visual effects for story 6Y.[337]

Thursday 26th:
Itinerary: Sarah Badel writes to John, thanking him for the invitation to play the Rani, but declining.

Friday 27th:
Commentary: Eric Saward begins a six-week break from today. As he is now between contracts as script editor and technically freelance, he sets about writing the scripts for 'Revelation of the Daleks' while on holiday in Greece. John will have to deputise for Saward during this six-week period.

John Nathan-Turner: 'I didn't enjoy being a script editor as well as producer, I have to say. All the stuff for the future could wait, but I had to deal with the job in hand, which was 'The Two Doctors'. So I had to attend to all the day-to-day script changes from the director, and suggestions from the actors.'[338]

---

[337] Kevin Molloy is ultimately allocated to story 6Y ('Timelash') as Visual Effects Designer.
[338] John Nathan-Turner and Eric Saward interview, *Doctor Who Magazine* #104.

Monday 30th:
Itinerary: Today is the Producer's Run at the BBC Television Rehearsal Rooms at Acton for the second studio block of 'Vengeance on Varos'.

Tuesday 31st:
Itinerary: In the morning, there is a script read-through of 'The Two Doctors' in the conference room in Threshold House, with cast and crew. Later, this is the first day of the three-day second studio block for 'Vengeance on Varos' in studio TC6 at BBC Television Centre.

AUGUST

Wednesday 1st:
Itinerary: Today is the second day of the three-day second studio block for 'Vengeance on Varos' in studio TC6 at BBC Television Centre. John writes to Jonathan Powell, explaining that there were 30-minute overruns during the first and third days of the first studio block for this story. He attributes this to enforced late starts of the same duration, which were demanded by the studio's Lighting Director.

Thursday 2nd:
Itinerary: Today is the third and final day of the second studio block for 'Vengeance on Varos' in studio TC6 at BBC Television Centre. John writes to Jonathan Powell, explaining that there was a 47-minute delay in the studio on the previous day, due to the overnight studio reset not being begun until 7.30am. John also writes to David Myers, thanking him for the make-up work he did with Nabil Shaban as Sil during the production of 'Vengeance on Varos'. He also writes to Charles Jeanes at BBC Visual Effects, asking that Sil's costume and water tank prop be retained, as he plans to bring the character back in a future story. Before recording concludes, John takes a flight from London to California, USA.

Friday 3rd – Saturday 4th:
Itinerary: Rehearsals for the location filming of 'The Two Doctors' take place at the BBC Television Rehearsal Rooms at Acton.

Friday 3rd – Sunday 5th:
Itinerary: John is a guest at the Timecon 84 convention, held at the Sainte Claire Hotel Convention Centre in San Jose, California. Other guests at the event include Jon Pertwee, Nicholas Courtney and Gerry Davis.

Monday 6th:
Itinerary: John takes a flight back from California to London

Wednesday 8th:
Itinerary: John gets a flight from London to Seville in Spain, along with the rest of the cast and crew of 'The Two Doctors'. They arrive at the Hotel Los Lebreros in Seville, which will be the unit hotel for the duration of the location filming.

Thursday 9th:
Itinerary: Today is the first day of location filming for 'The Two Doctors'. This was supposed to take place at a hacienda in Cortijos, El Garrobo, but a last-minute change of plan has been prompted by the discovery that the wigs needed for the characters of Chessene (played by Jacqueline Pearce), Dastari (Laurence Payne) and the second Doctor (Patrick Troughton) have been mislaid. Filming instead takes place with other characters in the grounds of another hacienda, in Dehera Boyar, while replacement wigs are ordered from the UK.

Friday 10th:
Itinerary: Location filming for 'The Two Doctors' resumes in the grounds of the hacienda in Dehera Boyar.

Saturday 11th:
Itinerary: Location filming for 'The Two Doctors' continues in the grounds of the hacienda in Dehera Boyar. No replacement wigs have arrived from the UK, however Cathy Davies, in charge of make-up for the story, has created replacements by adapting wigs purchased in Spain, so Jacqueline Pearce, Laurence Payne and Patrick Troughton can begin filming their scenes.

Sunday 12th: (John's thirty-seventh birthday)
Itinerary: Location filming for 'The Two Doctors' resumes in the grounds of the hacienda in Dehera Boyar. Cast members James Saxon, Carmen Gomez, Tim Raynham and Clinton Greyn all return to the UK, having completed all the location scenes featuring their characters.

Monday 13th:
Itinerary: Today is scheduled as a day off for the cast and crew. John is informed via a phone call that some of the film material shot last week of the characters Oscar and Anita in the olive groves has been spoiled by a serious scratch running along the length of the negative. John has to ask Sue Anstruther to arrange for the relevant cast members, James Saxon and Carmen Gomez, to return to Spain to re-film the affected scenes. Also on this

day, John signs off the commission for Peter Grimwade to write a scene breakdown for 'League of the Tandreds'.[339] He also receives a letter from Koo Stark's solicitors querying the non-payment as yet of her fee for 'Attack of the Cybermen'.

John Nathan-Turner: 'James Saxon (Oscar) and Carmen Gomez (Anita), having completed their sequences within a few days, were sent back to London, thus saving money. Then we heard the news; on two shots there was a scratch on the negative which I was informed was extremely bad, so back from England came the two actors. It cost us more than if we'd given them a paid holiday for the rest of the shoot. It was about this time that I was becoming a little disenchanted with filming on location for *Doctor Who* rather than taping the shoot. Many more minutes could be achieved per day [with taping], and despite the caravanserai of OB vehicles and the added staff, the economics were certainly in OB's favour. Not that I actually prefer the quality of picture, but for *Doctor Who* it made sound financial sense. My disenchantment was enhanced when, returning to England, we viewed the unacceptable shots to discover the scratch was virtually unnoticeable.'[340]

Tuesday 14th:
Itinerary: Location filming for 'The Two Doctors' continues, now in the streets of Santa Cruz. Part One of a version of 'The Five Doctors' re-edited into four episodes, previously prepared by director Peter Moffatt for BBC Enterprises for overseas sales purposes, is repeated on BBC1.

Wednesday 15th:
Itinerary: Location filming for 'The Two Doctors' continues in the streets of Santa Cruz. James Saxon and Carmen Gomez arrive back in Spain to re-film their olive grove scenes the following day. Part Two of the re-edited repeat of 'The Five Doctors' is transmitted on BBC1.

Thursday 16th:
Itinerary: Location filming for 'The Two Doctors' resumes and concludes in the area around Rio Guadiamar. Part Three of the re-edited repeat of 'The Five Doctors' is transmitted on BBC1.

Friday 17th:
Itinerary: The cast and crew of 'The Two Doctors' depart on an early-morning

---

[339] This is the date on the commissioning paperwork, but John must have signed the form either before he left for Spain or on his return. Grimwade's proposed story didn't progress beyond this scene breakdown.
[340] John Nathan-Turner Memoirs, *Doctor Who Magazine* #239.

flight from Spain, and arrive back at Heathrow airport in London at around 12.30pm local time. A coach takes them back to BBC Television Centre. Part Four of the re-edited repeat of 'The Five Doctors' is transmitted on BBC1. This is the last *Doctor Who* repeat on the BBC during John's time as producer.

Monday 20th – Wednesday 29th:
Rehearsals for the first studio block of 'The Two Doctors' take place at the BBC Television Rehearsal Rooms at Acton.

Tuesday 21st:
Itinerary: John accompanies Colin Baker as, given time off from rehearsals, the actor travels to Blackpool and – in costume as the sixth Doctor – opens a new Space Invader attraction at the Blackpool Pleasure Beach amusement park.

Monday 27th (bank holiday):
Itinerary: John is a guest at the Stoneleigh Agricultural Show at the National Agricultural Centre, alongside Jon Pertwee. This is the third day of the show, which has had *Doctor Who* guests on the previous two days as well: Saturday's were Colin Baker and Elisabeth Sladen, Sunday's were Colin Baker and Janet Fielding.

Wednesday 29th:
Itinerary: Today is the Producer's Run at the BBC Television Rehearsal Rooms at Acton for the first studio block of 'The Two Doctors'. John signs off the commission for Philip Martin to write a storyline for 'Mission to Magnus'.

Thursday 30th:
Itinerary: Today is the first day of the two-day first studio block for 'The Two Doctors' in studio TC1 at BBC Television Centre.

Friday 31st:
Itinerary: Today is the second and final day of the first studio block for 'The Two Doctors' in studio TC1 at BBC Television Centre.

SEPTEMBER

Monday 3rd – Wednesday 12th:
Rehearsals for the second studio block of 'The Two Doctors' take place at the BBC Television Rehearsal Rooms at Acton.

Tuesday 4th:
Itinerary: John writes to Sarah Bird at BBC Contracts, asking her to engage Kate O'Mara to play the Rani in 'The Mark of the Rani'.

Wednesday 12th:
Itinerary: Today is the Producer's Run at the BBC Television Rehearsal Rooms at Acton for the second studio block of 'The Two Doctors'.

Thursday 13th:
Itinerary: Today is the first day of the two-day second studio block for 'The Two Doctors' in studio TC6 at BBC Television Centre. On the same day, John writes to Jose Abaurre in Sevilla, Spain, thanking him for help he gave the crew during location filming of 'The Two Doctors'.

Friday 14th:
Itinerary: Today is the second and final day of the second studio block for 'The Two Doctors' in studio TC6 at BBC Television Centre.

Monday 17th – Wednesday 26th:
Rehearsals for the third studio block of 'The Two Doctors' take place at the BBC Television Rehearsal Rooms at Acton.

Wednesday 19th:
Itinerary: John, director Fiona Cumming and her husband Ian Fraser form Teynham Productions Ltd. This is a company through which they will put on their own theatre productions.

Commentary: Teynham House in Saltdean was where John and Gary first lived in Brighton. Fiona Cumming and Ian Fraser also had a flat in the same building, so they decided to name their company after the property. Teynham's first production would be the pantomime *Cinderella*, which would run over the Christmas period later in the year.

Friday 21st:
Itinerary: Sarah McNeill, editor of the Radio 4 documentary series *Wavelength*, writes to John, thanking him for setting up interviews with the cast and crew of 'The Two Doctors' that were carried out during the previous week during the story's final studio block.

Monday 24th:
Itinerary: John writes to Jonathan Powell, explaining that there was a 15-minute overrun on the final day of the second studio block of 'The Two Doctors'. He attributes this to a complex studio session with time-consuming

effects and make-up changes. Matthew Robinson writes to John, expressing interest in returning to direct further stories in the future. He suggests that John join him for lunch in the next fortnight to discuss.

Tuesday 25th:
Itinerary: John signs off the commission for Graham Williams to write a story breakdown for a 2 x 45-minute story, 'Arcade', set at Blackpool's Pleasure Beach.

Commentary: John came up with the idea of setting a *Doctor Who* story at Blackpool's Pleasure Beach following his visit there with Colin Baker the previous month.

Wednesday 26th:
Itinerary: Today is the Producer's Run at the BBC Television Rehearsal Rooms at Acton for the third studio block of 'The Two Doctors'.

Thursday 27th:
Itinerary: Today is the first day of the two-day third studio block for 'The Two Doctors' in studio TC6 at BBC Television Centre.

Friday 28th:
Itinerary: Today is the second and final day of the third studio block for 'The Two Doctors' in studio TC6 at BBC Television Centre.

OCTOBER

Monday 1st:
Itinerary: John writes to Sarah McNeill and Pete Brown, editor and producer respectively of the recent installment of the Radio 4 show *Wavelength* that covered the production of 'The Two Doctors'. He thanks them for the plug this gave to *Doctor Who*.[341]

Saturday 13th:
Itinerary: John is a guest (alongside Colin Baker) at the DWAS's Who Con 21 convention, held at the Bloomsbury Crest Hotel in London.

---

[341] The edition of *Wavelength* that covered 'The Two Doctors' was transmitted on Thursday 20 September 1984.

Wednesday 17th – Saturday 20th:
Rehearsals for the location filming of 'The Mark of the Rani' take place at Baden Powell House in Queens Gate, SW7.

Thursday 18th:
Itinerary: Jon Butcher, the Promotions and Entertainment Manager of Blackpool Pleasure Beach, writes to John. He mentions that script editor Eric Saward has recently visited the attraction, and asks if they are any further forward in their idea for a *Doctor Who* story set there. He outlines a possible filming window next year, between the Easter and Spring bank holidays, when the rides will be open and available and the crowds small and manageable. Today is also a cast read-through of the script of 'The Mark of the Rani' from 10.30am in the Conference Room in BBC Threshold House.

Friday 19th:
Itinerary: John and Gary Downie fly out to Singapore to recce possible locations for a planned *Doctor Who* story to be filmed there in 1985, for *Doctor Who*'s twenty-third season. They stay in the Hotel Meridien for the week.

John Nathan-Turner: 'I had met a Mr Tan of the Singapore tourist board through Brian Clifford of BBC Picture Publicity, who'd just returned from a trip to Singapore with the *Tenko* programme, and Ken Riddington, the producer of *Tenko*. Mr Tan was very keen that programmes which had good foreign sales considered Singapore as a location venue. He invited me to visit Singapore for a few days to assess whether it was viable for *Doctor Who*. He gave me a mass of literature and books, and I felt fairly confident we could make good use of the place, as long as finances could be made attractive. I asked the management to allocate a production manager who would be free for the trip and who they could guarantee would be the production manager on the actual show, which was ages away. I would have taken my production associate, but she was only doing one season of the show. I was delighted when they allocated Gary Downie, and the two of us set off on our travels. The Tourist Board couldn't have been more helpful and supplied us with a bevy of guides and a minibus. They took us everywhere; the tourist spots, the beauty spots, ruins of wartime forts and historical places, including the famous Raffles hotel. The only problem was the intense heat. Most evenings there were spent in meetings with people who could be helpful if the shoot went ahead: more Tourist Board officials, airline representatives and hotel managers. I left Singapore with the most wonderful deal: £300 per head for return flight and bed and breakfast accommodation in a top hotel and unlimited shipping for equipment etc. It was to be a ten-day trip which worked out as a seven-day shoot, because of a day off and time to recover from jet lag.'[342]

Commentary: Although John's relationship with Gary Downie was common knowledge inside the BBC, John was very discrete in how he referred to Downie in his dealings with fandom and the media. And while John doubtless pulled strings to get Downie attached to various *Doctor Who* productions, Downie was by now working as a Production Manager at the BBC, and may well have landed the assignments on his own merit.

Saturday 20th:
Itinerary: In Singapore, John and Gary visit the *Instant Asia* show and take a tour of the city.

Sunday 21st:
Itinerary: In Singapore, John and Gary visit the Botanic Gardens.

Monday 22nd:
Itinerary: In Singapore, John and Gary visit the Chinese Garden, the Jurong Bird Park, and some junks (Chinese sail ships). Back in the UK, today is the first day of location filming for 'The Mark of the Rani', at the Granville Colliery Spoil Heaps in Donnington Wood in Shropshire.

Tuesday 23rd:
Itinerary: John is still in Singapore, but he and Gary have a day off from their location scouting. Back in the UK, filming for 'The Mark of the Rani' resumes, now relocated to the Ironbridge Gorge Open Air Museum at Blists Hill in Telford, Shropshire.

Wednesday 24th:
Itinerary: Still on their overseas trip, John and Gary visit the Singapore Zoo, the National Orchid Garden and the local opera. Back in the UK, filming for 'The Mark of the Rani' continues at the Ironbridge Gorge Open Air Museum at Blists Hill in Telford, Shropshire.

Thursday 25th:
Itinerary: John and Gary return to London. They bring with them video footage they have recorded on a BBC camcorder of their location scouting trip to Singapore. Meanwhile, filming for 'The Mark of the Rani' continues at the Ironbridge Gorge Open Air Museum at Blists Hill in Telford, Shropshire.

Eric Saward: 'Bob Holmes and I sat in a viewing room and we watched [the

---

[342] John Nathan-Turner memoirs, *Doctor Who Magazine* #240.

Singapore location scouting footage shot by John and Gary Downie], which was about forty minutes long, and afterwards we just shrugged and thought, "Well, what is the point of all this?" They had literally just driven around in a taxi and shot from the window. As anyone knows, you can only do location work on foot.'[343]

Friday 26th:
Itinerary: Filming for 'The Mark of the Rani' continues at the Ironbridge Gorge Open Air Museum at Blists Hill in Telford, Shropshire. John signs off the commission for Robert Holmes to write the 50-minute script for 'Yellow Fever And How To Cure It' Part One, to be set in Singapore.[344]

Saturday 27th:
Itinerary: Filming for 'The Mark of the Rani' continues at the Ironbridge Gorge Open Air Museum at Blists Hill in Telford, Shropshire. John finally joins the cast and crew at the unit hotel that evening, and hosts a party for his colleagues.

Sunday 28th:
Itinerary: It's a day off from filming for the cast and crew of 'The Mark of the Rani'.

Monday 29th:
Itinerary: Filming for 'The Mark of the Rani' resumes, now relocated to the Coalport China Works in Coalport, Telford, Shropshire.

Tuesday 30th:
Itinerary: Filming for 'The Mark of the Rani' returns to the Ironbridge Gorge Open Air Museum at Blists Hill in Telford, Shropshire.

Wednesday 31st:
Itinerary: John writes to the producer of BBC1's *The Late, Late Breakfast Show*, offering an outtake from 'The Two Doctors' of Frazer Hines getting his kilt caught up on a doorhandle for use in the 'Golden Egg Awards' section of their programme. Filming for 'The Mark of the Rani' continues at the Ironbridge Gorge Open Air Museum at Blists Hill in Telford, Shropshire. In the evening, John hosts a Halloween party for cast and crew at the unit hotel.

---

[343] Eric Saward and Ian Levine interview, *DWB* #106.
[344] At Robert Holmes' request, it was subsequently agreed that this commission should be put on hold temporarily, pending a final decision being made about the story's filming location.

NOVEMBER

Thursday 1st:
Itinerary: Filming for 'The Mark of the Rani' continues at the Ironbridge Gorge Open Air Museum at Blists Hill in Telford, Shropshire. On the same day, John dictates letters to his secretary, Sarah Lee, to send to Frazer Hines (Jamie), Carmen Gomez (Anita) and Laurence Payne (Dastari), thanking them for their performances in 'The Two Doctors'.

Friday 2nd:
Itinerary: The final scheduled day of location filming for 'The Mark of the Rani' concludes early at the Ironbridge Gorge Open Air Museum at Blists Hill in Telford, Shropshire, due to disruption from heavy rain. Some scenes remain unfilmed, and so will need rescheduling.

Tuesday 6th:
Itinerary: John writes to Brian Turner in the BBC Copyright Department, asking him to negotiate with the estate of writer Brian Hayles for the use of his Celestial Toymaker character in a possible Graham Williams-scripted story of two 45-minute episodes. Colin Baker and Nicola Bryant are both contracted to appear in thirteen 45-minute episodes of the twenty-third season.

Commentary: The intention was for the Celestial Toymaker to feature as the villain in Graham Williams' 'Arcade', the story set partly at Blackpool Pleasure Beach.

Thursday 8th:
Itinerary: Today is a remount of the unfilmed scenes for 'The Mark of the Rani', in the new location of the Queen Elizabeth Country Park in Hampshire. Sometime on or before this date, John flies from the UK to New York City, USA.

Friday 9th – Sunday 11th:
Itinerary: John is a guest at the Buffalo Who Fest 1984 convention, held in the Executive Hotel Buffalo Airport in Buffalo, New York. Other guests include Jon Pertwee and Gary Downie.

Saturday 10th – Saturday 17th:
Rehearsals for the single studio block of 'The Mark of the Rani' take place at the BBC Television Rehearsal Rooms at Acton.

Monday 12th:
Itinerary: John flies back to London from New York. On his return to the *Doctor Who* Production Office, he writes to the Head of Copyright, requesting that negotiations take place with Pip and Jane Baker for the use of their character the Rani in a three-part story to be written by Robert Holmes. He also writes to BBC Contracts, asking that Terry Molloy be booked to play Davros in 'Revelation of the Daleks' in January.

Wednesday 14th:
Itinerary: John writes to Blackpool Pleasure Beach's Jon Butcher, informing him of his intention to film there from Monday 20 May to Friday 24 May 1985. He doesn't envisage monopolising any particular rides at this stage, and adds that a script for the story has now been commissioned.

Saturday 17th:
Itinerary: John writes two memos to the Manager of the BBC Series and Serials, Drama Department. The first asks that Fiona Cumming be engaged from 13 May to 6 September 1985 to direct story 7B (two 45-minute episodes); the second asks that Graeme Harper be engaged from 3 June to 15 November 1985 to direct story 7C (three 45-minute episodes). He also signs off the commission for Graham Williams to write two 45-minute scripts for 'The Nightmare Fair' – the new title for 'Arcade'. Today is the Producer's Run at the BBC Television Rehearsal Rooms at Acton for the single studio session of 'The Mark of the Rani'.

Sunday 18th:
Itinerary: John writes another memo to the Manager of the BBC Series and Serials, Drama Department. He asks that Bob Gabriel be engaged from 11 November 1985 to 9 March 1986 to direct story 7F (two 45-minute episodes). Today is the first day of the three-day studio block for 'The Mark of the Rani' in studio TC1 at BBC Television Centre.

Monday 19th:
Itinerary: In the morning, John attends a planning meeting for 'Revelation of the Daleks' in Threshold House. Today is the second day of the three-day studio block for 'The Mark of the Rani' in studio TC1 at BBC Television Centre.

Tuesday 20th:
Itinerary: Today is the third and final day of the studio block for 'The Mark of the Rani' in studio TC1 at BBC Television Centre.

Wednesday 21st – Monday 3rd December:
Rehearsals for the first studio block of 'Timelash' take place at the BBC Television Rehearsal Rooms at Acton.

Wednesday 21st:
Itinerary: In the morning, John attends a full-cast read-through of the scripts of both episodes of 'Timelash' at the BBC Television Rehearsal Rooms at Acton. Later in the day, he signs off the commission for Christopher H Bidmead to write two 45-minute scripts for a story called 'In The Hollows of Time'. He also writes to Peter Moffatt, thanking him for his work on 'The Two Doctors'. In addition, he writes to Jonathan Powell, informing him of a 16-minute overrun on the final studio day of 'The Mark of the Rani', which he attributes to the fact that some scenes originally intended to be shot on film had to be reworked for the studio, due to the bad weather encountered on location.

Thursday 22nd:
Itinerary: Sometime on or before this date, John flies from the UK to Chicago, Illinois, USA.

Friday 23rd – Sunday 25th:
Itinerary: John is a guest at the TARDIS 21 convention mounted by the Spirit of Light organisation at the Hyatt Regency O'Hare Hotel in Chicago. Other guests at the event include Patrick Troughton, Jon Pertwee, Peter Davison, Colin Baker, Frazer Hines, Nicholas Courtney, John Levene, Richard Franklin, Elisabeth Sladen, Ian Marter, Lalla Ward, Janet Fielding, Mark Strickson, Nicola Bryant, Anthony Ainley and Terrance Dicks.

Monday 26th:
Itinerary: John flies back to London from Chicago.

Tuesday 27th:
Itinerary: In the afternoon, John attends a planning meeting for 'Revelation of the Daleks' in Threshold House.

Friday 29th:
Itinerary: Cathy Davies, the make-up designer on 'The Two Doctors' and 'The Mark of the Rani', writes to John, telling him how much she enjoyed working on the shows and asking to be considered for *Doctor Who* again.

DECEMBER

Monday 3rd:
Itinerary: Jon Butcher of Blackpool Pleasure Beach writes to John. He is fine with the dates suggested for filming there next year, and notes that only around half of the attraction will be open to the public at that time, from 2pm to 6pm each day. Today is the Producer's Run at the BBC Television Rehearsal Rooms at Acton for the first studio block of 'Timelash'.

Tuesday 4th:
Itinerary: Today is the first day of the three-day first studio block for 'Timelash' in studio TC4 at BBC Television Centre.

Wednesday 5th:
Itinerary: Today is the second day of the three-day first studio block for 'Timelash' in studio TC4 at BBC Television Centre. On the same day, John writes to Marianne Craig, Cathy Davies' boss, praising her make-up work on 'The Two Doctors'.

Thursday 6th:
Itinerary: Today is the third and final day of the first studio block for 'Timelash' in studio TC4 at BBC Television Centre.

Friday 7th – Tuesday 18th:
Rehearsals for the second studio block of 'Timelash' take place at the BBC Television Rehearsal Rooms at Acton.

Monday 17th:
Itinerary: John accompanies director Graeme Harper and other members of the 'Revelation of the Daleks' crew on a recce for the story's location filming early next year. They visit the Queen Elizabeth Country Park and other possible sites nearby. John spends the night in the Dolphin and Anchor Hotel in Chichester.

Tuesday 18th:
Itinerary: John spends the first part of the day with Graeme Harper, scouting more potential filming locations for 'Revelation of the Daleks'. He then returns to London in the afternoon, for the Producer's Run at the BBC Television Rehearsal Rooms at Acton for the second studio block of 'Timelash'.

Wednesday 19th:
Itinerary: Today is the first day of the three-day second studio block for 'Timelash' in studio TC8 at BBC Television Centre.

Thursday 20th:
Itinerary: Today is the second day of the three-day second studio block for 'Timelash' in studio TC8 at BBC Television Centre.

Friday 21st:
Itinerary: Today is the third and final day of the second studio block for 'Timelash' in studio TC8 at BBC Television Centre.

Saturday 22nd:
Itinerary: John travels to Southampton for a day of rehearsals for his pantomime production of *Cinderella* at the Gaumont Theatre. He's joined by cast members Colin Baker, Nicola Bryant, Anthony Ainley, Mary Tamm and Jacqueline Pearce and director Fiona Cumming.

Monday 24th:
Itinerary: John attends another day of rehearsals for *Cinderella* at the Gaumont Theatre in Southampton.

Wednesday 26th:
Itinerary: *Cinderella* opens at the Gaumont Theatre in Southampton. The pantomime will be performed twice daily, apart from on Mondays, at 2.30pm and 7.30 pm, and will run until Saturday 12 January 1985.

Saturday 29th:
Itinerary: Matthew Robinson writes to John, informing him that he's only today received an offer from the BBC Contracts Department to direct the first story of Season 23. He tells John that he's opened negotiations, and suggests they meet up for lunch in the New Year.

1985

Setting the Scene:

John had spent 1984 working on *Doctor Who* in his accustomed manner. For the third year on the bounce, he'd stretched the show's budget to allow for the overseas filming of one story; he'd spent a week scouting possible locations in Singapore; and he'd attended seven US conventions. Coupled with his attendance at rehearsals, UK location filming days and studio recordings, the amount of time he was actually spending in the *Doctor Who* Production Office in Union House was probably at an all-time low.

How much this 'invisibility' was responsible for the storm that would break at the end of February 1985 can't be measured. But it's inconceivable that the cancellation crises that *Doctor Who* would face in just a few short weeks could have come about overnight. How far in advance the seeds were sown with Jonathan Powell, and to a lesser extent Michael Grade, isn't known. But if *Doctor Who* was being scrutinised carefully by senior people at the BBC, then it's hard not to imagine what conclusions they might have come to.

Were the annual overseas filming trips a good way of spending the show's budget? Or were they 'jollies' for the boys? The inclusion of John's partner, Gary Downie, on the trip to Spain, and then on the location scouting visit to Singapore, can't have gone unnoticed.

Then there was the perceived quality of the episodes themselves. The new, 45-minute format was still being adjusted to – in particular, the pacing of the scripts was still being fine-tuned – and doubts remained about how Colin Baker would be received as the new Doctor. It seemed that for many members of the viewing public, the show had undergone just too much upheaval recently. Season 22 would see *Doctor Who* return to its traditional Saturday teatime slot for the first time in just under four years, but although it would get off to a good start, ratings-wise, things would soon go downhill.

'Business as usual' wouldn't last very long in 1985 …

JANUARY

Wednesday 2nd:
Itinerary: John attends a planning meeting for 'Revelation of the Daleks' at 10.30am.

Thursday 3rd – Friday 4th:
Rehearsals for the location filming of 'Revelation of the Daleks' take place at the BBC Television Rehearsal Rooms at Acton. Colin Baker and Nicola Bryant are limited to making only brief appearances before rushing down to Southampton to appear in John's production of *Cinderella*.

Saturday 5th:
Itinerary: Colin Baker, Nicola Bryant, Mary Tamm and Jacqueline Pearce all appear as guests on the live BBC1 programme *Saturday Superstore*, plugging mainly the *Cinderella* pantomime, but also the start of the new season of *Doctor Who* on BBC1 later that day. Afterwards, the cast and John have to race back to Southampton for the first of the day's two performances of *Cinderella*. 'Attack of the Cybermen' Part One screens on BBC1 that evening.

Monday 7th:
Itinerary: Today is the first day of location filming for 'Revelation of the Daleks', at Bolinge Hill Farm and Butser Hill Farm in Hampshire. The cast and crew travel by coach from the BBC's Ealing Studio at 8.00am. John spends the night at the Langrish Hotel in Petersfield.

John Nathan-Turner: 'The pantomime that I was involved with that Christmas starred Colin Baker and Nicola Bryant. It did mean that for a few days of the final week of the run, Colin and Nicola were filming during the day and performing in the theatre at night. Graeme Harper, the director, chose *Who* locations near to the theatre, though, of course, the shooting days were so short anyway at that time of year. Also in the theatre show were Anthony Ainley, Mary Tamm and Jacqueline Pearce, and our posters proclaimed "The Stars of *Doctor Who*". Sarah Lee organised a coach trip from the office to see the show. I recall dear Nick Courtney joining in the spirit of the evening like mad, and Nabil Shaban leading the community singing.'[345]

Tuesday 8th:
Itinerary: Today is the second day of location filming for 'Revelation of the

---

[345] John Nathan-Turner memoirs, *Doctor Who Magazine* #240.

Daleks', now at the Queen Elizabeth Country Park and again Butser Hill Farm in Hampshire. John spends the night at the Langrish Hotel in Petersfield.

Wednesday 9th:
Itinerary: Today is the third day of location filming for 'Revelation of the Daleks', this time at the IBM headquarters in Portsmouth, Hampshire. John spends the night at the Langrish Hotel in Petersfield.

Thursday 10th:
Itinerary: Today is the fourth and final day of location filming for 'Revelation of the Daleks', which takes place at the Goodwood Estate and a disused aerodrome in West Sussex. It's the final time that 16mm film cameras will be used for location filming on *Doctor Who* – from the following season, up to the end of the 'classic' era, all location material will be recorded on OB 1-inch videotape.

Friday 11th:
Itinerary: John writes to Jonathan Powell, informing him that the there was a studio overrun of nine minutes on 21 December, the final day of recording for 'Timelash'. He attributes this to a late start the previous day due to part of the set not being ready in time.

Friday 11th – Wednesday 16th:
Rehearsals for the first studio block of 'Revelation of the Daleks' take place at the BBC Television Rehearsal Rooms at Acton.

Saturday 12th:
'Attack of the Cybermen' Part Two screens on BBC1. Today also sees the final performance of *Cinderella* take place in Southampton.

Wednesday 16th:
Itinerary: Today is the Producer's Run at the BBC Television Rehearsal Rooms at Acton for the first studio block of 'Revelation of the Daleks'. On the same day, Tim Raynham, who had played Varl in 'The Two Doctors', writes to John, enclosing details of his latest acting roles.

Thursday 17th:
Itinerary: Jon Butcher, the Promotions and Entertainment Manager of Blackpool Pleasure Beach again, writes to John, asking if there is any news on the planned *Doctor Who* location filming there (for 'The Nightmare Fair'), and if there has been any firming-up of the provisional dates given the previous month. Today is the first day of the two-day first studio block for 'Revelation of the Daleks' in studio TC8 at BBC Television Centre.

Friday 18th:
Itinerary: Today is the second and final day of the first studio block for 'Revelation of the Daleks' in studio TC8 at BBC Television Centre.

Saturday 19th:
'Vengeance on Varos' Part One screens on BBC1.

Wednesday 23rd – Tuesday 29th:
Rehearsals for the second studio block of 'Revelation of the Daleks' take place at the BBC Television Rehearsal Rooms at Acton.

Thursday 24th:
Itinerary: John writes to Jonathan Powell, explaining that there was a 15-minute overrun on the final day of the first studio block for 'Revelation of the Daleks'. He puts this down to the fact that some material originally planned to be shot on film had to be rescheduled for the studio due to poor weather on location, and also to a nine-minute delay to proceedings on the first studio day.

Saturday 26th:
'Vengeance on Varos' Part Two screens on BBC1.

Tuesday 29th:
Itinerary: Today is the Producer's Run at the BBC Television Rehearsal Rooms at Acton for the second studio block of 'Revelation of the Daleks'.

Wednesday 30th:
Itinerary: Today is the first day of the three-day second studio block for 'Revelation of the Daleks' in studio TC8 at BBC Television Centre. An additional TARDIS scene is also recorded for 'Timelash' Part Two, which in the edit has been found to be under-running.

Thursday 31st:
Itinerary: Today is the second day of the three-day studio second block for 'Revelation of the Daleks' in studio TC8 at BBC Television Centre. On the same day, the musician Dominic Glynn writes to John, enclosing samples of his music and expressing a desire to work on *Doctor Who* later in the year.

FEBRUARY

Friday 1st:
Itinerary: Today is the third and final day of the second studio block for 'Revelation of the Daleks' in studio TC8 at BBC Television Centre. This brings production on Season 22 of *Doctor Who* to a close, although there is still some post-production and editing to be done. Also on this day, John asks for a 'negative name check'[346] to be carried out on the character Inspector Trusscot, who features in Graham Williams' scripts for 'The Nightmare Fair'. John wants to make sure that there isn't a real policeman of that name working for the Lancashire constabulary. Sometime on or after this date, John flies from the UK to Florida, USA.

Friday 1st – Sunday 3rd:
Itinerary: John is a guest at the Omnicon VI convention, held at the Marriott Hotel in Tallahassee, Florida. Other guests include Peter Davison, Nicholas Courtney, Gary Downie and Michael Keating (a *Blake's 7* regular who had also had a guest part in the Season 15 *Doctor Who* story 'The Sun Makers').

Saturday 2nd:
'The Mark of the Rani' Part One screens on BBC1.

Monday 4th:
Itinerary: John flies back to the UK from Florida. [347]

Tuesday 5th:
Itinerary: John signs off the commission for Michael Feeney Callan to write the two 45-minute scripts for a story called 'The Children of January'.

---

[346] A standard BBC procedure to ensure that characters in drama productions don't accidentally resemble real-life people, as legal ramifications might otherwise ensue.
[347] There is some doubt as to whether or not John did actually take this flight; it is possible he instead stayed on in the USA to avoid having to make a separate trip for his attendance the following weekend at the Time Travellers Anonymous convention in Champagne, Illinois. Some support for this may be found in the fact that a letter he sent on 7 February to director Sarah Hellings (see below) was signed in his absence by his secretary, Sarah Lee. If so, the other letters and memos bearing dates during this week would either have been signed by him before he left for Florida or, again, dictated to Lee and signed by her on his behalf, before she too flew out to Illinois for the convention there.

Wednesday 6th:
Itinerary: John signs off the commission for Robert Holmes to write the three 45-minute scripts for 'Yellow Fever and How To Cure It'.

Thursday 7th:
Itinerary: John writes to director Sarah Hellings, thanking her for her work on 'The Mark of the Rani'.

Friday 8th:
Itinerary: John writes to Ron Jones, thanking him for his work on 'Vengeance on Varos'. On the same day, he sends a memo to Elizabeth Western, Deputy Manager of BBC Series and Serials, requesting that Llinos Wyn Jones be allocated as Production Assistant to director Matthew Robinson for the production of story 7A. He also writes to Robinson himself, expressing interest in a project called *The Manageress* and thanking him for the work he did on 'Attack of the Cybermen'. He asks that they meet for lunch later in the month. In addition, he writes to Jonathan Powell, explaining that during the final studio day of 'Revelation of the Daleks' there was a 15-minute overrun, which he attributes to waiting for a new power lead to be made for the TARDIS console, the original having been lost.[348] Finally, John writes to the editor of the *Radio Times*, informing him of the return of the Daleks in 'Revelation of the Daleks', due for transmission next month, and asking if he would consider running either a colour feature or a cover to promote the story. Sometime on or before this date, John flies from the UK to Illinois, USA.[349]

Saturday 9th:
'The Mark of the Rani' Part Two screens on BBC1.

Saturday 9th – Sunday 10th:
Itinerary: John is a guest at the Time Travellers Anonymous convention, held at the Chancellor Inn Convention Centre in Champagne, Illinois. Other guests at the event include Colin Baker and Production Secretary Sarah Lee. On the flight over to America, Colin Baker gets to read the rehearsal scripts for 'The Nightmare Fair'.

Monday 11th:
Itinerary: John flies back to London from Illinois.

---

[348] As there are no TARDIS scenes in 'Revelation of the Daleks', this probably referred to the remounted TARDIS scene from 'Timelash', also recorded during this studio block.
[349] But see footnote 340.

Saturday 16th:
'The Two Doctors' Part One screens on BBC1.

Monday 18th:
Itinerary: John sends a memo to Sarah Bird of Music Copyright, informing her of the address of the late composer John Lewis's estate, to whom any monies owed should be paid in future for his unused score for 'The Mark of the Rani'. On the same date, Brian Turner of the Copyright Department sends John a memo confirming that terms have now been agreed with Robert Holmes for him to write the three scripts for his 'Yellow Fever' story (the title having apparently been shortened from the original 'Yellow Fever and How to Cure It').

Wednesday 20th:
Itinerary: Matthew Robinson writes to John, explaining that he has not been able to come to an agreement with the BBC with regard to his proposed fee to direct two stories for Season 23. Consequently, he has to turn down the invitation to direct these stories (one of which would have been 'The Nightmare Fair'). In studio TC8 at Television Centre, Colin Baker and Janet Fielding – reprising her role as Tegan as a stand-in for Nicola Bryant, who is on holiday in Venice – record 'In A Fix With Sontarans' for the BBC show *Jim'll Fix It*.

John Nathan-Turner: 'They'd been wanting to do a *Doctor Who* "fix" for about four years. For various reasons, they all fell through. At one point, we were going to have the robot from "The Visitation" doing somebody's housework! This series, they had a very bright director called Marcus Mortimer, and he wanted to encompass the wishes of hundreds of kids who want to travel in the Doctor's TARDIS. I insisted that any sketch would have to be in character, and out of that evolved "In A Fix With Sontarans". I suggested that Eric [Saward] wrote it, for obvious reasons – it was easier, and he knows the continuity. It was originally written for Peri, but then Nicola booked a holiday, so Eric rewrote it for Janet. The name Group Marshall Nathan [for one of the featured Sontarans], by the way, came out of rehearsals; in the script he was called Stern.'[350]

Thursday 21st:
Itinerary: Robert Holmes calls Eric Saward in the *Doctor Who* Production Office to tell him that he's heard a rumour that *Doctor Who* is to be cancelled by the BBC. Ian Levine calls John around the same time, reporting the same rumour. Saward and John discuss the matter, but John dismisses the rumour as nonsense.

---

350 John Nathan-Turner interview, *Doctor Who Magazine* #104.

John Nathan-Tuner: 'Imagine the surprise you get when, on a Thursday, an independent record producer [Ian Levine] rings to tell *you* that *your* show has been cancelled. Half an hour later your script editor pops in to tell you that Bob Holmes has told him on the telephone that the show has been cancelled! "Cancelled" being the operative word at the time. I wasn't at all preoccupied with other concerns, apart from my usual responsibilities. I couldn't believe a *fan* and a writer had their fingers on the pulse more than any of us in the front office. It wasn't the way the BBC did things at all. I dismissed the whole thing out of court. Arrogance, maybe, but I couldn't believe that such a major decision had been made without any form of discussion with the front office. It was inconceivable. I had taken off the Friday of that week as part of my annual leave, to attend, with the BBC's knowledge, a US *Doctor Who* event. I left my US phone number behind, as usual, with a clear conscience.'[351]

Friday 22nd:
Itinerary: John takes a day of annual leave, and flies from the UK to Philadelphia, USA.

Saturday 23rd – Sunday 24th:
Itinerary: John is a guest at a Doctor Who Festival (formerly Whovian Festival Tour) event held at the Valley Forge Convention Centre in Philadelphia, Pennsylvania. Also guesting is Colin Baker. While at the event, John records an interview with Eric Luskin for the latter's documentary *Doctor Who's Who's Who*, which is being made by the New Jersey Network PBS station and will be sold to and screened on many other such stations.

Saturday 23rd:
'The Two Doctors' Part Two screens on BBC1.

Monday 25th:
Itinerary: John flies back to the UK from Philadelphia. In his absence, Sarah Lee sends a memo in his name to Charles Jeanes of the Visual Effects Department, thanking him for his work in bringing the character of Sil to life in 'Vengeance on Varos', and promising that the character will return. On arriving back in the *Doctor Who* Production Office, John is summoned to a meeting with Jonathan Powell, who informs him that *Doctor Who* is to be cancelled by the BBC, effective immediately. Work on the upcoming twenty-third season, due to start filming in five weeks' time, is suspended. John and Gary Downie go over to Ian Levine's house in the evening and start working on a strategy to gain press and public support for the show, in the hope of getting Powell to reverse his decision. Under John's guidance, Levine talks

---

[351] John Nathan-Turner memoirs, *Doctor Who Magazine* #239.

anonymously to Charles Catchpole at the *Sun* and Geoff Baker at the *Daily Star*, pretending to be a BBC insider.

John Nathan-Turner: 'I returned to the *Doctor Who* office straight from my trip to America. The weekend had been successful, and I'd managed to forget the ridiculous rumours emanating from record producer Ian Levine and the late Bob Holmes about *Doctor Who* being cancelled. I hadn't been in the office for long when my new Head of Department, Jonathan Powell, asked to see me. He told me that a vast amount of money was needed to open up daytime TV earlier than planned, to avoid ITV stealing a march on proceedings. I forget the number of millions of pounds involved, but it was a vast amount of money. He told me that many shows were being cut back and some were being dropped from the production schedule of the next financial year. *Doctor Who* was one of the casualties. After picking up my chin from the floor, I told him that I'd heard rumours of this the previous Thursday from *outside* the BBC. He said not to bother about this. I suspect he felt guilty. I felt gutted and asked if the programme was to blame. He reassured me it wasn't, and said I and my resident team should take a well-earned rest, start thinking about the next season and get rid of the amazing amount of leave I'd built up by hardly ever taking a long holiday.'[352]

Eric Saward: 'John came back from Powell's office looking very sheepish and said, "We've been cancelled." As producer he was told before anybody else. What truly aggravated me about it was that Powell was getting fraught without actually being constructive. Powell seemed to hate everything we were doing. John went to see Michael Grade soon after we were cancelled and Grade was apparently outraged by John's attitude and his demands to know why the show had been cancelled. The production team heard this through Grade's secretary.[353] Let me tell you how the procedure for commissioning a script works in Series and Serials. A script is commissioned by the Production Office; that was John and me. We both sign the commissioning form, which then goes upstairs to the Head of Department, who approves the commission. The script is then delivered by the author, and the producer and script editor read it and ask for rewrites if necessary. The finished script is typed up by the script typists, printed, and a copy (i.e. the final version of the script) is then sent back upstairs to Jonathan Powell. His job is to read everything, not just *Doctor Who*, but everything that is produced. The above procedure was followed with every script for *Doctor Who*. Before we were cancelled, we never had any comment from Jonathan Powell concerning scripts. Not one word of doubt or consideration, nothing at all. We were then cancelled and told we

---

[352] John Nathan-Turner memoirs, *Doctor Who Magazine* #240.
[353] Eric Saward and Ian Levine interview, *DWB* #107.

were doing it wrong. My supposition is that it was some kind of political argy-bargy going on within the BBC. It must have been. You can say that we cocked it up, but nothing was said till we were cancelled. The thing is, the man had the power, he could have said, "Look here, the scripts are crap, we don't want them, they're awful, get rid of the script editor, put John Nathan-Turner onto another job, get rid of both of them …", but he didn't. We were then, after we'd been cancelled, told we were staying on the show!'[354]

Ian Levine: 'The day it was cancelled, John and Gary [Downie] came round my house and spent the whole evening plotting what to do and how to get the press involved. John got me to phone Charles Catchpole of the *Sun*. He'd told me that there were codenames within the BBC that Catchpole would know, so I phoned him and said that I worked on the sixth floor under Michael Grade and that my name was Snowball. I said there was a plot to get rid of *Doctor Who*, and while I was talking, John and Gary were busy scribbling away, telling me what to say. I told Charles Catchpole how the show made profits for the BBC, how [it] was being used in a plot to defend the licence fee increase – John was even reeling off figures off the top of his head of the number of countries *Doctor Who* was sold to and the millions of pounds' worth of figures for me to quote at him. John was pulling the strings all the way, because he couldn't risk being identified as being involved. He knew this whole code thing and exactly what to say, and then we did the same thing with Geoff Baker of the *Daily Star*.'[355]

Eric Saward: '[John] was in a state of shock. That day, we were due to have a playback of "Revelation of the Daleks", which would air the following month. He said, "I don't think I can do this." I said, "Do you want me to do it?" During the playback, John just sat there. He had never been so quiet or unopinionated. It took him quite a while to recover.'[356]

Tuesday 26th:
Itinerary: The evening edition of the *London Evening Standard* is the first newspaper to break the news of *Doctor Who*'s cancellation.

Wednesday 27th:
Itinerary: The cancellation makes the headlines of the BBC's own news bulletins throughout the day. Patrick Troughton turns up at the *Doctor Who* Production Office to offer his support to the show, and helps field phone calls during the day.

---

[354] Eric Saward interview, *DWB* #58.
[355] Eric Saward and Ian Levine interview, *DWB* #107.
[356] Eric Saward interview, *Doctor Who Magazine* #348.

Thursday 28th:
Itinerary: Most of the national tabloid newspapers cover the cancellation of *Doctor Who* on the front pages. John suggests to Ian Levine that he should smash up his TV set in a protest stunt, and Levine is interviewed by Leonard Parkin on ITV's *News at One*.

Ian Levine: 'After I went on ITV's *News at One* when the cancellation had been announced, it caused such an outcry that Bill Cotton personally phoned the DWAS and assured them that the show was coming back. John then thought he'd won and that he was invincible.'[357]

MARCH

Friday 1st:
Itinerary: Bill Cotton, the Managing Director of BBC Television, issues a press statement, promising that *Doctor Who* will be back in the autumn of 1986 in its old 25-minute format, and will run for a greater number of weeks than it currently does. John writes to Elizabeth Western, Deputy Manager, BBC Series and Serials, detailing the costs for writing off production on the six stories intended for Season 23. The only actors under contract so far for the season are Colin Baker, Nicola Bryant and Nabil Shaban (who was to return to play Sil). Also included are costs for payment in full for all the scripts and story breakdowns already commissioned, and the costs for the long-term storage of the TARDIS sets and props. He notes that the Dalek props are stored free of charge by BBC Enterprises. The *Sun* and the *Daily Star* newspapers both start 'Save *Doctor Who*' campaigns in the editions out today. A Cyberman appears on the evening's live edition of *Wogan* on BBC1, praising Michael Grade.

Commentary: When the show did eventually return, it was reduced to a season of just fourteen 25-minute episodes – although that did technically meet Bill Cotton's promise, as it was one more episode than Season 22.

Saturday 2nd:
'The Two Doctors' Part Three screens on BBC1. This is followed by *Jim'll Fix It*, which contains the 'A Fix with Sontarans' segment.

Monday 4th:
Itinerary: John writes to Jon Butcher, the Promotions and Entertainment

---

[357] Eric Saward and Ian Levine Interview, *DWB* #107.

Manager of Blackpool Pleasure Beach. He explains that the next series of *Doctor Who* has been postponed, so his team won't now be filming on the dates they'd previously discussed. However, he tells Butcher that he intends to reschedule the Blackpool filming for early 1986, and that it will concentrate around the rides called Space Machine, Big Dipper and Goldmine.

Thursday 7th:
Itinerary: John writes to Brian Turner at BBC Copyright, informing him that Christopher Bidmead and Michael Feeney Callan have agreed to extend their respective planned stories from two 45-minute episodes to four 25-minute episodes, and that Robert Holmes has also agreed to extend his from three 45-minute episodes to six 25-minute episodes, in return for increased fees to cover the additional minutes of material.[358] During the evening, Ian Levine and Paul Mark Tams record the novelty record *Doctor in Distress* in Trident Studios in Soho. This is intended to raise interest in the show's plight. Colin Baker, Nicola Bryant, Anthony Ainley and Nicholas Courtney are persuaded to take part by John, and they record parts along with several other celebrities that Levine and Tams have secured. Sometime on or before this date, John flies from the UK to Florida, USA.

Friday 8th:
Itinerary: John guests at the *Doctor Who* Festival event in the Tampa Theatre, Tampa, Florida. He appears alongside Peter Davison.

Saturday 9th:
Itinerary: John guests at another *Doctor Who* Festival event, in the O'Connell Centre, Gainesville, Florida. Again, he appears alongside Peter Davison. 'Timelash' Part One screens on BBC1.

Sunday 10th:
Itinerary: John guests at a third *Doctor Who* Festival event, this one at the Civic Centre in Tallahassee, Florida. Once more, he appears alongside Peter Davison. After the event, he returns to the UK, arriving back in London the following day.

Monday 11th:
Itinerary: Jon Butcher, Promotions and Entertainment Manager, Blackpool Pleasure Beach, writes to John, enquiring about the status of the proposed

---

[358] Robert Holmes would withdraw from the commission to write 'Yellow Fever And How To Cure It' in early June 1985 with no scripts having been written; the fee he had received in advance would be offset against his next commission, which would come a few months later with 'Wasteland'.

filming there, in light of the recent announcement of *Doctor Who*'s postponement. (He must not have received John's letter of the 4 March.) On the same day, John signs off the commission for Pip and Jane Baker to write four 25-minute scripts for a story titled simply 'Gallifrey'.

Commentary: At this point, John seems to have been sure that Season 23 would consist of 26 episodes, and that the already-commissioned scripts and storylines would still be put into production. However, the commissioning of 'Gallifrey' could indicate that one of the previously-planned four-parters had been dropped. As far as can be ascertained, Pip and Jane Baker never wrote a single line of any script for 'Gallifrey' – in later interviews, they denied any knowledge of it – and it was soon dropped as a possible story when the curtailed nature of Season 23 became apparent.

Wednesday 13th:
Itinerary: John is interviewed in the *Doctor Who* Production Office by David Saunders and Patrick Mulkern of the DWAS. It's the first interview he has given following the cancellation of the original Season 23. Sometime after this date, John flies back out to the US.

Saturday 16th:
'Timelash' Part Two screens on BBC1.

Saturday 16th – Sunday 17th:
Itinerary: John is the sole guest at the Creation convention at the Roosevelt Hotel, New York City.

Saturday 23rd – Sunday 24th:
Itinerary: John is the sole guest at the Creation convention at the Gateway Inn, Rochester, New York.

Saturday 23rd:
'Revelation of the Daleks' Part One screens on BBC1.

Sunday 24th:
Itinerary: Royce Mills writes to John to thank him for casting him as a Dalek voice in 'Revelation of the Daleks', and expresses his sorrow that *Doctor Who* is to be rested for 18 months.

Monday 25th:
Itinerary: John flies back to London from New York.

Saturday 30th:
'Revelation of the Daleks' Part Two screens on BBC1.

APRIL

Saturday 6th:
Itinerary: John is a guest at the DWAS's DWASocial V convention at the Novatel in Hammersmith, London. Also in attendance are Colin Baker and Ian Levine. Levine takes to the stage to warn the audience that he's heard credible rumours that the next season will be only 20 episodes in length, and not the full 26 episodes that they were expecting. John then takes to the stage and angrily refutes this.

Ian Levine: 'At the DWASocial V at Hammersmith in April, I went on stage … I told the audience not to be complacent, to keep writing to the BBC, and although we'd lost a season, the show was coming back, but don't think it's coming back as 26 episodes because it's not. JNT came on stage shortly afterwards and literally tore me to pieces and got a huge round of applause for saying, "The idiot that was on before, worrying you all and telling you all it's coming back as 14 episodes, it's all nonsense, and I'm here to assure you that it's totally untrue and that no decision has been made about the episodes. Don't listen to him – he's winding you up with rubbish." I knew that John was lying through his teeth, so what does that tell you about the (lack of) respect for the fans? John publically humiliated me and later phoned me at home and said, "I hope you didn't take it personally. I had to humiliate you in public – *I* will decide when the fans know, not you. It's *my* choice, *my* show, and *I* will decide." After that, I didn't speak to him for a while.'[359]

Commentary: Paperwork would suggest that for at least another month or so, John was still expecting to make a 26-episode season when *Doctor Who* returned to production, so the decision to reduce the number of episodes was not a certainty at this point.

Thursday 11th:
Itinerary: John writes to Jonathan Powell, explaining that there was a 15-minute overrun on the final studio day of 'Revelation of the Daleks' on 1

---

[359] Eric Saward and Ian Levine interview, *DWB* #107. This interview was conducted some years after the convention took place, and Levine evidently misremembered the actual number of episodes he had spoken about in his warning to attendees.

February, due to 'highly complex visual effects.'[360]

Friday 19th:

Itinerary: Sometime on or before this date, John flies from the UK to Oregon, USA.

Saturday 20th:

Itinerary: John guests at a *Doctor Who* Festival event in Portland, Oregon, alongside Patrick Troughton.

Sunday 21st:

Itinerary: John guests at another *Doctor Who* Festival event, at the Civic Centre in San Jose, California, again alongside Patrick Troughton.

Monday 22nd:

Itinerary: John flies back to the UK from California.

MAY

Tuesday 7th:

Itinerary: John sends Jonathan Powell a proposed recording schedule for the 1986/87 season of *Doctor Who*, to be ready for transmission in autumn 1986 and continue into the first quarter of 1987. The schedule is for 26 episodes of 25 minutes' duration, broken into five four-part stories and one six-part story. Production is planned to begin in Week 13 (w/c 24 March 1986) and run through to Week 46 (w/c 10 November 1986), with a two-week break in early August.

Commentary: Despite the rumours circulating at the time of a reduction to a lower episode count, John seems still to have been holding out to produce a 26-episode season when *Doctor Who* re-entered production. And in order to get 26 episodes ready to begin transmission in autumn 1986, he proposed a March start date.

Thursday 23rd:

Itinerary: Brian Turner of the Copyright Department sends John a memo, confirming that terms have now been agreed with Pip and Jane Baker for them to write the four scripts for the proposed story with the working title

---

[360] This memo was signed by Sarah Lee, suggesting that John wasn't in the office at the time. He may have departed for the US well in advance of his 20 April convention appearance in Oregon.

'Gallifrey'.[361]

Saturday 25th:
Itinerary: John attends the shop Forbidden Planet 2 in London between 2.00pm and 4.00pm, to sign copies of his book *Doctor Who: The TARDIS Inside Out*.[362]

Wednesday 29th:
Itinerary: John appears as a guest on BBC1's *Breakfast Time* programme to discuss his book *Doctor Who: The TARDIS Inside Out*. On the same date, he sends a memo to Brian Turner of the Copyright Department, confirming a recent phone discussion in which he informed him that Robert Holmes wished to withdraw from writing 'Yellow Fever'. He goes on to ask if the fee already paid to Holmes can be set against his next commission, as he feels sure the writer will be asked to contribute further episodes.

JUNE

Monday 17th:
Itinerary: John, along with Colin Baker, Eric Saward, production secretary Sarah Lee and the actor Ian Ogilvy, takes part in a sponsored charity parachute jump organised by the Red Devils. At some point in the following few days, John flies from London to Florida, USA.

John Nathan-Turner: 'It's odd how fear takes people in different ways as we sped from the ground [for the parachute jump]. Sarah couldn't stop talking, I withdrew, as did Saward, Ogilvy kept laughing and Colin was distressingly ebullient. It was time to jump! Sarah leapt out with the largest plastic smile I've ever seen! Then Saward refused to jump – he didn't say a word, he grunted, bared his teeth and shook his head. Words from Sean (the parachute instructor) didn't affect him; he just kept grunting and shaking his head. It was frightening to watch, and had a devastating effect on those of us left in the plane. Then Sean took control, and Saward was dragged, still snarling, to the gaping hole (in the side of the plane) and pushed out! I gulped! Well, I thought, I've been thrown out of better places than this, and I'm not going to

---

[361] As previously mentioned, this story was soon abandoned, the Bakers having apparently done no work on it at all.
[362] *Doctor Who: The TARDIS Inside Out* was published by Piccadilly Press on 30 May 1985 in both hardback and paperback. Advance copies were made available for John's signing at Forbidden Planet 2.

be pushed, so I went through the rehearsed procedure with terrific determination ... Thankfully, I drifted reasonably safely down to the ground, but landed badly and sprained my ankle. The others had near-perfect landings, save for Sarah who broke a bone in her toe. The jump was an experience that I wouldn't have missed, but one that I never wish to repeat.'[363]

Saturday 29th:

Itinerary: John writes to Dominic May, the out-going editor of the DWAS's newsletter, *Celestial Toyroom*. He takes issue with the May 1985 edition's front page headline 'Who Do You Believe?' and the accompanying article, which detailed the onstage spat between him and Ian Levine at the DWASocial V event in April. He further objects to the fact that in the June 1985 edition May backtracked over criticisms he aimed at Levine in the earlier article. Nevertheless, he thanks May for the work he's done on the newsletter over the past 18 months.

JULY

Friday 5th:

Itinerary: John and Eric Saward jointly pen character outlines for the Valeyard and the Inquisitor, who will be recurring characters in the forthcoming season. John also writes a brief character description for Melanie Bush, the new companion he has devised. It relates a backstory of how Melanie first meets the Doctor in 1986, helping him defeat a plot by the Master to defraud all the banking houses in the world. She's into aerobics and health food, has red hair, and sings a lot in the TARDIS.

Eric Saward: 'I'd thought that the hiatus would be it. Three months later, I was still saying to John, "When are we getting the sack?" We didn't know what was happening. "What are we doing here? It's become pointless." Eventually, we started planning the next season. I came up with the theme of the Doctor being on trial, more from desperation than creativity. I started developing the opening episodes with Bob Holmes ... John had seen Bonnie [Langford] – or someone had mentioned her – and he had fallen in love with the idea. He came in and said, "I want a companion with red hair." By this time, I was getting a bit tired, and thinking that I really should have left last year, and I thought, "What nonsense is this now? Why a companion with red hair?" No

---

363 John Nathan-Turner memoirs, *Doctor Who Magazine* #245.

thought had gone into it.'[364]

Tuesday 9th:
Itinerary: John and Eric hold a meeting at BBC Threshold House with writers selected to script the all-new Season 23. In attendance are Robert Holmes, Philip Martin, David Halliwell and Jack Trevor Story. At some point after this meeting, John flies from London to New Orleans, Louisiana, USA.

Wednesday 10th:
Itinerary: John and Eric Saward circulate a Drama Script Classified List, which states that the only writers they are working with at this date for upcoming storylines and/or scripts are: Pip and Jane Baker, Christopher H Bidmead (scene breakdown), Michael Feeney Callan, Wally K Daly, Peter Grimwade (scene breakdown), Robert Holmes, Gary Hopkins (one episode), Ian Marter, Philip Martin, Pat Mills, Ingrid Pitt and Tony Rudlin, Andrew Smith (scene breakdown), Robin Squire, Graham Williams, Jonathan Wolfman, and Paula Woolsey (two episodes).

Friday 12th – Sunday 14th
Itinerary: John is a guest at the Panopticon New Orleans/1985 North American Time Festival convention, held at the International Hotel in New Orleans. Other guests at the event include Colin Baker (and his wife, Marion Wyatt), Nicholas Courtney, Gary Downie and Ian Levine. During the weekend, John records an interview for the WYES TV documentary *They All Axed for Who* and judges a 'John Nathan-Turner lookalike' competition.

Friday 26th:
Itinerary: John signs off the commission for Jack Trevor Story to write a story outline for a 2 x 25-minute story, 'The Second Coming'.[365]

Friday 26th – Sunday 28th:
Itinerary: John is a guest at the *Timecon 85* convention in San Jose, California. Other guests include Colin Baker, Sarah Sutton, Nicholas Courtney and Richard Franklin.

---

[364] Eric Saward interview, *Doctor Who Magazine* #348.
[365] Although this form is dated 26 July, it's doubtful that John actually signed it on that date, as he almost certainly stayed in the US between the Panopticon New Orleans event and the Timecon convention the following weekend.

AUGUST

Friday 2nd – Sunday 4th:
Itinerary: John is a guest at the Tampa Bay Who Fest 1985 convention, held at the Sheraton Tampa Motor Hotel in Tampa, Florida. Other guests at the event include Nicholas Courtney, John Levene, Richard Franklin, Ian Marter and Gary Downie. John returns to the UK in the days after this event.

Monday 12th: (John's thirty-eighth birthday)
Itinerary: Jacqueline Pearce throws a surprise birthday party for John on her houseboat in Chelsea. Eric Saward is invited but does not attend.

John Nathan-Turner: 'In August of the hiatus year, a surprise party for my birthday was arranged. A plot had been hatched where I was hijacked from my office by Sarah Lee, blindfolded, bundled into a car and told I was going to get a surprise. It's amazing, once unable to see, how you speculate on where the various twists and turns of the road are taking you. The car came to a stop. Someone else got in; another female. I could smell delicious perfume! The journey went on. The car finally stopped and I was herded across a busy wide road. By now I thought I was at an airport terminal. My sense of direction while blindfolded had led me to believe that, despite the detour to pick up Madam X (who never spoke), we were somewhere near Heathrow. Suddenly the floor beneath me was clearly wooden and there was great effort to make me walk in a very straight line. We went down some stairs and then warmth hit me. I thought, "Wherever we are, we're here." Off came the blindfold and before me was a sumptuous dinner table, beautifully laid out. Standing directly opposite me was the exquisite Jacqueline Pearce and a whole load of friends singing "Happy Birthday". We were all aboard Jacqui's Chelsea houseboat. It was a gorgeous moment. And Madam X? None other than Janet Fielding!'[366]

Saturday 17th:
Itinerary: John travels to Edinburgh by train with Terrance Dicks and a BBC Dalek prop to promote a *Doctor Who* day at the Edinburgh Book Festival.

Friday 23rd:
Itinerary: Several members of the Executive Committee of the DWAS are summoned by John to a meeting at the *Doctor Who* Production Office. A recent issue of the fanzine produced by the Society's Merseyside Local Group (MLG)

---

[366] John Nathan-Turner memoirs, *Doctor Who Magazine* #240.

has included a tasteless joke about the cot-death of Colin Baker's son, and John reads the riot act over the incident, which has already caused the cancellation of a DWASocial event planned to be held in Liverpool. John warns that any repeat of such an incident could result in legal action against the Society, and the withdrawal of all support and cooperation from the BBC.

Friday 30th:
Itinerary: John appears with Colin Baker and Nicola Bryant at Blackpool's *Doctor Who* Exhibition to sign autographs and raise money for the BBC's annual *Children in Need* fundraiser.

SEPTEMBER

Monday 2nd:
Itinerary: John signs off the commission for Roberts Holmes to write the four 25-minute scripts for 'Wasteland'.[367]

Wednesday 11th:
Itinerary: David Halliwell delivers his scripts for the first two episodes of 'Attack from the Mind' to the *Doctor Who* Production Office.[368]

Friday 13th:
Itinerary: John requests that Philip Martin be given staff clearance to write the scripts for 'The Planet of Sil'.[369]

Saturday 14th:
Itinerary: Musician Dominic Glynn writes to John, updating him on his recent projects and enquiring if there would be any work for him on the upcoming season of *Doctor Who*.

Tuesday 24th:
Itinerary: John sends a memo to Jenny Betts at the BBC's studio bookings office. He's heard a rumour that an upcoming *Doctor Who* story will be allocated studio space at Pebble Mill in Birmingham rather than as usual at

---

[367] This story would eventually be titled 'The Mysterious Planet', before becoming 'The Trial of a Time Lord' Parts One to Four.
[368] These scripts proved to be unsuitable, and Halliwell was asked to rewrite the one for the first episode and resubmit it the next month.
[369] This story would eventually be titled 'Mindwarp', before becoming 'The Trial of a Time Lord' Parts Five to Eight.

Television Centre in London. He cites his experience as Production Unit Manager on the 1977 story 'Horror of Fang Rock' – the only previous *Doctor Who* to be recorded at Pebble Mill – when stating that he considers the studio space in Birmingham too small for the show's needs.

OCTOBER

Friday 4th:
Itinerary: Philip Martin delivers his script for 'The Planet of Sil' Part One to the *Doctor Who* Production Office. At some point on or before this date, John flies from London to Florida, USA.

Saturday 5th – Sunday 6th:
Itinerary: John guests at a *Doctor Who* Festival event at the Curtis Hixon Centre in Tampa, Florida. The other guests include Patrick Troughton, Colin Baker and Richard Franklin.

Sunday 6th:
Itinerary: David Halliwell delivers his revised script for 'Attack from the Mind' Part One to the *Doctor Who* Production Office.[370]

Sunday 13th:
Itinerary: John guests at a *Doctor Who* Festival event in Connecticut. The other guests include Patrick Troughton and Colin Baker.

Tuesday 29th:
Itinerary: John signs off the commission for Christopher H Bidmead to write the scripts for four 25-minute episodes of 'The Last Adventure'. [371]

---

[370] On 18 October 1985, script editor Eric Saward informed Halliwell that both he and John found the scripts for 'Attack from the Mind' unacceptable for the show.
[371] This four-part story was a replacement for Jack Trevor Story's 'The Second Coming' and David Halliwell's 'Attack from the Mind', two two-part stories. It would be given the new title 'Pinocotheca' when the scripts were written.

NOVEMBER

Friday 8th – Sunday 10th:
Itinerary: John guests at the Buffalo Who Fest 1985 convention, held at the Executive Hotel in Buffalo, New York. Other guests include Ian Marter and Janet Fielding.

Monday 11th:
Itinerary: John flies back to the UK on or around this date.

Saturday 16th:
Itinerary: John attends the one-day Genesis convention in Manchester.

Friday 22nd:
Itinerary: Colin Baker, Peter Davison, Jon Pertwee and Patrick Troughton headline a total of twenty *Doctor Who* guests (plus, in model form, a Dalek and K-9) in an appearance on the live BBC1 *Children in Need* programme in the evening, handing over a cheque for the money raised when John accompanied Baker and Nicola Bryant on their trip to Blackpool earlier in the year.

Thursday 28th:
Itinerary: Sometime on or before this date, John flies from the UK to Chicago, USA. Nicola Bryant is contracted to appear in eight 25-minute episodes of Season 23.

Friday 29th – Sunday December 1st:
Itinerary: John is a guest at the TARDIS 22 convention, organised by Spirit of Light, held at the Hyatt Regency Hotel in Chicago, Illinois. Other guests include Patrick Troughton, Jon Pertwee, Colin Baker, John Levene, Richard Franklin, Elisabeth Sladen, Louise Jameson, Lalla Ward, Sarah Sutton, Janet Fielding, Mark Strickson, Nicola Bryant, Anthony Ainley, Paul Darrow, Jacqueline Pearce and stuntman Terry Walsh.

Saturday 30th:
Itinerary: Sarah Lee, acting on John's instructions, writes to Jonathan Powell, asking him to book Matthew Robinson to direct story 7A during weeks 15 to 31 in 1986.[372]

---

[372] Story 7A will eventually become the first four episodes of 'The Trial of a Time Lord', and will be directed by Nicholas Mallett.

DECEMBER

Thursday 12th:
Itinerary: Now back in the UK, John requests that Dave Chapman be allocated to produce video effects for the entire twenty-third season of *Doctor Who*, and that Alec Wheal and his camera crew be allocated to all the studio sessions. Also on this day, he writes to Jonathan Powell to ask that Ron Jones be allocated to direct story 7B, from 31 March to 18 July 1986.

Friday 20th:
Itinerary: John writes to Jonathan Powell to ask that Nicholas Mallett be allocated to direct 'Wasteland', from 10 February to 6 June 1986.

Undated:
John Nathan-Turner: 'I devised Melanie as a character in July of 1985. As it wasn't too important at that point, I never started to think about casting. In December, I happened to be up in the West End, when I phoned Barry Burnett, Colin Baker's agent, to see if he wanted to meet for a chat. I thought, as one does when meeting agents, about who else was on his books, so [I could] make polite conversation. My mind went through a few names that I remembered, and I suddenly thought of Bonnie Langford, and realised that she fitted my concept of Melanie as this health fanatic person. I asked about Bonnie, but said that I doubted it was the sort of thing that she'd want to do. But Barry thought it was just the sort of different thing that she'd been looking for, and so it went from there.'[373]

Colin Baker: 'Eventually, John conceded that I'd said to him about six months earlier, "How about Bonnie Langford as the new companion?" And he'd said, "Over my dead body." Six months later, he claimed to have had a great idea for a new companion – Bonnie Langford! Hah!'[374]

---

[373] John Nathan-Turner interview, *Doctor Who Magazine* #131.
[374] Colin Baker interview, *Doctor Who Magazine* #324.

1986

Setting the Scene:

The 'cancellation' of *Doctor Who* in February 1985 was a bitter blow to John, and he probably realised that his career prospects within the BBC were now limited. It was clear that Jonathan Powell had little time either for *Doctor Who* in general, or for John in particular.

Once the plug had been pulled on the original Season 23, which would have been in production during the financial year April 1985 to March 1986, there was no BBC budget or resources allocated to the show during this period. The curtailed new Season 23 was instead scheduled to be made in the financial year April 1986 to March 1987. All that John and script editor Eric Saward could do before that time was organise the commissioning of scripts.

But, on its reduced count of 14 episodes per year, *Doctor Who* was no longer a 52-week rolling production. The producer's job now took up, at best, only around seven months of the year; consequently, John was left with far more downtime than he'd had in the past six or seven years. With only 14 episodes to commission, rather than the usual 26, and the luxury of a longer run-up than had ever been afforded before, this season of *Doctor Who* should have been the best-prepared production ever – but no sense of urgency was apparent. John spent most of 1985 jetting to and from the USA; the lack of a series to produce meant that he could indulge himself to his heart's content on the US convention circuit. Only later in the year did he and Eric Saward eventually get down to the nitty-gritty of planning the new season and commissioning scripts.

If John had been damaged by *Doctor Who*'s cancellation, then so too had Saward. The flaws in their working relationship were soon to develop into wholesale fissures, and what should have been a triumphant return for *Doctor Who* was soon marred by bitter conflict.

JANUARY

Wednesday 8th:
Itinerary: John writes to Jonathan Powell to ask that Chris Clough be allocated to direct story 7C from 14 April to 26 September.

Thursday 9th:
Itinerary: Christopher H Bidmead delivers his four scripts for 'Pinocotheca' to the *Doctor Who* Production Office.

Wednesday 15th:
Itinerary: Robert Holmes delivers his four scripts for 'Wasteland' to the *Doctor Who* Production Office.

Thursday 16th:
Itinerary: Colin Baker is contracted to appear in fourteen 25-minute episodes of Season 23.

Friday 17th:
Itinerary: Peter Pegrum, the Design Manager at the BBC Visual Effects Department, writes to John, apologising for not being able to allocate the specific designers that John had requested for the upcoming season. Pegrum informs him that Mike Kelt will handle story 7A, Peter Wragg story 7B and Kevin Molloy story 7C.

Wednesday 22nd:
Itinerary: John writes to Sharon Miskith at the BBC Costume Department, asking that Dennis Ado be allocated as the regular male costume dresser for the upcoming season, and that Sheila Cullen be allocated as senior dresser.

Thursday 23rd:
Itinerary: A press photocall, which John oversees, is held at the Aldwych Theatre in London, with Colin Baker and Bonnie Langford on Kirby wires, to announce Langford's casting as Melanie Bush, the new companion to replace Nicola Bryant's Peri. On the same day, he writes to Jonathan Powell regarding Ron Katz and the DWFCA. Katz has recently made an offer for the DWFCA to co-produce *Doctor Who*, and Powell wants to know if the proposal is serious. John notes that the offer has already been declined by the BBC, and says that this makes it difficult for him to try to ascertain if it was serious. However, he adds that he would consider filming a story in America in the future. At some point in the following week, John flies out to Florida, USA.

Commentary: For her introductory photocall, Bonnie Langford wore her costume from the Mark Furness-produced *Peter Pan* musical in which she was starring at the time. Furness got to know John here. Later they would have discussions that resulted in the 1989 stage production *Doctor Who: The Ultimate Adventure*.

Thursday 30th – Sunday 2nd February:
Itinerary: John guests at the Omnicon VII convention, held at the Miami Airport Hilton in Miami, Florida. Other guests include Patrick Troughton and Paul Darrow.

Friday 31st:
Itinerary: Philip Martin delivers his scripts for 'The Planet of Sil' Parts Two to Four to the *Doctor Who* Production Office.

FEBRUARY

Sunday 2nd:
Itinerary: Eric Saward sends John a note regarding Christopher Bidmead's scripts for 'Pinocotheca'. He urges their rejection as, having read them three times, he considers them 'boring', adding that they are 'jibberish and totally out of character with the first eight episodes of the season'.

Tuesday 4th:
Itinerary: Now back in the UK, John signs off the commission for Robert Holmes to write the two 25-minute scripts for 'Time Inc'.[375]

Thursday 6th:
Itinerary: John writes to the BBC Costume Design Manager, requesting that John Hearne be allocated to design the costumes for story 7B, and Judy Pepperdine those for story 7C.

Friday 7th:
Itinerary: John having accepted his recommendation regarding the scripts for 'Pinocotheca', Eric Saward writes to Christopher Bidmead to reject the story, offering to phone him to explain the reasons. A dispute subsequently ensues, Bidmead arguing that the circumstances entitle him to receive his final acceptance fee for the scripts and the BBC disagreeing.

Thursday 13th:
Itinerary: Roger Reece from the BBC Costume Department writes to John, confirming John Hearne as Costume Designer for story 7B but letting him know that Judy Pepperdine will be unavailable for story 7C. He proposes

---

[375] The commission stipulated delivery by Friday 28 February. Holmes delivered only the first episode before being taken ill; he subsequently passed away, on 24 May.

Andrew Rose as an alternative.[376]

Saturday 15th:
Commentary: Today is the birthday of actress Anita Graham, one of John's oldest friends.[377]

Tony Selby: 'I went to Australia with the Theatre of Comedy – that's a Ray Cooney organisation, which does mostly farce, and it was with "Run for your Wife", which was a big smash hit. I got to know one of the girls, Anita Graham, who was a great friend of John Nathan-Turner, and had a birthday party when we got back. It was at Lynda Bellingham's restaurant, and I met John Nathan-Turner there. He said, "I've got a wonderful character, and I've got this idea that I'd like you to play him. But you've lost weight … !" People always think I'm bigger than I am, because television makes you look two stone heavier, but I suppose I'd lost about a stone from what he expected. He said, "I want you to put a bit of weight on if you want to play this part, but it's a marvellous character." The first time ever I've got a job through being somewhere socially. It was a great party.'[378]

Lynda Bellingham: 'I only got to do *Doctor Who* because John Nathan-Turner knew my actress friend Anita Graham. She had a birthday party at my ex-husband's North London restaurant. I'd never met JN-T before, but we had a jolly evening. The next day, he rang Anita to ask, "Do you think Lynda can be evil and imposing enough to play the Inquisitor?" Anita quite rightly told him, "John, it's called acting," and thank God he accepted that …'[379]

Monday 17th:
Itinerary: John signs off the commission for P J Hammond to write four 25-minute scripts for 'End of Term'.[380] On the same day, John rings Roger Reece and agrees Andrew Rose's selection as Costume Designer for story 7C.

Monday 24th:
Itinerary: Brian Turner sends John a memo, seeking his views on the dispute with writer Christopher Bidmead regarding his fees for the rejected story 'Pinocotheca'. On the same day, Jonathan Powell writes to John, having read Robert Holmes' scripts for 'The Mysterious Planet' and Philip Martin's for the

---

[376] Rose was indeed given the task of designing the costumes for 7C.
[377] Anita Graham would go on to appear in the minor role of Bollitt in 'Delta and the Bannermen'.
[378] Tony Selby interview, *Doctor Who Magazine* #282.
[379] Lynda Bellingham interview, *Doctor Who Magazine* #346.
[380] 'End of Term' was a story considered to replace Christopher H Bidmead's 'Pinocotheca' in the season's line-up.

first three episodes of 'Mindwarp'. On the evidence of the latter, he thinks 'Mindwarp' to be a good, strong story. However, he has many criticisms, reservations and issues with the scripts of 'The Mysterious Planet', which he proceeds to detail over three pages of A4 paper.

Eric Saward: 'When you're not told what you're doing wrong, it's very difficult to think where you've gone wrong in the way that it was implied but never explained. We tried to make it funnier. Bob Holmes wrote the first four episodes, which given the pressures were okay on paper, but Jonathan Powell didn't like them. The scripts had disappeared for weeks and we thought they had been accepted. The director had even joined. Then we got this memo saying, "Didn't like this, or that, thought this was silly ..." and all the rest of it. So alterations were made, which he accepted and which went into the final programme. But I think by that time Bob Holmes ... he wasn't ill then, but he was, like me, absolutely pissed off with the whole way it had gone.'[381]

Friday 28th:
Itinerary: John writes to BBC Publicity's Kevin O'Shea, suggesting Thursday 10 April as the best date to organise a press visit to the location recording of 'The Mysterious Planet'. He also writes to graphic designer Oliver Elms, thanking him for his thoughts on a new title sequence and logo for the show but explaining that he's decided not to change these for the upcoming season. On the same day, he writes to the BBC Contracts Department, asking that Lynda Bellingham be engaged to play the Inquisitor.

MARCH

Wednesday 5th:
Itinerary: Eric Saward sends John a memo setting out his assessment of the rights and wrongs of the ongoing dispute with writer Christopher Bidmead regarding his fees for the rejected story 'Pinocotheca'.

Thursday 6th:
Itinerary: John signs off the commission for Pip and Jane Baker to write the storyline for 'The Ultimate Foe'. He also sends the Copyright Department's Brian Turner a memo, explaining that this storyline has superseded the Bakers' proposed story 'Gallifrey', which was put on hold a year earlier.

---

[381] Eric Saward interview, *DWB* #58.

Pip Baker: 'We'd been abroad for two months. On our return, we popped in to see [BBC Head of Series and Serials] Bill Slater, and we bumped into John in a lift at the BBC. "Where on Earth have you been?" he exclaimed. We'd been staying in a Spanish villa, without access to a telephone. "I've got a problem," he said. "I need you to write me a script." Our brief was to provide the Doctor's defence, and we had to set the story entirely within the confines of a studio. John wanted an Agatha Christie-style country-house whodunit, so we hit on the idea of setting it on an intergalactic liner.'[382]

Thursday 13th:
Itinerary: John signs off the commission for Pip and Jane Baker to write the four scripts of 'The Ultimate Foe' (which will eventually become Parts Nine to Twelve of 'The Trial of a Time Lord').

Monday 17th:
Itinerary: Dominic Glynn writes to John, enclosing a demo cassette of music composed for the first episode of 'The Mysterious Planet'.

Wednesday 19th:
Itinerary: John writes a lengthy 'Producer's Diary' article for Ron Katz and the DWFCA, for inclusion in their latest newsletter.

APRIL

Tuesday 1st:
Itinerary: John has Eric Saward commissioned to write Part Fourteen of 'The Trial of a Time Lord' as a staff contribution. This will later be revised to a freelance contribution. John also writes to the BBC Contracts Department, asking that Anthony Ainley be engaged to play the Master in the last two episodes of story 7C.

Commentary: Robert Holmes, the writer originally commissioned to supply Part Fourteen of 'The Trial of a Time Lord', had been taken seriously ill shortly after delivering his first draft script for Part Thirteen, sometime the previous month. He had been taken into hospital, and would eventually pass away on Thursday 24 May. In recent years, he had become good friends with Eric Saward, and Saward felt partly responsible for triggering his ill health, because of the pressure of writing of his scripts for this season. Holmes's death

---

[382] Pip and Jane Baker interview, *Doctor Who Magazine* #303.

would be the catalyst for the final breakdown of Saward's relationship with John, although things had been problematic between the two of them for some considerable time.

Wednesday 2nd:
Itinerary: Dominic Glynn writes to John, enclosing a demo cassette of a revamped version of the *Doctor Who* theme tune. Brian Turner of the Copyright Department also sends John a memo, confirming that terms have now been agreed with writer P J Hammond for him to write one 25-minute script for his proposed story 'Paradise Five', previously 'End of Term'. On the same day, Eric Saward writes to Jonathan Powell, offering his resignation as *Doctor Who* script editor with immediate effect.

Eric Saward: 'Bob [Holmes] and I had discussed the last two episodes of the trial … [We] had agreed … that we were going to have a negative end. Like Sherlock Holmes and Moriarty going over the Falls, the Doctor and the Master would be locked in mortal combat, and we'd go out with this question mark hanging over the resolution. And John who hadn't been present at the meeting said, "All right, go ahead and write it and see how it works." But it was never written, because Bob became ill, and John later reneged on the idea. During my time on *Doctor Who*, I had become friends with Robert Holmes and was greatly distressed by his illness. What with that, and the show in such a mess, and little or no support from the producer, I felt I had had enough.'[383]

John Nathan-Turner: 'I was asked to accompany the licensing executives on an unannounced visit to a store that was selling unlicensed *Doctor Who* gear. When we arrived there, to our surprise, we were expected. My secretary, not realising we had been caught in a traffic jam, had called the shop requesting to speak to me immediately. This rather put paid to the licensing brigade's attempt to find illegal merchandise, though certain totally empty shelves were a little suspicious. More to the point, though, the news from base was that Saward had submitted his resignation. He had said that he hated *Doctor Who* and the way that it was run. I returned to the office to see the letter myself and went to see Jonathan Powell. Jonathan suggested I try to woo Saward back, particularly as he had no other script editors available. And, of course, there was also the question of the concluding episode to the season. Bob Holmes was still unwell, so Saward had taken over the responsibility for writing Part Fourteen. I agreed to Jonathan's suggestion and tried to persuade Saward to return, but to no avail – although he agreed to continue with the unfinished script. So along with my other duties, I was now to be *Doctor Who*'s script

---

[383] Eric Saward interview, *DWB* #58.

editor as well.'[384]

Eric Saward: 'I was certainly experiencing burnout when we were in the planning stages of Season 23. I felt that I was going around in circles, and not getting a lot of support from John. I'd have loved to go out on a high note, but I got up one morning and thought, "What am I doing? This is mad." I went to see John, and he was very good, telling me to go away and think about it, which I did. In fact, I went home for two weeks. But it was much the same. I needed someone to say, "Yeah, that's good" or "I like that," but that was never forthcoming. I was getting no support. I'd had enough.'[385]

Gary Downie: 'Eric had a lot of problems he had to work through, and was taking it out on everybody. I can see that now. His personal life interfered with his work. He was involved romantically with John's secretary, Jane Judge. Things that Jane heard in the office she would inadvertently tell Eric – things that shouldn't be heard were discussed. There was a lot of resentment.'[386]

Eric Saward: 'Gary Downie had a lot of fantasies and ideas as to where his career was going. He used to say, "I will be the next producer of *Doctor Who*. John is grooming me." He would be sat there with production managers and directors, amongst others, going on and on. I stopped going to the pub with them. It just got embarrassing. Gary had an enormous effect on John. He was often stirring it. I think John and Gary fed off each other, which became dangerous.'[387]

Friday 4th:
Itinerary: Rehearsals for location OB recording of 'The Trial of a Time Lord' Parts One to Four take place at the BBC Television Rehearsal Rooms at Acton.

Sunday 6th:
Itinerary: Pip and Jane Baker deliver their scripts for 'The Ultimate Foe' Parts One and Two to the *Doctor Who* Production Office.

Monday 7th:
Itinerary: Rehearsals for the location OB recording of 'The Trial of a Time Lord' Parts One to Four take place at the Butser Ancient Farm Project, Butser Hill in Hampshire.

---

[384] John Nathan-Turner memoirs, *Doctor Who Magazine* #245.
[385] Eric Saward interview, *Doctor Who Magazine* #348.
[386] Gary Downie interview, *Doctor Who Magazine* #338.
[387] Eric Saward interview, *Doctor Who Magazine* #348.

Tuesday 8th:
Itinerary: Today is the first day of location OB recording for 'The Trial of a Time Lord' Parts One to Four. The location is the area around Holt Pond and Gravel Hill in the Queen Elizabeth Country Park in Hampshire. John stays overnight at The Spread Eagle Hotel in Midhurst, West Sussex.

Wednesday 9th:
Itinerary: Today is the second day of location OB recording for 'The Trial of a Time Lord' Parts One to Four. The location is once again the area around Holt Pond and Gravel Hill in the Queen Elizabeth Country Park in Hampshire. John again stays overnight at The Spread Eagle Hotel in Midhurst, West Sussex.

Thursday 10th:
Itinerary: Today is the third day of location OB recording for 'The Trial of a Time Lord' Parts One to Four. The location now switches to the Butser Ancient Farm Project, Butser Hill in Hampshire. John organises a press photocall to take place during the day's recording. He once more stays overnight at The Spread Eagle Hotel in Midhurst, West Sussex.

Friday 11th:
Itinerary: Today is the fourth and final day of location OB recording for 'The Trial of a Time Lord' Parts One to Four. The location is again the Butser Ancient Farm Project, Butser Hill in Hampshire. John travels home after recording concludes.

Monday 14th – Wednesday 23rd:
Rehearsals for the first studio block of 'The Trial of a Time Lord' Parts One to Four take place at the BBC Television Rehearsal Rooms at Acton.

Tuesday 15th:
Itinerary: John writes to *Doctor Who Monthly* editor Sheila Cranna at Marvel UK, expressing his dissatisfaction with the first installment of a proposed series of articles entitled 'Who to be ...'.

Thursday 17th:
Itinerary: At some point prior to this date, Eric Saward has delivered his reworked script for Part Thirteen of 'The Trial of a Time Lord'. Today, the typed-up script is returned from the BBC typists to the *Doctor Who* Production Office. John, along with Colin Baker, Nicola Bryant and Janet Fielding, attends the press launch of a new US *Doctor Who* Exhibition trailer/truck at the BBC's Elstree studios.

Sunday 20th:
Itinerary: Dominic Glynn writes to John, enclosing a cassette of further remixes and reworkings of the *Doctor Who* theme tune.

Monday 21st:
Itinerary: Eric Saward writes to John. He says that he can't bring himself to write the script for Part Fourteen, and suggests that John get Pip and Jane Baker to do it episode instead. He adds that, alternatively, John could abandon the Robert Holmes script for Part Thirteen that Saward has revised, and get the Bakers to write the last two episodes of 'The Trial of a Time Lord' from scratch. Up until now, John has left Saward's resignation as script editor on hold, but Saward now tells him that it is final.

Tuesday 22nd:
Itinerary: John writes to Eric Saward. He tries to persuade him to continue writing the script for Part Fourteen of 'The Trial of a Time Lord', but accepts his final resignation as script editor. He also writes to the BBC Copyright Department, confirming that Philip Martin has delivered an additional three minutes of script for Part Two of 'Mindwarp', as requested, as the episode was found to be underrunning.

Wednesday 23rd:
Itinerary: Today is the Producer's Run at the BBC Television Rehearsal Rooms at Acton for the first studio block of 'The Trial of a Time Lord' Parts One to Four.

Thursday 24th:
Itinerary: Today is the first day of the two-day first studio block for 'The Trial of a Time Lord' Parts One to Four in studio TC6 at BBC Television Centre. John writes to Ron Jones, informing him that an additional three minutes of script for 'Mindwarp' will be available to him next week.

Friday 25th:
Itinerary: Today is the second and final day of the first studio block for 'The Trial of a Time Lord' Parts One to Four in studio TC6 at BBC Television Centre. Eric Saward's contract as script editor expires today. Saward is paid in full up to this date.

Sunday 27th:
Itinerary: Philip Martin writes to John, enclosing a further four minutes of script for Part Two of 'Mindwarp'.

Monday 28th – Friday 9th May:
Rehearsals for the second studio block of 'The Trial of a Time Lord' Parts One to Four take place at the BBC Television Rehearsal Rooms at Acton.

John Nathan-Turner: 'I recall that during the rehearsals for the second and final recording of this story, there came a panic phone-call from the rehearsal block. Two episodes were under-running! So, as Saward was on leave at the time and Bob Holmes had been taken ill, I decided that there was only one thing to do: write the material myself. I will never reveal which two-and-a-half minutes were written by me!'[388]

Wednesday 30th:
Itinerary: John writes to the BBC Copyright Department, confirming that Philip Martin has delivered an additional four minutes of script for Part Two of 'Mindwarp'. He also writes to Martin to thank him for sending in this additional material. In addition, he writes to the BBC Contracts Department, asking that Tony Selby's contract for the part of Glitz be extended to cover also the final two episodes of story 7C. On the same day, Laurence J Bennett from the US Spirit of Light conventions group writes to John though his company, Aerosport Ltd, asking to have two photos of John exclusively licensed to them for sale at the *Doctor Who* events they run, with the profits to be split equally between John and the company. Accompanying the letter is a contract for John's appearance at the Whovent 86 convention next month. John declines the request to supply photos of himself.[389]

MAY

Thursday 1st:
Itinerary: Sometime on or before this date, John flies from the UK to Atlanta, Georgia, USA.

Friday 2nd – Sunday 4th:
Itinerary: John is a guest at the Dixie Trek 86 convention, held at the Sheraton Century Center Hotel in Atlanta. The other main guest is Peter Davison.

---

[388] John Nathan-Turner memoirs, *Doctor Who Magazine* #245. The material written by Nathan-Turner for this story can be found in Part Three, where Katryca, Balazar and Broken Tooth – plus the Tribe of the Free – can't decide on the best route to Drathro's headquarters.
[389] This letter was addressed to John at the BBC, but all subsequent correspondence and payments from Laurence J Bennett were sent to John's home address.

Monday 5th:
Itinerary: John flies back to London from Atlanta.

Thursday 8th:
Itinerary: John writes to Philip Martin, advising him of the studio dates for 'Mindwarp', should he wish to attend any of the recordings. Laurence J Bennett writes to John to confirm the travel arrangements for the Spirit of Light-run Whovent 86 convention in New Brunswick later this month. He also points out that if John were to appear at any other US events, this might contravene an exclusivity clause in the contract. On the same day, John writes to Sheila Cranna at Marvel UK, raising concerns about a retrospective article by Gary Russell on the Target range of *Doctor Who* books, which is intended for publication in *Doctor Who Monthly*.

Friday 9th:
Itinerary: Today is the Producer's Run at the BBC Television Rehearsal Rooms at Acton for the second studio block of 'The Trial of a Time Lord' Parts One to Four. Pip and Jane Baker deliver their scripts for 'The Ultimate Foe' Parts Three and Four to the *Doctor Who* Production Office. The *Doctor Who* Travelling Exhibition trailer is launched in Washington DC, USA by Peter Davison and Michael Grade. Laurence J Bennett again writes to John, informing him that an event that he was due to attend in July in Los Angeles has now been cancelled. Bennett instead invites him to appear at another event, planned for San Antonio, Texas, between 22 and 24 August, which he says is covered in John's exclusivity contract.[390]

Saturday 10th:
Itinerary: Today is the first day of the three-day second studio block for 'The Trial of a Time Lord' Parts One to Four in studio TC3 at BBC Television Centre.

Sunday 11th:
Itinerary: Today is the second day of the three-day second studio block for 'The Trial of a Time Lord' Parts One to Four in studio TC3 at BBC Television Centre.

Monday 12th:
Itinerary: Today is the third and final day of the second studio block for 'The Trial of a Time Lord' Parts One to Four in studio TC3 at BBC Television Centre.

---

[390] No event seems to have been run by Spirit of Light in Texas in August 1986, so this must have been cancelled too.

Wednesday 14th – Monday 26th:
Rehearsals for the first studio block of 'The Trial of a Time Lord' Parts Five to Eight take place at the BBC Television Rehearsal Rooms at Acton.

Wednesday 14th:
Itinerary: Laurence J Bennett again writes to John, finalising the details of the exclusivity contract for John to attend only Spirit of Light events during the year – aside from any he is required to attend by arrangement with the BBC or BBC Enterprises. Enclosed is a cheque for several thousand pounds, as an initial payment under this contract.

Monday 19th:
Itinerary: John writes to Pip and Jane Baker, thanking them for the quick rewrites they have done on their scripts for 'The Trial of a Time Lord' Parts 9 to 12.

Tuesday 20th:
Itinerary: Eric Saward writes a letter to John. He states that he cannot act on some of John's notes on his script for Part Fourteen of 'The Trial of a Time Lord', as he has many points of contention with the requested rewrites.

Commentary: Sometime in the weeks immediately prior to this date, Saward had delivered his script for Part Fourteen of 'The Trial of a Time Lord' and John had had the opportunity to read it and request alterations.

Thursday 22nd
Itinerary: Eric Saward writes again to John. He has not had a reply to his letter of the 20 May, and wants to know if this means that John has accepted his various points regarding the script for Part Fourteen of 'The Trial of a Time Lord'. John asks the BBC Legal Department to run a negative check on 'Melanie Bush, computer programmer, Pease Pottage.'

Friday 23rd:
Itinerary: John writes to Eric Saward and tries to rebut all of the writer's objections to his original notes on the script for Part Fourteen of 'The Trial of a Time Lord'. Later that day, he flies from the UK to New Jersey, USA.

Saturday 24th:
Writer Robert Holmes dies in Stoke Mandeville hospital from liver failure.

Sunday 25th – Monday 26th:
Itinerary: John is a guest at the Whovent 86 convention, organised by Spirit of Light and held at the Hyatt Regency Hotel in New Brunswick, New Jersey.

The other guests include Patrick Troughton, Carole Ann Ford, Frazer Hines, Louise Jameson, Sarah Sutton, Mark Strickson and Bonnie Langford (who has yet to record any scenes as Mel at this point). John flies back to the UK on the Sunday evening.

Eric Saward: 'When he goes to these conventions he has to get permission from the head of department to do so. I gather that usually goes through on the nod. At first, it didn't encroach upon his work in that way. He started going to more and more of them. A lot of them would be at weekends. What did become apparent, though, if he'd gone off for a weekend convention to America, he would come into work on Monday straight from the 'plane. It was as though he wanted to go to the conventions, but wanted to show everyone that nothing was distracting him from his duties as producer, so he would do the lunatic thing of coming back Sunday/Monday morning, coming into the office, and just shutting the door and going to sleep. He is obsessed with the American fans ... I think the main draw for him, apart from the fact that he has got his fingers in so many pies, is the income from the conventions in America, which I think is quite a lot of money. I think that is something he is reluctant to give up ... He went through a phase a couple of years ago of spending a lot of time on the 'phone I think to America, certainly to the various convention organisers – most of them are in America – and we had the lunatic situation one day [that] I was standing outside the office, I needed to see him, and two of his directors needed to see him, and he'd been there chatting on the 'phone, as far as the secretary was concerned, for at least an hour. It wasn't just once, it was often, and with people waiting to see him – waiting to make the goddamn show he was supposed to be the producer of. It was anything that would come up – I mean, he'd rather read a manuscript from W H Allen, or spend hours piddling about with some crappy piece of merchandising from Enterprises, than willingly become involved in talking about what we were doing. I can't understand it.'[391]

Monday 26th:
Itinerary: Eric Saward writes to John. He encloses a revised version of his script for 'The Trial of a Time Lord' Part Fourteen, which takes on board some of John's notes on his original script but leaves the ending unchanged. He goes on to say that he is open to discussing alternative suggestions for the ending, but refuses point blank to consider John's preferred 'happy walk down' option.

Eric Saward: 'Did I leave on bad terms? The initial departure, no. I mean, [John] said "Well, perhaps it is time to go," and I was sorry I was going as I

---

[391] 'The Revelations of a Script Editor', *Starburst* #97.

was, but this thing remained of the last episode and there were other things looming up about material that had been used that shouldn't have been used, and I think it began to get silly. I agreed to write the last episode but on the understanding of what we'd discussed, and he said "Yes, fine," and I went away and did my version of the last episode, pulling the threads together. To Bob's formula, I rewrote the [second] half of the previous episode, which he'd already written, because I couldn't link up exactly with what he'd done; I think the first 12 minutes of episode thirteen is his and the rest is mine. Then I wrote the last episode and delivered it, and John said "Yes, that's all right I suppose." Then he turned around and said "I can't stand this ending, you can't have them going out like this." It was a definite renege on what had been agreed, and I said "Well, find someone else to do it." I had not signed the contract to write the thing anyway, and then, I think, he got rather annoyed. It was a terrible mess, a pain in my life that I really hated, and then at the end of it all Bob Holmes died, so it was a *wonderful* sort of conclusion to my time on *Doctor Who*.'[392]

Tuesday 27th:
Itinerary: Today is the first day of the three-day first studio block for 'The Trial of a Time Lord' Parts Five to Eight in studio TC1 at BBC Television Centre.

Wednesday 28th:
Itinerary: Today is the second day of the three-day first studio block for 'The Trial of a Time Lord' Parts Five to Eight in studio TC1 at BBC Television Centre. The recording is followed by a crew from the French TV channel TF-1, who are covering *Doctor Who* for a documentary for the show *Temps X*. John is interviewed by the *Temps X* crew during the day.

Thursday 29th:
Itinerary: Today is the third and final day of the first studio block for 'The Trial of a Time Lord' Parts Five to Eight in studio TC1 at BBC Television Centre. Also on this day, John writes to the BBC Music Copyright Department, asking that Richard Hartley be engaged to write the incidental music for 'Mindwarp'.

Friday 30th:
Itinerary: On or before this date, John flies to Wisconsin, USA. On the same date, he writes to Ron Katz at the DWFCA, asking him to resolve a longstanding dispute with Mayflower Travel in London revolving around plane tickets for guests from the UK to attend events organised by the DWFCA in the US. John was the one who introduced Katz to Mayflower

---

[392] Eric Saward interview, *DWB* #58.

Travel, and so finds himself compromised by the situation.

Friday 30th – Sunday June 1st:
Itinerary: John is a guest at the Whovent 86 convention, organised by Spirit of Light, which is held at the Wisconsin Union Theatre in Madison, Wisconsin. The other guests include Peter Davison, Louise Jameson, Lalla Ward, Sarah Sutton, Mark Strickson and Bonnie Langford.

Friday 30th – Tuesday 10th June:
Rehearsals for the second studio block of 'The Trial of a Time Lord' Parts Five to Eight take place at the BBC Television Rehearsal Rooms at Acton.

JUNE

Sunday 1st:
Itinerary: Eric Saward writes to John and accuses him of making untrue claims to a third party (referred to simply as 'AR' in the letter) about the script of Part Fourteen of 'The Trial of a Time Lord'. Saward acknowledges that they can't reach agreement on how to end the season, so he withdraws permission for his script to be used by the BBC. Saward also points out that Mr Popplewick is wholly his creation, and therefore his copyright, as he has rewritten the final 15 minutes of Robert Holmes' script for Part Thirteen and added the character into the narrative. John flies back to London from Wisconsin late this evening.

Eric Saward: 'I finished Part Fourteen, and John, who was not a script editor, sent it back covered in silly comments. I said, "Oh fuck off! I've had enough of this. Get someone else. I can live without these really trite comments." His comments were ill-considered. Given that I'd worked so hard in pulling Bob's stuff together, and given my five years' service, I deserved better than the silly remarks that were fed back via the scripts ... I felt the only thing I could do was withdraw the script.'[393]

Tuesday 3rd
Itinerary: Now back in the UK, John writes to Eric Saward, denying all of Saward's claims regarding speaking to a third party about the script for Part Fourteen. He asks Saward to ring him as soon as possible.

---

[393] Eric Saward Interview, *Doctor Who Magazine* #348.

Wednesday 4th:
Itinerary: Eric Saward writes to John, rejecting John's denial about the third party referred to as 'AR', suggesting that he 'chew on a name with the initials AW', which he is sure will 'bring back tragic memories', and reiterating that he is withdrawing his script for Part Fourteen.

Thursday 5th:
Itinerary: Eric Saward writes to Brian Turner at the BBC Copyright Department, informing him that he has withdrawn his script for Part Fourteen of 'The Trial of a Time Lord'. He adds that he also wants to withdraw the extra material he wrote for Part Thirteen (more or less all the scenes set inside the Matrix), and asks for confirmation that this will happen.

Jane Baker: 'John rang me up one day, and said, "I'm having a script biked over to you. I want you to read it, and come into the office first thing tomorrow morning." He wouldn't say any more ... The script was for Part Thirteen of "The Trial of a Time Lord" by Robert Holmes. We went into John's office the next day ...'[394]

Friday 6th:
Itinerary: John meets with Pip and Jane Baker, and signs off the commission for them to write a script for 'The Trial of a Time Lord' Part Fourteen. A representative from the BBC Legal Department sits in on the meeting, to ensure that no details from Eric Saward's withdrawn script are divulged to the Bakers.

John Nathan-Turner: 'I called in Pip and Jane Baker, who are intensely professional, and they immediately agreed to tackle the problem. I insisted that the entire briefing session was witnessed and minuted so that no-one could say that the new writers had been passed information about what had been planned or written before. Naturally they saw no earlier versions of Part Fourteen. All scripts remaining in the production office were shredded, and Pip and Jane disappeared home.'[395]

Pip Baker: 'A severe-looking woman was sitting in on our meeting. She was a lawyer. John explained, "We're supposed to be rehearsing Parts Thirteen and Fourteen at the moment, but we have no Part Fourteen!" We discovered afterwards that Eric had accepted a commission to script Part Fourteen practically from scratch, but he never signed that contract. Until he signed that contract, the script was his property. We went across the corridor to Eric's

---

[394] Pip and Jane Baker interview, *Doctor Who Magazine* #304.
[395] John Nathan-Turner memoirs, *Doctor Who Magazine* #245

now-vacant office and devised an ending. John told us that he needed the script within three days.'[396]

Monday 9th:
Itinerary: Stephen Edwards from the BBC Copyright Department sends John a copy of Eric Saward's letter of 5 June, and of the response to be sent back from the Copyright Department. This response states that the rewrites Saward did on the script of Part Thirteen were done as part of his normal duties as script editor, and so the copyright on the material belongs to the BBC.

Tuesday 10th:
Itinerary: Today is the Producer's Run at the BBC Television Rehearsal Rooms at Acton for the second studio block of 'The Trial of a Time Lord' Parts Five to Eight.

Wednesday 11th:
Itinerary: Today is the first day of the three-day second studio block for 'The Trial of a Time Lord' Parts Five to Eight in studio TC6 at BBC Television Centre.

Thursday 12th:
Itinerary: Eric Saward writes to Stephen Edwards. Saward notes that he understands that Brian Turner is away on leave, and so asks Edwards to deal with the matter raised in his letter of 5 June. (Presumably Saward has not yet not received the reply of 9 June.) Today is also the second day of the three-day second studio block for 'The Trial of a Time Lord' Parts Five to Eight in studio TC6 at BBC Television Centre.

Colin Baker: 'Brian [Blessed, playing King Yrcanos] did something one night that I've never seen any other actor get away with ... At around 10pm, the plugs are pulled in studio. If you have any scenes still to record [as that time approaches], you have to get them done bloody quickly. No retakes. There was a scene where Brian and I had to run along a corridor, grab Nicola [Bryant], and Brian had to say, "Right, let's find the Mentors." That was all he had to say. The line was tied in with lots of special effects. It was two-minutes-to-ten. "*Action!*" Explosions! Open door, grab Nicola, look at Brian – and he can't remember the word "Mentor", so he says, "*Right, lets find the Fuckerons!*" The Fuckerons don't exist, of course, and that isn't a word we can use in *Doctor Who*. But it's ten o'clock, and we've run out of time. If I'd done that, or if Nicola had done that, the producer would have come down to the studio floor and flayed us alive. We would have been in deep doo-doo. As it was, John

---

[396] Pip and Jane Baker interview, *Doctor Who Magazine* #304.

tiptoed down and said, "That wasn't terribly helpful, Brian." "*Sorry, old boy. I couldn't remember the fucking word! Bloody things! Who wrote this?*" All John could say was, "Well, never mind. We'll remount the scene tomorrow. Don't worry about it, Brian." He said "*What! I'm not fucking worried! I'll tear your head off and eat your brains if you annoy me!*" So they had to remount that scene, which must have cost thousands …'[397]

Friday 13th:
Itinerary: Eric Saward writes to Stephen Edwards, having now presumably received the letter of 9 June. He restates that the material he has written for Part Thirteen of 'The Trial of a Time Lord' is to be withdrawn. He gives Edwards seven days notice to comply with this, or he threatens further action. Today is the third and final day of the second studio block for 'The Trial of a Time Lord' Parts Five to Eight in studio TC6 at BBC Television Centre.

Sunday 15th:
Itinerary: Today is the first day of location OB recording for 'The Trial of a Time Lord' Parts Five to Eight. The location is the beach and shoreline at Telscombe Cliffs in East Sussex, very close to John's house in Brighton. Pip and Jane Baker deliver their script for 'The Trial of a Time Lord' Part Fourteen to the *Doctor Who* Production Office.

Commentary: Unusually, the location recording for this story was done after all the studio segments had been completed.

Monday 16th:
Itinerary: Eric Saward writes to Jonathan Powell, setting out his case for claiming the copyright on the material he has written for Part Thirteen of 'The Trial of a Time Lord'. Today is the second and final day of location OB recording for 'The Trial of a Time Lord' Parts Five to Eight. The location is once again the beach and shoreline at Telscombe Cliffs in East Sussex. It's Nicola Bryant's last day working on the series, and John throws a farewell party for her at his house in nearby Brighton after recording concludes.

Thursday 19th – Saturday 21st:
Rehearsals for the OB location recording of 'The Trial of a Time Lord' Parts Thirteen and Fourteen take place at the BBC Television Rehearsal Rooms at Acton.

Thursday 19th:
Itinerary: Jonathan Powell sends John a copy of Eric Saward's letter of 16 June,

---

[397] Colin Baker interview, *Doctor Who Magazine* #324.

with a short memo asking him to draft a reply. Stephen Edwards is also sent copies of Powell's memo and Saward's letter. Lisa Pieri from the Negative Check Department writes back to John, informing him that it is virtually impossible to check the names of all the computer programmers in the UK. However, they have found no-one famous with the name Melanie Bush.

Saturday 21st:
Itinerary: Actor James Bree writes to John to voice his disappointment that the part of the Keeper of the Matrix in the new version of Part Fourteen's script has been vastly reduced from what was initially outlined to him.

Monday 23rd:
Itinerary: Today is the first day of location OB recording for 'The Trial of a Time Lord' Parts Thirteen and Fourteen. The location is Camber Sands in East Sussex. After recording, John stays the night at The Saltings Hotel in Rye, East Sussex.

Tuesday 24th:
Itinerary: Stephen Edwards sends Jonathan Powell a draft of a letter that he wants Powell to send to Eric Saward. Edwards points out that John Nathan-Turner went to great lengths to check with him that they could use the material that Saward wrote in his script for Part Thirteen. The letter that Edwards has drafted accuses Saward of being grossly defamatory to John, and to the BBC. The letter restates that the work Saward did on the script of Part Thirteen was done as part of his script editing duties, and so the copyright belongs to the BBC. Today is also the second day of location OB recording for 'The Trial of a Time Lord' Parts Thirteen and Fourteen. The location is once again Camber Sands in East Sussex. After recording, John returns to London.

Monday 30th:
Itinerary: Jonathan Powell writes to Eric Saward, using the text of Stephen Edwards' proposed response from 24 June. Today is the third day of location OB recording for 'The Trial of a Time Lord' Parts Thirteen and Fourteen. The venue has now switched to the Gladstone Pottery Museum in Longton, Staffordshire, and the recording takes place at night, beginning in the early evening and finishing at around 3.00am. After recording, John spends the night at the Thomas Foreshore Hotel in Newcastle-Under-Lyme.

JULY

Tuesday 1st:
Itinerary: Today is the fourth day of location OB recording for 'The Trial of a Time Lord' Parts Thirteen and Fourteen. The location is again Gladstone Pottery Museum in Longton, Staffordshire, and the recording again finishes at around 3.00am. After recording, John once more spends the night at the Thomas Foreshore Hotel.

Wednesday 2nd:
Itinerary: Today is the fifth day of location OB recording for 'The Trial of a Time Lord' Parts Thirteen and Fourteen. The location is again unchanged, and the recording again finishes at around 3.00am. After recording, John again spends the night at the Thomas Foreshore Hotel.

Thursday 3rd:
Itinerary: Today is the sixth day of location OB recording for 'The Trial of a Time Lord' Parts Thirteen and Fourteen. The location and recording end time are the same as previously. After recording, John once more spends the night at the Thomas Foreshore Hotel.

Friday 4th:
Itinerary: Today is technically the seventh and final day of location OB recording for 'The Trial of a Time Lord' Parts Thirteen and Fourteen. However, the last of the required material has already been completed during the previous night's session, so once rested, the cast and crew are free to depart. John returns to London later in the day.

John Nathan-Turner: 'Recording late at night at the Gladstone Pottery Museum was bizarre … The place had such a strange atmosphere and it seemed weird to be recording *Doctor Who* with hardly any non-speaking artistes. However, it resulted in a close-knit community who got up after lunch and usually went to bed as dawn broke. I say usually, for after the last night-shoot, Mike Jayston, Geoff Hughes, Tony Selby, Colin [Baker, Chris Clough, myself and company said "goodnight" to Pip and Jane [Baker] at about four in the morning and we were still in the bar when they passed through, having had breakfast, several hours later!'[398]

---

[398] John Nathan-Turner Memoirs, *Doctor Who Magazine* #245

Monday 7th – Tuesday 15th:
Rehearsals for the first studio block of 'The Trial of a Time Lord' Parts Nine to Fourteen take place at the BBC Television Rehearsal Rooms at Acton.

Tuesday 15th:
Itinerary: Today is the Producer's Run at the BBC Television Rehearsal Rooms at Acton for the first studio block of 'The Trial of a Time Lord' Parts Nine to Fourteen.

Wednesday 16th:
Itinerary: Today is the first day of the two-day first studio block for 'The Trial of a Time Lord' Parts Nine to Fourteen in studio TC1 at BBC Television Centre. All the material needed to complete Parts Thirteen and Fourteen is recorded in this block, along with some trial room scenes for Parts Nine to Twelve.

Thursday 17th:
Itinerary: Today is the second and final day of the first studio block for 'The Trial of a Time Lord' Parts Nine to Fourteen in studio TC1 at BBC Television Centre.

Friday 18th – Tuesday 29th:
Rehearsals for the second studio block of 'The Trial of a Time Lord' Parts Nine to Twelve take place at the BBC Television Rehearsal Rooms at Acton. The second and third studio blocks are exclusively to record material for the Vervoid segment of the story.

Tuesday 29th:
Itinerary: Today is the Producer's Run at the BBC Television Rehearsal Rooms at Acton for the second studio block of 'The Trial of a Time Lord' Parts Nine to Twelve.

Wednesday 30th:
Itinerary: Today is the first day of the three-day second studio block for 'The Trial of a Time Lord' Parts Nine to Twelve in studio TC3 at BBC Television Centre.

John Nathan-Turner: 'I had nipped to the office early to deal with urgent problems before proceeding to Wood Lane for the studio, Just as I was going out of the door the press officer, Kevin O'Shea, called and said there was an article in a science fiction magazine, *Starburst,* in which [Eric] Saward was interviewed and it was extremely nasty stuff. Kevin met me in the tea bar next to the studio and gave me the magazine in an envelope. He said he would come into the producer's studio office in an hour, adding ominously, "There are follow-up enquiries from other publications!" I sipped my coffee and ate a ham roll. Pip and Jane [Baker] advised, nay begged, me not to read it. I went to that office, turned down the talkback, and read the article. Kevin had been right. It was nasty. Saward attacked not only the show, but my own decisions, abilities and motives in an extremely personal and abusive way. I shook with rage ... Kevin came in with a superbly written statement and I signed it. I asked him to get a copy of the article to Jonathan Powell as quickly as possible. At lunch I realised that everyone was treating me with kid gloves; clearly the news had got around, and copies of said magazine were doubtless being read in costume rooms, under the booms, in the scenic service docks, etc ... I sought advice from both the BBC and an independent solicitor, who both thought the issue should be pursued. I discussed this with Jonathan Powell and he told me not to bother. He kept saying, "*He's* gone and you're still here!"'[399]

Thursday 31st:
Itinerary: Today is the second day of the three-day second studio block for 'The Trial of a Time Lord' Parts Nine to Twelve in studio TC3 at BBC Television Centre.

AUGUST

Friday 1st:
Itinerary: Today is the third and final day of the second studio block for 'The Trial of a Time Lord' Parts Nine to Twelve in studio TC3 at BBC Television Centre.

Friday 1st – Sunday 3rd:
Itinerary: John is supposed to be a guest at the TARDIScon/Time Festival 1986 convention in St Louis, Missouri this weekend. However, he pulls out of this.

Commentary: John's withdrawal was probably due either to him having signed the exclusivity contract in May to appear only at Spirit of Light events this year, or to the fallout over the Eric Saward *Starburst* interview.

---

[399] John Nathan-Turner memoirs, *Doctor Who Magazine* #245. Issue 97 of the sci-fi magazine *Starburst*, with a cover date of September 1986, contained the interview with Eric Saward under the title 'The Revelations of a Script Editor'.

Monday 4th – Monday 11th:
Rehearsals for the third studio block of 'The Trial of a Time Lord' Parts Nine –
Twelve take place at the BBC Television Rehearsal Rooms at Acton.

Tuesday 5th:
Itinerary: Bob Davis, Design Resource Manager at the BBC, writes to John,
informing him that the scenic costs for story 7C will come in at £7,556 over the
available budget. He says that designer Dinah Walker has made some cuts
that have saved £3,632 on this cost, but asks that the balance of £3,924 be met
by the *Doctor Who* production team.

Wednesday 6th:
Itinerary: John replies to Bob Davis, refusing to agree to the design overspend.

Thursday 7th:
Itinerary: The BBC launch their Autumn Season line up with a press
conference at the Lancaster Gate Hotel in London. John attends, as does
Michael Grade, who congratulates him on the first episode of the new season.

John Nathan-Turner: 'When he saw the first episode of "The Trial of a Time
Lord", Michael [Grade] congratulated me publically at the Lancaster Gate
Hotel where the BBC1 Drama launch was being held, though he attracted my
attention from amongst a group of journalists by calling me "J". I thought of
responding by calling him "M", but Mr Fleming had got there first!'[400]

Friday 8th:
Itinerary: John writes to Peter Seddon, Head of Design at the BBC, enclosing
copies of his recent correspondence with Bob Davis. John maintains that the
overspend is down to an error in arithmetic made by the Design Department
after the final costings were talked through at a design meeting on Wednesday
16 July. He cannot see why the *Doctor Who* budget should have to bear the cost
of the Design Department's error.

Monday 11th:
Itinerary: Today is the Producer's Run at the BBC Television Rehearsal Rooms
at Acton for the third studio block of 'The Trial of a Time Lord' Parts Nine to
Twelve.

Tuesday 12th: (John's thirty-ninth birthday)
Itinerary: Today is the first day of the three-day third studio block for 'The Trial
of a Time Lord' Parts Nine to Twelve in studio TC1 at BBC Television Centre.

---

[400] John Nathan-Turner Memoirs, *Doctor Who Magazine* #240.

Wednesday 13th:
Itinerary: Today is the second day of the three-day third studio block for 'The Trial of a Time Lord' Parts Nine to Twelve in studio TC1 at BBC Television Centre.

Thursday 14th:
Itinerary: Today is the third and final day of the third studio block for 'The Trial of a Time Lord' Parts Nine to Twelve in studio TC1 at BBC Television Centre. This concludes production on the twenty-third season of *Doctor Who*, although there is still some editing and post-production work to be done. Sometime on or before this date, John flies from the UK to Washington, USA.

Friday 15th – Sunday 17th:
Itinerary: John is a guest at the Time Fest '86 convention, held at the Spokane Sheraton Hotel in Spokane, Washington. The other guests at this event include Nicholas Courtney, John Levene, Richard Franklin, Katy Manning, Ian Marter and Anthony Ainley. John returns to the UK shortly after the event finishes.

Commentary: By all accounts, this event was poorly organised and poorly attended. The guests ended up having to pay their own travel costs, and although they were promised that they would be reimbursed, payments were never made.

Tuesday 19th:
Itinerary: The BBC Press Office confirms that there will be a Season 24 of *Doctor Who*, which will air on BBC1 in 1987.

Thursday 28th:
Itinerary: John is copied in to correspondence from Mayflower Travel, instigating legal proceedings against Ron Katz and the DWFCA over the ongoing dispute regarding plane tickets for guests to fly to US conventions.

SEPTEMBER

Saturday 6th – Sunday 7th:
Itinerary: John attends the DWAS's PanoptiCon VII convention at Imperial College in South Kensington in London. He announces that he will be leaving *Doctor Who* at the end of the year, and that a new producer will take over for Season 24. He makes it very clear that he is expecting to leave the show to work on other projects at the BBC. Other guests at the event include Colin

Baker, Nicola Bryant, Peter Davison and Jon Pertwee.

Saturday 6th:
'The Trial of a Time Lord' Part One screens on BBC1.

Saturday 13th:
'The Trial of a Time Lord' Part Two screens on BBC1.

Saturday 20th:
'The Trial of a Time Lord' Part Three screens on BBC1.

Saturday 27th:
'The Trial of a Time Lord' Part Four screens on BBC1.

Monday 29th:
Itinerary: Tom Rivers, the BBC's Assistant Head of Copyright, sends John a memo, requesting his help in resolving a dispute that has arisen with writer Peter Grimwade. With Eric Saward's support, Grimwade is contesting the BBC's claim to ownership of the companion character Turlough, who was introduced in his story 'Mawdryn Undead'.

OCTOBER

Saturday 4th:
'The Trial of a Time Lord' Part Five screens on BBC1.

Wednesday 8th:
Itinerary: Philip Martin writes to John, expressing his enjoyment at watching Part Five of 'The Trial of a Time Lord' on Saturday. He goes on to say how remarkable the alien landscape scenes looked.

Friday 10th:
Itinerary: Tom Rivers of the Copyright Department again writes to John about the ongoing dispute with Peter Grimwade over ownership of the character of Turlough. Attempts are being made to establish that the production team gave a briefing note on the character to other writers, such as Stephen Gallagher, Terence Dudley and Eric Pringle, in advance of Grimwade submitting his scripts for 'Mawdryn Undead', and that he could not therefore have been the character's creator.

Saturday 11th:
'The Trial of a Time Lord' Part Six screens on BBC1.

Saturday 18th:
Itinerary: John attends the shop Forbidden Planet 2 in London between 1.00 and 2.00pm, to sign copies of his book *Doctor Who: The Companions.*[401] 'The Trial of a Time Lord' Part Seven screens on BBC1.

Monday 20th:
Itinerary: John, along with Janet Fielding and Nicola Bryant, is a guest on the BBC's *Breakfast Time* programme, plugging his new book *Doctor Who: The Companions*. Afterwards, he attends a press launch for Part Nine of 'The Trial of a Time Lord', to publicise the introduction of new assistant Mel. Colin Baker and writers Pip and Jane Baker also attend.

Wednesday 22nd:
Itinerary: John writes the recap narration to be spoken by the BBC1 continuity announcer prior to the broadcast of Part Ten of 'The Trial of a Time Lord'. Sometime in the next few days, he flies out to New York City, USA.

Saturday 25th:
'The Trial of a Time Lord' Part Eight screens on BBC1.

Saturday 25th – Sunday 26th:
Itinerary: John is a guest at the Fall-Con I 86 convention, held at the Best Western Red Jacket Hotel, Niagara Falls in New York. The other main guest is Janet Fielding. He returns to the UK after the event finishes.

Tuesday 28th:
Itinerary: Writer Christopher Bidmead sends John a letter, complaining about the fact that, in his book *Doctor Who: The Companions*, John thanked him for his co-operation with the project, something that he denies having agreed to. He also repeats the allegation, previously made by Eric Saward, that John has received fees for the showing of *Doctor Who* episodes at conventions.

Wednesday 29th:
Itinerary: Now back in the UK, John is informed by Jonathan Powell that the BBC's option on Colin Baker's contract will not be taken up for the following year. He is instructed to break the news to Baker. He phones Baker and duly

---

[401] This was John's follow-up book to *Doctor Who: The TARDIS Inside Out*. It was again published by Piccadilly Press, and came out on 1 November May 1986 in both hardback and paperback. Advance copies were again made available for John's signing at Forbidden Planet 2.

informs him of the BBC's decision. He also phones Christopher Bidmead to discuss his letter of the previous day's date.

John Nathan-Turner: 'At the end of November 1986 it was agreed I could leave *Doctor Who* once and for all. I was pleased, until Jonathan [Powell] said there was one last thing he'd like me to do, other than keeping an eye on the remaining transmissions and dealing with any resultant queries. I was to tell Colin Baker that there was going to be a new Doctor. Jonathan said that three years was now the optimum period for a Doctor, and Colin's three were over. Despite my protestations to the contrary, Jonathan said the hiatus year should be counted as part of the Doctor's reign. I called Colin, fixed lunch as soon as he could make it – certainly within two days, and it might have even been the following day. On the day of our meeting, there was an enquiry from Fleet Street to our press officer, asking if Colin was to be replaced. The BBC fan moles were at it again, I suspect! The enquirer was stalled, and I decided to tell Colin straight away by telephone, rather than risk his embarrassment should he start getting peculiar calls at home. Not surprisingly, Colin decided to postpone lunch. He was offended, annoyed and upset. I sympathised and had more of the same feeling myself. I felt that Colin was being treated shoddily.'[402]

Colin Baker: 'John told me over the phone, which I'm sure he would have acknowledged wasn't the best way to tell me! "I've got some good news," he said, "and some bad news. The good news is that the series is happening again next year." "Oh, thank God! John, I'm so pleased," I said. "What's the bad news?" He said, "I've been asked by Michael Grade to replace you." I waited for him to say, "But I refused, and I insisted that you must stay," but he said, "It's non-negotiable. I've asked them to reconsider. I tried hard, but they're immovable. They think it's time for a new Doctor." That was kind of a shock to the system … Actually, Peter Davison told me this – and Peter isn't the most forthcoming of people. He doesn't rush up and fling his arms around you. But he did tell me that he sat next to Michael Grade on an aeroplane, and got a strong impression that it wasn't me but John Nathan-Turner that Grade was after. The difference in style between Grade, the new man at the BBC, and Nathan-Turner, the populist TV drama producer, was tremendous. I think John was an irritant. Being a kind of corporate game-player, Grade thought that by telling the producer to sack his lead actor, he'd force him to resign. He wanted John to point-blank refuse to sack me – but John called his bluff. He sacked me instead.'[403]

---

[402] John Nathan-Turner Memoirs, *Doctor Who Magazine* #240.
[403] Colin Baker interview, *Doctor Who Magazine* #324. John recalled in interviews that it was Jonathan Powell who instructed that Baker's contract not be renewed,

NOVEMBER

Saturday 1st:
'The Trial of a Time Lord' Part Nine screens on BBC1.

Monday 3rd:
Itinerary: John writes to the BBC Contracts Department, informing them that a short flashback clip of Brian Blessed and Nicola Bryant from Part Eight of 'The Trial of a Time Lord' will be used in Part Fourteen. He also writes a second memo to them, asking them to take up Bonnie Langford's contract option for the 1987 season of *Doctor Who*.

Tuesday 4th:
Itinerary: John writes to the Head of BBC Copyright, informing him that Pip and Jane Baker's script for 'The Trial of a Time Lord' Part Fourteen will run for 29 minutes and 30 seconds, five minutes longer than normal. As it will be transmitted at this length, he asks that any additional payment they require be paid.

Wednesday 5th:
Itinerary: John writes to director Chris Clough, thanking him for the work he did on the final six episodes of 'The Trial of a Time Lord'.

Thursday 6th:
Itinerary: Over lunch, Colin Baker has a one-on-one meeting with Jonathan Powell to discuss the non-renewal of his contract. John had persuaded Powell to allow Baker to record one more story – the opening installment of Season 24 – as the sixth Doctor, before regenerating into the new Doctor at its conclusion. Powell makes this offer to Baker. Baker declines, but makes a counter-offer to remain as the Doctor for the entirety of the twenty-fourth season and to depart in its final story. Powell declines this, and urges Baker to reconsider doing the first story of the season. Baker leaves the meeting with no agreement reached.

Commentary: Baker's reasoning was that if he were to agree to appear in just one further story, he'd have to commit to the four weeks work in April 1987 and this could potentially prevent him accepting a longer contract elsewhere. Matters were left dangling for several weeks until John had to accept that Baker wouldn't be returning, and so the new Doctor would have to be introduced in the new season's opening story. However, he envisaged this would be someone else's problem, as he still hoped to be replaced as producer

but Baker attributes this to Michael Grade.

of *Doctor Who* and be allowed to move on to another project. Baker, meanwhile, was just about to start rehearsals for his starring role in *Cinderella*, the pantomime John was putting on in Southampton over Christmas and New Year. His ousting from *Doctor Who* would lead to a potentially awkward situation between him and John for the duration of the pantomime's run.

Saturday 8th:
'The Trial of a Time Lord' Part Ten screens on BBC1.

Monday 10th:
Itinerary: John replies in writing to Christopher Bidmead's letter of 28 October, asserting that Bidmead gave prior agreement to him including in his book *Doctor Who: The Companions* the character outlines that they wrote together while Bidmead was script editor, hence the thanks credit he received in the book.

Thursday 13th:
Itinerary: Bonnie Langford is contracted to appear in all 14 episodes of Season 24. At some point on or around this date, John flies from London to Nashville, Tennessee, USA. Meanwhile, Christopher Bidmead again writes to John, disputing his recollection of having had his co-operation in the preparation of *Doctor Who: The Companions* and citing support from Eric Saward.

Friday 14th – Sunday 16th:
Itinerary: John is the sole guest at an unknown convention in Nashville.

Saturday 15th:
'The Trial of a Time Lord' Part Eleven screens on BBC1.

Wednesday 19th:
Itinerary: John writes to the BBC Presentation Department, providing the recap narrations he's written to be spoken by the BBC1 continuity announcer prior to the broadcasts of Parts Twelve, Thirteen and Fourteen of 'The Trial of a Time Lord'. He also writes again to Christopher Bidmead about the ongoing dispute over the book *Doctor Who: The Companions* and the screening of *Doctor Who* episodes at fan conventions.

Friday 21st – Sunday 23rd:
Itinerary: John is the sole guest at an unknown convention in Louisiana, New Orleans, USA. He returns to London early the following week.

Saturday 22nd:
'The Trial of a Time Lord' Part Twelve screens on BBC1.

Friday 28th:
Itinerary: John is about to begin a period of annual leave, so that he can direct the Colin Baker-starring pantomime *Cinderella* in Brighton. He is informed in a meeting with Jonathan Powell that he is to stay on as *Doctor Who*'s producer for the show's twenty-fourth season in 1987.

John Nathan-Turner: 'I was spending two weeks of that year's leave back in the theatre with what was to be a record-breaking panto in Brighton, staring Colin [Baker], Wendy Richard, Hugh Lloyd and Carol Kaye. On the Friday before the first Monday of rehearsals, I was called again to see Jonathan Powell. Guess what! No, he hadn't changed his mind about Colin … He wanted to tell me that I was to produce Season 24 of *Doctor Who*. Again, I was left with no choice. I protested that I didn't have enough time – there were no scripts on the shelf, no script editor, no Doctor, no nothing. My mind was in turmoil. By the time the Brighton show opened, there'd be Christmas itself, and then New Year … And what of the other projects I'd been promised? Jonathan said something quite brief like "You'll cope," as I was shown out.'[404]

Saturday 29th:
Itinerary: Colin Baker is a guest on this morning's live BBC1 programme *Saturday Superstore*. His imminent departure from *Doctor Who* is still not public knowledge. 'The Trial of a Time Lord' Part Thirteen screens on BBC1.

DECEMBER

Saturday 6th:
'The Trial of a Time Lord' Part Fourteen screens on BBC1.

Monday 8th:
Itinerary: John phones in to the live BBC1 programme *Open Air* from Brighton (where he is conducting rehearsals for *Cinderella*) as they discuss the conclusion of the latest *Doctor Who* season Writers Pip and Jane Baker are in the studio, defending the just-concluded season from criticisms from viewers and fans.

Friday 12th:
Itinerary: John's pantomime *Cinderella*, starring Colin Baker as Buttons, opens at the Theatre Royal in Brighton. Also in the cast are Wendy Richard

---

[404] John Nathan-Turner Memoirs, *Doctor Who Magazine* #245.

(*EastEnders, Are You Being Served*), Carol Kaye, and Hugh Lloyd (soon to be cast as Garonwy in the Season 24 *Doctor Who* story 'Delta and the Bannermen'). The pantomime is produced by Teynham Productions, John's newly-formed production company.

Tuesday 16th:
Itinerary: John writes to the Contracts Department, asking them to engage Kate O'Mara to return as the Rani in story 7D, with her availability to be between 30 March and 5 May 1987. He agrees to work around her theatre commitments in the play *King Lear* in Bath between 30 March and 4 April.

Thursday 18th:
Itinerary: News of Colin Baker's departure from *Doctor Who* is finally made public. BBC producer Clive Doig calls John and recommends Sylvester McCoy as Baker's replacement, based on McCoy's work for Doig on the BBC programme *Eureka*. John also writes to Jonathan Powell to ask that Chris Clough be engaged to direct the final six episodes of the twenty-fourth season.

John Nathan-Turner: 'My casting of Sylvester McCoy as the Doctor in most ways followed the usual route; quality-listing, endless interviews, brainstorming sessions, wading through piles of suggestions and so on. One of my theatre trips, at the behest of former agent Brian Wheeler, was to see "The Pied Piper" at the National Theatre, in which Sylvester was playing the title role. I was very impressed, though slightly perturbed, as minutes after Brian had suggested Sylvester to me, I received a phone-call from a producer, Clive Doig, giving me much the same sales pitch about Mr McCoy as Brian Wheeler. It turned out there was no collusion whatsoever, but I did wonder about this at the time.'[405]

Monday 22nd:
Itinerary: John signs off the commission for Pip and Jane Baker to write the four scripts for 'Strange Matter'.[406] He writes to Jonathan Powell's office to ask that Andrew Morgan be engaged to direct the story.

---

[405] John Nathan-Turner memoirs, *Doctor Who Magazine* #246. John's trip to see 'The Pied Piper' didn't actually take place until the following month, but he might well have been spoken to by Wheeler around the same time as Doig phoned him.
[406] 'Strange Matter' was retitled 'Time and the Rani' by the time it was shown on BBC1.

1987

Setting the Scene:

John's enthusiasm for *Doctor Who* must have been at an all-time low at the end of 1986. Still reeling from the fall-out of the acrimonious departure of Eric Saward, he had been juggling both producer and script editor duties for the past nine months. His desire to leave the show at the end of Season 23 had been not just an act to appease the – by now – many voices within fandom clamouring for him to quit, but a genuine desire to move on from *Doctor Who* and let the show become someone else's problem. But because of the machinations of his boss Jonathan Powell, the man who decided who worked on what programme in the BBC Drama Department, his departure was blocked, while at the same time his leading man was removed from the show without him being consulted.

Having been boxed into a corner, John must have at least toyed with the notion of quitting the BBC, thus forcing Powell to sort out the mess that *Doctor Who* was in by either appointing a new producer or cancelling the show for good. But John was, if nothing else, a career BBC man, and he was not easily going to throw away the career he had spent the previous two decades building up.

So John was forced to take up the reins of *Doctor Who* once again. As there were no scripts on the shelf, he quickly turned to the trusted duo of Pip and Jane Baker to provide at least an initial four-part story to launch the new season. At the same time, he had to find both a new Doctor – Colin Baker having understandably resisted his pleas to return in just that one story, in line with the concession won from Jonathan Powell, so that the Doctor could regenerate at its conclusion – and a new script editor.

It would seem that, once both of those vacancies had been filled, by Sylvester McCoy and Andrew Cartmel respectively, the combined influence of their 'new blood' managed to reinvigorate John's enthusiasm for the show ...

JANUARY

Tuesday 6th:
Itinerary: John and Gary Downie attend a performance of 'The Pied Piper', starring Sylvester McCoy, at the National Theatre in London.

Sylvester McCoy: 'I was at the National Theatre playing the Pied Piper, in a part written specially for me by Adrian Mitchell, a great poet, playwright and novelist. It was a very good audition piece for *Doctor Who*. I wore an extraordinary, wonderful, multicoloured coat, which I think, visually, must have tingled something in John's mind when he came to see the play. There was this multicoloured coat, which in a sense was like Colin's, which wasn't actually very popular, but it was a *Doctor Who*-ish thing. John went back and – he told me this much later – he said, "I've found my new Doctor." But then I had to go through lots and lots of bureaucratic things.'[407]

Wednesday 7th:
Itinerary: Christopher Bidmead sends John a further letter about their dispute over the book *Doctor Who: The Companions*.

Thursday 8th:
Itinerary: Ken Campbell's agent contacts John to suggest his client for the role of the seventh Doctor. John writes to the Camera Organiser at BBC Television Centre, requesting that Alec Wheal and his camera crew (Crew 11) be allocated to work on all four stories of the twenty-fourth season.

Saturday 10th:
Today is the final performance of John's production of *Cinderella* at the Theatre Royal in Brighton.

Monday 12th:
Itinerary: Pip and Jane Baker deliver their script for 'Strange Matter' Part One to the *Doctor Who* Production Office. The Camera Organiser at BBC Television Centre confirms to John that Alec Wheal and Crew 11 have been allocated to all of the stories of Season 24

Friday 16th:
Itinerary: Andrew Cartmel begins work as the new script editor on *Doctor Who*.

---

[407] Sylvester McCoy interview, *Doctor Who Magazine* #316

John Nathan-Turner: 'Richard Wakely – formerly of Peters, Fraser and Dunlop, who later represented me – was someone I had known from the moment I arrived in London in nineteen-hundred-and-frozen-to-death! I had always respected his judgement. He asked me to meet a young man called Andrew Cartmel, which I duly did, and found him bursting with many ideas and, indeed, firm opinions about the show. Although we didn't always agree, we instantly struck up a rapport – which I do think is a good sign. I invited Andrew to join the team and I have never regretted it.'[408]

Thursday 22nd:
Itinerary: Christopher Bidmead sends John yet another letter about their dispute over the book *Doctor Who: The Companions*.

Monday 26th:
Itinerary: John and Andrew Cartmel draft a character outline for Alf, a teenage London checkout girl who is swept off to another world in a time storm and becomes the Doctor's new companion.

Tuesday 27th:
Itinerary: John writes to Jonathan Powell's office, asking that Nick Mallett be engaged to direct story 7E.

Thursday 29th:
Itinerary: Pip and Jane Baker deliver their script for 'Strange Matter' Part Two to the *Doctor Who* Production Office. John writes to the couple the same day, enclosing a copy of the rehearsal script for Part One and detailing the changes that have been made to it since they submitted it.

Friday 30th:
Itinerary: John signs off the commission for Stephen Wyatt to write the scripts for 'Paradise Towers' Part One.

Saturday 31st:
Itinerary: John signs off the commission for Malcolm Kholl to write a scene breakdown for an unnamed story with the code 7F.[409]

---

[408] John Nathan-Turner memoirs, *Doctor Who Magazine* #246.
[409] This story will eventually be titled 'Delta and the Bannermen'.

FEBRUARY

Monday 2nd:
Itinerary: John sends Christopher Bidmead a letter (signed on his behalf by secretary Kate Easteal), apologising for not replying sooner to the writer's letters of 7 and 22 January. John maintains that Bidmead gave his prior written agreement for *Doctor Who: The Companions* to include character outlines that they wrote together during Bidmead's time as script editor, and that while he himself does not recall seeing that written agreement, his former secretary Sarah Lee would be prepared to swear as much on oath. This appears to draw a line under the dispute.

Wednesday 4th:
Itinerary: Tom Rivers from the BBC Copyright Department writes to John, suggesting that all future *Doctor Who* scriptwriters be asked to sign a disclaimer acknowledging that the character of Alf is BBC copyright. At some point on or before this date, John flies out to Florida, USA.

Thursday 5th – Sunday 8th:
Itinerary: John is a guest at the Omnicon convention in Fort Lauderdale, Florida, alongside Gary Downie.

Friday 6th:
Itinerary: Pip and Jane Baker deliver their scripts for 'Strange Matter' Part Three to the *Doctor Who* Production Office.

Monday 9th:
Itinerary: Stephen Wyatt delivers his script for 'Paradise Towers' Part One to the *Doctor Who* Production Office.

Thursday 12th:
Itinerary: Now back in the UK, John writes to Sylvester McCoy, sending him copies of two Andrew Cartmel-written audition scripts for him to learn, and details of the camera test to be recorded the following week. He also drafts a contract for whoever is cast as the new Doctor, to run for an initial period of 14 episodes in the first year, with renewable options in the BBC's favour for a further two years of 14 episodes each.

Friday 13th:
Itinerary: John writes to Tom Rivers of the BBC Copyright Department, informing him that only one writer, so far, has been engaged to write a story

outline featuring Alf, and that he has already been asked to sign a waiver over the character's ownership.[410]

Monday 16th:
Itinerary: Pip and Jane Baker deliver their scripts for 'Strange Matter' Part Four to the *Doctor Who* Production Office. Stephen Wyatt delivers his scripts for 'Paradise Towers' Parts Two to Four to the *Doctor Who* Production Office.

John Nathan-Turner: 'Pip and Jane Baker had to write the first story of the season without knowing who the new Doctor would be and with no knowledge of what he would bring to the part. Naturally, the script was adjusted as things became clearer, but they really did have to work blind for most of the time.'[411]

Tuesday 17th:
Itinerary: The BBC's Head of Copyright writes to John, stating that the DWFCA have breached various clauses in their merchandise agreement with the BBC. He copies John in on a letter he is sending about this to the DWFCA's Ron Katz, which also states that no episodes of *Doctor Who* can be screened at any future DWFCA events. John attends a pre-production meeting for 'Strange Matter', along with the director and other relevant departmental staff.

Wednesday 18th:
Itinerary: Camera test auditions for the new Doctor are held in Presentation Studio B at BBC Television Centre, directed by Andrew Morgan. Sylvester McCoy, Dermot Crowley and David Fielder all test for the role, with Janet Fielding playing both the 'companion' and the 'adversary' parts in the short Andrew Cartmel-written scripts.

Thursday 19th:
Itinerary: John signs off the (retrospective) commission for Stephen Wyatt to write the scripts for 'Paradise Towers' Parts Two to Four.

Friday 20th:
Itinerary: John attends a meeting with Andrew Cartmel, Andrew Morgan and Pip and Jane Baker to discuss the scripts for 'Strange Matter'.

---

[410] Presumably Ian Briggs was the writer in question, he being the one who would script the character's debut story, although he was not formally commissioned until the next month to provide an outline.
[411] John Nathan-Turner memoirs, *Doctor Who Magazine* #246.

Monday 23rd:
Itinerary: John attends another meeting with Andrew Cartmel and Pip and Jane Baker to discuss the scripts for 'Strange Matter'. Sylvester McCoy accepts John's offer to become the seventh Doctor.

Friday 27th:
Itinerary: John attends a preliminary planning meeting for 'Strange Matter' in the conference room at BBC Threshold House at 10.30am, along with the director and other relevant departmental staff.

MARCH

Monday 2nd:
Itinerary: At around 11.45am there is a press photocall in the *Blue Peter* Garden at BBC Television Centre to announce that Sylvester McCoy has been cast as the seventh Doctor. McCoy is joined by Bonnie Langford, and is pictured with her outside the TARDIS prop. John also attends and takes part in some of the photographs. Later that day, McCoy appears live in studio on BBC1's *Blue Peter* and is interviewed by presenter Janet Ellis. Malcolm Kholl delivers his scene breakdown for story 7F to the *Doctor Who* Production Office.

Tuesday 3rd:
Itinerary: John and Sylvester McCoy travel up to BBC Pebble Mill in Birmingham to appear as guests on the BBC2 afternoon *Pamela Armstrong* chat show.

Wednesday 4th:
Itinerary: Andrew Cartmel hands John a storyline from Ian Briggs titled 'The Pyramid's Treasure'. John doesn't like the story idea, and asks Cartmel to get Briggs to come up with a different one.

Friday 6th:
Itinerary: Sylvester McCoy is contracted to appear as the Doctor in 14 *Doctor Who* episodes during 1987, with further options in the BBC's favour for 14 more episodes in both 1988 and 1989. On or before this date, John and Sylvester McCoy fly out to Atlanta, Georgia, USA.

Saturday 7th – Sunday 8th:
Itinerary: John and Sylvester McCoy are guests at the *Doctor Who* Festival convention in Atlanta.

Monday 9th:
Itinerary: Back in the UK, John signs off the commission for Ian Briggs to write a scene breakdown for an unnamed story with the code 7F.

Monday 16th:
Itinerary: John signs off the commission for Malcolm Kholl to write the script for 'Delta and the Bannermen' Part One.[412]

Wcdnesday 18th:
Itinerary: John travels down to Frome in Somerset, along with director Andrew Morgan and various other personnel working on the story 'Strange Matter'. They spend the day visiting quarries to use as possible locations for the story's OB recording.

Friday 20th:
Itinerary: John has a pub lunch with Andrew Cartmel, director Nicholas Mallet and writer Stephen Wyatt to discuss the production of the upcoming story 'Paradise Towers'.

Monday 23rd:
Itinerary: Ian Briggs delivers his scene breakdown for story 7F to the *Doctor Who* Production Office. John writes to the Contracts Department, asking that Keff McCulloch be engaged to compose the incidental music for 'Strange Matter'. He also writes to the senior members of production on all of Season 24's stories, telling them he has been made aware that copies of scripts for the upcoming season have been circulated to members of the DWAS, and warns them to keep their offices and desks locked.

Tuesday 24th:
Itinerary: Malcolm Kholl delivers his script for 'Delta and the Bannermen' Part One to the *Doctor Who* Production Office.

Wednesday 25th:
Itinerary: John meets with Andrew Cartmel to discuss the script for 'Delta and the Bannermen' Part One. John decides to move the opening sequence from the bridge of Delta's spaceship, which would be recorded in the studio, to an alien planet, which could be represented by a quarry and so shot on location.

---

[412] Although the story starts life with the title 'Delta and the Bannermen', this alters to 'Flight of the Chimeron' before it enters production, before reverting back to 'Delta and the Bannermen' shortly before transmission.

Thursday 26th:
Itinerary: John writes to agent Elizabeth Shepherd, thanking her for a letter she has sent him about the composer David Snell, whom she represents, and for sending examples of his work. John tells her he's looking for composers who work in the electronic music field to work on *Doctor Who*.

Monday 30th – Friday 3rd April:
Itinerary: OB rehearsals for the location recording of 'Strange Matter' take place at the BBC Television Rehearsal Rooms at Acton.

Monday 30th:
Itinerary: John attends the first day of rehearsal for 'Strange Matter', along with script editor Andrew Cartmel and writers Pip and Jane Baker.

Tuesday 31st:
Itinerary: John signs off the commission for Malcolm Kholl to write the scripts for 'Delta and the Bannermen' Parts Two and Three.

APRIL

Thursday 2nd:
Itinerary: John signs off the commission for Ian Briggs to write the script for 'Dragonfire' Part One. On the same day, he contacts Tony Selby's agent and discusses the possibility of Selby returning to the series to play Glitz in 'Dragonfire', as one of the characters in Briggs' script is written in such a way that Glitz could be quite easily substituted.

Saturday 4th:
Itinerary: Today is the first day of OB recording for 'Strange Matter' on location in Cloford Quarry, near Frome in Somerset. John spends the night with the cast and crew at The Mendip Lodge Hotel in Frome.

Sunday 5th:
Itinerary: Today is the second day of OB recording for 'Strange Matter' at Cloford Quarry, near Frome in Somerset. John again spends the night with the cast and crew at The Mendip Lodge Hotel in Frome.

John Nathan-Turner: 'We had varied weather on this shoot, some of it quite unpleasant, but many a happy evening was spent with the unit in our warm hotel. One evening Richard Gauntlett (who played Urak, and who is an immensely talented juggler, acrobat and actor) and Sylvester did an impromptu cabaret of bizarre tricks and knock-about comedy. At one point, Sylvester got hold of some spoons and started playing them quite brilliantly. It was Geoff Posner, the designer, who suggested we incorporate the spoons into the mad capers of the seventh Doctor's regeneration crisis, and he promptly designed some futuristic spoons on the back of a table napkin.'[413]

Monday 6th:
Itinerary: Today is the third day of OB recording for 'Strange Matter' at Cloford Quarry, near Frome in Somerset. John once more spends the night with the cast and crew at The Mendip Lodge Hotel in Frome. Malcolm Kholl delivers his scripts for 'Delta and the Bannermen' Parts Two and Three to the *Doctor Who* Production Office.

Tuesday 7th:
Itinerary: This is the fourth day of OB recording for 'Strange Matter' at Cloford Quarry, near Frome in Somerset. Today, a news crew from the BBC's *Breakfast Time* programme is also on location, following the recording. John is interviewed by them about the new *Doctor Who* season and the new Doctor.[414] John spends a final night with the cast and crew at The Mendip Lodge Hotel in Frome.

Wednesday 8th:
Itinerary: Today is the fifth and final day of OB recording for 'Strange Matter' at Cloford Quarry, near Frome in Somerset. John returns to London after recording finishes. Ian Briggs delivers his script for 'Dragonfire' Part One to the *Doctor Who* Production Office.

Thursday 9th – Saturday 18th:
Itinerary: Rehearsals for the first studio block of 'Strange Matter' take place at the BBC Television Rehearsal Rooms at Acton.

Thursday 9th:
Itinerary: John gets the chance to read the script for 'Dragonfire' Part One. He meets with Andrew Cartmel, and agrees that the rest of the story can be commissioned.

Friday 10th:
Itinerary: John meets with Andrew Cartmel to discuss Malcolm Kholl's scripts

---

[413] John Nathan-Turner Memoirs, *Doctor Who Magazine* #246.
[414] The report on the recording of 'Strange Matter' is shown on the edition of *Breakfast Time* broadcast on BBC1 on Tuesday 5 May 1987.

for 'Delta and the Bannermen' Parts Two and Three. There are particular problems with Part Two, which John calls '… the worst script I've ever read'. Cartmel works with Kholl on restructuring the script's structure, and asks him to do a rewrite to address the problems.

Monday 13th:
Itinerary: John attends a preliminary planning meeting for 'Paradise Towers' at Acton. Malcolm Kholl delivers his revised script for 'Delta and the Bannermen' Part Two to the *Doctor Who* Production Office. John signs off the (retrospective) commission for Ian Briggs to write the script for 'Dragonfire' Parts Two and Three. Briggs delivers his script for 'Dragonfire' Part Three to the *Doctor Who* Production Office on the same day.

Tuesday 14th:
Itinerary: John sits in on interviews/auditions for actresses to play the various Kangs in 'Paradise Towers'. He tells Andrew Cartmel that he thinks he's found the ideal actress to play Ace in 'Dragonfire'.

Wednesday 15th:
Itinerary: Today is a wake for Patrick Troughton at Television Centre, organised by John. Nicholas Courtney and Janet Fielding are amongst the attendees.

Commentary: Patrick Troughton had died suddenly of a heart attack on 28 March 1987, while attending the Magnum Opus II convention in Columbus, Georgia in the USA. Troughton's enthusiasm for *Doctor Who* had been reawakened following his appearances in 'The Five Doctors' and 'The Two Doctors', and he had become a regular on the US *Doctor Who* convention circuit. He had also been a regular visitor to the *Doctor Who* Production Office, popping in to see John on a whim. His last visit had been just a few weeks prior to his death, when he'd met new script editor Andrew Cartmel for the first time.

Thursday 16th:
Itinerary: Ian Briggs delivers his script for 'Dragonfire' Part Two to the *Doctor Who* Production Office. Today is the Producer's Run at the BBC Television Rehearsal Rooms at Acton for the first studio block of 'Strange Matter'.

Monday 20th:
Itinerary: Today is the first day of the first two-day studio block for 'Strange Matter' in studio TC8 at BBC Television Centre.

Tuesday 21st:
Itinerary: Today is the second and final day of the two-day first studio block for 'Strange Matter' in studio TC8 at BBC Television Centre.

Wednesday 22nd – Friday 1st May:
Itinerary: Rehearsals for the second studio block of 'Strange Matter' take place at the BBC Television Rehearsal Rooms at Acton.

Friday 24th:
Itinerary: John writes to the Contracts Department, asking that David Snell be booked to compose the incidental music for 'Paradise Towers' and that Dominic Glynn be booked to do likewise for story 7G ('Dragonfire').

Monday 27th:
Itinerary: John writes to the BBC Copyright Department, informing them that Pip and Jane Baker have written an additional one minute of material for Part Three of 'Strange Matter', as the episode was found to be under-running. The writers will need paying for the additional work as per their contract.

MAY

Friday 1st:
Itinerary: Today is the Producer's Run at the BBC Television Rehearsal Rooms at Acton for the second studio block of 'Strange Matter'.

Sunday 3rd:
Itinerary: Today is the first day of the three-day second studio block for 'Strange Matter' in studio TC1 at BBC Television Centre.

Commentary: Andrew Cartmel notes in his book *Script Doctor* that, around the time of this second studio block, '… John Nathan-Turner was a pillar of strength when you consider the stress he was under. He had been flying up to Birmingham to see his father, who had had a stroke while trying to escape from hospital after minor surgery. His father had knocked down two nurses and a security guard before they could subdue him. Now he was paralysed. And John's mother was on the verge of the latest of a series of nervous breakdowns.'[415]

---

[415] *Script Doctor* by Andrew Cartmel, published by Reynolds & Hearn, 2005.

Monday 4th (bank holiday):
Itinerary: Today is the second day of the three-day second studio block for 'Strange Matter' in studio TC1 at BBC Television Centre.

Tuesday 5th:
Itinerary: Today is the third and final day of the second studio block for 'Strange Matter' in studio TC1 at BBC Television Centre.

Wednesday 6th:
Itinerary: John meets with Andrew Carmel and Stephen Wyatt to discuss a story idea for Season 25, to be made in 1988.

Andrew Cartmel: '... My blood ran cold when I heard about the story that John was proposing ... John was talking to Stephen about a story set in a fairground. I couldn't imagine a worse location. It was so trite and kitsch and boring. As I said, my blood ran cold. But halfway through the meeting, which proved to be a rather dead-end discussion, John suddenly said, of his own volition, "I'm going off the idea as we talk about it." So we ended up with a circus instead of a fairground.'[416]

Commentary: It's possible John was thinking back to the aborted story 'The Nightmare Fair', which had been set in a fairground and been due to be filmed in Blackpool in 1985, shortly before *Doctor Who* was put on hiatus by the BBC's sixth floor management. That story had begun with an idea from John, which he had then passed to Graham Williams to develop.

Friday 8th:
Itinerary: John signs off the commission for Stephen Wyatt to write the script for 'The Greatest Show in the Galaxy' Part One.

Monday 11th:
Itinerary: John attends a pre-production meeting for 'Flight of the Chimeron' at 2.00pm in the conference room at BBC Threshold House. He also writes to Brian Turner at the BBC Copyright Department, asking that the use of the character Glitz in 'Dragonfire' be negotiated with the estate of his creator, Robert Holmes. The actor Nigel Miles-Thomas writes to John, having heard on the grapevine that the series is looking to cast 'large' actors in a story, and asks to be considered. John passes his details to Chris Clough, and Miles-Thomas is later offered – and accepts – the role of Pudovkin in 'Dragonfire'.

---

[416] *Script Doctor* by Andrew Cartmel, published by Reynolds & Hearn, 2005.

Tuesday 12th:
Itinerary: John writes notes to thank Lesley Rawstone for her make-up work, Ken Trew for his costume work and Geoff Powell for his design work, all on 'Strange Matter'.

Monday 18th:
Itinerary: John, Andrew Cartmel, Chris Clough and Gary Downie attend auditions in the conference room at BBC Threshold House for singers to play a group called the Lorells in 'Flight of the Chimeron'. The Wilson sisters are the successful candidates.

Tuesday 19th – Wednesday 20th:
Rehearsals for the OB location recording of 'Paradise Towers' take place at the BBC Television Rehearsal Rooms at Acton.

Tuesday 19th:
Itinerary: John attends a planning meeting for the first studio block of 'Paradise Towers' at 9.30am at the BBC Television Rehearsal Rooms at Acton.

Wednesday 20th:
Itinerary: John attends a pre-production meeting for 'Flight of the Chimeron' at 10.30am in the conference room at BBC Threshold House.

Thursday 21st:
Itinerary: Today is the first day of OB recording for 'Paradise Towers' at the outdoor swimming pool at Elmswell House in Chalfont St Giles, Buckinghamshire.

Friday 22nd:
Itinerary: Today is the second and final day of OB recording for 'Paradise Towers' at the outdoor swimming pool at Elmswell House in Chalfont St Giles, Buckinghamshire.

Saturday 23rd – Wednesday 3rd June:
Rehearsals for the first studio block of 'Paradise Towers' take place at the BBC Television Rehearsal Rooms at Acton.

Thursday 28th:
Itinerary: In the *Doctor Who* Production Office, John and Chris Clough audition actors to play the role of Billy in 'Flight of the Chimeron'. On the same day, John previews the new *Doctor Who* title sequence produced by CAL video.

Friday 29th:
Itinerary: John writes to the BBC Contracts Department, asking that Keff McCullough be engaged to compose the incidental music for 'Flight of the Chimeron', and also to appear on location with three other musicians of his choice to play the camp band in the same story. Today is also the Producer's Run at the BBC Television Rehearsal Rooms at Acton for the first studio block of 'Paradise Towers'.

JUNE

Monday 1st:
Itinerary John attends a planning meeting for the second studio block of 'Paradise Towers' at the BBC Television Rehearsal Rooms at Acton.

Wednesday 3rd:
Itinerary: John attends the final rehearsals for the first studio session of 'Paradise Towers' for the Producer's Run, along with Andrew Cartmel.

Andrew Cartmel: '[During the Producer's Run] John Nathan-Turner snapped at me, the first of several such incidents as the season moved on and tension mounted up. It left me feeling sour and angry for the rest of the day.' [417]

Thursday 4th:
Itinerary: Today is the first day of the two-day first studio block for 'Paradise Towers' in studio TC1 at BBC Television Centre. On the same day, John writes to the BBC Contracts Department, asking that Sophie Aldred be engaged to play Ace in story 7G. He asks that additional options in the BBC's favour be included in the contract, to cover 14 more episodes in 1988 and 8 out of 14 episodes in 1989.

Andrew Cartmel: 'Stephen [Wyatt] was very concerned that the Caretakers [in his story "Paradise Towers"] should be suitably seedy looking and slovenly and shambolic … I'd already spoken to John about this once on Stephen's behalf. But still nothing seemed to have been done … Stephen urged me to repeat the observation. So I moved forward in the control room darkness to remind John. He turned to me and snarled, "Listen. Don't you check on me. I'm the producer." I retreated and sat down again, feeling humiliated and angry. That was the second time in two days that John had

---

[417] *Script Doctor* by Andrew Cartmel, published by Reynolds & Hearn, 2005.

snapped at me … Looking back with the hindsight of years … the enormous pressure of making the show for John had been compounded by the even more enormous pressure of events in his family.'[418]

Friday 5th:
Itinerary: Today is the second and final day of the second studio block for 'Paradise Towers' in studio TC1 at BBC Television Centre.

Saturday 6th – Tuesday 16th:
Rehearsals for the second studio block of 'Paradise Towers' take place at the BBC Television Rehearsal Rooms at Acton.

Wednesday 10th:
Itinerary: John takes Andrew Cartmel and a writer friend of his (unnamed) to the Bush pub in Shepherd's Bush for a working lunch to discuss the writer perhaps contributing a story for the show. After the writer departs, John and Andrew talk over the problems they've had with each other during the previous week, and resolve the issues amicably.

Tuesday 16th:
Itinerary: Today is the Producer's Run at the BBC Television Rehearsal Rooms at Acton for the second studio block of 'Paradise Towers'. Also on this day, Sylvester McCoy attends a photo studio where he is photographed for the new title sequence.

Wednesday 17th:
Itinerary: Today is the first day of the three-day second studio block for 'Paradise Towers' in studio TC1 at BBC Television Centre. Following John's request on 4 June, Sophie Aldred is contracted to play the part of Ace for three episodes during this season, with further options in the BBC's favour for 14 more episodes in 1988 and 8 more in 1989.

Thursday 18th:
Itinerary: Today is the second day of the three-day second studio block for 'Paradise Towers' in studio TC1 at BBC Television Centre.

Friday 19th:
Itinerary: Today is the third and final day of the second studio block for 'Paradise Towers' in studio TC1 at BBC Television Centre. After recording concludes, John hosts a wrap party for the cast and crew.

---

[418] *Script Doctor* by Andrew Cartmel, published by Reynolds & Hearn, 2005.

Saturday 20th – Tuesday 23rd:
Itinerary: Rehearsals for the OB location recording of 'Flight of the Chimeron' take place at the BBC Television Rehearsal Rooms at Acton.

Wednesday 24th:
Itinerary: Today is the first day of OB recording for 'Flight of the Chimeron' at Springwell Lock Quarry in Rickmansworth, Buckinghamshire. John directs some second-unit material of the Bannermen descending from the clifftop in the opening battle sequence.

Thursday 25th:
Itinerary: Today is the second day of OB recording for 'Flight of the Chimeron' at Sutton Farm in Penarth, South Glamorgan in Wales. John spends the night at the Hotel International in Barry, South Glamorgan.

Commentary: John has his dog, Pepsi, with him during the entire location shoot for this story. Today, Pepsi gets to appear on-screen in the story as camp manager Burton's pet pooch.

Friday 26th:
Itinerary: Today is the third day of OB recording for 'Flight of the Chimeron' at Psygollyn Mawr in Hensol Forest, South Glamorgan in Wales. John again spends the night at the Hotel International in Barry, South Glamorgan.

Saturday 27th:
Itinerary: Today is the fourth day of OB recording for 'Flight of the Chimeron' at Sutton Farm in Penarth, South Glamorgan in Wales. John once more spends the night at the Hotel International in Barry, South Glamorgan.

Sunday 28th:
Itinerary: Today is a day off from recording for cast and crew. However, everyone remains in Wales for the day, and John spends a further night at the Hotel International in Barry, South Glamorgan.

Monday 29th:
Itinerary: Today is the fifth day of OB recording for 'Flight of the Chimeron' at Coed Y Wallas, Castle-Upon-Alum, South Glamorgan in Wales. John directs some second-unit material of the Doctor and Mel riding the Vincent motorcycle in the fields. John spends a fifth night at the Hotel International in Barry, South Glamorgan.

Tuesday 30th:
Itinerary: Today is the sixth day of OB recording for 'Flight of the Chimeron'

at the Majestic Holiday Camp on Barry Island, South Glamorgan in Wales. John spends a sixth night at the Hotel International in Barry, South Glamorgan.

Andrew Cartmel: 'I went and said hello to John Nathan-Turner. "I've just bitten [the director] Chris Clough's fucking head off," he told me. According to him, Chris, an eminently nice guy, had been going on about how cheap *Doctor Who* was. "We're only £28,000 over budget," said John.'[419]

JULY

Wednesday 1st:
Itinerary: Today is the seventh day of OB recording for 'Flight of the Chimeron' at the Majestic Holiday Camp on Barry Island, South Glamorgan in Wales. John spends a seventh night at the Hotel International in Barry, South Glamorgan.

Thursday 2nd:
Itinerary: Today is the eighth day of OB recording for 'Flight of the Chimeron' at the Majestic Holiday Camp on Barry Island, South Glamorgan in Wales. John spends an eighth night at the Hotel International in Barry, South Glamorgan.

Friday 3rd:
Itinerary: Today is the ninth day of OB recording for 'Flight of the Chimeron' at the Majestic Holiday Camp on Barry Island, South Glamorgan in Wales. John, along with Sylvester McCoy, is interviewed for an item to be shown on the regional *Wales Today* BBC news programme later that evening. After the scenes of the band and campers dancing from Part One are recorded, and the day's work has concluded, John hosts an evening cabaret in the holiday camp, where he performs a duet on stage with Hugh Lloyd. Other members of the cast and crew also get a chance to perform their 'party pieces'. John spends a ninth night at the Hotel International in Barry, South Glamorgan.

Saturday 4th:
Itinerary: Today is the tenth day of OB recording for 'Flight of the Chimeron' at the Majestic Holiday Camp on Barry Island, South Glamorgan in Wales. John directs some additional material that will be used in the BBC's

---

[419] *Script Doctor* by Andrew Cartmel, published by Reynolds & Hearn, 2005.

promotional trailer for the new *Doctor Who* season. John spends a tenth night at the Hotel International in Barry, South Glamorgan.

Sunday 5th:
Itinerary: Today is a day off for the cast and crew of 'Flight of the Chimeron'. Most remain on location, although some of the cast are now released and can return to London. John spends an eleventh night at the Hotel International in Barry, South Glamorgan.

Monday 6th:
Itinerary: Today is the eleventh day of OB recording for 'Flight of the Chimeron' at the Majestic Holiday Camp on Barry Island, South Glamorgan in Wales. John spends a twelfth night at the Hotel International in Barry, South Glamorgan.

Tuesday 7th:
Itinerary: Today is the twelfth and final day of OB recording for 'Flight of the Chimeron'. The venue is now Hanger 50 in Llandow Industrial Estate, South Glamorgan in Wales. The production is joined by a camera crew from the BBC1 children's show *But First This*, who interview John and film behind-the-scenes items of a good section of the OB recording, including Ken Dodd's arrival on location. John spends a final night at the Hotel International in Barry, South Glamorgan.

Wednesday 8th:
Itinerary: The cast and crew of 'Flight of the Chimeron' decamp from Wales and return to London.

Monday 13th:
Itinerary: John attends a planning meeting for the first studio block of 'Dragonfire' at 11.00am in the conference room at BBC Threshold House.

Thursday 16th – Monday 27th:
Rehearsals for the first studio block of 'Dragonfire' take place at the BBC Television Rehearsal Rooms at Acton.

Thursday 16th:
Itinerary: John attends the first read-through of 'Dragonfire' at the BBC Rehearsal Rooms in Acton.

Friday 17th:
Itinerary: John writes to Tony Redston (Production Manager), Jo Newbury (Assistant Floor Manager), Colin Mapson (Visual Effects), Henry Barber

(Studio Lighting) and Joy Sinclair (Production Assistant), thanking them all for their work on 'Time and the Rani'. He also writes to Simon Taylor (Visual Effects Designer), Shaunna Harrison (Make-up), Janet Tharby (Costumes), Ian Fraser (Production Manager), Martin Collins (Designer) and Val McCrimmon (Assistant Floor Manager), thanking them for their work on 'Paradise Towers'.

Tuesday 21st:
Itinerary: John writes to Oliver Elmes, thanking him for his work on the show's new title sequence.

Friday 24th:
Itinerary: John writes to director Andrew Morgan, expressing his satisfaction with the completed edit of Part One of 'Time of the Rani'. However, he does suggest that a scene with Bonnie Langford being dragged by a rope by Mark Greenstreet needs post-synching.

Monday 27th:
Itinerary: Today is the Producer's Run at the BBC Television Rehearsal Rooms at Acton for the first studio block of 'Dragonfire'.

Tuesday 28th:
Itinerary: Today is the first day of the three-day first studio block for 'Dragonfire' in studio TC1 at BBC Television Centre. After recording concludes, John takes Sophie Aldred to one side and asks her if she would like to continue to play Ace as the new companion to the Doctor in the forthcoming twenty-fifth season. Aldred agrees, so John begins making the necessary arrangements, and Andrew Cartmel and Ian Briggs work on altering the script of the story's final episode so that Mel departs and Ace joins the Doctor in the TARDIS.

Wednesday 29th:
Itinerary: Today is the second day of the three-day first studio block for 'Dragonfire' in studio TC1 at BBC Television Centre.

Thursday 30th:
Itinerary: Today is the third and final day of the first studio block for 'Dragonfire' in studio TC1 at BBC Television Centre.

Friday 31st:
Itinerary: John attends a planning meeting for the second studio block of 'Dragonfire' at 2.00pm in the conference room at BBC Threshold House.

AUGUST

Monday 3rd – Tuesday 11th:
Rehearsals for the second studio block of 'Dragonfire' take place at the BBC Television Rehearsal Rooms at Acton.

Tuesday 4th:
Itinerary: John writes to Brian Turner at the BBC Copyright Department, informing him that Ian Briggs has had to rewrite approximately three minutes of the final episode of 'Dragonfire' to accommodate the departure of Bonnie Langford, and asking him to arrange appropriate payment for this additional work.

Friday 7th:
Itinerary: John meets with Andrew Cartmel and the writer Graeme Curry to discuss Curry being commissioned to write a story for the show's next season.

Monday 10th:
Itinerary: John attends a meeting with Jonathan Powell and Andrew Cartmel, where Cartmel's contract as script editor is discussed and extended. Today is also the Producer's Run at the BBC Television Rehearsal Rooms at Acton for the second studio block of 'Dragonfire'. John is also now planning the announcement to the press of Sophie Aldred as new companion Ace.

Wednesday 12th: (John's fortieth birthday)
Itinerary: Today is the first day of the two-day second studio block for 'Dragonfire' in studio TC3 at BBC Television Centre. The TARDIS scenes for 'Delta and the Bannermen' are also recorded. John writes to director Andrew Morgan, expressing his satisfaction with the completed edits of Parts One and Two of 'Time and the Rani'. He informs him that 'the Headmaster' (i.e. Jonathan Powell) has also seen both episodes and is pleased with them as well. He also writes to director Nick Mallet, expressing his satisfaction with the completed edit of 'Paradise Towers' Part Three. In addition, he writes to Doug Whittaker (Sound), Ian Dow (Lighting), Alistair Mitchell (Camera Operator), Chas Snare (Camera Operator) and John Wilson (Engineering Manager), to thank them for their work on 'Delta and the Bannermen'.

Thursday 13th:
Itinerary: At 10.30am there is a press photocall in the *Blue Peter* Garden at BBC Television Centre with Sophie Aldred and Sylvester McCoy, to announce Aldred's casting as the new companion, Ace. John fields questions from the

journalists in attendance. Today is also the second and final day of the second studio block for 'Dragonfire' in studio TC3 at BBC Television Centre. This completes production on the twenty-fourth season of *Doctor Who,* although there is some editing and post-production still to be done. After the studio session is concluded, the cast and crew hold a dual wrap party and farewell party for Bonnie Langford.

Saturday 15th – Monday 31st:
Itinerary: John takes a fortnight of annual leave away from the BBC.

Wednesday 19th:
Itinerary: Today is the BBC's press launch at BBC Television Centre for its Autumn Season of programmes. John doesn't attend, due to being on leave.

SEPTEMBER

Thursday 3rd:
Itinerary: John signs off the commission for Graeme Curry to write the script for 'The Crooked Smile' Part One.[420]

Monday 7th:
'Time and the Rani' Part One screens on BBC1.

Tuesday 8th:
Itinerary: John informs Andrew Cartmel that he wants to bring the Daleks back for a story during the following year's season. Cartmel tells John that he wants a writer new to the series, Ben Aaronovitch, to provide the script.

Thursday 10th:
Itinerary: John and Andrew Cartmel watch a fully dubbed VHS copy of 'Paradise Towers' Part One with Colin Rogers, the Assistant Head of the Drama Department. They all come to the conclusion that the incidental music, by David Snell, just doesn't work for this story.

John Nathan-Turner: 'I originally engaged another composer to provide the incidental music for this story. At the first dub I was totally surprised by his work. It was genuinely atmospheric, but also rather weird, and I wasn't too

---

[420] This story will be retitled as 'The Happiness Patrol' by the time it screens on BBC1.

sure about it. After we dubbed the second episode and I still had strong doubts, I asked Colin [Rogers] to view the first one for a second opinion. He agreed with me that we should change the music, so sadly we had to replace the composer.'[421]

Friday 11th:
Itinerary: John writes to composer David Snell and informs him, with great regret, that he's not happy with his incidental music score for 'Paradise Towers'. He notes that while the music is very atmospheric, he finds it is also very repetitive, which he feels distracts from the main action of the story.

Saturday 12th:
Itinerary: An article by DWAS Coordinator Andrew Beech appears in today's edition of the *Daily Mail*. It criticises certain aspects of the new season, and questions the competency of the current production team. Today is also the first day of the DWAS's PanoptiCon VIII convention at Imperial College in London. John is due to appear as a guest, but as a result of the *Daily Mail* article he decides at the last minute not to do so. Also on this day, John writes to the Contracts Department, asking that Keff McCulloch be engaged to provide a new incidental music score for 'Paradise Towers'.

Monday 14th:
'Time and the Rani' Part Two screens on BBC1.

Friday 18th:
Itinerary: Composer David Snell replies to John's 11 September letter. He expresses surprise and disappointment at the rejection of his score for 'Paradise Towers'.

Sunday 20th:
Itinerary: John signs off the commission for Stephen Wyatt to write the scripts for 'The Greatest Show in the Galaxy' Parts Two to Four.

Monday 21st:
'Time and the Rani' Part Three screens on BBC1.

Wednesday 23rd:
Itinerary: Graeme Curry delivers his script for 'The Crooked Smile' Part One, and Stephen Wyatt delivers his script for 'The Greatest Show in the Galaxy' Part One, to the *Doctor Who* Production Office.

---

[421] John Nathan-Turner memoirs, *Doctor Who Magazine* #246.

Monday 28th:
'Time and the Rani' Part Four screens on BBC1.

Tuesday 29th:
Itinerary: John travels to Manchester to appear on the BBC1 daytime TV review programme *Open Air* alongside Sylvester McCoy and Bonnie Langford. The new *Doctor Who* season is the main topic of discussion, and John defends it from the criticism it has received from some quarters.

Wednesday 30th:
Itinerary: John signs off the commission for Graeme Curry to write the scripts for 'The Crooked Smile' Parts Two and Three.

OCTOBER

Friday 2nd:
Itinerary: Jonathan Powell writes to John, thanking him for sending him a videotape of 'Paradise Towers' Part One. He informs John that he feels the episode is absolutely first rate.

Monday 5th:
'Paradise Towers' Part One screens on BBC1.

Wednesday 7th:
Itinerary: John sends the Copyright Department's Brian Turner a memo to put on record that, although it was previously agreed to accept writer Peter Grimwade's claim to ownership of the copyright in Turlough (presumably following the dispute that arose the previous September), he maintains that he himself created the character. He also confirms that there are no plans for Turlough to return to *Doctor Who*.

Monday 12th:
'Paradise Towers' Part Two screens on BBC1.

Thursday 15th:
Itinerary: John discusses with Andrew Cartmel the possibility of re-editing a scene in 'Paradise Towers' Part Three of Mel being threatened by a knife by the Rezzies. They ultimately decide against this.

Commentary: This debate was triggered by the murder of four people in

Bristol the previous day by Kevin Weaver, which came only weeks after the Hungerford massacre, where Michael Ryan killed 16 people before shooting himself. The effect that televised violence might possibly have played in both atrocities was suddenly a very hot topic within Government and with broadcasters.

Friday 16th:
The UK is battered overnight by an unusually violent storm, which has particularly serious effects in London and the South East. John's home in Brighton suffers some minor damage.

Monday 19th:
'Paradise Towers' Part Three screens on BBC1.

Monday 26th:
'Paradise Towers' Part Four screens on BBC1.

Tuesday 27th:
Itinerary: Today is the press screening of 'Delta and the Bannermen' Parts One and Two at Light Fantastic in The Trocadero on Coventry Street in London, from 10.30am. Cast members Don Henderson, Stubby Kaye, Ken Dodd, Hugh Lloyd and Sylvester McCoy are amongst those attending, alongside John.

Wednesday 28th:
Itinerary: Jonathan Powell writes to John to inform him that the Controller of BBC1 has requested that the scene of Mel being threatened with a knife in 'Paradise Towers' be edited down, or out, should the story be repeated.

Commentary: Despite this request, the episode was never edited, whether for overseas sales, for screenings on UK GOLD or for its commercial releases.

Friday 30th:
Itinerary: John signs off the commission for Ben Aaronovitch to write the script for 'Nemesis of the Doctor' Part One.[422] John shows Andrew Cartmel a letter from a viewer who was disturbed by the scene of Mel being threatened by a knife in 'Paradise Towers' Part Three. Cartmel agrees with the letter, and John recalls that Cartmel did try to flag up the problem during the studio recording, and that he failed to address it.

---

[422] This story will be retitled 'Remembrance of the Daleks' by the time it airs on BBC1.

NOVEMBER

Monday 2nd:
Itinerary: John writes to Dick Mills (Special Sounds, BBC Radiophonic Workshop), Brian Clarke (Studio Sound), Dave Chapman (Video Effects), Alec Wheal (Camera Supervisor) and High Parson (Videotape Editor), who all worked on the entire twenty-fourth season, thanking them for their work on the show. He also writes to John Asbridge (Design, 'Delta and the Bannermen' and 'Dragonfire'), Andy McVean (Visual Effects, 'Delta and the Bannermen' and 'Dragonfire') Richard Croft (Costume Design, 'Delta and the Bannermen' and 'Dragonfire'), Don Babbage (Studio Lighting, 'Dragonfire'), Karen King (Production Assistant, 'Dragonfire') and Rosemary Parsons (Production Assistant, 'Delta and the Bannermen' and 'Dragonfire'), thanking them for their work on those stories. 'Delta and the Bannermen' Part One screens on BBC1.

Wednesday 4th:
Itinerary: John, Andrew Cartmel and Stephen Wyatt meet with stuntman Roy Scammel, who demonstrates a new stunt he's devised, whereby he dresses as a giant Japanese robot, with roller skates hidden in oversized boots, as an assistant pulls him along by a cord. The demonstration ends abruptly when the cord snaps.

Commentary: It's possible that the robot idea was being investigated for 'The Greatest Show in the Galaxy', as a huge buried robot was a plot point in that story.

Thursday 5th:
Itinerary: John writes a lengthy article for Ron Katz for inclusion the latest DWFCA newsletter. He also writes a reply to a viewer by the name of Mr Stewart, who has written into the *Doctor Who* Production Office to complain about the scene in Part Three of 'Paradise Towers' of Mel being threatened with a knife. John defends the scene as an example of bad people (i.e. those who use knives to threaten other people) eventually getting their come-uppance for their actions. He also writes to Nick Mallett, informing him of the diktat to edit Part Three of 'Paradise Towers' for repeats, and now also for overseas sales. He enquires about Mallett's availability for him to come in and supervise the edit.

Monday 9th:
'Delta and the Bannermen' Part Two screens on BBC1.

Monday 16th:
'Delta and the Bannermen' Part Three screens on BBC1.

Tuesday 17th:
Itinerary: John signs off the commission for Kevin Clarke to write the script for 'The Harbinger' Part One.[423]

Kevin Clarke: 'They were looking for something special. I said, "Well, I've got just the thing." Outside the Mobil garage on Shepherd's Bush Green, a thought struck me, so when we sat down in the office, and John Nathan-Turner and Andrew [Cartmel] looked at me expectantly, I said, "The question we have all been asking ourselves for 25 years is Doctor who? Who is the Doctor?" They both leaned forward and said, "Well, who is he?" "Exactly," I said. They sat back and digested this. John said, "But we don't know who he is." Neither did I. Another silence followed, and I came out with, "It's obvious. He came among us, mucked things up because he's so forgetful, but is sort of working it out in the end. He is God!" John and Andrew both looked terrified. Eventually John said, "You can do that, as long as you don't say it." I've always thought that sums up the attitude toward writers at the BBC.'[424]

Thursday 19th:
Itinerary: The BBC takes up the option for Sylvester McCoy to appear as the Doctor in 14 new episodes to be made in 1988.

Sunday 22nd:
Itinerary: The BBC2 review programme *Did You See ...?* focuses on *Doctor Who*'s upcoming birthday the following day, with a programme critical of the new season and John's producership in particular. John is asked to participate, but declines.

Monday 23rd:
'Dragonfire' Part One screens on BBC1.

Tuesday 24th:
Itinerary: John and Andrew Cartmel attend a playback of 'Dragonfire' Part Three with Colin Rogers, the Assistant Head of the BBC Drama Department. At some point after this, John flies from London to New York City, USA.

---

[423] This story will be retitled 'Nemesis' before finally becoming 'Silver Nemesis' by the time it airs on BBC1.
[424] Kevin Clarke interview, *Doctor Who Magazine* #244.

Friday 27th – Sunday 29th:
Itinerary: John is the sole guest at the Creation convention, held at the Penta Hotel in New York.

Monday 30th:
'Dragonfire' Part Two screens on BBC1.

DECEMBER

Tuesday 1st:
Itinerary: The BBC takes up the option for Sophie Aldred to appear as Ace in 14 new episodes to be made in 1988.

Thursday 3rd:
Itinerary: Now back in the UK, John writes letters of response to a number of viewers who have written to the BBC to complain about the violent nature of the death of Ken Dodd's character in 'Delta and the Bannermen' Part One. John points out that the Tollmaster isn't seen to die on screen, and says that he is considering bringing the character back in a future story.

Commentary: The Tollmaster is shown being shot in the back, with appropriate pyrotechnic charges exploding from Dodd's costume, before slumping to the floor. For John to suggest that this wasn't an on-screen death was somewhat disingenuous. The suggestion that the character might return was even less credible.

Friday 4th:
Itinerary: John writes to actor Howard Cooke, who played Pex in 'Paradise Towers', thanking him for an invitation to his party (date unknown), which he says he will attend. He tells him he is considering the possibility of Pex returning in a future story.

Commentary: Like his recent comments about the Tollmaster in response to viewers' letters, this suggestion by John that the clearly killed-off character Pex could return was scarcely credible. As this came a few months after the BBC had screened the episodes of the US soap *Dallas* in which the dead-and-buried Bobby Ewing comes back to life in a contrived plot involving a season-long dream and a shower, maybe John – a big fan of soap operas – was jokily riffing on the idea.

Monday 7th:
'Dragonfire' Part Three screens on BBC1.

Wednesday 9th:
Itinerary: Graeme Curry delivers his script for 'The Crooked Smile' Part Two to the *Doctor Who* Production Office. On the same day, David Williams, the BBC's Assistant Legal Advisor, writes to Gary Leigh, editor of *DWB*. The fanzine's November edition, Issue 49, published this same day, carries a front-page article entitled 'JNT Must Go Now!', written by Ian Levine, in which Levine questions John's competence as a producer. Williams asserts that the article goes beyond fair comment and could be considered a malicious attack on John's reputation. He asks that Leigh write John an apology and refrain from such personal attacks in the future.[425]

Friday 11th:
Itinerary: John replies apologetically to a disgruntled viewer named Dorothy, who has written to the BBC to complain about the disparaging remarks made by Ace about this name – her real forename – in 'Dragonfire' Part Two.

Monday 14th:
Itinerary: Stephen Wyatt delivers his scripts for 'The Greatest Show in the Galaxy' Parts Two and Three to the *Doctor Who* Production Office.

Wednesday 16th:
Itinerary: Ben Aaronovitch delivers his script for 'Nemesis of the Doctor' Part One to the *Doctor Who* Production Office.

Friday 18th:
Itinerary: John signs off the commission for Ben Aaronovitch to write the script for 'Nemesis of the Doctor' Parts Two to Four.

Monday 21st:
Itinerary: John sends Terry Nation's agent Roger Hancock the storyline for the forthcoming Dalek story (which would ultimately be retitled 'Remembrance of the Daleks'), seeking Nation's approval and comments.

---

[425] Leigh wrote back to Williams in early January 1988, but stood by the criticism levelled at John in Levine's article and flatly refused either to apologise or to refrain from publishing further criticism in the future.

1988

Setting the Scene:

Having had his arm well and truly twisted by Jonathon Powell into producing *Doctor Who*'s twenty-fourth season, John had clicked back into full professional mode, and had got on with the job to the best of his abilities. His new script editor, Andrew Cartmel, seemed to get along with him reasonably well, despite a few early wobbles, and his new leading man, Sylvester McCoy, had certainly injected a new dynamism into proceedings.

However, John's relationship with the show's fans was at an all-time low. He felt that UK fandom had turned against him in the wake of Eric Saward's departure, and he declined all UK convention invitations in 1987, a stance he would maintain for all of 1988 as well. In the US, his convention appearances had been limited to just four events in 1987, and all but one of those had come in the months when *Doctor Who* wasn't in production, so his attendances can't have impeded on the making of the show in any significant way. However, these issues were to remain an uncomfortable backdrop to John's professional life in the months ahead.

Despite not having wanting to produce the twenty-fourth season, John needed little persuasion to stay on for the twenty-fifth, seeing the show's silver anniversary as an opportunity to indulge himself in its history. He quickly ruled out the notion of doing an anniversary story with any old Doctors, on the grounds that he didn't want to recast Patrick Troughton as well as William Hartnell; that Jon Pertwee was busy filming *Worzel Gummidge Down Under* in New Zealand; that Tom Baker probably would give another anniversary story as wide a berth as he had 'The Five Doctors'; that Peter Davison was busy starring in the BBC's *Campion*; that Colin Baker probably wasn't well-disposed toward the show that had dispensed with his services; and that in any case he had only 14 episodes to play with. Instead, John planned to try to celebrate *Doctor Who*'s silver anniversary in any other way, shape or form that he could. Once that was all done and dusted, then that would be an ideal point for him to step away from the show for good. Season 25 would definitely be John's last as producer of *Doctor Who*; of that, he had no doubt …

JANUARY

Tuesday 5th:
Itinerary: In the evening, John goes to see the pantomime *Jack and the Beanstalk* at the Grand Theatre in Wolverhampton.

Commentary: The cast of this pantomime included Roy Hudd, Geoffrey Hughes (Mr Popplewick in 'The Trial of a Time Lord' Parts Thirteen and Fourteen), Maurice Colbourne (Lytton in 'Resurrection of the Daleks' and 'Attack of the Cybermen'), Lyn Paul, Jack Tripp, Gary Lovine, Alan Christie, Debbie Flitcroft and Gail Mortley.

Friday 8th:
Itinerary: Stephen Wyatt delivers his script for 'The Greatest Show in the Galaxy' Part Four to the *Doctor Who* Production Office.

Tuesday 12th:
Itinerary: Ben Aaronovitch delivers his script for 'Nemesis of the Doctor' Part Two to the *Doctor Who* Production Office.

Wednesday 13th:
Itinerary: Sylvester McCoy, Sophie Aldred, Andrew Cartmel, Ben Aaronovitch, Graeme Curry, Stephen Wyatt, Kevin Clarke, Andrew Morgan, Chris Clough and Alan Wareing meet up for an informal chat about the upcoming season in a café in Shepherd's Bush. This is done with John's knowledge, although he elects not to get involved.

Commentary: Ben Aaronovitch, Graeme Curry, Stephen Wyatt and Kevin Clarke were the writers who would contribute scripts to the forthcoming season. Only Wyatt had written for *Doctor Who* before (with 'Paradise Towers'). Andrew Morgan, Chris Clough and Alan Wearing would be directing the stories. Morgan and Clough had directed for the show before, and Alan Wearing has just made the jump from Production Manager (in which capacity he had worked on 'Timelash') to director.

Thursday 14th:
Itinerary: John has a working lunch at the BBC Club bar with David Saunders.[426]

---

[426] Saunders was the ex-Coordinator of the DWAS and was in the process of writing the multi-volume reference work *The Encyclopaedia of the Worlds of Doctor*

Tuesday 12th:
Itinerary: John writes notes to thank Lesley Rawstone for her make-up work, Ken Trew for his costume work and Geoff Powell for his design work, all on 'Strange Matter'.

Monday 18th:
Itinerary: John, Andrew Cartmel, Chris Clough and Gary Downie attend auditions in the conference room at BBC Threshold House for singers to play a group called the Lorells in 'Flight of the Chimeron'. The Wilson sisters are the successful candidates.

Tuesday 19th – Wednesday 20th:
Rehearsals for the OB location recording of 'Paradise Towers' take place at the BBC Television Rehearsal Rooms at Acton.

Tuesday 19th:
Itinerary: John attends a planning meeting for the first studio block of 'Paradise Towers' at 9.30am at the BBC Television Rehearsal Rooms at Acton.

Wednesday 20th:
Itinerary: John attends a pre-production meeting for 'Flight of the Chimeron' at 10.30am in the conference room at BBC Threshold House.

Thursday 21st:
Itinerary: Today is the first day of OB recording for 'Paradise Towers' at the outdoor swimming pool at Elmswell House in Chalfont St Giles, Buckinghamshire.

Friday 22nd:
Itinerary: Today is the second and final day of OB recording for 'Paradise Towers' at the outdoor swimming pool at Elmswell House in Chalfont St Giles, Buckinghamshire.

Saturday 23rd – Wednesday 3rd June:
Rehearsals for the first studio block of 'Paradise Towers' take place at the BBC Television Rehearsal Rooms at Acton.

Thursday 28th:
Itinerary: In the *Doctor Who* Production Office, John and Chris Clough audition actors to play the role of Billy in 'Flight of the Chimeron'. On the same day, John previews the new *Doctor Who* title sequence produced by CAL video.

Friday 29th:
Itinerary: John writes to the BBC Contracts Department, asking that Keff McCullough be engaged to compose the incidental music for 'Flight of the Chimeron', and also to appear on location with three other musicians of his choice to play the camp band in the same story. Today is also the Producer's Run at the BBC Television Rehearsal Rooms at Acton for the first studio block of 'Paradise Towers'.

JUNE

Monday 1st:
Itinerary John attends a planning meeting for the second studio block of 'Paradise Towers' at the BBC Television Rehearsal Rooms at Acton.

Wednesday 3rd:
Itinerary: John attends the final rehearsals for the first studio session of 'Paradise Towers' for the Producer's Run, along with Andrew Cartmel.

Andrew Cartmel: '[During the Producer's Run] John Nathan-Turner snapped at me, the first of several such incidents as the season moved on and tension mounted up. It left me feeling sour and angry for the rest of the day.' [417]

Thursday 4th:
Itinerary: Today is the first day of the two-day first studio block for 'Paradise Towers' in studio TC1 at BBC Television Centre. On the same day, John writes to the BBC Contracts Department, asking that Sophie Aldred be engaged to play Ace in story 7G. He asks that additional options in the BBC's favour be included in the contract, to cover 14 more episodes in 1988 and 8 out of 14 episodes in 1989.

Andrew Cartmel: 'Stephen [Wyatt] was very concerned that the Caretakers [in his story "Paradise Towers"] should be suitably seedy looking and slovenly and shambolic ... I'd already spoken to John about this once on Stephen's behalf. But still nothing seemed to have been done ... Stephen urged me to repeat the observation. So I moved forward in the control room darkness to remind John. He turned to me and snarled, "Listen. Don't you check on me. I'm the producer." I retreated and sat down again, feeling humiliated and angry. That was the second time in two days that John had

---

[417] *Script Doctor* by Andrew Cartmel, published by Reynolds & Hearn, 2005.

Friday 15th:
Itinerary: Ben Aaronovitch visits the *Doctor Who* Production Office to deliver in person his script for 'Nemesis of the Doctor' Part Four. He meets up with John and they discuss the upcoming story.

Monday 18th:
Itinerary: John writes a letter to director Peter Grimwade, enquiring about his health after a recent operation. Grimwade has earlier sent John a copy of his novel *Robot*[427] to see if there is any mileage in trying to get the BBC to dramatise it, but John states that he feels it wouldn't fit into any of the available drama slots. He goes on to remind Grimwade that he previously said he was going to send a copy also to Anna Holme[428], which he thought might be more productive, as he had heard that the BBC Children's Department were seeking more 'teenage orientated' dramas. John concludes by suggesting that they meet up for a drink sometime soon. Ben Aaronovitch delivers his script for 'Nemesis of the Doctor' Part Three to the *Doctor Who* Production Office.

Tuesday 19th:
Itinerary: Kevin Clarke delivers his script for 'The Harbinger' Part One to the *Doctor Who* Production Office.

Wednesday 20th:
Itinerary: John entertains DWAS Coordinator Andrew Beech at the BBC Club bar.[429] John signs off the commission for Kevin Clarke to write the script for 'The Harbinger' Parts Two and Three.

Monday 25th:
Itinerary: John writes to the BBC Head of Copyright, Brian Turner, asking that the rights to use the Cybermen in 'The Harbinger' be negotiated with the agents/estates of their creators Gerry Davis and Kit Pedler.

Who. The first volume, covering the letters A-D, had been published in hardback by Piccadilly Press in November 1987, and the second was being written at this point. Saunders was one of a very small number of fans who had John's ear at this point in time. He regularly supplied him with VHS video copies of old *Doctor Who* stories for reference purposes, as John found this easier than obtaining them through official BBC channels.
[427] *Robot* by Peter Grimwade, published by Star Books (a division of W H Allen) in 1987
[428] Head of the BBC Children's Television Department.
[429] Beech had written the scathing *Daily Mail* article some months previously – this presumably was a 'clear the air' meeting between the two parties.

FEBRUARY

Friday 5th – Sunday 7th:
Itinerary: John is a guest at the Omnicon VIII convention, held at the Oceanside Holiday Inn in Fort Lauderdale, Florida, USA. Other guests include Frazer Hines, Nicola Bryant and Gary Downie.[430]

Friday 12th:
Itinerary: John meets with Andrew Cartmel and Ben Aaronovitch to discuss and time the scripts for 'Remembrance of the Daleks' Parts One and Two.

Monday 15th:
Itinerary: Graeme Curry delivers his script for 'The Crooked Smile' Part Three to the *Doctor Who* Production Office.

Tuesday 16th:
Itinerary: John meets with Andrew Cartmel and director Andrew Morgan to discuss the recording of 'Remembrance of the Daleks.'

Andrew Cartmel: '"He was pissed. He must have been pissed," whispered Andrew [Morgan, referring to the fact that] John had fallen over the night before and smashed his ribs on his metal Garfield briefcase … '[431]

Wednesday 17th:
Itinerary: at the BBC Club bar, John entertains John Freeman (Designer, and soon-to-be-Editor) and Sheila Cranna (Editor, and soon-to-be-Magazine Group Editor) from Marvel Comics' *Doctor Who* Magazine.

Thursday 18th:
Itinerary: John entertains director Peter Moffatt at the BBC Club bar.[432] In the

---

[430] This was tied in with a holiday that John and Gary were taking, visiting Florida and Honolulu in early February. Within weeks of his return to the UK, John elected to shave off his trademark beard – a look he'd sported since before becoming *Doctor Who* producer. He remained clean-shaven for the remainder of his time at the BBC, and for the rest of his life for that matter.

[431] *Script Doctor* by Andrew Cartmel, published by Reynolds & Hearn, 2005.

[432] Moffatt had directed the stories 'State of the Decay', 'The Visitation', 'Mawdryn Undead', 'The Five Doctors', 'The Twin Dilemma' and 'The Two Doctors', all for Nathan-Turner. It's possible there was some discussion at this meeting about him directing one of the upcoming Season 25 stories, but if so, nothing came of it, and Moffatt did not direct for the show again.

evening, he goes to see a theatre production of *Babes in the Wood*.

Friday 19th:
Itinerary: John attends a meeting with Andrew Cartmel, Andrew Morgan and Ben Aaronovitch to discuss the scripts for 'Remembrance of the Daleks'. He objects to a scene where the Doctor destroys a Dalek with a rocket launcher, and he and Andrew Cartmel come very close to having a full-on argument over the matter. [433]

Monday 22nd:
Itinerary: John sends Visual Effects Designers Stuart Brisdon, Steve Bowman and Perry Brahan a memo, welcoming them back to *Doctor Who* for its twenty-fifth anniversary year, setting out how he would like the costings for the season's visual effects to be agreed as work progresses and asking them to make sure that they stay within budget.

Thursday 25th:
Itinerary: John has a working lunch with an (unnamed) writer at the Muswell Restaurant in Goldhawk Road, Shepherd's Bush, London

Friday 26th:
Itinerary: John goes to the cinema to see the science-fiction film *Robocop*.[434]

MARCH

Wednesday 2nd:
Itinerary: John has a working lunch with director Chris Clough at the BBC Club bar.[435]

Tuesday 8th:
Itinerary: In the evening, John goes to see the play *The Rink* at the Cambridge Theatre in London.

Commentary: The cast of *The Rink* included Richard Bodkin, Peter Edbrook,

---

[433] The scene was eventually rewritten to have Ace use the rocket launcher on the Dalek.
[434] *Robocop* is an ultra-violent sci-fi tale directed by Paul Verhoeven.
[435] Clough had directed 'The Trial of a Time Lord' Parts Nine to Fourteen, 'Delta and the Bannermen' and 'Dragonfire', and would direct 'The Happiness Patrol' and 'Silver Nemesis' in the upcoming Season 25.

James Gavin, Michael Gyngell, Steve Hervieu, Gareth Snook, Diane Langton, Josephine Blake and Caroline O'Connor.

Wednesday 9th:
Itinerary: John meets up with actor Tony Selby. It would appear that the venue for the meeting was somewhere in the vicinity of Piccadilly Circus.[436]

Thursday 10th:
Itinerary: John travels by tube to the BBC's Rehearsal Rooms at Acton.

Commentary: The start of work on 'Remembrance of the Daleks' was still some weeks away, so John's trip may have been just to check out plans for the rehearsals for the upcoming Season 25.

Wednesday 16th:
Itinerary: John has a meeting with author Tony Gillett in the BBC Club bar.[437] In the evening, he goes to see Barry Humphries, as his *alter ego* Dame Edna Everage, at the Strand Theatre in London, in his show *Dame Edna: Back with a Vengeance.*

Friday 18th:
Itinerary: John travels from Union House to Hammersmith by tube, then returns later in the day.

Commentary: This was probably for a location recce for the recording of 'Remembrance of the Daleks' in a few weeks' time.

Sunday 20th:
Itinerary: Kevin Clarke delivers his script for 'The Harbinger' Part Two to the *Doctor Who* Production Office.

Friday 25th:
Itinerary: John writes to the Press Secretary at Buckingham Palace, asking for permission to record sections of 'The Harbinger' at Windsor Castle later in the summer. He also writes to HRH Prince Edward, asking if he would like to appear in the story as himself for a brief cameo scene.

Monday 28th – Saturday 2nd April:
Rehearsals for the OB location recording of 'Remembrance of the Daleks' take place at the BBC Television Rehearsal Rooms at Acton.

---

[436] Selby had played Glitz in 'The Trial of a Time Lord' and 'Dragonfire'.
[437] No author of that name seems to have had any works published or performed.

Monday 28th:
Itinerary: John takes the short tube ride from Union House to the BBC's Rehearsal Rooms at Acton for the first day of OB rehearsals for 'Remembrance of the Daleks'. Lieutenant Colonel Sean O'Dwyer from Buckingham Palace writes to John on behalf of HRH Prince Edward, thanking him for the offer of a role for the Prince in 'The Harbinger', but declining the invitation.

John Nathan-Turner: 'Via his equerry, I had suggested that Prince Edward might care to appear in this story; with half-a-dozen lines, he was to play himself. I got a ticking-off, because there is a special royal liaison office at the BBC and all such requests should be made through them. I was aware of its existence but was under the misapprehension that they merely arranged liaison for location shoots on royal premises and did not deal with individuals. I don't think that the prince was offended. His equerry wrote back to say that Edward was most amused by the idea, but nevertheless had to decline the offer.'[438]

APRIL

Friday 1st (Good Friday – bank holiday):
Itinerary: John takes the short tube ride from Union House to the BBC's Rehearsal Rooms at Acton for the ongoing OB rehearsals for 'Remembrance of the Daleks'.

Monday 4th (Easter Monday – bank holiday):
Itinerary: Today is the first day of OB recording for 'Remembrance of the Daleks'. This takes place in Theed Street, Lambeth in London. John drives to and from the location.

John Nathan-Turner: 'Much has been written about the battle under Waterloo Bridge, which set off the station's alarm system. Although we had previously warned the emergency services what we'd be doing, a stream of fire engines, ambulances and police cars turned up. It was funny at the time, and not just in retrospect. My only concern was that because so many car alarms had been set off by the explosions – some at least a mile away – cars might have been left

---

[438] John Nathan-Turner memoirs, *Doctor Who Magazine* #247. HRH Prince Edward having declined the invitation to appear in the story, a lookalike of the Queen was ultimately used instead.

for the day and we'd never get their alarms turned off at all!'[439]

Tuesday 5th:
Itinerary: Today is the second day of OB recording for 'Remembrance of the Daleks' in Theed Street, Lambeth in London. John drives to and from the location. During the afternoon, John directs some second-unit action involving the grey Daleks patrolling the streets and opening fire on the white Daleks.

Wednesday 6th:
Itinerary: Today is the third day of OB recording for 'Remembrance of the Daleks', now in the grounds of the Kew Bridge Steam Museum in Hounslow, London. John drives to and from the location. On arrival at the museum, John is disappointed to discover that the prop junkyard gates created for the shoot have been painted with the words 'L. M. FORMAN', rather than the intended 'I. M. FOREMAN' as seen in *Doctor Who*'s very first episode back in 1963, and he arranges for them to be repainted.[440]

Thursday 7th:
Itinerary: Today is the fourth day of OB recording for 'Remembrance of the Daleks'. This takes place in both of the previous locations, the Kew Bridge Steam Museum in Hounslow and Theed Street in Lambeth. John drives to and from the shoot. On the same day, he writes to the BBC Contracts Department, asking them to engage David Banks to play the Cyberleader in 'The Harbinger'.

Friday 8th:
Itinerary: Today is the fifth day of OB recording for 'Remembrance of the Daleks', now in and around the grounds of Willesden Lane Cemetery in Brent, London. John directs some second-unit material of the Doctor and Ace driving along the streets of London in a commandeered army van. John drives to and from the location.

Saturday 9th:
Itinerary: Today is the sixth day of OB recording for 'Remembrance of the Daleks', this time at St John's CE Junior & Infant School in Hammersmith, London. John drives to and from the location, and also makes a detour to the BBC's Elstree studios at some point during the day.

---

[439] John Nathan-Turner memoirs, *Doctor Who Magazine* #247.
[440] Despite this, 'FOREMAN' was still misspelt 'FORMAN' in some shots when the story reached the screen.

Monday 11th:
Itinerary: Today is the seventh day of OB recording for 'Remembrance of the Daleks', again in St John's CE Junior & Infant School in Hammersmith, London. John drives to and from the location. Kevin Clarke delivers his script for 'The Harbinger' Part Three to the *Doctor Who* Production Office.

Tuesday 12th:
Itinerary: Today is the eighth day of OB recording for 'Remembrance of the Daleks'. This time, the action is at Macbeth Street in Hammersmith, London. John drives to and from the location.

Wednesday 13th:
Itinerary: Today is the ninth and final day of OB recording for 'Remembrance of the Daleks', back in St John's CE Junior & Infant School in Hammersmith, London. John drives to and from the location.

Thursday 14th:
Itinerary: John receives a letter from Eric Hoffman[441], detailing various items of gossip from the US *Doctor Who* convention circuit.

Friday 15th – Tuesday 26th:
Rehearsals for the single studio block of 'Remembrance of the Daleks' take place at the BBC Television Rehearsal Rooms at Acton.

Saturday 16th:
Itinerary: John travels in by car for a non-duty day at Television Centre.

Wednesday 20th:
Itinerary: John entertains Eric Luskin at the BBC Club bar.[442]

Monday 25th:
Itinerary: John travels by tube to the BBC Television Rehearsal Rooms at Acton for the Producer's Run of the single studio block of 'Remembrance of the Daleks'. He also attends a pre-production meeting for 'The Harbinger' at the home of Jane Wellesley, the Production Assistant on the story.

---

[441] Hoffman was a prominent US *Doctor Who* fan.
[442] Luskin was a staff member at the US PBS Station New Jersey Network (NJN). He had already produced the documentaries *Doctor Who's Who's Who* in 1985 and *Doctor Who Then & Now* in 1987, both of which had screened on various PBS stations around the US. In 1988, he would make his third and final documentary about the show, *The Making of Doctor Who*, which would follow the production of the twenty-fifth anniversary story, 'Silver Nemesis'. His meeting with Nathan-Turner was almost certainly to discuss this latter project.

Wednesday 27th:
Itinerary: Today is the first day of the three-day studio block for 'Remembrance of the Daleks' in studio TC8 at BBC Television Centre. After recording, John joins the cast in the BBC Club bar.

Thursday 28th:
Itinerary: Today is the second day of the three-day studio block for 'Remembrance of the Daleks' in studio TC8 at BBC Television Centre. After recording, John joins the cast in the BBC Club bar.

Friday 29th:
Itinerary: Today is the final day of the three-day studio block for 'Remembrance of the Daleks' in studio TC8 at BBC Television Centre. After recording, John joins the cast in the BBC Club bar.

Andrew Cartmel: 'There was a memo from John lying around, complaining about Sophie's badges on her costume. Ace's bomber jacket featured an assortment of badges, both as souvenirs of her travels and as a kind of advertisement for her personality. The problem was that Sophie had been adding some badges of her own without going through the channels (i.e. the Costume Department) and there had been continuity problems as a result. And John had flipped. When I went into the producer's booth, I found John and Alan Wareing talking about Sophie. "And now she's complaining because I won't let her have a late-night taxi." Alan waves a disgusted, dismissive hand. For some reason, perhaps because this was the first proper story they'd done together, John and Sophie were totally in conflict. John talked to me about Sophie, and he was being very diplomatic and good about it all. But he said, "It's the worst relationship I've had with any of the companions." God knows why they'd got each other's backs up, but they had ... I wished they weren't at loggerheads. They weren't for long. Sophie and John would bury the hatchet over several drinks in a country pub during the shoot for "The Greatest Show in the Galaxy" and they remained on good terms thereafter.'[443]

MAY

Friday 6th – Thursday 12th:
Rehearsals for the OB location recording of 'The Greatest Show in the Galaxy' take place at the BBC Television Rehearsal Rooms at Acton.

---

[443] *Script Doctor* by Andrew Cartmel, published by Reynolds & Hearn, 2005.

Friday 6th:
Itinerary: John travels by tube to the BBC Television Rehearsal Rooms at Acton for the first day of rehearsals for the OB location recording of 'The Greatest Show in the Galaxy'.

Monday 9th:
Itinerary: John writes to Eric Hoffman, explaining that he was due to attend the 1988 North American Time Festival convention in the US in July but has had his invitation cancelled.[444]

Friday 13th:
Itinerary: John entertains writer Chris Beebee in the BBC Club bar.[445]

Saturday 14th:
Itinerary: John drives to Weymouth, Dorset for the OB Location recording of 'The Greatest Show in the Galaxy', which begins today at the ECC Quarry in Warmwell. He spends the night in the unit hotel.

Sunday 15th:
Itinerary: Today is the second day of OB Location recording for 'The Greatest Show in the Galaxy' at the ECC Quarry in Warmwell, Dorset. John directs some second-unit material of kites flying in the sky, and of the characters Bellboy and Flowerchild trying to evade them. He again spends the night in the unit hotel.

Monday 16th:
Itinerary: Today is the third day of OB Location recording for 'The Greatest Show in the Galaxy' at the ECC Quarry in Warmwell, Dorset. John spends a third night in the unit hotel.

Tuesday 17th:
Itinerary: Today is the fourth day of OB Location recording for 'The Greatest Show in the Galaxy' at the ECC Quarry in Warmwell, Dorset. John once more spends the night in the unit hotel. The same hotel is being used as a base tonight by another BBC programme, *Crimewatch*. The *Doctor Who* crew challenge the *Crimewatch* crew to an evening darts match at a nearby country pub.

---

[444] The 1988 North American Time Festival convention took place between 1 and 3 July at the Radisson Hotel in Minneapolis, Minnesota. Jon Pertwee, Frazer Hines and Janet Fielding did attend.
[445] Chris Beebee was a UK science fiction author who wrote the books *The Hub* (1987) and *The Main Event* (1989). It's possible that Beebee was looking to pitch story ideas for *Doctor Who* at the time, or alternatively that John was looking at using him and/or his books as a project to move on to after *Doctor Who*.

Wednesday 18th:
Itinerary: Today is the fifth and final day of OB Location recording for 'The Greatest Show in the Galaxy' at the ECC Quarry in Warmwell, Dorset. John spends a final night in the unit hotel.

John Nathan-Turner: 'Our end-of-location-shoot party at the unit hotel included the then-traditional cabaret. The leading light was Jessica Martin, who did an act all about *Doctor Who*, featuring impressions of many of the ladies who'd appeared in the show's past – and present, for she included Sophie Aldred, make-up artist Helen [Johnson] and our Production Manager, Susannah Shaw. The general consensus was that this was one of the most happy groups of cast and crew ever assembled. Everyone, without exception, was eagerly looking forward to the studio sessions ... '[446]

Thursday 19th:
John drives back to London.

Friday 20th – Monday 30th:
Rehearsals for the first studio block of 'The Greatest Show in the Galaxy' take place at the BBC Television Rehearsal Rooms at Acton.

Friday 20th:
Itinerary: John receives a letter from the BBC Personnel Department, thanking him for an application he has made for the position of Executive Producer, Children's Programmes, BBC Television. He is invited to an 'appointment board'[447] on the morning of Thursday 26 May at BBC Television Centre. On the same day, Davros actor Terry Molloy writes to John. John has previously asked Molloy if he would mind being credited under a false name in the BBC's weekly listings magazine *Radio Times*, to avoid spoiling the surprise of the character's return in the final episode of 'Remembrance of the Daleks'. Molloy doesn't object, and suggests they use 'Roy Morterlly', an anagram of his name.[448]

Thursday 26th:
Itinerary: John has his interview/appointment board for the position of Executive Producer, Children's Programmes, BBC Television. He doesn't get the job.

---

[446] John Nathan-Turner memoirs, *Doctor Who Magazine* #247.
[447] The BBC's terminology for a job interview.
[448] Molloy was eventually billed as 'Roy Tromelly' both in the *Radio Times* and in the end credits of Part Three of 'Remembrance of the Daleks'.

364

Tuesday 31st:
Itinerary: Today was due to be the start of the three-day first studio session for 'The Greatest Show in the Galaxy' at BBC Television Centre. However, a safety inspection on 27 May has revealed that there is asbestos in the ceilings of various Television Centre studios, so these have all been unexpectedly closed until it can be safely removed. John is informed that the first studio block of 'The Greatest Show in the Galaxy' has been lost as a result, and that the second block is now very unlikely to go ahead. Rehearsals for the first block began at Acton on Friday 20 May, and they continue while John tries to find a way of salvaging the production.

JUNE

Wednesday 1st:
Itinerary: John again entertains writer Chris Beebee in the BBC Club bar.

Commentary: Sometime around this point, John was informed that no alternative studio dates would be made available for the recording of 'The Greatest Show in the Galaxy' – a situation similar to the one that had led to the cancellation of 'Shada' back in 1979. He decided not to release the cast but to keep them in rehearsals with director Alan Wareing while he tried to get the BBC's Planning Resources Department to reconsider. Initial plans to remount the studio material in a tent close to the M40 were discussed, but were scuppered when the BBC's Director General issued an edict that any remounts had to take place on BBC premises. Designer David Lasky suggested instead erecting a tent in one of the car parks at the BBC's Elstree studios, which would meet this criterion. Planning then began to see if this could be achieved.

Thursday 2nd:
Itinerary: Nicola Bryant has recently written to John, informing him of her latest projects and generally updating him on things that are going on in her life. John writes back today, wishing her well with an upcoming play tour and promising to try to see one of the Richmond performances. However, he notes that he will be away on location in Arundel at the time, so it might be tricky.

Friday 3rd:
Itinerary: John travels from Union House to the BBC Rehearsal Rooms at Acton, where the cast of 'The Greatest Show in the Galaxy' are still rehearsing the still-to-be-recorded scenes. He also writes to noted American actress Dolores Gray's agent, confirming that she will have a 'single slide' credit for a

cameo appearance she has agreed to make in 'Silver Nemesis'.

Monday 6th:
Itinerary: To rescue the production of 'The Greatest Show in the Galaxy' after the closure of the BBC Television Centre studios, John has arranged for a huge marquee to be erected in the car park of the BBC Film Studios at Elstree. As most of the studio sets were designed to represent the inside of a circus tent, they have been fairly easily rejigged to fit inside the marquee. Today is the first day of what should have been the studio recording session, now revised to an OB one. John drives to and from the venue.

Tuesday 7th:
Itinerary: Today is the second day of the remounted OB recording of 'The Greatest Show in the Galaxy' at the Elstree marquee. John drives to and from location.

Wednesday 8th:
Itinerary: Today is the third day of the remounted OB recording of 'The Greatest Show in the Galaxy' at the Elstree marquee. John drives to and from location.

Thursday 9th:
Itinerary: Today is the fourth day of the remounted OB recording of 'The Greatest Show in the Galaxy' at the Elstree marquee. John drives to and from location.

Friday 10th:
Itinerary: Today is the fifth day of the remounted OB recording of 'The Greatest Show in the Galaxy' at the Elstree marquee. John drives to and from location.

Monday 13th:
Itinerary: John writes to Dolores Gray's agent, confirming the order of the final credits on her episode, and that the size of her credit will be no smaller than any other participant's. He also agrees to change the name of her character from Miss Hackensack to something else.

Tuesday 14th:
Itinerary: Eric Saward writes to Paul Fox, Deputy Head of Copyright at the BBC. He informs Fox that John is being paid large sums to appear at US conventions and to take tapes of *Doctor Who* stories to be shown at said events. Saward wants to know when the writers of the stories shown at these events will be paid accordingly.

Wednesday 15th:
Itinerary: Today is the first of three days' worth of OB recording at the studios at BBC Elstree, to complete the cancelled studio scenes for 'The Greatest Show in the Galaxy'. It is also the first day of rehearsals for the OB location recording of 'Silver Nemesis', but director Chris Clough has to start these without either Sylvester McCoy or Sophie Aldred, owing to their continued involvement in the Elstree recording.

Thursday 16th:
Itinerary: Tom Rivers, Deputy Head of Copyright at the BBC, writes to Eric Saward, replying to his letter of 14 June to Paul Fox. He sets out the BBC's position regarding the screening of *Doctor Who* episodes at fan events. As there is no further charge to watch the episodes once a fan has paid to attend a convention, there is no specific payment for this, as far as the BBC are concerned. Rivers goes on to point out that this scenario seems to have been already agreed with the Writer's Guild as a fair exemption, and so no fees to the writers are due. Additionally, he asserts, the rights that the BBC buy in the scripts in the first place allow them to use the stories for the BBC's own private purposes, including publicity; and fan conventions fall under this category. Today is also the second of three days' OB recording at the studios at BBC Elstree, to complete the cancelled studio scenes for 'The Greatest Show in the Galaxy'.

Friday 17th:
Itinerary: John receives a letter from Janet Fielding; this is a general 'catch up' missive on her latest career projects, and also contains some home decor suggestions.

Saturday 18th:
Itinerary: Today is the final day of the three-day OB recording at the studios at BBC Elstree, to complete the cancelled studio scenes for 'The Greatest Show in the Galaxy'.

Sunday 19th – Tuesday 21st:
Rehearsals for the OB location recording of 'Silver Nemesis' continue at the BBC Television Rehearsal Rooms at Acton, now with McCoy and Aldred in attendance. With John's blessing, some of the rehearsal is covered by a camera crew working on the NJN documentary *The Making of Doctor Who*.

Tuesday 21st:
Itinerary: Eric Saward writes back to Tom Rivers, Deputy Head of Copyright at the BBC. He refutes the points made by Rivers in his response regarding John's showing of *Doctor Who* episodes at US conventions.

Wednesday 22nd:
Itinerary: Glynne Price, Head of Personnel at the BBC, writes to John enclosing copies of the recent correspondence between Eric Saward and Tom Rivers. He says that he wants to talk to John about the concerns raised by Saward. Today is also the first day of OB recording for 'Silver Nemesis'; this takes place at the Gas Works in Greenwich, London. The recording is covered by the crew for the NJN documentary *The Making of Doctor Who*.

Thursday 23rd:
Itinerary: John writes to US fans Gail Bennett[449] and Laurie Haldeman[450]. He explains that his non-appearance at a recent convention in Cleveland, Ohio was due to him not being sent a plane ticket, and also getting no phone call or letter from the organisers to explain what was going on.[451] Today is also the second day of OB recording for 'Silver Nemesis' at the Gas Works in Greenwich, London. It is again covered by the crew for the NJN documentary *The Making of Doctor Who*.

Friday 24th:
Itinerary: Today is the third day of OB recording for 'Silver Nemesis' at the Gas Works in Greenwich, London. It was due to be covered once more by the crew for the NJN documentary *The Making of Doctor Who*, but they have been asked not to attend, to allow the production to try to make up for lost time.

Sunday 26th:
Itinerary: Today is the fourth day of OB recording for 'Silver Nemesis', now relocated to the Arundel Castle Estate, Arundel in West Sussex. The recording is covered by the crew for the NJN documentary *The Making of Doctor Who*. John stays overnight at Beach Hotel in Worthing.

John Nathan-Turner: 'When we moved our location to Worthing, we stayed at the Beach Hotel, which was very old fashioned, reeked of Eau de Cologne and Devon Violets, and was chiefly occupied by old ladies. Anton [Diffring, playing the part of De Flores in the story,] arrived before everyone else and informed the production manager: "I love it at this hotel. I am the youngest

---

[449] Gail Bennett had previously provided the illustrations for Gary Downie's 1986 book *The Doctor Who Cookbook* (WH Allen, 1986), and cover illustrations for some of the *Make Your Own Adventure With Doctor Who* books (published by Severn House).
[450] Laurie Haldeman was the co-author of the 1986 book *Doctor Who: Travel Without The TARDIS* (published by Target Books).
[451] John was meant to be a guest at an event in Cleveland called *A Day With the Doctor* in October 1988, but his appearance was cancelled, as was the event itself shortly after. This convention would seem to be the likely candidate for the events John describes in his letters.

here!"'[452]

Monday 27th:
Itinerary: Today is the fifth day of OB recording for 'Silver Nemesis', again at the Arundel Castle Estate, Arundel in West Sussex. The recording is covered by the crew for the NJN documentary *The Making of Doctor Who*. John again stays overnight at Beach Hotel in Worthing. On the same day, BBC producer and director Vere Lorrimer writes John a letter of thanks for being invited to attend the Arundel Castle recording.[453]

John Nathan-Turner: 'Many people have asked why so many Equity and Writer's Guild members made up a troop of visitors at "Windsor Castle". The answer, dear reader, you will find hard to believe, but it is true. Again, I thought – and I had been led to understand – that this was to be my farewell to *Who*. So we contacted the various directors, associates, producers, writers and production managers who held the necessary union cards, and took them out on a fun day by coach as part of my farewell.'[454]

Tuesday 28th:
Itinerary: Today is the sixth day of OB recording for 'Silver Nemesis' at the Arundel Castle Estate, Arundel in West Sussex. John again stays overnight at the Beach Hotel in Worthing. On the same day, Eric Saward writes again to Paul Fox at the BBC Copyright Department, complaining of a lack of satisfactory answers from Tom Rivers regarding his complaints regarding John's screening of old *Doctor Who* stories at US conventions. On the same day, Anne Gilchrist from the BBC1 Saturday night entertainment show *Noel Edmonds Saturday Roadshow* writes to John, requesting his help with an upcoming item, specifically a running gag that a duck is loose in BBC Television Centre and at various TV locations. The idea is that the duck will be claimed to feature in a number of BBC shows, cropping up in the background of certain shots, and the viewing audience will be encouraged to try to spot these throughout the week. In fact, two versions of each of the shots will be recorded, one with the duck and one without; the one with the duck will be screened only on the *Noel Edmonds Saturday Roadshow*, in the pretence that it is the real version.[455]

---

[452] John Nathan-Turner memoirs, *Doctor Who Magazine* #247.
[453] Vere Lorrimer took part in this day's recording at Arundel, playing a non-speaking role in a crowd on a guided tour of the Castle. It is believed to have been his last professional engagement, as he died three months later. Also in the crowd were actor Nicholas Courtney, director Peter Moffatt and writers Kevin Clarke and Graeme Curry.
[454] John Nathan-Turner memoirs, *Doctor Who Magazine* #247.
[455] It would appear that the duck-in-the-background gag idea was ultimately

Wednesday 29th:
Itinerary: Today is the seventh day of OB recording for 'Silver Nemesis' at the Arundel Castle Estate, Arundel in West Sussex. John once more stays overnight at Beach Hotel in Worthing.

Commentary: Andrew Cartmel initially joined the team on location for this shoot, but at some point during the week decided to return to London, having noted something of a poisonous atmosphere hanging over the crew. This had culminated in a conversation between the story's writer Kevin Clarke and John, when Clarke suggested something and John told him to mind his own business. Cartmel later explained that he understood that this was largely down to the pressure John was under at the time, but that he wanted no part of it, so he returned home. The following day (which Cartmel notes as 'National Defence Bonds Day' in his book *Script Doctor*, so probably 30 June, the date when these bonds were launched in 1932), John rang up his script editor and asked him why he'd left. Cartmel explained his reasons, and John persuaded him to return to Arundel the next day. On arriving back at the location, Cartmel noted that the atmosphere had changed markedly for the better, and Kevin Clarke later noted that it was Cartmel's departure that had been the catalyst for resolving the problems.

Thursday 30th:
Itinerary: Today is the eighth day of OB recording for 'Silver Nemesis', now in the streets around Arundel in West Sussex. Material to be shot today includes the cameo by Dolores Gray as the now-renamed Mrs Remington. After the completion of recording, John drives to Bournemouth to watch the play *Holiday Swap* at the Pier Theatre. Also on this day, Tom Rivers from the BBC Copyright Department writes again to Eric Saward. He explains that Saward's allegations regarding John receiving payments for the screening of *Doctor Who* episodes at US conventions come under the auspices of the BBC Personnel Department's Glynne Price, who will look into the matter. Rivers goes on to detail that when the BBC previously discovered that Lionheart (the US distributor of *Doctor Who* stories) were providing tapes for US convention screenings, the practice was stopped. He concludes that the only way the BBC could stop third parties showing material supplied from elsewhere, or taped off-air, at these events would be to take legal action, which it has elected not to do.

---

dropped from the *Noel Edmonds Saturday Roadshow*. But it may explain why, on 5 July, a (subsequently cut) scene was recorded for 'Silver Nemesis' Part One of the Doctor shooing a duck out of the TARDIS. Perhaps the gist of the gag wasn't fully explained to John?

John Nathan-Turner: 'I had made an arrangement with the *Daily Mail*, through our press and publicity officers, to give the newspaper exclusive pictures of Miss Gray, Sylvester and the limo. This was to be done at lunchtime with the artistes' blessing. During the morning, a London taxicab appeared pootling along the road where we were [recording] the scene in which Lady Peinforte and Richard meet the skinheads. I recognised the passenger: Gary Levy (aka Gary Leigh). Now it just so happened that the latest issue of Levy's magazine *DWB* had been shown around the set the previous day; cast and crew alike had been horrified by some of the personal comments and so on within. I advised the four actors of the arrival of the London taxi and its occupants. All four said that they did not want to be photographed by this magazine. Gary Levy stayed at a distance. Strictly speaking, you can't stop the press from taking photos of anything, but some would argue that that the publication in question was not *bona fide* press. Anyway, without any request whatsoever from anyone on the production team, the lighting van backed up and huge sheets of white polystyrene – usually used for reflecting what little light there is on dark days – were held up, totally surrounding the action.'[456]

Gary Leigh: 'Perhaps we should have known better than to travel to the historic town in [fan] Sheldon [Collins]'s distinctive red London cab, for no sooner had we arrived in Arundel in search of a mobile BBC canteen than we turned a corner and found ourselves bang in the middle of an OB unit with JNT's face leering in through the window as I innocently proceeded to fumble with my shoelace, whispering to Sheldon to keep driving! We continued for a further 150 yards, where we disembarked and casually proceeded to stretch out on a glade of grass in the glorious sunshine, pretending to ignore Gary Downie's shrieks of "It's them, it's them!" Almost immediately, half a dozen reflector shields appeared from nowhere as members of the crew formed a semicircle around the recording in process (the scene with the skinheads at the gate), the harsh sunlight bouncing off the shields and effectively blinding all onlookers.'[457]

John Nathan-Turner: 'The unit then moved to the private estate of the Duke of Norfolk. The two visitors tried to follow at a distance. Every time you turned round, they'd moved nearer. Requests both polite and impolite were ignored. The *Daily Mail* photographer arrived and asked who the paparazzi were. I said it was a fan magazine. He wasn't convinced, and kept going off to call his editor. And when we did the photoshoot in the lunch break, I kept reassuring him that this was still an exclusive. I think I knew deep down that

---

[456] John Nathan-Turner memoirs, *Doctor Who Magazine* #247.
[457] 'The Alternative Making of Silver Nemesis' by Gary Leigh, *DWB* #114.

the damage had already been done, but hoped for the best. The photos, which were stunning, never appeared in any *Mail* publication as far as I know ... On the day, having refused to leave the location we were renting, and claiming public rights of way to pass through – but standing still – they were eventually escorted from the estate by a shotgun-toting gamekeeper.'[458]

Gary Leigh: 'Enquiries with the local farmer, who happily gave us permission to enter his land, eventually led us to the miniature castle where the crew were clearly taking advantage of the baking heat during a break in recording. Again we settled down some way from the ensemble, or at least we thought we had. Our nap was rudely broken by the purring of an obviously large car and the bleatings of an almost, by now, manic Gary Downie, literally pleading with us not to photograph the vehicle ... "You hate the programme – well, we hate you!" screamed Downie, and eventually two constables arrived to restore order, routinely pointing out to the frenzied Downie that since neither myself nor Sheldon were committing any kind of offence, would he kindly stop wasting their time!'[459]

JULY

Friday 1st:
Itinerary: Today is the ninth day of OB recording for 'Silver Nemesis', now at the new location of St Mary's in Bamber, West Sussex. John again stays overnight at Beach Hotel in Worthing.

Saturday 2nd:
Itinerary: Today is the tenth day of OB recording for 'Silver Nemesis', now at Casa Del Mar, Goring-by-Sea in West Sussex. John returns home after recording concludes.

Tuesday 5th:
Itinerary: Today is the eleventh and final day of OB recording for 'Silver Nemesis'. This takes place at Black Jack's Mill Restaurant in Harefield in Uxbridge.

Thursday 7th:
Itinerary: John writes to Vere Lorrimer, thanking him for his cameo

---

[458] John Nathan-Turner memoirs, *Doctor Who Magazine* #247.
[459] 'The Alternative Making of Silver Nemesis' by Gary Leigh, *DWB* #114.

appearance in 'Silver Nemesis'.

Monday 11th:
Itinerary: John entertains Philip Ettinger from the Ettinger Brothers agency at the BBC Club bar.

Commentary: Ettinger was Jon Pertwee's agent, so John's discussions today may have revolved around the upcoming stage production *Doctor Who: The Ultimate Adventure*, in which Pertwee would eventually reprise the role of the Doctor for the initial 1989 tour. In its inception, John was advising the play's producers, and was in discussions to direct it. It is possible that, at this point, Sylvester McCoy may have been still in the frame for the starring role.

Tuesday 12th
Itinerary: Eric Saward again writes to Tom Rivers at the BBC Copyright Department. He continues to argue that as US conventions charge people to attend, part of this charge covers the viewing of any episodes screened. He also claims that John's fees to attend these events are linked in proportion to the number of tapes he provides.

Wednesday 13th:
Itinerary: John entertains Lorne Martin and Julia Jones at the BBC Club bar. Martin and Jones, formally of BBC Enterprises, have just set up their own company, M & J Media Ventures, which will take over the running of the *Doctor Who* Exhibition at Longleat House. On the same day, Tom Rivers writes back to Eric Saward. He restates that the Writer's Guild were happy that screenings of episodes of *Doctor Who* at conventions should be considered as showings to a non-paying public, and says that he now considers the matter closed. In the evening, John goes to see the play *World Story Time* at the Theatre Royal, Windsor.

Thursday 14th – Monday 25th:
Rehearsals for the first studio block of 'The Happiness Patrol' take place at the BBC Television Rehearsal Rooms at Acton.

Thursday 14th:
Itinerary: John travels from Union House to the BBC Rehearsal Rooms at Acton, where the cast of 'The Happiness Patrol' are doing a script read-through.

Tuesday 19th:
Itinerary: John has a working lunch with writers Pip and Jane Baker at the

BBC Club bar.[460]

Wednesday 20th:
Itinerary: John entertains Sean Franks from the DWAS at the BBC Club bar.

Thursday 21st:
Itinerary: John travels by tube to High Street, Kensington for a meeting with the agent of author Derek Tangye.

Commentary: Tangye wrote a large number of semi-autobiographical books, known collectively as *The Minack Chronicles*, about his life on a cliff-top daffodil farm in Cornwall. *A Gull on the Roof*, the first in the series, was published in 1961, and Tangye followed this up with a new book nearly every two years until his death in 1996. John was interested in producing a dramatisation of *A Gull on the Roof* as a project that would enable him to leave *Doctor Who* at the end of the twenty-fifth season.

Friday 22nd:
Itinerary: John travels from Union House to the BBC Rehearsal Rooms at Acton, where rehearsals for the first studio block of 'The Happiness Patrol' are under way. On the same day, he writes to Mark Shivas[461] to request two weeks of annual leave for weeks 33 and 34 (15 to 26 August 1988).

Monday 25th:
Itinerary: John travels from Union House to the BBC Rehearsal Rooms at Acton for the Producer's Run of the first studio block of 'The Happiness Patrol'.

Tuesday 26th:
Itinerary: Today is the first day of the three-day first studio block for 'The Happiness Patrol' in studio TC3 at BBC Television Centre. John overrules director Chris Clough's initial intention to shoot some scenes using Dutch (i.e. tilted) camera angles to give them the feel of a classic film noir movie. Conventional shots are used instead. On the same day, John writes back to Janet Fielding, thanking her for her home decor tips.

---

[460] Pip and Jane Baker had last written for *Doctor Who* the previous year, scripting Sylvester McCoy's debut story 'Time and the Rani'. That would prove to be their last contribution to the show, but it would appear they were still looking to pitch story ideas to John.

[461] Earlier in 1988, Mark Shivas had replaced Jonathan Powell as BBC Television's Head of Drama. He had worked as a BBC drama producer since the late 1960s, helming such shows as *Play for Today*, *Telford's Change* and *The Borgias*.

John Nathan-Turner: 'The set, I think, should be discussed … The whole place was supposed to be a façade, pretending to be something that it wasn't. The design was splendid as an idea, splendid on paper, but looked wrong on the studio floor … When we got to the studio it looked rather like we'd run out of money, which we hadn't. Much additional work was done to the sets and, at my behest, Andrew Cartmel added a few lines of pertinent explanatory dialogue to the Doctor and Ace's arrival scene.'[462]

Wednesday 27th:
Itinerary: Today is the second day of the three-day first studio block for 'The Happiness Patrol' in studio TC3 at BBC Television Centre. After recording, John joins the cast in the BBC Club bar.

Thursday 28th:
Itinerary: Today is the third and final day of the first studio block for 'The Happiness Patrol' in studio TC3 at BBC Television Centre. After recording, John joins the cast in the BBC Club bar.

AUGUST

Monday 1st – Tuesday 9th:
Rehearsals for the second studio block of 'The Happiness Patrol' take place at the BBC Television Rehearsal Rooms at Acton.

Thursday 4th:
Itinerary: Today is the press launch of the BBC's Autumn schedule of new programmes; this is held at BAFTA in Piccadilly, London. John travels by tube to the venue, and arranges a taxi to pick up actress Jessica Martin (Mags in 'The Greatest Show in the Galaxy') from her home to take her there, so that she can also appear at the launch.

Friday 5th:
Itinerary: John again entertains writer Chris Beebee in the BBC Club Bar.

Monday 8th:
Itinerary: John travels from Union House to the BBC Rehearsal Rooms at Acton for the Producer's Run of the second studio block of 'The Happiness Patrol'.

---

[462] John Nathan-Turner memoirs, *Doctor Who Magazine* #247.

Wednesday 10th:
Itinerary: This is the first day of the two-day second studio block for 'The Happiness Patrol' in studio TC8 at BBC Television Centre. After recording, John joins the cast in the BBC Club bar.

Thursday 11th:
Itinerary: Today is the second and final day of the second studio block for 'The Happiness Patrol' in studio TC8 at BBC Television Centre. This concludes production on the twenty-fifth season of *Doctor Who*, although there is some editing and post-production work still to be concluded. After recording, John joins the cast in the BBC Club bar for his 'farewell' party.

John Nathan-Turner: 'We had a special visitor on one studio day – P D James, the famous novelist, then a member of the BBC's Board of Governors. She'd insisted on including *Doctor Who* on her tour of Television Centre, apparently; she came in, visited the gallery, and chatted to Sheila [Hancock, [playing Helen A in the story] and Sylvester [McCoy]. When Special Services suggested that it was time she leave in order to watch the news going out live, Phyllis said: "Oh no, I'm not leaving yet, not without meeting the monster!" So she waited until David John Pope – the Kandyman – had finished his scene and chatted away to him before heading to the news studio, which was now in mid-transmission.'[463]

Friday 12th:
(Today is John's forty-first birthday.)

Monday 15th – Friday 26th:
Itinerary: John takes two weeks of annual leave from the BBC.

SEPTEMBER

Wednesday 7th:
Itinerary: John goes to visit writer Derek Tangye. He travels by tube to Euston Station, catches a train down to Penzance Station in Cornwall, then gets a taxi from there to the Mount Prospect Hotel, where he stays the night.

Commentary: In the book *JN-T: The Life and Scandalous Times of John Nathan-Turner* by Richard Marson, Andrew Cartmel recalls accompanying John on

---

[463] John Nathan-Turner memoirs, *Doctor Who Magazine* #247.

this visit to Tangye in Cornwall. They later invited Ian Briggs to write a script based on Tangye's novel, but the proposal was turned down by Mark Shivas and Jonathan Powell. [464]

Thursday 8th:
Itinerary: In the morning, John travels by taxi from his hotel to Derek Tangye's home in Dorminack. After his meeting, he gets a taxi to Penzance Station, from where he catches a train back to London. On the same day, Mark Shivas's office confirms to the fanzine *DWB* that John will be staying on as producer of *Doctor Who* for the twenty-sixth season.

Monday 12th:
Itinerary: John travels by tube to London Bridge to meet with Lorne Martin of M & J Media Ventures. Martin is in the process of putting the finishing touches to his plans to open a new *Doctor Who* Exhibition, which will be hosted at the Space Adventure[465] attraction in Tooley Street in London.

Thursday 15th:
Itinerary: John entertains Andrew Beech and Andrew Hair from the DWAS in the BBC Club bar.[466]

Friday 16th:
Itinerary: John writes to David Hatch, Managing Director of BBC Radio and the Vice-Chairman of BBC Enterprises. He previously accepted an invitation from Hatch to attend the recent launch event for the BBC Radio Collection[467] (an umbrella title for a range of releases, mainly of classic radio programmes, on audio cassette). However, on the evening prior to the event, he was mugged on his journey home from the BBC. He was still too shaken the

---

[464] After his experience of working on *All Creatures Great and Small*, it's hard not to imagine John looking to pitch a similar series of his own, based on Tangye's books, as he was fully intent on leaving *Doctor Who* after completion of the twenty-fifth season. However, he was informed within days of his return from annual leave that he would be staying on *Doctor Who* for another year.

[465] Space Adventure was a simulated space shuttle ride. Participants sat in a shuttle cockpit mounted on hydraulics, which tilted and shook in time to a short animated movie of simulated spaceflight. The *Doctor Who* exhibition was presented in the 'departure' area of the ride, and remained at Tooley Street well into 1989.

[466] Almost certainly this meeting was to discuss the Panopticon IX convention that the duo were organising for the DWAS that coming weekend (16-19 September). John declined the invitation to attend.

[467] The BBC Radio Collection released in November 1988 a *Doctor Who* double audio cassette containing the 1986 radio play 'Slipback' alongside the LP version of 'Genesis of the Daleks', so John's invite to the range's launch was probably connected to this.

following day to go to Hatch's event. John apologises for his non-appearance, but explains the reason.[468] On the same day, John signs off the commission for Ben Aaronovitch to write the four scripts for 'Storm over Avallion' for Season 26.

Tuesday 20th:
Itinerary: John spends the evening at the Savoy Theatre in London, to see the play *Sugar Babies*.

Commentary: The cast of *Sugar Babies* included Mickey Rooney, Peter Reeves, Steve Rawlings, Ann Miller, Len Howe, Chris Emmett, Bryan Burdon and Rhonda Burchmore.

Wednesday 21st:
Itinerary: John entertains Kevin Clarke, the writer of 'Silver Nemesis', at the BBC Club bar.

Thursday 22nd:
Itinerary: Peter Litten of Coast to Coast Productions, the company who currently have the rights to make a *Doctor Who* film, sends John a copy of the proposed script, entitled *Doctor Who – The Movie*.

Wednesday 28th:
Itinerary: Today is the Press Launch at BAFTA in Piccadilly for Season 25 of *Doctor Who*. John travels by tube to the event, where he is joined by Sylvester McCoy and Pamela Salem (who plays Professor Rachel Jensen in 'Remembrance of the Daleks'). The first episodes of 'Remembrance of the Daleks' and 'The Happiness Patrol' are screened for the press. In the evening, John goes to the Adelphi Theatre in central London to see the play *Me and My Girl*.

Commentary: The cast of *Me and My Girl* included David Schofield, Bonnie Langford, Sheila Mathews, Graham Seed, Roy Macready, Tracy Collier, Jeremy Hawk and Patrick Cargill.

Thursday 29th:
Itinerary: John writes to Bonnie Langford, praising her performance in *Me and My Girl*.

---

[468] The exact date of the launch event, and therefore that of the mugging, isn't known. The incident occurred as John was walking between Union House and Shepherd's Bush tube station; the mugger stuck a lit cigarette into the back of his neck in order to distract him, then grabbed his wallet from the back pocket of his trousers.

OCTOBER

Wednesday 5th:
Itinerary: John entertains David Saunders in the BBC Club bar. Earlier in the day, Saunders and Sylvester McCoy were interviewed by Jeremy Paxman on BBC1's *Breakfast Time* to publicise the start of the new *Doctor Who* season that evening. Later, John takes writer Ben Aaronovitch out for a drink at the Bush pub. 'Remembrance of the Daleks' Part One screens on BBC1.

Andrew Cartmel: 'Just before "Remembrance of the Daleks" was transmitted, John took Ben [Aaronovitch] out to the Bush, the local pub for BBC drama series and serials. He proceeded to buy Ben drink after drink, getting him drunk as a skunk, and telling him story after story about true transmission disasters that had befallen shows in the past. Ben reeled home, deeply intoxicated and profoundly paranoid, to join a riotous party of his friends, get drunker still, and watch the first episode of his first television script go out without a hitch.'[469]

Thursday 6th:
Itinerary: John entertains writers Pip and Jane Baker in the BBC Club bar.

Monday 10th:
Itinerary: Pat Dyer from the BBC Personnel Department writes to John, acknowledging receipt of two articles that he has forwarded the previous week. Dyer informs John that the articles have been passed on to Glynne Price, also from the Personnel Department, who will be writing to Eric Saward about them. John is promised that he will be kept abreast of any developments.[470]

Wednesday 12th:
Itinerary: John entertains Lorne Martin of M & J Media Ventures and Richard Class from the Space Adventure attraction in Tooley Street at the BBC Club bar, to discuss the *Doctor Who* exhibition at the latter venue. 'Remembrance of the Daleks' Part Two screens on BBC1.

---

[469] *Script Doctor* by Andrew Cartmel, published by Reynolds & Hearn, 2005.
[470] It's not known for sure what these 'articles' were, but issue 57 of the fanzine *DWB*, published on 26 August 1988, had covered the ongoing spat between Saward and the BBC regarding the showing of *Doctor Who* stories at US conventions. That same issue had also featured the first part of an interview with Saward (his first since the *Starburst* one in 1986), in which many new perceived criticisms of John's competence as *Doctor Who*'s producer were aired. The interview with Saward continued and concluded in issue 58 of *DWB*, published 16 September 1988.

Wednesday 19th:
'Remembrance of the Daleks' Part Three screens on BBC1.

Tuesday 25th:
Itinerary: John gets a taxi from Threshold House to Chelsea Wharf to have lunch with Richard Wakeley.[471]

Wednesday 26th:
'Remembrance of the Daleks' Part Four screens on BBC1.

Friday 28th:
Itinerary: Pat Dyer from the BBC Personnel Department writes to John to tell him it has been agreed that he may attend the forthcoming *Doctor Who* Cruise event in the USA, which is scheduled to take place between 20 and 25 November. This agreement is on the understanding that John is not to be paid a fee for attending, though it is acknowledged that the cost of his air fare and the cruise itself will be met by the organisers. Dyer also makes clear that John's attendance at the event will be strictly as a private person and not as a member of BBC staff, and that the days he spends away from the BBC on the cruise will be treated as annual leave.

NOVEMBER

Undated:
John and Andrew Cartmel circulate a Drama Script Classified List, which states that the only writers they are working with at this time for upcoming storylines and/or scripts are: Ben Aaronovitch ('Storm Over Avallion' – four episodes), Ian Briggs ('Wolf-Time' – four episodes), Kevin Clarke ('Silver Nemesis' – three episodes), Robin Mukherjee ('Alixion'), Stephen Wyatt ('The Greatest Show in the Galaxy' – four episodes), and Graeme Curry ('The Happiness Patrol' – three episodes).

Wednesday 2nd:
'The Happiness Patrol' Part One screens on BBC1.

---

[471] Richard Wakeley was Andrew Cartmel's agent, and also an old friend of John's. He would eventually become John's agent too, and this meeting may have been a precursor to that.

Thursday 3rd:
Itinerary: John entertains Andrew Beech of the DWAS in the BBC Club bar.

Monday 7th:
Itinerary: John entertains director Graeme Harper ('The Caves of Androzani' and 'Revelation of the Daleks') in the BBC Club bar.

Commentary: It is possible that John was trying to entice Harper back to work on the series again, but if so, this was to no avail.

Tuesday 8th:
Itinerary: John entertains director Peter Moffatt in the BBC Club bar.

Commentary: Again, John was possibly trying to entice Moffatt back to work on the show again. If so, this also was to no avail.

Wednesday 9th:
Itinerary: John signs off the commission for Ian Briggs to write the four scripts for 'Wolf Time'.[472] 'The Happiness Patrol' Part Two screens on BBC1.

Thursday 10th:
Itinerary: John travels by tube to London Bridge to visit the *Doctor Who* Exhibition at Tooley Street. Meanwhile, Bev Stokes, the Chairman and Chief Executive of Bassett Foods PLC, writes to John to complain of the visual similarities between the Kandyman character in 'The Happiness Patrol' and Bassett's own liquorice allsorts character Bertie Bassett, and hints at legal action should the character reappear. John passes the letter to Brian Turner, Senior Assistant, Contracts, to assess and respond to.

Monday 14th:
Itinerary: John travels by tube to London Bridge for the official opening of the *Doctor Who* exhibition at Tooley Street. Sylvester McCoy and Sophie Aldred are present to talk to the press and pose for photographs, cutting a birthday cake for *Doctor Who*'s silver anniversary, and the first episode of 'Silver Nemesis' is given a preview screening. John is interviewed at the event for the BBC2 series *Behind the Screen*.[473] He also chats to David J Howe, Mark Stammers and Stephen James Walker of the *Doctor Who* fanzine *The Frame*, who have been commissioned by the Space Adventure team to produce a

---

[472] 'Wolf Time' would become 'The Wolves of Fenric' and then 'The Curse of Fenric' by the time it was screened on BBC1.
[473] This edition of *Behind the Screen* was shown on BBC2 on Monday 28 November 1988.

booklet for the attraction (although this idea will later be dropped for cost reasons). As he's running behind schedule, John then gets a taxi back to the BBC. There he meets Alan Wareing, who directed 'The Greatest Show in the Galaxy' and will go on to direct 'Ghost Light' and 'Survival' the following season, for a late lunch at the BBC Club bar.

Tuesday 15th:
Itinerary: Director Derek Martinus writes to John, telling him that a recent hoped-for assignment has collapsed, so he now could be available for a project in 1989.[474]

Wednesday 16th:
Itinerary: John signs off the commissions for Rona Munro to write the script for 'Blood-Hunt' Part One[475] and for Marc Platt to write the three scripts for 'Life Cycle'.[476] At some point in the next day or so, he flies from London to the US. 'The Happiness Patrol' Part Three screens on BBC1.

Friday 18th:
Itinerary: John writes to Julie Dixon at BBC Enterprises regarding the upcoming licence renewal for Marvel UK to keep publishing *Doctor Who Monthly*. He states that he would hate for the title to disappear, but thinks that they currently pay 'a pittance' to the BBC for the rights. On the same date, Make-Up Designer Dorka Nieradzik, who designed the Kandyman for 'The Happiness Patrol', sends John a letter refuting that the character's appearance was in any way inspired by that of Bassett Foods' Bertie Bassett.

Saturday 19th:
Itinerary: John is a guest at the 25th Anniversary Birthday Party convention at the Newark Airport Marriott hotel in New Jersey, along with Sylvester McCoy and Sophie Aldred.

Sunday 20th – Friday 25th:
Itinerary: John is a guest at the Silver Anniversary Cruise event, which takes place on board the SS *Galileo* as it sails around the coastline of Miami and

---

[474] Martinus had directed the stories 'Galaxy 4', 'Mission to the Unknown', 'The Tenth Planet', 'The Evil of the Daleks', 'The Ice Warriors' and 'Spearhead from Space' in the 1960s. It's possible that John was considering him for a return to *Doctor Who* for the twenty-sixth season; his recent lunches with Peter Moffatt, Graeme Harper and Alan Wareing would suggest that he was starting to look for directors at this point . Or perhaps Martinus was just trying his luck.

[475] 'Blood Hunt' would become 'Catflap' before being retitled 'Survival' by the time it aired on BBC1

[476] 'Life Cycle' would become 'Ghost Light' by the time it aired on BBC1.

Florida. Other guests include Sylvester McCoy, Frazer Hines and Sarah Sutton.

Monday 21st – Friday 2nd December:
Itinerary: John takes two weeks of annual leave from the BBC, part of which is spent on the Florida cruise.

Wednesday 23rd:
'Silver Nemesis' Part One screens on BBC1.

Friday 25th:
Itinerary: Ben Aaronovitch delivers his script for 'Storm over Avallion' Part One to the *Doctor Who* Production Office. Meanwhile the Copyright Department's Brian Turner responds to Bev Stokes at Bassett Foods, refuting any similarities between the Kandyman and Bertie Bassett and giving assurances that the character has been killed off in the final episode of 'The Happiness Patrol' and therefore will not be returning to the show.

Wednesday 30th:
'Silver Nemesis' Part Two screens on BBC1.

DECEMBER

Tuesday 6th:
Itinerary: Back from leave, and back in the UK, John travels with Sophie Aldred by train from London to Brighton. They are both guests on BBC Radio Sussex today, generally publicising Season 25 of *Doctor Who*. John writes to the BBC Copyright Department, asking them to negotiate with Mervyn Haisman and Henry Lincoln for the rights to use their character Brigadier Lethbridge-Stewart in 'Storm over Avallion'.

Wednesday 7th:
'Silver Nemesis' Part Three screens on BBC1.

Monday 12th:
Itinerary: John writes to the BBC Contracts Department, asking that Nicholas Courtney be engaged to play the Brigadier in 'Storm over Avallion', due for production between 23 March and 28 April 1989.

Commentary: These dates were for when 'Storm over Avallion' was due to be the first story to go into production for Season 26. At some later point, the story was swapped in production with 'The Wolves of Fenric', which then occupied these dates. 'Storm over Avallion' was actually recorded between the end of April and the beginning of June 1989.

Tuesday 13th:
Itinerary: John writes to director Derek Martinus, promising to keep him in mind for the future.

Wednesday 14th:
'The Greatest Show in the Galaxy' Part One screens on BBC1.

Monday 19th:
Itinerary: John entertains actor Anthony Ainley in the BBC Club bar.[477] On the same day, Mark Furness, producer of the proposed *Doctor Who: The Ultimate Adventure* stage play, writes to John, saying that he understands the reasons why he has had to withdraw from directing the play.

John Nathan-Turner: 'While Season 25 was still on air, I had a meeting with Mark Furness, the theatrical producer I'd met back in 1986 when Colin Baker and Bonnie Langford were lifted on wires for the press on the *Peter Pan* set. Mark wanted to instigate a new *Doctor Who* play to feature some musical numbers, and he approached me to direct it. I agreed, and Mark asked who I wanted to write the show. I suggested Andrew Cartmel, my script editor, and Andrew asked if I'd consider both he and Ben Aaronovitch as co-writers. Mark and I concurred, and we had various meetings discussing what could be achieved on stage, as opposed to on TV. The script that Andrew and Ben delivered, despite being an early draft, was going to be splendid. Ambitious, but splendid. Originally the plan was to star Sylvester McCoy, with *Neighbours* heartthrobs Jason Donovan and Kylie Minogue as the Doctor's companions. We intended to do a tour in the UK before recording Season 26, to be followed by a run in Australia when the season was complete. That was the idea – but, as with most things, the best laid plans … Over the months, Jason and Kylie concentrated, with great success, on their pop careers – and then our recording dates for Season 26 were moved forward and the play's schedule delayed, thereby preventing both Sylvester and myself from taking part.'[478]

---

[477] Ainley had last played the Master in 1986, in the final two episodes of 'The Trial of a Time Lord'. John was presumably sounding him out for a return to the show in 1989's 'Survival'.
[478] John Nathan-Turner memoirs, *Doctor Who Magazine* #248.

Wednesday 21st:
Itinerary: John writes to the BBC Contracts Department, asking that Anthony Ainley be booked to play the Master in 'Blood-Hunt', with production dates in June 1989. 'The Greatest Show in the Galaxy' Part Two screens on BBC1.

Wednesday 28th:
'The Greatest Show in the Galaxy' Part Three screens on BBC1.

Friday 30th:
Itinerary: Nick Mallett writes to John, having heard on the grapevine that he will be producing another series of *Doctor Who* after all. He notes that perhaps there might be a chance of him directing for John again.[479]

---

[479] Mallett had previously directed 'The Trial of a Time Lord' Parts One to Four and 'Paradise Towers'. He would indeed work for John once more, directing 'The Curse of Fenric' for Season 26.

1989

Setting the Scene:

It's difficult to assess what John's frame of mind might have been as he prepared for the ninth season of *Doctor Who* to go into production under his watch. He'd tried and failed to leave the show twice now, and could no longer have believed that he was being kept on it simply because his bosses thought he was doing a good job. A half-hearted search had been carried out around the BBC to see if there was another producer willing to take on the show, but no-one had put their name forward. *Doctor Who* was not the popular brand that it had been in the 1960s and 1970s, and John was saddled with the job.

Doctor Who's unpopularity within the BBC began to take on a new dimension during this year, as the Drama Department began actively looking at ways in which it could divest itself of the responsibility of actually making the show. Yet *Doctor Who* wasn't unpopular enough that anyone at the BBC was seriously considering actually cancelling it – those who could have wielded the axe were probably mindful of the public furore that had erupted back in 1985, when cancellation had been a hair's breadth away.

So *Doctor Who* was caught in limbo, and John was stuck in limbo right along with it. He must have realised that the show was now living on borrowed time, and that once it disappeared, the future of his BBC career was in serious doubt. He'd never managed to interest his bosses in any of his alternative programme ideas, and the possibility that he might be handed a new series to produce that wasn't one he had devised himself seemed unlikely.

The backdrop to all this was a growing shift within the industry, and the BBC itself, toward buying-in programmes made by independent production companies. John Birt, who had been made the BBC's Deputy Director-General in 1987, was known to be pushing forward this agenda. One upshot of this was that the BBC would in future need fewer staff producers and directors, and would ultimately lose whole departments, such as Costume, Make-up and Visual Effects, which no longer had sufficient in-house programmes to service. But all this was still to come. For now, in 1989, John was part of a production-line of programme-making that was beginning to be slowly wound down.

JANUARY

Wednesday 4th:
'The Greatest Show in the Galaxy' Part Four screens on BBC1.

Thursday 5th:
Itinerary: John entertains actor Nicholas Courtney in the BBC Club bar.

Commentary: John was almost certainly using today's meeting to assess Courtney's willingness and availability to reprise his role as the Brigadier in the upcoming story 'Storm over Avallion'.

Friday 6th:
Itinerary: John writes a letter of condolence to Hilda Dudley, the recently-widowed wife of Terence Dudley, the director of 'Meglos' and the writer of 'Four to Doomsday', 'Black Orchid', 'The King's Demons' and *K-9 and Company*. He tells her how saddened he was to learn of Dudley's death[480], and praises him as one of the great 'all-rounders of British television'. He concludes by confirming that he'll attend the Memorial Service being held later in the month.

Monday 9th:
Itinerary: John entertains director Michael Kerrigan in the BBC Club bar.

Commentary: John was almost certainly looking to see if Kerrigan would be interested in directing a story for the twenty-sixth season. Kerrigan would end up helming 'Storm over Avallion' (later retitled 'Battlefield').

Tuesday 10th:
Itinerary: Ian Briggs delivers his script for 'Wolf-Time' Part One to the *Doctor Who* Production Office. On the same day, Rona Munro delivers her script for 'Blood-Hunt' Part One.

Wednesday 11th:
Itinerary: John signs off the commission for Rona Munro to write the scripts for 'Blood-Hunt' Parts Two and Three. He also entertains director Nicholas Mallett in the BBC Club bar.

---

[480] Terence Dudley had died just over a week earlier, on Christmas Day, 25th December 1988.

Commentary: Again, John was almost certainly looking to see if Mallett would be interested in returning to *Doctor Who* to direct a story for the twenty-sixth season. Mallett would end up helming 'Wolf-Time' (later retitled 'The Curse of Fenric').

Thursday 12th:
Itinerary: John entertains a freelance journalist, Roger Smethurst, in the BBC Club bar.[481] Ben Aaronovitch delivers his script for 'Storm over Avallion' Part Two to the *Doctor Who* Production Office.

Friday 13th:
Itinerary: John entertains Malcolm Prince from the Birmingham BBC local radio station, Radio WM, in the BBC Club bar.[482] On the same day, he writes to the BBC Contracts Department, asking that Nicholas Courtney's dates for playing the Brigadier in 'Storm over Avallion' be revised to run now from 28 April to 1 June. He also writes to Mark Shivas, asking that Michael Kerrigan be booked to direct 'Storm over Avallion'.

Monday 16th:
Itinerary: John entertains Andrew Beech of the DWAS in the BBC Club bar. On the same day, he writes again to Mark Shivas, asking that Nicholas Mallett be booked to direct 'Wolf-Time'.

Tuesday 17th:
Itinerary: John entertains Peri actress Nicola Bryant in the BBC Club bar.

Commentary: Presumably John was just being sociable on this occasion – there were no plans for Peri to return to the show.

Wednesday 18th:
Itinerary: John entertains agent Tim Scott in the BBC Club bar.

Commentary: Tim Scott, while working as an actor, had appeared as the Forum Doorman in 'The Happiness Patrol' the previous year. He was at this point in the process of setting himself up as an actor's agent, and John's expenses form for the meeting lists him as an agent rather than an actor.

---

[481] It is unknown for which newspaper or magazine Roger Smethurst was writing, or why John met him.
[482] Like John, Malcolm Prince hailed from Birmingham. In 1983 he had hosted for Radio WM a special *Doctor Who* twentieth anniversary retrospective programme, with John featuring as the main guest in the studio. Prince later moved away from presenting and into radio production, and was responsible for the BBC Radio 2 documentaries *Project Who* in 2005 and *Who on Who?* in 2009.

Thursday 19th:
Itinerary: John entertains director Brian Morgan in the BBC Club bar.[483] On the same day, Ian Briggs delivers his script for 'Wolf-Time' Part Two to the *Doctor Who* Production Office.

Sunday 22nd:
Itinerary: John entertains director Michael Kerrigan in the BBC Club bar.

Tuesday 24th:
Itinerary: John writes to Stephen James Walker of *The Frame* fanzine to give his approval for the text of a forthcoming article about the design of the Kandyman, based on information gleaned from an interview he has previously sanctioned with the character's designer Dorka Nieradzik.

Commentary:
John may have considered that this article could serve as useful ammunition in the BBC's defence in the event of any further complaints from Bassett Foods over the character's alleged similarity to their Bertie Bassett marketing device.

Wednesday 25th:
Itinerary: Ben Aaronovitch delivers his script for 'Storm over Avallion' Part Three to the *Doctor Who* Production Office.

Thursday 26th:
Itinerary: John travels by tube from Union House to Covent Garden (for reasons unknown), then returns to the BBC. On the same day, Marc Platt delivers his script for 'Life Cycle' Part One to the *Doctor Who* Production Office.

Friday 27th:
Itinerary: John entertains director Alan Wareing in the BBC Club bar. On the same day, Ian Briggs delivers his script for 'Wolf-Time' Part Three to the *Doctor Who* Production Office.

Commentary: John was almost certainly looking to see if Wareing would be interested in returning to the show to direct for the twenty-sixth season. Wareing would end up helming the stories 'Ghost Light' and 'Survival' this year.

---

[483] Brian Morgan had previously directed episodes of shows including *Angels*, *Crossroads*, *EastEnders* and *Boon*. He was possibly being sounded out by John about directing for *Doctor Who*, although probably not for the upcoming season.

Monday 30th:
Itinerary: John writes to the BBC Music Copyright Department, asking that Mark Ayres be engaged to compose the incidental music for 'Wolf-Time'.

FEBRUARY

Thursday 2nd:
Itinerary: Ian Briggs delivers his script for 'Wolf-Time' Part Four to the *Doctor Who* Production Office.

Monday 6th:
Itinerary: John sends a memo to Julie Dixon at BBC Enterprises regarding the posters for the *Doctor Who* stage play *The Ultimate Adventure*. He states that he requires a credit as Creative Consultant, and corrects the spelling of Terry Nation's name.

Thursday 9th:
Itinerary: Rona Munro delivers her script for 'Blood-Hunt' Part Two to the *Doctor Who* Production Office. On the same day, Marc Platt delivers his script for 'Life Cycle' Part Two.

Friday 10th:
Itinerary: John travels by tube from Union House to Oxford Street (for reasons unknown), then returns to the BBC.

Tuesday 14th:
Itinerary: John entertains John Freeman and Sheila Cranna from Marvel Comics' *Doctor Who Magazine* at the BBC Club bar.

Monday 20th:
Itinerary: John writes a letter to Peter Litten at Coast to Coast Productions regarding a 'replacement' script for *Doctor Who: The Movie*, which he has recently been sent, and is just in the process of reading. He notes that, although he's only two-thirds of the way through, he thinks the script is terrific, exciting and ambitious. On the same day, he writes to Carole Todd, c/o Mark Furness, regarding the script for the *Doctor Who* stage play *The Ultimate Adventure*, which she is now down to direct. He notes the aspects he feels that Jon Pertwee would want to ensure are retained in any rewrites, namely the Doctor's use of the sonic screwdriver, of a lullaby to pacify a monster, of hypnosis, of the 'reverse the polarity of the neutron flow' line, and

of the Venusian Aikido martial art.

Tuesday 21st:
Itinerary: John attends a planning meeting for 'Wolf-Time' at BBC Threshold House.

Friday 24th:
Itinerary: Ben Aaronovitch delivers his script for 'Storm over Avallion' Part Four to the *Doctor Who* Production Office.

Monday 27th:
Itinerary: John writes again to the Music Copyright Department, asking that Keff McCulloch be engaged to provide the incidental music for 'Storm over Avallion'.

Tuesday 28th:
Itinerary: John entertains actor Nicholas Courtney in the BBC Club bar.

MARCH

Wednesday 1st:
Itinerary: John entertains members of the DWAS executive committee in the BBC Club bar.

Thursday 2nd:
Itinerary: John entertains Lorne Martin of M & J Media Ventures in the BBC Club bar.

Commentary: The *Doctor Who* exhibition at Space Adventure in Tooley Street in London was still running at this time, and the long-running one at Longleat House in Wiltshire was due to reopen over Easter, restocked with new exhibits and props from the previous *Doctor Who* season. Presumably this day's meeting was to discuss both attractions.

Monday 6th:
Itinerary: John travels by train to Brighton station, then gets a taxi from there to Brighton Conference Centre for an industry showcase event. He returns to London by train later in the evening.

Commentary: This was almost certainly the latest of the annual events where BBC Enterprises tried to interest overseas broadcasters in buying BBC programmes for screening on their channels. According to the BBC Yearbook 1989/90, over 300 international buyers attended this year's event in Brighton, and sales in excess of £10 million of revenue were secured. It was at this event that representatives from German broadcaster RTL decided to purchase a package of twelve Sylvester McCoy *Doctor Who* stories. The deal was brokered by BBC Enterprises' Arthur Jearum and was possibly being worked on prior to the event, which might explain John's attendance, possibly at Jearum's request, to help cement it. As it depended on the completion and inclusion of the four Season 26 stories, RTL wouldn't be able to screen the package until after that season began airing in the UK. Part One of 'Time and the Rani' eventually went out on RTL+ on 22 November 1989.

Wednesday 8th:
Itinerary: John travels by tube to London Bridge.[484]

Thursday 9th:
Itinerary: John travels with Nicholas Mallet and other production personnel on a recce for possible recording locations for 'The Wolves of Fenric' in the Folkestone area.

Friday 10th:
Itinerary: Today is the second day of scouting possible locations for 'The Wolves of Fenric' in Folkstone. Afterwards, John returns to London.

John Nathan-Turner: '["The Curse of Fenric"] was scheduled as a mixture of outside broadcast and studio recording, but when the army camp location was found, we discovered a vast section, totally unoccupied, with stark period décor – so the designer, director and production manager put forward a proposal to do the whole thing as OB. June Collins, who'd returned as my Production Associate, examined the cost implications with me, and in the end we agreed – extracting some financial promises that were never kept. This story went substantially over budget!'[485]

Monday 13th:
Itinerary: Rona Munro delivers her script for 'Blood-Hunt' Part Three to the *Doctor Who* Production Office. On the same day, Sylvester McCoy is issued a new contract, covering the 14 episodes to be made for the show's twenty-sixth

---

[484] Almost certainly to visit the *Doctor Who* Exhibition in Tooley Street.
[485] John Nathan-Turner memoirs, *Doctor Who Magazine* #248. The original production schedule for 'The Wolves of Fenric' was for location OB shooting between 1 and 11 April 1989, then rehearsals at Acton from 14 to 24 April, and three studio days at Television Centre from 25 to 27 April.

season and including an option in the BBC's favour for 14 more episodes to be made in 1990.

Commentary: There seems to be no indication at this point that *Doctor Who* wouldn't return for a twenty-seventh season on BBC1 in 1990.

Saturday 18th:
Itinerary: John is a guest at the DWAS's A Day at the Forum convention, held at St John's School in Hammersmith (the location used as Coal Hill School in 'Remembrance of the Daleks' the previous year). This is John's first UK convention appearance since Panopticon VII over 6-7 September 1986.

Monday 20th:
Itinerary: Marc Platt delivers his script for 'Life Cycle' Part Three to the *Doctor Who* Production Office.

Tuesday 21st:
Itinerary: John writes to the BBC Music Copyright Department, asking that Dominic Glynn be engaged to produce the incidental music for story 7P.

Thursday 23rd – Thursday 30th
Rehearsals for the OB location recording of 'The Wolves of Fenric' take place at the BBC Television Rehearsal Rooms at Acton.

Thursday 23rd:
Itinerary: In the morning, John attends a script read-through of 'The Wolves of Fenric' at the BBC Rehearsal Rooms at Acton. In the afternoon, back in the *Doctor Who* Production office in Union House, he hosts a meeting that is covered by cameras for the BBC's *Take Two* programme. The meeting is between John, director Nick Mallett, costume designer Ken Trew, make-up artist Dee Baron and visual effects designer Graham Brown, and the topic is the visualisation of the Haemovores in 'The Wolves of Fenric'. In the evening, John attends the opening night of the play *Doctor Who: The Ultimate Adventure,* starring Jon Pertwee as the Doctor, at the Wimbledon Theatre in London.

Thursday 30th:
Itinerary: In the morning, John attends a planning meeting for 'Storm over Avallion' at BBC Threshold House. In the afternoon, he travels to the BBC Rehearsal Rooms at Acton, where OB rehearsals for 'The Wolves of Fenric' are under way.

Friday 31st:
Itinerary: John entertains David Saunders in the BBC Club bar.

APRIL

Undated:
John and Andrew Cartmel circulate a Drama Script Classified List, which states that the only writers they are working with at this time for upcoming storylines and/or scripts are: Ben Aaronovitch ('Storm over Avallion' – four episodes), Ian Briggs ('Wolves of Fenric' – four episodes), Marc Platt ('Life-Cycle' – three episodes) and Rona Munro ('Blood-Hunt' – three episodes).

Monday 3rd:
Itinerary: John travels to Crowborough in East Sussex for the OB recording of 'The Curse of Fenric' (as 'The Wolves of Fenric' has now been retitled). The first day of recording takes place at Crowborough Training Camp. Afterwards, John stays overnight at The Calverley Hotel in Tunbridge Wells.

Tuesday 4th:
Itinerary: Today is the second day of OB recording at the Crowborough Training Camp for 'The Curse of Fenric'. John again stays overnight at The Calverley Hotel in Tunbridge Wells.

Wednesday 5th:
Itinerary: Today is the third day of OB recording at the Crowborough Training Camp for 'The Curse of Fenric'. John spends a third night at The Calverley Hotel in Tunbridge Wells.

Thursday 6th:
Itinerary: Today is the fourth day of OB recording at the Crowborough Training Camp for 'The Curse of Fenric'. John spends a fourth night at The Calverley Hotel in Tunbridge Wells.

Friday 7th:
Itinerary: Today is the fifth day of OB recording at the Crowborough Training Camp for 'The Curse of Fenric'. John spends a fifth night at The Calverley Hotel in Tunbridge Wells.

Saturday 8th:
Itinerary: Today is the sixth day of OB recording at the Crowborough Training Camp for 'The Curse of Fenric'. Today, the production is joined by a camera team from the BBC2 children's magazine programme *Take Two*, who cover the sequence where the vampiric Jean and Phyllis disintegrate. John is unhappy with how the sequence looks, and the material will be remounted

later in production, but *Take Two* get some shots of the now unused version. John spends a sixth night at The Calverley Hotel in Tunbridge Wells.

Sunday 9th:
Itinerary: John travels back to London from Tunbridge Wells.

Monday 10th:
Itinerary: John spends a day catching up with work at the *Doctor Who* Production Office.

Tuesday 11th:
Itinerary: John travels back to Tunbridge Wells in the morning. Today is the seventh day of OB recording at the Crowborough Training Camp for 'The Curse of Fenric'. John once more stays overnight at The Calverley Hotel in Tunbridge Wells.

Wednesday 12th:
Itinerary: Today is the eighth day of OB recording for 'The Curse of Fenric' now at the Church of St Lawrence in Hawkhurst, Kent. John organises a press call for the national tabloid newspapers during today's lunch break, and arranges for Sylvester McCoy to wear the Doctor's old cream jacket for the photo session, so as not to reveal the switch to a brown one for this new season. Later, John spends another night at The Calverley Hotel in Tunbridge Wells.

Thursday 13th:
Itinerary: Today is the ninth day of OB recording for 'The Curse of Fenric', again at the Church of St Lawrence in Hawkhurst, Kent. John spends a further night at The Calverley Hotel in Tunbridge Wells.

Friday 14th:
Itinerary: Today is the tenth day of OB recording for 'The Curse of Fenric'. The main location is now Bedgebury Lower School in Lillesden, Kent. However, John remains at the Church of St Lawrence in Hawkhurst, directing a second-unit crew, mopping up some uncompleted scenes from the previous day's recording, of Sorin's escape from the church crypt. Later, he stays again at The Calverley Hotel in Tunbridge Wells.

Saturday 15th:
Itinerary: The latest location is Rose's Farm in Hawkhurst, Kent. John's dog, Pepsi, manages to get into shot during a scene of Ace and the Doctor approaching Mrs Hardaker's cottage. John returns to London after the recording is completed.

Monday 17th:
Itinerary: John spends the day in the *Doctor Who* Production Office, then travels by train from London to Wareham. He then gets a taxi to The Bishop's Cottage Hotel, West Lulworth in Warsham, in readiness for the continuation of OB recording for 'The Curse of Fenric' the following day.

Tuesday 18th:
Itinerary: Today is the twelfth day of OB recording for 'The Curse of Fenric', now at Lulworth Cove in Dorset. John spends a second night at The Bishop's Cottage Hotel in West Lulworth.

Wednesday 19th:
Itinerary: Today is the thirteenth day of OB recording for 'The Curse of Fenric', and the second at Lulworth Cove in Dorset. John again stays overnight at The Bishop's Cottage Hotel in West Lulworth.

Thursday 20th:
Itinerary: Today is the fourteenth and final day of OB recording for 'The Curse of Fenric', again at Lulworth Cove in Dorset. John directs a second-unit crew, recording all the underwater scenes needed for the story. During the day, he also buys a box of Liquorice Allsorts on BBC expenses to 'check copyright infringement'.[486] In the evening, he returns to The Bishop's Cottage Hotel in West Lulworth.

John Nathan-Tuner: 'The underwater filming was strange. I could still talk to the cameraman underwater, but of course he couldn't talk back to me. There was a tiny little monitor in the boat for me to watch, and because the water was so cold, we would line up the shots with our effects team clad in wet-suits and only put the artists in the freezing water at the last minute. We tried to keep the number of takes to a minimum, not always successfully, but everyone in the water was exceedingly patient. The person who should have been near the submerged Viking longboat, pretending to be dead, didn't feel comfortable with the idea, and so one of the effects boys, John [Van Der Pool], volunteered. Now, John is not black, but most certainly not white; all eyes in the boat turned on me. There was no time to go back to shore to get someone else, but would there really be black Russians in the Second World War? I made the decision there and then: "White him up!" I ordered. When John

---

[486] This presumably was a tongue-in-cheek reference to the controversy regarding the resemblance between the Kandyman from the previous season's story 'The Happiness Patrol' and the Bertie Bassett character used by Bassetts on its boxes of Liquorice Allsorts.

laughed, I knew I hadn't offended him.'[487]

Friday 21st:
Itinerary: John gets a taxi from The Bishop's Cottage Hotel to Wareham station, then gets a train back to London.

Tuesday 25th:
Itinerary: John travels with Michael Kerrigan and other members of the 'Battlefield' production team for to recce potential locations for the story's OB recordings. They visit Fulmer Plant Park, Little Paston and Black Park, all in Buckinghamshire.

Friday 28th – Thursday 4th May:
Rehearsals for the OB location recording of 'Battlefield' take place at the BBC Television Rehearsal Rooms at Acton.

Friday 28th:
Itinerary: John travels from Union House to the BBC Rehearsal Rooms at Acton, where a script read-through for 'Battlefield' takes place. This is followed by a planning meeting for the story's three-day studio recording block, scheduled for late next month.

MAY

Monday 1st (bank holiday):
Itinerary: In the evening, John directs a charity gala show at the Dome Theatre in Brighton to raise funds for the Hillsborough disaster.[488] He is joined by Colin Baker, Sylvester McCoy and Sophie Aldred, who appear on stage.

Wednesday 3rd:
Itinerary: John travels from Union House to the BBC Rehearsal Rooms at Acton, for the Producer's Run of the OB material for 'Battlefield'.

---

[487] John Nathan-Turner memoirs, *Doctor Who Magazine* #248.
[488] Just a few weeks previously, on 15 April 1989, 94 Liverpool fans died while attending the FA Cup semi-final between their club and Nottingham Forest at the Hillsborough football stadium in Sheffield. Overcrowding in the stadium led to fans being crushed to death as they were forced against the perimeter safety barriers of the terraces. In the weeks and months that followed, three more supporters died as a result of the injuries they received that day, taking the final death toll to 97.

Friday 5th:
Itinerary: John writes to Riitta Lynn, Production Manager for 'Battlefield', informing her that he's arranged a press photocall to take place during the location OB recording on Monday 15 May.

Saturday 6th:
Itinerary: John drives to Fulmer Plant Park in Fulmer, Buckinghamshire for the first day of OB recording for 'Battlefield'. After recording, he drives home to London.

Sunday 7th:
Itinerary: John drives to Stamford in Lincolnshire for the second day of OB recording for 'Battlefield'. Recording takes place at Dowager House in St Martin Without. John stays overnight at the unit hotel, The Crown Hotel in Oakham.

Monday 8th:
Itinerary: Today is the third day of OB recording for 'Battlefield', now at Hambleton Old Hall in Upper Hambleton, Leicestershire. John again stays at The Crown Hotel in Oakham.

Tuesday 9th:
Itinerary: Today should have been the fourth day of OB recording for 'Battlefield', but industrial action by the Broadcasting and Entertainments Trades Alliance (BETA) and the National Union of Journalists (NUJ) forces this to be abandoned and the production be put on hold. Although booked into The Crown Hotel in Oakham, John returns home that evening, along with the cast and crew, to await the end of the strike.

Wednesday 10th:
Itinerary: Today should have been the fifth day of OB recording for 'Battlefield', but industrial action by BETA and the NUJ continues, forcing it to be abandoned.

Thursday 11th:
Itinerary: With industrial action now over, the cast and crew return to Oakham for the rescheduled fourth day of OB recording for 'Battlefield'. This takes place at Rutland Water, Upper Hambleton in Leicestershire. To help get the production back on schedule, director Michael Kerrigan asks John to direct a number of second-unit sequences throughout the day. John again stays overnight at The Crown Hotel.

Friday 12th:
Itinerary: Today is a scheduled day off, and despite losing two days of recording to industrial action, this is still observed. John organises a day trip to nearby Skegness, and is joined by Sylvester McCoy and Nicholas Courtney, amongst others. Despite the pouring rain, they enjoy the day. The cast and crew still stay at The Crown Hotel in Oakham overnight.

Saturday 13th:
Itinerary: Today is the fifth day of OB recording for 'Battlefield', now in Twyford Woods, Lincolnshire. During the day, John directs some second-unit action of the 2CV and Range Rover cars driving around Twyford Woods, encountering Mordred's troops. This time, he spends the night at The Stamford Poste Hotel in Stamford.

John Nathan-Turner: 'I got to supervise more second-unit shooting on this story, my fondest memory being an interior car shot: five people in a Land Rover and about half-a-page of dialogue. Later, a great deal of mirth was had at our expense, because we just couldn't get this simple one-shot scene right. Tree reflections blocked out faces at first, then light reflections ... by the time we'd done ten takes, all for technical reasons, hysteria had set in amongst the actors, and they just couldn't get through it. Take followed take followed take ... when we did finally have a good take the actors cheered so loudly that they ruined the main unit's sound-take – from a couple of hundred yards away!'[489]

Sunday 14th:
Itinerary: Today is the sixth day of OB recording for 'Battlefield', which again takes place in Twyford Woods, Lincolnshire. During the day, John directs some second-unit action of the battle between Ancelyn and Mordred and his troops from Part One. He again stays overnight at The Stamford Poste Hotel in Stamford.

Monday 15th:
Itinerary: Today is the seventh day of OB recording for 'Battlefield', now back in Upper Hambleton, Leicestershire. John has invited journalists and photographers from a number of the national daily tabloid newspapers to attend the location during the lunch break. A photoshoot takes place with most members of the cast and the Doctor's car Bessie. John again spends the night at The Stamford Poste Hotel in Stamford.

---

[489] John Nathan-Turner nemoirs, *Doctor Who Magazine* #248. A large proportion of this footage that John directed is included in the *Doctor Who: The Collection – Season 26* Blu-ray boxset.

Tuesday 16th:
Itinerary: Today is the eighth day of OB recording for 'Battlefield'. This again takes place in Rutland Water, Upper Hambleton in Leicestershire. John spends a last night at The Stamford Poste Hotel in Stamford.

Wednesday 17th:
Itinerary: Today is the ninth and final day of OB recording for 'Battlefield', at Hambleton Ridge, Upper Hambleton in Leicestershire. After recording concludes, John drives home to London.

Thursday 18th – Monday 29th:
Rehearsals for the single studio block of 'Battlefield' take place at the BBC Television Rehearsal Rooms at Acton.

Friday 19th:
Itinerary: John entertains Colin Baker in the BBC Club bar.[490]

Tuesday 23rd:
Itinerary: John attends a planning meeting for 'Ghost Light' at BBC Threshold House in the morning.

Wednesday 24th:
Itinerary: John heads down to Dorset with director Alan Wareing and other members of the production team of 'Survival' to recce possible locations for OB recording. On the same day, Marc Platt writes to John with script rewrites for 'Ghost Light' Parts One and Three.

Thursday 25th:
Itinerary: John remains in Dorset with director Alan Wareing and other members of the production team of 'Survival' to recce possible locations for OB recording.

Friday 26th:
Itinerary: John returns from Dorset. He writes to a woman named Jill Champion to arrange for Sylvester McCoy to appear in a photoshoot with a 'cuddly monster' on the afternoon of Tuesday 30 May, during a break in the second studio day of 'Battlefield'. Because of further industrial action by the BETA trade union, rehearsals for the studio session of 'Battlefield' have to be cancelled for the day.

---

[490] Baker was by now preparing to enter rehearsals to take over from Jon Pertwee as the Doctor in the stage tour of *Doctor Who: The Ultimate Adventure*. His tenure in the show's lead role would begin on Monday 5 June 1989, at the Newcastle Opera House in Newcastle Upon Tyne.

Commentary: The nature of the planned photoshoot involving Sylvester McCoy is something of a mystery, as is Jill Champion's role in the matter. It could possibly have been something for BBC Enterprises, or perhaps for the BBC's annual *Children in Need* telethon.

Monday 29th (bank holiday):
Itinerary: John travels from Union House to the BBC Rehearsal Rooms at Acton for the Producer's Run for the single studio block of 'Battlefield'.

Tuesday 30th:
Itinerary: Today is the first day of the three-day studio block for 'Battlefield' in studio TC3 at BBC Television Centre.

Wednesday 31st:
Itinerary: Today is the second day of the three-day studio block for 'Battlefield' in studio TC3 at BBC Television Centre.

JUNE

Thursday 1st:
Itinerary: Today is the third and final day of the studio block for 'Battlefield' in studio TC3 at BBC Television Centre. As studio time begins to run out, John decides to cut a major effects shot from the running order. This would have featured at the end of the first episode, as Mordred and his knights burst through a wall of the hotel's brewery. This dictates a change to several camera set-ups during the rest of the scene, which confuses the cast. Later in the evening, a water tank in the studio breaks while Sophie Aldred is inside it. Aldred escapes with minor lacerations, but the studio is flooded. John negotiates an overrun beyond the usual 10.00pm finish time so that all the scenes needed to complete the story can be recorded.

John Nathan-Turner: 'In studio, we started running very short of time. At the end of Part One a wall was supposed to tumble down as the knights marched in. Throughout the years, I'd always told production managers not to instigate recording orders where the final scenes were essential to the plot. "Talk to the script editor and ask, if push comes to shove, whether any scenes could be mounted in another set that has yet to be recorded, for example." Sometimes these conversations took place, sometimes they didn't. In this case, however, we were shooting a vital scene that couldn't take place anywhere else last thing at night and over-running. I suggested we alter the angle, cut the wall effect and add a noisy entrance on the dub. It's not ideal, but we had a limited over-run and we couldn't afford to bring the set back, nor to store it for a fortnight. Then, of course, there was the terrible business involving the water tank, where Sophie only narrowly avoided serious injury after the glass cracked and threatened to shatter ... The reason it happened? The contractor who had built the tank had not used the precise thickness of glass specified, hence it gave way under the pressure of the gallons of water.'[491]

Friday 2nd – Thursday 8th:
Rehearsals for the OB location recording of 'Survival' take place at the BBC Television Rehearsal Rooms at Acton.

Friday 2nd:
Itinerary: John travels from Union House to the BBC Rehearsal Rooms at Acton for a script read-though for 'Survival'. In spite of the accident with the water tank the previous evening, Sophie Aldred is also in attendance.

Monday 5th:
Itinerary: Unbeknown to John, on this day Mark Shivas writes to Cliff Taylor, the BBC's Director of Resources, informing him in confidence that the BBC are considering having *Doctor Who* made by an independent production company for the 1990/1991 production year.

Tuesday 6th:
Itinerary: John writes to Peter Cregeen regarding the studio overrun of 12 minutes on the last studio day for 'Battlefield'. He attributes this to the cumulative effect of late starts due to costume, make-up and lighting issues over the three days in the studio.

Commentary: Surprisingly, John didn't cite the accident with Sophie Aldred and the water tank as an excuse for the studio overrun. Was this a case of him sticking his head in the sand over the incident – and who could be to blame for it – or did he genuinely believe that other factors were more significant in necessitating the overrun?

Wednesday 7th:
Itinerary: John attends the Producer's Run for 'Survival' at the BBC's Television Rehearsal Rooms at Acton.

Thursday 8th:
Itinerary: John appears before a BBC Safety Committee panel to discuss the

---

[491] John Nathan-Turner memoirs, *Doctor Who Magazine* #248.

accident with the water tank during the final studio session of 'Battlefield'.

Saturday 10th:
Itinerary: John drives to Medway Parade in Perivale for the first day of OB location recording for 'Survival' in and around the area. He is dissatisfied with the animatronic cat prop made by Visual Effects and agrees with director Alan Wareing to use actual 'trained' cats instead during the day's shooting. The animatronic cat undergoes more work before it is ready for use again.

Sunday 11th:
Itinerary: John drives to The Avenue in Ealing, and then to Medway Parade in Perivale, for the second day of OB location recording for 'Survival'. He has invited most of the national tabloid press to attend the shoot today, but the *Daily Mirror* is the only newspaper to send a photographer. Sylvester McCoy poses with guest stars Hale and Pace for a series of photos.

Monday 12th:
Itinerary: John drives to Perivale for the third day of OB location recording for 'Survival'. The animatronic cat prop now gets its first outing.

Tuesday 13th:
Itinerary: John drives to Perivale for the fourth day of OB location recording for 'Survival'. John's dog, Pepsi, makes another cameo appearance in the show during today's recording.

John Nathan-Turner: 'My dog, Pepsi, appeared in "Survival". It was her last TV appearance; she died not long after, at the ripe old age of 19 … Alan Wareing asked how I could train a dog to ignore all the shouting. I, basking in Pepsi's reflected glory, said, "She was given the note. She's a professional, with a long list of credits." Well, I'll now confess – Pepsi, at this late stage of her life, was deaf!'[492]

Wednesday 14th:
Itinerary: John drives to the E Y J Martial Arts Centre in Ealing for the fifth day of OB location recording for 'Survival'. During breaks in recording, he chats from time to time with David J Howe, Mark Stammers and Stephen James Walker, whom he has invited to cover the day's proceedings for their fanzine *The Frame*.

Thursday 15th:
Itinerary: John drives to Horsenden Hill in Perivale for the sixth day of OB

---

[492] John Nathan-Turner memoirs, *Doctor Who Magazine* #248.

location recording for 'Survival'. The motorcycle stunt rider Eddie Kidd has been booked for the day to perform a number of stunts for the shoot, but this causes a problem for the show's regular stuntman, Tip Tipping, when he realises that Kidd doesn't have the correct union membership to perform in a TV programme. Tipping raises the matter with John, and the pair become embroiled in a full-on argument over the matter, which leads to Tipping walking off the production in protest.

Friday 16th:
Itinerary: John has to find a replacement for Tip Tipping at short notice for the upcoming OB shoot in Dorset. The new stuntman is Paul Heasman, who does the remaining horse stunts for 'Survival' and will return for the stunt work on 'Ghost Light'.

Saturday 17th:
Itinerary: John leaves home at around midday and drives to the unit hotel – The Bishop's Cottage Hotel in West Lulworth, previously used for 'The Curse of Fenric' – for the resumption of OB location recording for 'Survival', due to start the next day.

Sunday 18th:
Itinerary: John drives to the ECC Quarry in Warmwell, Dorset for the seventh day of OB recording for 'Survival'. He again stays overnight at The Bishop's Cottage Hotel.

Monday 19th:
Itinerary: John drives to the ECC Quarry in Warmwell in Dorset for the eighth day of OB recording for 'Survival'. During the afternoon's shoot, one of the actresses playing a Cheetah Person decides that she can no longer cope with wearing her hot and bulky costume in the blistering Dorset temperatures. She rips off the costume and leaves the location. On the same day, Paul Stone, producer of the BBC drama *The Chronicles of Narnia*, writes to John, thanking him for co-operating in the casting of John Hallam in his show, during the making of which Hallam will also be recording scenes as Light in 'Ghost Light'. Stone confirms the mutually agreed dates on which the two productions will each have call on Hallam's services in the coming weeks.[493] John spends a third night at The Bishop's Cottage Hotel in West Lulworth.

Tuesday 20th:
Itinerary: John drives to the ECC Quarry in Warmwell in Dorset for the tenth

---

[493] Hallam played Captain Drinian in *The Chronicles of Narnia: Prince Caspian*, which aired on BBC1 over four weeks in November 1989.

day of OB recording for 'Survival'. The NUJ and BETA unions announce that there will be a nine-hour strike from 3.00pm onwards, so the day's schedule is tweaked to ensure that all the shots required are completed by that cut-off time. Because the day's shoot has wrapped early, John decides to organise an impromptu party and barbecue that evening for the cast and crew on the beach at Lulworth Cove. After the party, John returns to The Bishop's Cottage Hotel in West Lulworth.

Wednesday 21st:
Itinerary: John drives to the ECC Quarry in Warmwell in Dorset for the eleventh day of OB recording for 'Survival'. A small amount of recording for 'Ghost Light' also takes place today at 11 Greenhill in Weymouth, Dorset, which doubles as the exterior of the story's Gabriel Chase setting. John again stays overnight at The Bishop's Cottage Hotel.

Thursday 22nd:
Itinerary: John drives to the ECC Quarry in Warmwell in Dorset for the twelfth day of OB recording for 'Survival'. He then spends a further night at The Bishop's Cottage Hotel.

Friday 23rd:
Itinerary: John drives to the ECC Quarry in Warmwell in Dorset for the thirteenth and final day of OB recording for 'Survival'. After recording concludes, he drives back to London, arriving home at around 7.00pm.

John Nathan-Turner: 'The morning of the last day of the shoot, when we were due to both record *and* travel home, I was in discussion with our OB engineering managers. There was likely to be a strike involving all OB crews, and they thought there'd be a telephone instruction at 3.30pm ordering them to down tools. If this happened, we had to stop, obviously, but the OB crew couldn't even then drive the vehicles back to London; they would have to get home by other means – and all the OB vehicles would have to remain on site 'til the strike was over, when we'd all have to come back. As we were going virtually straight into rehearsals of "Ghost Light", this would pose tremendous problems. I talked to Alan [Wareing], who agreed we might just be able to finish at 3.15pm, if everyone worked at breakneck speed. No-one on the show wanted to come back just for a couple of hours' work! Normally cables and rigging are packed away at the end of the day ... well, suddenly the location became the tidiest I'd ever seen. People were packing up as they went along. You see, what was essential was that the OB vehicles were travelling home by 3.30pm, because their telephone wouldn't have to be switched on ... By lunchtime, thanks to everyone's efforts, we were left with one scene to do – a tightly contained scene between the Master and the Doctor (the one where the Master howls, I think). We wrapped at 3.10pm, people moved like the clappers, and stuff was being shunted left, right and centre. I drove away at 3.25pm, realising that mine was the last but one vehicle to leave, and had a very satisfactory journey home, overtaking a caravanserai of huge trucks – and was tooted by OB staff giving me the thumbs-up sign.'[494]

Tuesday 27th:
Itinerary: John entertains several members of the executive committee of the DWAS in the BBC Club bar.

Friday 30th:
Itinerary: John attends a script read-through of 'Ghost Light' along with writer Charles Vincent[495], who helps time the script to check if is running under- or over-length.

JULY

Tuesday 4th:
Itinerary: John entertains David Saunders in the BBC Club bar.

Friday 7th:
Itinerary: John entertains Lorne Martin of M & J Media Ventures in the BBC Club bar.

Saturday 8th – Monday 17th:
Rehearsals for the first studio block of 'Ghost Light' take place at the BBC Television Rehearsal Rooms at Acton.

Saturday 8th:
Itinerary: John drives in to Television Centre by car, as it's a non-duty day at work, then gets a tube to the Television Rehearsal Rooms at Acton to attend a script read-through of 'Ghost Light'.

Monday 10th:
Itinerary: John entertains Susan Rosenberg from Lionheart, *Doctor Who*'s US distributors, in the BBC Club bar.

---

[494] John Nathan-Turner memoirs, *Doctor Who Magazine* #248.
[495] Vincent was a writer whom Andrew Cartmel hoped would provide a story for consideration for inclusion in Season 27.

Thursday 13th:
Itinerary: John writes to Dominic Glynn and Mark Ayres, asking that they send their respective music mastertapes for 'Survival', 'Ghost Light' and 'The Curse of Fenric' to the *Doctor Who* Production Office, so that they can then be passed on to BBC Enterprises for use in the production of foreign language versions of the stories.

Friday 14th:
Itinerary: John travels to the Television Rehearsal Rooms at Acton to attend the Producers' Run for the first studio block of 'Ghost Light'

Saturday 15th:
Itinerary: John drives in to Television Centre by car, as it's a non-duty day at work, then gets a tube to the Television Rehearsal Rooms in Acton to attend the rehearsals for the first studio block of 'Ghost Light'.

Tuesday 18th:
Itinerary: Today is the first day of the two-day first studio block for 'Ghost Light' in studio TC3 at BBC Television Centre. Also on this day, John writes to all the main production personnel who worked on 'The Curse of Fenric', thanking them for their efforts and letting them know the planned broadcast dates for the story.

Wednesday 19th:
Itinerary: Today is the second and final day of the first studio block for 'Ghost Light' in studio TC3 at BBC Television Centre. John joins the cast in the BBC Club bar after recording concludes.

Friday 21st – Monday 31st:
Rehearsals for the second studio block of 'Ghost Light' take place at the BBC Television Rehearsal Rooms at Acton.

Friday 21st:
Itinerary: John entertains writer Chris Guard in the BBC Club bar.

Commentary: John specified on his expenses claim that Guard was a writer. It's possible that this was the same Christopher Guard who had played Bellboy in 'The Greatest Show in the Galaxy', now looking to pitch a story idea for the show. Alternatively, it could actually have been Chris Jury, who had played Deadbeat in the same story, and John had simply got the two surnames mixed up; later, after he left *Doctor Who*, he and Jury would work together on a number of script ideas, none of which ever got off the ground.

Monday 24th:
Unknown to John, Leslie Arnold, Head of Finance Planning for BBC Television, writes to the Jonathan Powell, the Controller of BBC1, with a breakdown of proposed costs and budgets should *Doctor Who* be produced by an independent production company in the 1990/1991 financial year. The budget for a 20-episode series made outside the BBC is estimated at £4.1 million.

Wednesday 26th:
Itinerary: John writes to the BBC Music Copyright Department, asking that Mark Ayres be engaged to provide the incidental music for 'Ghost Light'. He also writes to Ayres, letting him know that he'd originally wanted to ask him if it would be possible to use genuine period instruments on the story's soundtrack, but that the cost prohibit such an idea.

Thursday 27th:
Itinerary: John entertains writer Charles Vincent in the BBC Club bar. He also writes to Vincent later the same day, thanking him for his help in timing the 'Ghost Light' script reading on Friday 30 June. On the same day, unknown to John, Patricia Southam, the Planning Manager of BBC1, writes to the BBC's Head of Financial Planning regarding the proposed outsourcing of *Doctor Who* as an independent production. She points out that the Controller of BBC1, Jonathan Powell, wants to commit to only 14 new episodes per year, beginning in 1990/1991, but that if production blocks of 20 episodes are more economical, then monies from the 1991/1992 budget could be bought forward to cover the extra six episodes. Additionally, Southam stipulates that any shortfall between the in-house budget for an all-film series and the cost of making the show as an outside production must be met by BBC Enterprises. A meeting with Verity Lambert, the independent producer favoured to take on the making of the show, is scheduled for later the same day.[496]

Friday 28th:
Itinerary: John sends director Alan Wareing a memo setting out some brief sections of dialogue that he would like him to get Sylvester McCoy and Sophie Aldred to record, in sound only and with minimal rehearsal needed, at some point during the second studio block for 'Ghost Light', to be post-dubbed onto certain scenes of 'The Curse of Fenric'.

---

[496] Verity Lambert had been *Doctor Who*'s very first producer in 1963. Since leaving the BBC, she'd set up her own production company, Cinema Verity, in 1985, and was considered by the industry a very safe pair of hands. Her connection to *Doctor Who* had put her company in prime position for consideration to make the show for the BBC.

Saturday 29th:
Itinerary: As it's a non-duty day at work, John drives in by car to the Television Rehearsal Rooms at Acton to attend the rehearsals for the second studio block of 'Ghost Light'.

Monday 31st:
Itinerary: John travels from Union House to the BBC Rehearsal Rooms at Acton for the Producer's Run of the second studio block of 'Ghost Light'.

AUGUST

Tuesday 1st:
Itinerary: Today is the first day of the three-day second studio block for 'Ghost Light' in studio TC3 at BBC Television Centre.

Wednesday 2nd:
Itinerary: Today is the second day of the three-day second studio block for 'Ghost Light' in studio TC3 at BBC Television Centre. John joins the cast in the BBC Club bar after recording concludes.

Thursday 3rd:
Itinerary: Today is the third and final day of the second studio block for 'Ghost Light' in studio TC3 at BBC Television Centre. John joins the cast in the BBC Club bar after recording concludes, and hosts an end-of-season wrap party. This marks the end of production on Season 26 of *Doctor Who*, although there is still some editing and post-production remaining to be done. No-one realises it yet, but it also marks the end of *Doctor Who* as a BBC production, at least until 2004.

Commentary: Around this time, John had a meeting in the *Doctor Who* Production Office with writer Stephen James Walker. This was for the dual purpose of being interviewed by Walker for a future issue of *Doctor Who Magazine*[497] and of approving the text for some behind-the-scenes features that were shortly to appear in the fanzine *The Frame*. At this stage, John still appeared confident that *Doctor Who* would be returning for a further season the next year, but that he would no longer be the producer, leaving him free to

---

[497] Walker's interview with John (co-written by David Auger, who wasn't present when it was conducted but helped out with the transcription) appeared in *Doctor Who Magazine* #153, cover-dated October 1989.

move on to other projects. Noticing that Walker was carrying his wallet in the back pocket of his trousers, he cautioned him against doing this, telling him about how he was mugged the previous September.

Saturday 12th: (John's forty-second birthday)

Sunday 13th:
Itinerary: John travels in by car for a non-duty day at Television Centre.

Commentary: David Bingham records some additional ADR voice-over dialogue for 'Battlefield' today, so presumably John comes in to work to supervise this.[498]

Tuesday 15th:
Itinerary: John entertains David Saunders in the BBC Club bar.

Wednesday 16th:
Itinerary: Today is the BBC Autumn Season press launch at BBC Television Centre. John is joined by Jean Marsh (Morgaine from 'Battlefield') and Sophie Aldred (who gets time off from recording an episode of her new show *Corners* in order to be there) to help publicise the new *Doctor Who* season. John returns to the *Doctor Who* Production Office afterwards and writes to both Sophie Aldred and Jean Marsh, thanking them for attending.

Tuesday 22nd:
Itinerary: John travels in by car for a non-duty day at Television Centre.

Thursday 24th:
Itinerary: John writes to director Michael Kerrigan, asking that the countdown shots seen on screen in Part Four of 'Battlefield' be changed so that any viewers counting down with the clock will reach '1' at the same point as it appears on screen.

Tuesday 29th:
Itinerary: John travels in by car for a non-duty day at Television Centre.

---

[498] ADR is an acronym for additional dialogue recording. Bingham's role in 'Battlefield' was uncredited, but it's presumed that he provided some of the ethereal voices heard in the story's first episode. At the time, Bingham was appearing in the stage production *Doctor Who – The Ultimate Adventure* as an extra in crowd scenes, but was also understudy for the role of companion character Jason.

Wednesday 30th:
Itinerary: John writes to Peter Darvill-Evans at W H Allen, having been copied in to a mass of correspondence between him and Judy Nash at BBC Enterprises on the subject of copyright. John confirms that the characters of the Master and Ace are both BBC copyright. He also points out the interest that Terry Nation has in the characters of the Daleks, and the share of royalties he has historically asked for in relation to new Dalek stories. He concludes by saying that he has no objection to W H Allen publishing original *Doctor Who* fiction, as long as all the televised *Doctor Who* stories have already been novelised, which he acknowledges is now very nearly the case.

Thursday 31st:
Itinerary: John flies to Berlin with Sylvester McCoy, arriving at 4.25pm local time.

SEPTEMBER

Friday 1st:
Itinerary: John and Sylvester McCoy spend the day with executives from the German television station RTL+, then catch an evening flight back to London. They depart from Berlin at 7.20pm local time and arrive back in London at 9.45pm. The whole trip is paid for by BBC Enterprises.[499]

Saturday 2nd:
Itinerary: John travels in by car for a non-duty day at Television Centre. He later joins Sylvester McCoy at the Space Adventure exhibition in Tooley Street for the press launch of Season 26, which would begin on BBC1 later that week.

Wednesday 6th:
Itinerary: John entertains director Michael Kerrigan in the BBC Club bar. 'Battlefield' Part One screens on BBC1.

Monday 11th:
Itinerary: John writes to Sylvester McCoy and Sophie Aldred, informing them the BBC will not be taking up the options on their contracts for the 1990 season of *Doctor Who*.

---

[499] This trip was a follow-up to the BBC Enterprises showcase event on 6 March, when a deal had been agreed with RTL for them to purchase a package of *Doctor Who* episodes. Starting on 22 November 1989, RTL+ screened all 42 episodes featuring McCoy's Doctor over the next 12 months, all dubbed into German.

Commentary: This is the first indication in the paperwork that the future of *Doctor Who* beyond Season 26 was in doubt, as far as John was concerned. It's now clear that other conversations were going on over his head regarding the show's long-term future. The BBC's plan at this time was to have the next season made by an independent production company, with Verity Lambert's Cinema Verity seemingly in pole position to take on that role. The initial thinking was that production might take place in the 1990/91 financial year; a schedule that could even have seen *Doctor Who* return to the screen as usual as part of BBC1's next Autumn Season of programmes. However, by the time a definite decision was taken not to produce *Doctor Who* in-house during the 1990/91 financial year – with McCoy's and Aldred's contracts being cancelled in consequence – it was too late for that schedule to be met. The BBC were still expecting that a 14-episode season would be made for airing on BBC1 in 1991, and a commitment would be there on the BBC's part for the show to continue into 1992 and beyond, as long as the chosen independent production company was still happy making it. These prospective future episodes would almost certainly not have involved John in any capacity, but might have seen McCoy and even Aldred re-contracted to appear if they had been agreeable. How much of any of this would have been apparent to John at this point in time isn't clear. He certainly had an inkling that the show was being prepared for outside production – but this meant that it would now no longer be made in-house, leaving John as a BBC staff producer with no show to produce.

Wednesday 13th:
Itinerary: John writes to Hale and Pace, inviting them to a press preview screening at BAFTA on Thursday 19 October. 'Battlefield' Part Two screens on BBC1.

Thursday 14th:
Itinerary: John writes to Peter Darvill-Evans at W H Allen with his feedback on the first 35 pages of Ben Aaronovitch's manuscript for the Target novelisation of 'Remembrance of the Daleks'.

Friday 15th:
Itinerary: A farewell party is held at BBC Television Centre for Andrew Cartmel, who is leaving *Doctor Who* to work as script editor on the BBC1 drama *Casualty*.

Commentary: Cartmel had planned to leave *Doctor Who* even before the show was put on its second hiatus by the BBC, so his move to *Casualty* would have happened regardless.

Tuesday 19th:
Itinerary: John attends a viewing of 'Battlefield' Part Four with Mark Shivas.

Wednesday 20th September – Friday 6th October
Itinerary: John takes two-and-a-half weeks of annual leave from the BBC. He flies out to Ohio, USA on or sometime after the 20 September.

Wednesday 20th:
'Battlefield' Part Three screens on BBC1.

Thursday 21st:
Itinerary: In a memo dated today's date but written before he went on leave, John asks the BBC Contracts Department to book Sylvester McCoy to perform a new post-synched voiceover for the closing moments of 'Survival' Part Three. The studio session is booked for Thursday 23 November.

Friday 22nd:
Itinerary: In a letter dated today's date but written before he went on leave, John thanks director Michael Kerrigan for his work on 'Battlefield'. In similarly post-dated letters, he also writes to all the main production personnel who worked on 'Ghost Light' and 'Survival', thanking them for their efforts and letting them know the stories' planned broadcast dates.

Friday 22nd – Sunday 24th:
Itinerary: John is a guest at the Timelord '89/North American Time Festival convention held at the Ramada Inn in Columbus, Ohio. Other guests include Anthony Ainley and Terry Nation. Sylvester McCoy, Nicholas Courtney and Gary Downie were also supposed to appear, but Courtney was dropped from the guest list some days before the event, and the others never received their plane tickets and so never left the UK.

Wednesday 27th:
'Battlefield' Part Four screens on BBC1.

Friday 29th:
Commentary: While John is away on annual leave, Jonathan Powell writes to the Director General of Television, telling him that he has been informed by Roger Laughton, Director of BBC Enterprises, that Columbia Pictures Television in the US are interested in co-producing *Doctor Who*.

OCTOBER

Wednesday 4th:
'Ghost Light' Part One screens on BBC1.

Wednesday 11th:
'Ghost Light' Part Two screens on BBC1.

Friday 13th:
Itinerary: US fan Eric Hoffman writes to John, attempting to piece together the behind-the-scenes problems that beset the Timelord '89/North American Time Festival convention the previous month. He recommends to John a new US convention group, Gallifrey One. John writes to actress Katharine Schlesinger, apologising for her name having been misspelt on the end credits of the first two episodes of 'Ghost Light', and also in the *Radio Times* billings for the story. He assures her that no such error will occur in the end credits of Part Three when it screens next week. On the same day, Mark Shivas writes to Jonathan Powell, confirming that a twenty-seventh season of *Doctor Who* is not being put forward by BBC Drama for the 1990/1991 production year. He also writes to the BBC's Head of Television Publicity, informing him of this decision, so that he is aware should he start getting calls on the subject. Shivas goes on to say that they are looking at bringing *Doctor Who* back in the early 1990s.

Tuesday 17th:
Itinerary: John entertains writer Charles Vincent in the BBC Club bar.

Wednesday 18th:
'Ghost Light' Part Three screens on BBC1.

Thursday 19th:
Itinerary: John attends a press screening of 'The Curse of Fenric' Part One and 'Survival' Part One at BAFTA in London. On the same day, Jonathan Powell writes to the Managing Director of Network Television, letting him know that the BBC Drama group are not offering up *Doctor Who* for production the following year. He says that a three-way deal between the BBC Drama Department, BBC Enterprises and Verity Lambert for production of the show the following year has stalled, and blames BBC Enterprises for being less than helpful in this matter. However, if funding can be achieved at a later date, then the show is open for revival. He warns of an impending PR problem when the news gets out that *Doctor Who* won't be returning to BBC1 the following year.

Commentary: It seems that *Doctor Who*'s fate had now been sealed. In the expectation of a deal being done to shift the show's production to an independent company, the BBC had divested itself of its commitment to make it in-house; but that deal had now failed to materialise. Reading between the lines, it appears that the budget to buy in the show from an external producer had to be met jointly by the BBC Drama Department – committing the same resources as it usually did when the production was in-house – and BBC Enterprises, whose contribution would be recouped through overseas and home media sales; however, it would seem that BBC Enterprises had baulked at this up-front cost/investment, which would probably have been well in excess of a million pounds, and this had now caused the whole deal to collapse.

Saturday 21st:
Itinerary: John, along with Sylvester McCoy and Sophie Aldred, attends *Doctor Who Magazine*'s 10th Birthday Party event at Centrepoint in London.

Tuesday 24th:
Itinerary: John entertains writer Marc Platt in the BBC Club bar.

Wednesday 25th:
'The Curse of Fenric' Part One screens on BBC1.

Monday 30th:
Itinerary: US fan Eric Hoffman writes to John with more gossip from the American *Doctor Who* convention circuit.

Tuesday 31st:
Itinerary: John writes to Mark Ayres, thanking him for providing the incidental music for 'Ghost Light'.

NOVEMBER

Wednesday 1st:
'The Curse of Fenric' Part Two screens on BBC1.

Thursday 2nd:
Itinerary: John writes to Eric Hoffman, thanking him for his recent letter, and for his recommendation of the Gallifrey One US event.

Wednesday 8th:
'The Curse of Fenric' Part Three screens on BBC1.

Wednesday 15th:
'The Curse of Fenric' Part Four screens on BBC1.

Saturday 18th:
Itinerary: John attends the *Doctor Who* Mega-Quiz '89 event at Aston University in Birmingham, organised by West Midlands-based fan group the Whonatics.[500]

Wednesday 22nd:
Itinerary: John writes to Julie Dixon at BBC Enterprises to give his approval for a proposal from Marvel UK to produce a *Doctor Who* comic strip for a national tabloid newspaper. 'Survival' Part One screens on BBC1.

Thursday 23rd:
Itinerary: Sylvester McCoy comes in to the BBC to record the new post-synched dialogue, written by Andrew Cartmel, for the final few moments of Part Three of 'Survival'.

Wednesday 29th:
Itinerary: John writes to director Nick Mallett, thanking him for his work on 'The Curse of Fenric'. 'Survival' Part Two screens on BBC1.

DECEMBER

Wednesday 6th:
'Survival' Part Three screens on BBC1. This marks the end of *Doctor Who*'s original run on BBC1, which stretches back to 1963.

Monday 11th:
Itinerary: John writes to Peter Darvill-Evans at W H Allen regarding Ben Aaronovitch's manuscript for the upcoming Target novelisation of 'Remembrance of the Daleks'. Although he is happy with the manuscript, he states that he doesn't hold with some of the 'theories' Aaronovitch has incorporated into the text, making the fiction a 'fact'. He adds that he will be

---

[500] John probably took the opportunity to visit his parents for the weekend while attending this event.

talking to BBC Books shortly about the 'invented fiction' problem.[501]

Thursday 28th – Friday 29th:
Itinerary: John takes two days of annual leave from the BBC.

Saturday 30th:
Itinerary: In the evening, John goes to the Connaught Theatre in Worthing to see their production of *Snow White and the Seven Dwarfs*.

---

[501] John's mention of the 'invented fiction' problem seems to hint at him paving the way for W H Allen to be given a licence to publish original *Doctor Who* novels, which would ultimately lead to their New Adventures range, featuring the further adventures of the seventh Doctor and Ace.

1990

Setting the Scene:

As 1989 drew to a close, John found himself in limbo at the BBC. He had no series to produce anymore, or script editor with whom to plan upcoming projects. The *Doctor Who* Production Office no longer had any purpose, but it was still John's official place of work. Production Associate June Collins and John's secretary Clare Kinmont had both left the show by the end of 1989.

If, in 1990, John was still pitching new programme ideas to his bosses as alternatives for him to produce, then almost nothing is recorded to that effect in the surviving paperwork. In contemporary correspondence with others, he maintained that he was still developing new projects for the BBC. Was he putting a brave face on things, and giving a positive spin to events, or was he in denial about what was happening?

He must have known that the next step was, inevitably, for him to be made redundant by the BBC. The Corporation, for whom he had worked for over two decades, was about to cast him aside for good …

JANUARY

Saturday 6th:
Itinerary: In the evening, John goes to the Lyric Theatre in Hammersmith, London, to see the play *Thark*.

Commentary: The cast of *Thark* included Sonia Ritter, Hugh Lloyd (Goronwy in 'Delta and the Bannermen'), Peter Carlisle, Belinda Lang, Helen Lindsay, Ramsay Gilderdale, Linda Polan (Juno Baker in *K-9 and Company*), Griff Rhys Jones, Dinsdale Landen (Dr Judson in 'The Curse of Fenric'), Eva Griffith and Charles Pemberton.

Sunday 7th – Sunday 14th:
Itinerary: John is a guest on the Omnicon British Fantaseas Cruise, which takes place on a cruise ship sailing around the coast of Miami, Florida. Gary Downie is the other main guest.

Commentary: John must have flown out to the US today to join up with this cruise, after seeing the play *Thark* on the Saturday night.

FEBRUARY

Thursday 1st:
Itinerary: John entertains director Alan Wareing and novelist Susan Lewis[502] in the BBC Club bar.

John Nathan-Turner: 'Alan Wareing and I took out an option on a marvellous book which we were developing; the BBC were making charming noises about the project in our direction so, for me, the end [of *Doctor Who*] wasn't as painful as you might think. I'd been attempting to get off the *Doctor Who* merry-go-round for many, many years, and Alan and I were genuinely excited about our new project. Andrew [Cartmel] and I had several ideas at various stages of readiness too – one favourite being an exposé drama concerning the world of fine art. As the months passed, many of these projects bit the dust; such is the way of the TV world ...'

Wednesday 14th:
Itinerary: John meets with his Personnel Manager, who informs him that he will be made redundant from the BBC. He will be formally notified of this at a later date.

Wednesday 21st:
Itinerary: In the evening, John attends the Old Red Lion Theatre Club in St John Street, London (although it's not known what play he went to see).

MARCH

Friday 30th:
Itinerary: US fan Eric Hoffman writes to John, looking forward to meeting him in Los Angeles at the Gallifrey One event in May, along with Jon Pertwee and John Levene, who are also due to attend.

---

[502] Susan Lewis had previously worked as a secretary, first at HTV in Bristol and then at Thames Television in London. While at Thames, she had written her first novel, *A Class Apart*, published in 1988. It's possible that this was the novel that John, along with director Alan Wareing, was looking at adapting for television.

APRIL

Monday 2nd:
Itinerary: Eric Hoffman, now working at the New Jersey Network (NJN) PBS Station, writes again to John, thanking him for introducing him to Bill Sellars, the producer of *All Creatures Great and Small*. Eric has recently visited the UK and met with Sellars to discuss potentially making a behind-the-scenes documentary about the show, to be titled *The Making of Creatures*.

Tuesday 10th:
Itinerary: John writes to John Gau Productions in order to reclaim rail expenses he has incurred in travelling to and from the *Doctor Who* Exhibition at Longleat House to record an interview to feature in a programme being made by them for the newly-launched British satellite TV station BSB.

Commentary: One of the BBC shows that BSB had purchased to launch its service was *Doctor Who*, and specifically a package of 1960s episodes starring William Hartnell and Patrick Troughton as the Doctor. Consequently, these featured very prominently in their launch publicity.

Monday 30th:
Itinerary: John receives a letter from the BBC Personnel Department, giving him one month's notice of dismissal on the grounds of redundancy, which is then to be followed by his three-month contractual notice period. The letter states that John's last day of employment by the BBC will therefore be Friday 31 August 1990.

MAY

Monday 14th – Friday 25th:
Itinerary: Sylvester McCoy and Sophie Aldred return to the BBC to play the Doctor and Ace for an edition of the BBC's children's science series *Search Out Science*, recorded over these two weeks. This programme has no input from the *Doctor Who* Production Office, of which John is now the last remaining occupant.

Friday 18th:
Itinerary: John writes to Eric Hoffman at NJN, wishing him well in his

proposed production of an *All Creatures Great and Small* documentary. John explains that he's currently looking after the business side of *Doctor Who* for the BBC while working in 'development' on several other projects, some for the BBC, and some for other TV companies.

Friday 25th – Monday 28th:
Itinerary: John is a guest at the Gallifrey One convention held at the Los Angeles Airport Hilton hotel in Los Angeles, California, USA. Other guests include Jon Pertwee, John Levene and writer Jean-Marc L'officier.

JUNE

Monday 4th:
Itinerary: John writes to Eric Hoffman, thanking him for his MC-ing at the recent Gallifrey One convention that he attended in LA. He explains he is trying to get used to working in 'development' – coming up with new ideas for programmes – but is finding it a frustrating experience. He hopes to see Eric again at a US convention in August.

Friday 8th:
Itinerary: John writes to Stephen Phelps, editor of the BSB programme *31 West*, at John Gau Productions.[503] Giving the details of his and Sian Lloyd's series *Glitz & Bitz* for Radio Sussex[504], he asks to be considered as a guest presenter of *31 West*. In the evening, he visits the Westminster Theatre in London to see the play *Temptation*.

Commentary: The cast of *Temptation* includes Sylvester McCoy, Frank Middlemass, Aden Gillett, Rula Lenska (Styles in 'Resurrection of the Daleks'), Robert Longden, Christopher Adamson, Mark Montinaro, Anna Barnes, Sukie Smith, Angela Clerkin, Sara Stewart, Andrew Lawden, Jerome Turner, Tristram Davies, Toby Simkin, Franc Fioli and Penelope Diamond.

---

[503] *31 West* was a half-hour magazine programme shown on weekday evenings on BSB's *Galaxy* Channel. It was a bit like a cross between the BBC's *Nationwide* and *The One Show* programmes.
[504] *Glitz and Bitz* was a semi-regular radio spot on BBC Radio Sussex, with John and Sian Lloyd (wife of comedian Hugh Lloyd) playing the two titular characters. It was described by the fanzine *DWB* (issue 79) as a show '… hosted by two anonymous Hinge & Bracket-type characters, who bitch about showbiz personalities.' When exactly John and Sian Lloyd first started performing these two characters, and for how long they continued, isn't known.

Friday 15th – Sunday 17th:
Itinerary: John is a guest at the Timewarp 90 convention, held at the Penn Towers Hotel in Philadelphia, Pennsylvania, USA.

JULY

Tuesday 3rd:
Itinerary: In the evening, John visits the Soho Poly Theatre in London to see a play (title unknown).

Tuesday 31st:
Itinerary: Bob Furnell, organiser for a Canadian *Doctor Who* convention due to take place in November, writes to John. The event's main guest is planned to be Nicola Bryant, and Furnell asks John if he has any outtakes or bloopers of her from her time in the show that they can screen.

AUGUST

Friday 10th:
Itinerary: John writes to Bob Furnell, telling him that there are no *Doctor Who* blooper tapes available featuring Nicola Bryant. He also expresses an interest in attending, as a guest, one of Furnell's events in the future.

Sunday 12th: (John's forty-third birthday)

Monday 13th:
Itinerary: John writes to Penny Mills at BBC Enterprises. He reminds her that he's leaving the staff of the Corporation at the end of the month, and says that as he was asked to take seven weeks' leave prior to that date, he has rarely been in the *Doctor Who* Production Office of late. He points out to Mills that he should be due some additional payment for upcoming post-production work that he'll be doing for BBC Enterprises, on the VHS release of 'The Curse of Fenric'.

Commentary: John was commissioned by Penny Mills of BBC Enterprises sometime in spring 1990 to produce an extended version of 'The Curse of Fenric' for its first home video release. He insisted on the story's director Nick

Mallett being part of the project, and on any new music being provided by its composer Mark Ayres. In total, around six minutes of deleted material was ultimately reinstated by John in the extended version. In order to keep costs down, he used an outside edit suite in Soho for this work, rather than BBC facilities. For the same reason, he reneged on the agreed fee due to Mark Ayres for the additional music he supplied; and this so enraged Nicholas Mallett that he walked off the project and didn't attend the final dubbing sessions.

John Nathan-Turner: 'I insisted director Nick Mallett be involved also, and we did all our preparatory work together, reinserting as much as possible [of the originally deleted material], adapting the soundtrack and adding the small amount of new music we could afford. We did the edit and agreed to dub the show somewhere off Oxford Street. However, Nick didn't turn up to this session and has never to this day told me why.'[505]

Thursday 30th:
Itinerary: John, along with Deborah Watling, attends the press launch for the BSB *Doctor Who Weekend* at BSB Marco Polo House in London.[506]

Undated memo from John Nathan-Turner to Peter Cregeen:
'Thank you for agreeing to a party with regard to my leaving the Corporation. On reflection, I've decided I'd rather leave in a quieter fashion. It suddenly occurred to me that these parties have a dreadful finality about them, and, after all, I do hope to return! Nevertheless, I would like to see you before my departure on 31st August to say my farewells, and discuss one or two things with you.'

Friday 31st:
Itinerary: Today is John's final day at the BBC. He packs up the contents of the *Doctor Who* Production Office, removing as much in the way of photos, scripts, files and paperwork as he can, as anything left behind is due to be thrown into a skip, leaving the office empty in readiness for whatever new use the BBC will put it to …

John Nathan-Turner: 'I had declined the BBC's offer of a lavish party – but, on my last day, and much to my complete surprise, friends, colleagues and several *Doctor Who* regulars descended on the office, laden with drink and

---

[505] John Nathan-Turner memoirs, *Doctor Who Magazine* #248.
[506] The *Doctor Who Weekend* was a strand of programmes shown on BSB's Galaxy Channel on 22 and 23 September 1990. Numerous 1960s and 1970s episodes were screened alongside interviews with various *Doctor Who* guests. John was one of the on-screen hosts.

food, to wish me well for the future.'[507]

Commentary: Whatever one thinks of John Nathan-Turner, this was undoubtedly a sad - some would say tragic - way for his career at the BBC to end. He would spend the next twelve years working at the periphery of various other *Doctor Who* projects, but he never managed to shoulder his way back into the world of television.

---

[507] John Nathan-Turner memoirs, *Doctor Who Magazine* #249.

APPENDIX
PRODUCER'S CREDITS

Viewing figures are in millions

Doctor Who – Season 18

Story Title	Episode	BBC1 Air Date	Viewers
The Leisure Hive	Part One	30 August 1980	5.9
The Leisure Hive	Part Two	6 September 1980	5.0
The Leisure Hive	Part Three	13 September 1980	5.0
The Leisure Hive	Part Four	20 September 1980	4.5
Meglos	Part One	27 September 1980	5.0
Meglos	Part Two	4 October 1980	4.2
Meglos	Part Three	11 October 1980	4.7
Meglos	Part Four	18 October 1980	4.7
Full Circle	Part One	25 October 1980	5.9
Full Circle	Part Two	1 November 1980	3.7
Full Circle	Part Three	8 November 1980	5.9
Full Circle	Part Four	15 November 1980	5.4
State of Decay	Part One	22 November 1980	5.8
State of Decay	Part Two	29 November 1980	5.3
State of Decay	Part Three	6 December 1980	4.4
State of Decay	Part Four	13 December 1980	5.4
Warrior's Gate	Part One	3 January 1981	7.1
Warrior's Gate	Part Two	10 January 1981	6.7
Warrior's Gate	Part Three	17 January 1981	8.3
Warrior's Gate	Part Four	24 January 1981	7.8
The Keeper of Traken	Part One	31 January 1981	7.6
The Keeper of Traken	Part Two	7 February 1981	6.1
The Keeper of Traken	Part Three	14 February 1981	5.2
The Keeper of Traken	Part Four	21 February 1981	6.1
Logopolis	Part One	28 February 1981	7.7
Logopolis	Part Two	7 March 1981	7.7
Logopolis	Part Three	14 March 1981	5.8
Logopolis	Part Four	21 March 1981	6.1

K-9 and Company

Story Title	Episode	BBC1 Air Date	Viewers
A Girl's Best Friend	N/A	28 December 1981	8.4

Doctor Who – Season 19

Story Title	Episode	BBC1 Air Date	Viewers
Castrovalva	Part One	4 January 1982	9.1
Castrovalva	Part Two	5 January 1982	8.6
Castrovalva	Part Three	11 January 1982	10.2
Castrovalva	Part Four	12 January 1982	10.4
Four to Doomsday	Part One	18 January 1982	8.4
Four to Doomsday	Part Two	19 January 1982	8.8
Four to Doomsday	Part Three	25 January 1982	8.9
Four to Doomsday	Part Four	26 January 1982	9.4
Kinda	Part One	1 February 1982	8.4
Kinda	Part Two	2 February 1982	9.4
Kinda	Part Three	8 February 1982	8.5
Kinda	Part Four	9 February 1982	8.9
The Visitation	Part One	15 February 1982	9.1
The Visitation	Part Two	16 February 1982	9.3
The Visitation	Part Three	22 February 1982	9.9
The Visitation	Part Four	23 February 1982	10.1
Black Orchid	Part One	1 March 1982	9.9
Black Orchid	Part Two	2 March 1982	10.1
Earthshock	Part One	8 March 1982	9.1
Earthshock	Part Two	9 March 1982	8.8
Earthshock	Part Three	15 March 1982	9.8
Earthshock	Part Four	16 March 1982	9.6
Time-Flight	Part One	22 March 1982	10.0
Time-Flight	Part Two	23 March 1982	8.5
Time-Flight	Part Three	29 March 1982	8.9
Time-Flight	Part Four	30 March 1982	8.1

Doctor Who – Season 20

Story Title	Episode	BBC1 Air Date	Viewers
Arc of Infinity	Part One	3 January 1983	7.2
Arc of Infinity	Part Two	5 January 1983	7.3
Arc of Infinity	Part Three	11 January 1983	6.9

Arc of Infinity	Part Four	12 January 1983	7.2
Snakedance	Part One	18 January 1983	6.7
Snakedance	Part Two	19 January 1983	7.7
Snakedance	Part Three	25 January 1983	6.6
Snakedance	Part Four	26 January 1983	7.4
Mawdryn Undead	Part One	1 February 1983	6.5
Mawdryn Undead	Part Two	2 February 1983	7.5
Mawdryn Undead	Part Three	8 February 1983	7.4
Mawdryn Undead	Part Four	9 February 1983	7.7
Terminus	Part One	15 February 1983	6.8
Terminus	Part Two	16 February 1983	7.5
Terminus	Part Three	22 February 1983	6.5
Terminus	Part Four	23 February 1983	7.4
Enlightenment	Part One	1 March 1983	6.6
Enlightenment	Part Two	2 March 1983	7.2
Enlightenment	Part Three	8 March 1983	6.2
Enlightenment	Part Four	9 March 1983	7.3
The King's Demons	Part One	15 March 1983	5.8
The King's Demons	Part Two	16 March 1983	7.2

Doctor Who – **Anniversary Special**

Story Title	Episode	BBC1 Air Date	Viewers
The Five Doctors	N/A	25 November 1983	7.7

Doctor Who – **Season 21**

Story Title	Episode	BBC1 Air Date	Viewers
Warriors of the Deep	Part One	5 January 1984	7.6
Warriors of the Deep	Part Two	6 January 1984	7.5
Warriors of the Deep	Part Three	12 January 1984	7.3
Warriors of the Deep	Part Four	13 January 1984	6.6
The Awakening	Part One	19 January 1984	7.9
The Awakening	Part Two	20 January 1984	6.6
Frontios	Part One	26 January 1984	8.0
Frontios	Part Two	27 January 1984	5.8
Frontios	Part Three	2 February 1984	7.8
Frontios	Part Four	3 February 1984	5.6
Resurrection of the Daleks	Part One	8 February 1984	7.3
Resurrection of the Daleks	Part Two	15 February 1984	8.0
Planet of Fire	Part One	23 February 1984	6.1

Planet of Fire	Part Two	24 February 1984	6.1
Planet of Fire	Part Three	1 March 1984	7.4
Planet of Fire	Part Four	2 March 1984	7.0
The Caves of Androzani	Part One	8 March 1984	6.9
The Caves of Androzani	Part Two	9 March 1984	6.6
The Caves of Androzani	Part Three	15 March 1984	7.8
The Caves of Androzani	Part Four	16 March 1984	7.8
The Twin Dilemma	Part One	22 March 1984	7.6
The Twin Dilemma	Part Two	23 March 1984	7.4
The Twin Dilemma	Part Three	29 March 1984	7.0
The Twin Dilemma	Part Four	30 March 1984	6.3

Doctor Who – Season 22

Story Title	Episode	BBC1 Air Date	Viewers
Attack of the Cybermen	Part One	5 January 1985	8.9
Attack of the Cybermen	Part Two	12 January 1985	7.2
Vengeance on Varos	Part One	19 January 1985	7.2
Vengeance on Varos	Part Two	26 January 1985	7.0
The Mark of the Rani	Part One	2 February 1985	6.3
The Mark of the Rani	Part Two	9 February 1985	7.3
The Two Doctors	Part One	16 February 1985	6.6
The Two Doctors	Part Two	23 February 1985	6.0
The Two Doctors	Part Three	2 March 1985	6.9
Timelash	Part One	9 March 1985	6.7
Timelash	Part Two	16 March 1985	7.4
Revelation of the Daleks	Part One	23 March 1985	7.4
Revelation of the Daleks	Part Two	30 March 1985	7.7

Doctor Who – Season 23

Story Title	Episode	BBC1 Air Date	Viewers
The Trial of a Time Lord	Part One	6 September 1986	4.9
The Trial of a Time Lord	Part Two	13 September 1986	4.9
The Trial of a Time Lord	Part Three	20 September 1986	3.9
The Trial of a Time Lord	Part Four	27 September 1986	3.7
The Trial of a Time Lord	Part Five	4 October 1986	4.8
The Trial of a Time Lord	Part Six	11 October 1986	4.6
The Trial of a Time Lord	Part Seven	18 October 1986	5.1
The Trial of a Time Lord	Part Eight	25 October 1986	5.0
The Trial of a Time Lord	Part Nine	1 November 1986	5.2

The Trial of a Time Lord	Part Ten	8 November 1986	4.6
The Trial of a Time Lord	Part Eleven	15 November 1986	5.3
The Trial of a Time Lord	Part Twelve	22 November 1986	5.3
The Trial of a Time Lord	Part Thirteen	29 November 1986	4.4
The Trial of a Time Lord	Part Fourteen	6 December 1986	5.6

Doctor Who – Season 24

Story Title	Episode	BBC1 Air Date	Viewers
Time and the Rani	Part One	7 September 1987	5.1
Time and the Rani	Part Two	14 September 1987	4.2
Time and the Rani	Part Three	21 September 1987	4.3
Time and the Rani	Part Four	28 September 1987	4.9
Paradise Towers	Part One	5 October 1987	4.5
Paradise Towers	Part Two	12 October 1987	5.2
Paradise Towers	Part Three	19 October 1987	5.0
Paradise Towers	Part Three	26 October 1987	5.0
Delta and the Bannermen	Part One	2 November 1987	5.3
Delta and the Bannermen	Part Two	9 November 1987	5.1
Delta and the Bannermen	Part Three	16 November 1987	5.4
Dragonfire	Part One	23 November 1987	5.5
Dragonfire	Part Two	30 November 1987	5.0
Dragonfire	Part Three	7 December 1987	4.7

Doctor Who – Season 25

Story Title	Episode	BBC1 Air Date	Viewers
Remembrance of the Daleks	Part One	5 October 1988	5.5
Remembrance of the Daleks	Part Two	12 October 1988	5.8
Remembrance of the Daleks	Part Three	19 October 1988	5.1
Remembrance of the Daleks	Part Four	26 October 1988	5.0
The Happiness Patrol	Part One	2 November 1988	5.3
The Happiness Patrol	Part Two	9 November 1988	4.6
The Happiness Patrol	Part Three	16 November 1988	5.3
Silver Nemesis	Part One	23 November 1988	6.1
Silver Nemesis	Part Two	30 November 1988	5.2
Silver Nemesis	Part Three	7 December 1988	5.2
The Greatest Show in the Galaxy	Part One	14 December 1988	5.0
The Greatest Show in the Galaxy	Part Two	21 December 1988	5.3
The Greatest Show in the Galaxy	Part Three	28 December 1988	4.8
The Greatest Show in the Galaxy	Part Four	4 January 1989	6.6

Doctor Who – Season 26

Story Title	Episode	BBC1 Air Date	Viewers
Battlefield	Part One	6 September 1989	3.1
Battlefield	Part Two	13 September 1989	3.9
Battlefield	Part Three	20 September 1989	3.6
Battlefield	Part Four	27 September 1989	4.0
Ghost Light	Part One	4 October 1989	4.2
Ghost Light	Part Two	11 October 1989	4.0
Ghost Light	Part Three	18 October 1989	4.0
The Curse of Fenric	Part One	25 October 1989	4.3
The Curse of Fenric	Part Two	1 November 1989	4.0
The Curse of Fenric	Part Three	8 November 1989	4.0
The Curse of Fenric	Part Four	15 November 1989	4.2
Survival	Part One	22 November 1989	5.0
Survival	Part Two	29 November 1989	4.8
Survival	Part Three	6 December 1989	5.0

ABOUT THE AUTHOR

Richard Molesworth was hooked by *Doctor Who* when he first saw the Daleks menacing Jon Pertwee in 'Day of the Daleks' in 1972. He acted as a researched for *Thirty Years in the TARDIS*, the BBC documentary celebrating *Doctor Who*'s thirtieth anniversary, and was a producer of *Doctor Who: The Ultimate Guide*, which helped celebrate *Doctor Who*'s fiftieth anniversary on the BBC. Working as part of the unofficial Restoration Team, he was responsible for a multitude of special features on the BBC's *Doctor Who* DVD releases; producing audio commentaries with cast and crew, and writing, directing and producing a number of documentary features. Most recently he has been Project Manager for the BBC's classic *Doctor Who: The Collection* Blu Ray boxsets. He has written the books *Robert Holmes: A Life in Words*, *Wiped! Doctor Who's Missing Episodes*, and *Surf 'N' Turf: The Unofficial Skins Companion*. He has also written articles for numerous magazines, including *Doctor Who Magazine*, *Starburst*, *SFX*, *Sci Fi Now*, and *Dreamwatch*, and has a regular monthly column in *Infinity* magazine.